Conversation and Brain Damage

Conversation and Brain Damage

Edited by
Charles Goodwin

WITHDRAWN

OXFORD
UNIVERSITY PRESS

2003

OXFORD
UNIVERSITY PRESS

Oxford   New York
Auckland   Bangkok   Buenos Aires   Cape Town   Chennai
Dar es Salaam   Delhi   Hong Kong   Istanbul   Karachi   Kolkata
Kuala Lumpur   Madrid   Melbourne   Mexico City   Mumbai
Nairobi   São Paulo   Shanghai   Taipei   Tokyo   Toronto

Published by Oxford University Press, Inc.
198 Madison Avenue, New York, New York 10016

www.oup.com

Oxford is a registered trademark of Oxford University Press

Library of Congress Cataloging-in-Publication Data
Conversation and brain damage / edited by Charles Goodwin.
p. cm.
ISBN 0-19-512953-9
1. Aphasia.   2. Conversation.   3. Brain damage.   I. Goodwin, Charles.
RC425 .C65 2002
616.85'52—dc21   2001052100

2 4 6 8 9 7 5 3 1

Printed in the United States of America
on acid-free paper

CONTENTS

CONTRIBUTORS

Jan Anward is professor of language and culture at Linköping University, Sweden. He is the author of *Språkbruk och språkutveckling i skolan* (Language use and language development in school) and a number of scholarly articles on various aspects of linguistics. His principal interests are languages as dynamic systems, with particular reference to part-of-speech systems and grammatical constructions, the use and development of linguistic resources in specific interactional contexts, such as classrooms and speech therapy sessions, the places of individual voices in various interactional and cultural contexts, and story-telling as an open-ended activity.

Suzanne Beeke is a research speech and language therapist, whose expertise lies in the field of aphasia. She is interested in using conversation analysis as a tool for the study of interactions between speakers with aphasia and their significant others, and is currently engaged in doctoral research into the nature of aphasic syntax in the contexts of everyday conversation and clinical language testing.

Jack S. Damico holds the Doris B. Hawthorne Eminent Scholar Professorship in Communicative Disorders and Special Education at the University of Louisiana at Lafayette. He received an M.S. in communicative disorders from the University of Oklahoma Health Sciences Center and a Ph.D. in linguistics from the University of New Mexico. He has been a keynote speaker at national conferences in Australia, New Zealand, Great Britain, and Canada, and he has published more than 90 articles in scholarly journals in the areas of linguistics, second language acquisition, language assessment and intervention, conversation analysis, and qualitative research methodology. His primary interests are in clinical aphasiology and the study of language as a synergistic phenomenon. He has co-authored six recent books, including *Limiting Bias in the Assessment of Bilingual Students* with Else Hamayan and *Childhood Language Disorders* with Michael Smith.

Charles Goodwin is professor of applied linguistics at UCLA. He is the author of *Conversational Organization: Interaction Between Speakers and Hearers* and co-editor (with Alessandro Duranti) of *Rethinking Context: Language as an Interactive Phenomenon*, and author of numerous articles. His interests include study of the discursive practices used by hearers and speakers to construct utterances, stories and other forms of talk, language in the professions (for example analysis of the courtroom arguments used to free the policemen who beat Rodney King), the ethnography of science (including studies of archaeological field excavations and oceanographers working in the mouth of the Amazon), cognition in the workplace (he spent two years as a member of the Workplace Project at Xerox PARC), and aphasia in discourse.

Claus Heeschen was trained as a formal linguist and worked for many years as a researcher at the Max Planck Institute for Psycholinguistics in Nijmegen, the Netherlands. After making many important contributions to the analysis of how aphasia might provide a window into how language is organized in the brain, he began to investigate how the agrammatic speech of aphasics might be an adaptation to the task of making meaning within talk-in-interaction.

Anu Klippi is professor of speech and language pathology in the University of Helsinki. She has published numerous articles about aphasia and aphasic conversation and has been a visiting researcher at the University of Arizona. Her research focuses on how people with aphasia are able to make meaning through the use of talk, gesture, the environment, and other aspects of context.

Minna Laakso is a senior lecturer in logopedics (speech and language pathology) at the University of Helsinki. She has worked as a clinical speech-and-language therapist at Helsinki University Hospital and at Turku City Hospital. She has also held several research positions at the Universities of Helsinki and Turku, an acting professorship at the University of Oulu, and visiting research appointments at the University of Arizona and the Max-Planck-Institute for Psycholinguistics in the Nertherlands. She is the author of *Self-Initiated Repair by Fluent Aphasic Speakers in Conversation* (1997). Her research interests are in the organization of repair in ordinary and aphasic institutional and everyday conversation, and currently she is interested in studying the emergence and development of repair practices in children's conversations.

Jane Maxim is a speech and language therapist, senior lecturer, and head of the Department of Human Communication Science at University College London. Her interests include all aspects of aphasia, but in particular the relationship between language skills/deficits and communication breakdown. She has also written about syntax in normally aging older people and semantic processing in people with Alzheimer's Disease.

Lise Menn teaches linguistics at the University of Colorado, Boulder. She is the co-author of *Non-fluent Aphasia in a Multi-lingual World* and co-editor of the books *Agrammatic Aphasia—A Cross-Language Narrative Sourcebook*; *Phonological Development: Models, Research, Implications*; and *Methods for Studying Language Production*. She is also an associate editor of the journal *Aphasiology*. She has held visiting research appointments in Japan and at UCLA, the University of Arizona, and the University of Hawaii. Her principal interests are the psycholinguistic accounts of the development of phonology and morphology, and psycholinguistic models of aphasic and normal language production.

Mary Oelschleager's interest is in clinical aphasiology, investigating clinical populations, assessment procedures, and the development of social approaches to clinical management of aphasia (spontaneous verbal repetition, joint productions, word search and laughter strategies in aphasic conversation). Her work with Jack Damico has concentrated on explicating how persons with aphasia and their partners achieve communicative success despite the disruptive effects of aphasia. She is an associate professor in the Department of Communication Sciences and Disorders at Northern Arizona University.

Lisa Perkins is a speech and language therapist working with people with acquired neurological conditions, and she has combined research work with clinical practice throughout her career. Her research interests reflect this clinical focus; they include exploring the impact of different linguistic and cognitive impairments on interaction through the use of conversation analysis (CA), investigation of how people with language or cognitive impairments and their interactional partners negotiate disordered speech and the impact of this on quality of life for those living with aphasia or dementia, and the use of CA to measure the impact of improving language skills on interaction. She has applied research findings to the development of assessment materials for clinicians to use with people with aphasia and dementia.

Gail Ramsberger's research focuses on understanding the linguistic, cognitive, social, environmental, and emotional factors that contribute to communicative success for people with acquired languages and cognitive disorders. The ultimate goal of her research program is to develop more effective rehabilitation programs. Her work reflects a paradigm shift in three dimensions of traditional aphasia rehabilitation research focus. First, instead of emphasizing the production and comprehension of linguistically well-formed sentences in laboratory situations, she focuses on functional communication in real-life situations. Second, instead of emphasizing the role of purely linguistic processes, her approach recognizes the importance of nonlinguistic process in real-life communication. Finally, she seeks to better understand the role that communicative partnerships play in the communicative success rather than focusing solely on the person with aphasia. She has been awarded the certificate of clinical competence from the American Speech Language Hearing Association (ASHA) and is board certified in adult disorders by the Academy of Neurogenic Communication Disorders and Sciences (ANCDS). She is associate professor in the Department of Speech, Language and Hearing Sciences at the University of Colorado in Boulder.

Emanuel A. Schegloff is professor of sociology with a joint appointment in applied linguistics at the University of California, Los Angeles (UCLA). Educated at Harvard and the University of California, Berkeley, he has taught at Columbia University as well as UCLA. His interests center on the naturalistic study of interaction and what we can learn about humans and the organization of social life and experience from it. Within the last five years, his articles have appeared in *American Journal of Sociology, American Anthropologist, Applied Linguistics, Aphasiology, Discourse & Society, Discourse Stufies, Discourse Processes, Journal of Pragmatics, Journal of Narrative and Life History, Language, Language and Speech, Linguistics, Research on Language and Social Interaction, Social Problems, Social Psychology Quarterly, and Social Research*, and in various edited volumes, among them *Interaction and Grammar*, which he co-edited with Elinor Ochs and Sandra Thompson. His book *A Primer in Conversation Analysis: Sequence Organization* is soon to appear from Cambridge University Press.

Ray Wilkinson is a speech and language therapist whose main research interest is in the area of conversation analysis and communication disorders, particularly aphasia. He is currently investigating changes over time in couples where one partner has aphasia and the efficacy of conversation-focused intervention.

PART I

GENERAL PERSPECTIVES

CHARLES GOODWIN

Introduction

The chapters in this volume focus on the analysis of how the talk of parties suffering from aphasia, and other language impairments resulting from trauma to the brain, is organized within talk-in-interaction. This volume provides a new, pragmatic, and interactive perspective for the analysis of aphasia and other neurological deficits (see also the special issue of *Aphasiology*, *13*, nos. 4/5 [1999] edited by Ray Wilkinson and Lesser and Milroy 1993). Most research into the effects of brain damage on linguistic abilities has focused primarily on processes inside the individual patient, for example, what patterns of language breakdown can tell us about the cognitive architectures and brain structures implicated in normal language processing. Methodologically, patients' abilities have typically been assessed in isolation from relevant interactive and pragmatic contexts. However, damage to the brain has equally important consequences for the organization of talk-in-interaction, the primordial site where language emerges as action in the lived social world, and the place where the results of brain damage become both visible and consequential for people's lives. Moreover, it has long been recognized that traditional assessment measurements of language deficit do not correlate well with actual ability to engage successfully in real-world interaction. On the one hand, people with fairly intact syntactic and semantic ability have difficulty in engaging in social interaction outside the laboratory. On the other hand, parties with very severe language impairments are nonetheless able to say quite complicated things by successfully using the social and cognitive resources provided by the sequential organization of conversation to tie their talk to the talk of their interlocutors, as this volume shows. A focus on how damage to the brain shapes discourse sheds new light on both the practices participants use to accomplish meaning and action through temporally unfolding sequences of interaction and the diverse range of cognitive activities implicated in the production and understanding of language.

Theoretical point of departure: Conversation Analysis

In recent years a new and important perspective for the analysis of language impairment within discourse has emerged in the work of scholars in a number of different countries, many of whom are contributors to this volume. A central resource for much of this work can be found in the theories, methods, and theoretical perspectives of the field that has come to be known as Conversation Analysis (CA). Conversation Analysis emerged within sociology in the late 1960s through intense collaboration between Harvey Sacks and his colleagues Emanuel Schegloff and Gail Jefferson. While addressing sociology's long neglect of how talk was central to the constitution of social action and the organization of human interaction, conversation analysts developed a unique theoretical framework for the analysis of talk. Rather than restricting analysis to the isolated sentence and its constituents, they took as their point of departure *sequential organization*, the way in which individual utterances are understood by being embedded within larger sequences of talk and other action.[1] Such an analytic framework provides powerful resources for the analysis of talk in which the language abilities of one or more participants are impaired. Thus, I have analyzed (1995, chap. 4) how a man able to speak only three words (*Yes, No,* and *And*) is nonetheless able to say quite complicated things by embedding his talk within sequences of action co-constructed with his interlocutors. By way of contrast, if analysis were restricted to the structure of his utterances in isolation, most of his competence to understand and use language to build meaningful action in concert with others would be hidden. Similarly Wilkinson, Beeke, and Maxim (chap. 3) demonstrate how shortly after a stroke a man with limited vocabulary was able to carry on coherent conversation by using deictic expressions. By replacing words he has difficulty producing with terms that point to phenomena in the local context, he is able to incorporate into the structure of his utterance gestures he makes, which get their sense from the unfolding sequential structure of the conversation in progress.

Repair

During the past thirty years, the central analytic frameworks of conversation analysis have proved remarkably robust and productive and have led to the detailed study of a host of phenomena that can shed new light on the structure of the talk of impaired speakers. One major stream of research within Conversation Analysis has focused on the organization of *repair* (Goodwin, 1981; Goodwin & Goodwin, 1986;

Jefferson, 1987; Schegloff, 1987; Schegloff, Jefferson, & Sacks, 1977). Rather than studying repair mechanisms, including what others have sometimes treated as "speech errors," from a purely psychological perspective, or as instances of performance failures, conversation analysts have stressed the interactive organization of repair and its central importance as the self-righting mechanism of conversation, that is, the system that gives parties the ability to themselves recover from the systematic troubles that emerge within the social activity of sustaining a state of talk. Participants have systematic methods for displaying entry into repair by both a current speaker who can note upcoming trouble with speech perturbations such as cut-offs and sound stretches, and by one of his or her interlocutors who can initiate repair on what has been said in a next turn (Schegloff, 1992). Moreover, through structures such as the Error Correction Format (Jefferson, 1974), speakers are able to show that consequential lexical alternatives are being weighed. This body of research has provided detailed explication of the interactive organization of the repair process as a local, party-administered social activity, one that has its major home within the ordinary conversations of non-impaired speakers (Schegloff, Jefferson, & Sacks, 1977).

The approach to the study of repair developed within CA constitutes one major analytic point of departure for the investigation of discourse in which the language abilities of one or more participants are impaired. First, the way in which impairment becomes visible, salient, and consequential for the parties themselves is through the production of phenomena associated with repair. Indeed, visible problems in producing the appropriate word at the point where it is due within a conversation is perhaps the most pervasive feature of all forms of language impairment. Word searches have received extensive study within CA (Goodwin & Goodwin, 1986; Sacks, 1995/1992). Such research provides a comparative framework for the investigation of problems of lexical retrieval in the talk of speakers who have suffered brain damage. More crucially, CA has demonstrated how the process of finding a word is not restricted to a single party, but instead constitutes a systematic interactive activity in which interlocutors are very active co-participants (Goodwin & Goodwin, 1986). Through this process, participants are able to build meaning and action together that may be beyond the capacity of an isolated actor[2] (cf. Vygotksy's situating study of the child's intelligence within a social milieu). Aphasic speakers who are unable to produce a relevant lexical item themselves display great ingenuity in using other semiotic resources, including gesture, writing, and graphic representations (Klippi, 1996; chap. 5), to guide their addressees toward recovery of what they want to say. Rather than simply manifesting trouble in language production, repair constitutes a major organizational framework for the collaborative constitution of meaning and action.

Embodiment, participation, and activity

Within this process, visible displays of the body (gesture, facial expressions, and head positions that can alternatively display that the speaker is in the midst of a search and does not want to be interrupted, even though he or she is not producing talk, versus a request that others actively help in the search, etc.) play a most important role. Thus, CA provides a theoretical framework in which the visible displays of the body are thoroughly integrated into language practice, something that is especially important for the analysis of the language ability of parties whose speech production is impaired.

Also, CA has devoted considerable analysis to the interactive organization of *participation frameworks* (C. Goodwin, 1981, 1984; M. H. Goodwin, 1997; Goodwin & Goodwin, 1992) and situated *activity systems* (M. H. Goodwin, 1990). The collaborative activity of evaluating or assessing something incorporates into a single course of action a diverse collection of heterogeneous phenomena including the hearer's use of syntax to project what a speaker is about to say next, the use of intonation to display stance, the use of overlap to demonstrate rather than claim understanding, language choices that make visible congruent evaluations of what is being assessed while simultaneously displaying that each party has different access to and experience of the assessable, the interactive organization of affect, and so on (Goodwin & Goodwin, 1987). Through changing participation displays, including concurrent assessments and appropriate use of the visible body, hearers not only co-construct an assessment being given voice by another speaker but, more important, display through their embodied actions their detailed understanding of the events in progress (Goodwin & Goodwin, 2000). Such processes provide important resources for analysis of the language abilities of participants whose speech is impaired. For example, someone not able to produce multi-word utterances on his own might nonetheless display detailed understanding of the talk in progress, including aspects of its emerging syntax, by performing relevant participation displays at appropriate places (Goodwin & Goodwin, 2000). Once again, CA provides an analytic framework capable of studying the sometimes limited linguistic displays of a speaker suffering from brain trauma as integral components of larger, socially organized language practices. The way in which affect and intonation have a prominent role in the organization of participation also creates the possibility for comparative analysis of the effects of different kinds of brain trauma within interaction.

Pragmatic competence and social life

More generally, CA offers unparalleled resources for the analysis of pragmatic competence. Levinson (1983: 284) in his classic survey of the field of pragmatics notes that "It is not hard to see why one should look to conversation for insight into pragmatic phenomena, for conversation is clearly the prototypical kind of language usage, the form in which we are all first exposed to language—the matrix for language acquisition." The way in which CA sheds light on pragmatic abilities is one of the central themes of Schegloff's chapter in this volume.

From a slightly different perspective, conversation is the place where language impairment emerges as a visible phenomenon in the natural world. Moreover, because of such placement at the interstices of human life and action, it has very real consequences for not only the afflicted party but also for those who interact with him or her, and most especially spouses and others who share a life with that person. Within talk-in-interaction, language impairment not only is rendered visible and consequential but also acquires a profound moral dimension, as all participants are forced to come to terms with how they are to treat someone manifesting troubles in the most central domain of human competence, the ability to use language to engage in relevant social action.

Methodology

Methodologically, CA has developed procedures for recording talk-in-interaction within the consequential settings where people actually live their lives (the home, meals, medical encounters, the workplace, relevant social settings from children's peer groups to scientific laboratories, etc.) and rigorous analytical methods for describing the procedures participants use to construct meaningful talk and action in such environments. Central to such methodology is recording and analysis of multiple, differentiated participants who are relevant to the organization of a strip of talk (e.g., not just the party speaking, for example, an aphasic patient, but also his or her interlocutors), as well as relevant features of the setting where talk occurs. Such resources are especially important for the analysis of a range of phenomena implicated in the organization of aphasia from repair to the co-construction of meaning. Recording in the homes of parties suffering from brain trauma sheds new light on the importance of particular kinds of co-participants such as spouses. For example, a person with limited vocabulary can nonetheless tell an intricate narrative by getting his or her spouse to recall events from the past and then commenting on the telling. When the spouse is removed, an important part of that person's memory as something that can be mobilized socially within talk also disappears. Similarly, some participants who have difficulties saying certain things use resources in the setting where talk occurs (maps, objects, points in relevant directions, etc.; see Klippi, chap. 5) to make themselves understood.

A number of innovative scholars, Audrey Holland and her colleagues in particular, have long recognized the importance of situating language impairment within a conversational context (e.g., Holland, 1977, 1982, 1991). Accumulating research within CA provides important new resources for the analysis of how brain impairment is manifested within discourse. Such work sheds light simultaneously on basic pragmatic processes implicated in the general organization of talk-in-interaction and on the distinctive patterns of discourse that arise when a participant suffers from brain trauma.

The chapters in this book

A number of common themes run through the essays in this collection. First, a particular geography of cognition is invoked. Instead of focusing just on the language abilities of a single individual, the person whose brain has been damaged, all of the chapters take as their basic unit of analysis sequences of talk constructed through the collaborative actions of multiple parties. Such frameworks for the organization of talk-in-interaction provide parties whose language abilities have been impaired in some fashion a greatly expanded set of resources for accomplishing meaning and action. First, as demonstrated in most of the chapters, they can use the words of others to say what they cannot. Thus, though Chil in chapter 4 can speak only three words, he can say quite complicated things by getting others to produce the words he needs. More generally, through processes of repair (see chapters 6, 7, 8, and 3), the interlocutors of a person with language impairment can provide candidate versions of what their partner appears to be trying to say. Rather than being unique to talk that includes a person with language impairment, these processes build upon an organization of repair that is generally used in talk-in-interaction. However, as noted by Anward, Perkins, Laakso, and Oelschlaeger and Damico, repair becomes much more elaborated when one participant suffers from language impairment. Indeed, Schegloff has suggested that because of such repair's pervasiveness and centrality in such conversations it might not be appropriate to think of it as equivalent to the more limited repair that occurs in conversations without impaired participants. It nonetheless draws upon the same basic set of practices for accomplishing meaning through human interaction.

In addition to its cognitive and meaning-making practices, such repair has important consequences for how the parties are constituting each other as skilled or incompetent social actors. This issue is given particular attention by Oelschlaeger and Damico and is present in many other chapters as well. The ability to produce relevant speech can be seen as a major failing in human competence. By producing candidate words in a way that treats the party with a language impairment as nonetheless the ultimate source and judge of what is being said (for example, with rising intonation as a guess that can be rejected as well as accepted), others can continue to treat that party as a competent and consequential social actor. The way in which persons with language impairment can use the talk of others to make themselves understood also has important consequences for therapy. For example, conducting therapy in an environment that systematically removes such resources can lead to a very biased picture of someone's actual abilities to participate relevantly in interaction.

All of this depends upon the way in which the talk of separate parties is constituted as meaningful and relevant through organization into larger sequences of action. Thus, what B says is heard as a candidate guess of what A might be trying to say by virtue of its placement right after A's efforts. Spoken elsewhere, these exact same words could have a very different meaning and relevance. Such sequential organization seems to provide a master matrix for the constitution of meaning and action within interaction. Moreover, it can encompass far more than talk. This can be very consequential for the ability of persons with language impairment to make themselves understood. In face-to-face interaction, participants have not only their voices but also their bodies. Chapter 2 focuses on someone who has had a commisurotomy, an operation that severs the *corpus callosum*, the pathway between the two hemispheres of the brain. He is being tested for pragmatic abilities. Schegloff demonstrates that, independent of the test itself, this man demonstrates a crucial range of pragmatic competence through the finely tuned way in which he performs relevant action with his body at precisely the place such action is called for by the emerging sequences of action in which he is embedded. Formal analysis of interactive practices, developed on a range of materials drawn from vernacular conversation, is able to shed important light on basic abilities of parties with brain damage.

Gesture provides another class of embodied practices that can provide crucial resources for making meaning. It is important to recognize that gesture rarely stands alone but instead becomes meaningful by elaborating, and being elaborated by, other meaning-making practices that it is tied to through sequential organization. Thus, Wilkinson, Beeke, and Maxim (chap. 3) demonstrate how even a very short time after a stroke a man is able to produce fluent conversation by 1) using proterms (e.g., deictic expressions such as "do that") in his talk to 2) instruct his hearer to take into account his hand, which is pointing toward 3) an enactment (of someone walking) being made by his legs. Rather than existing entirely in the stream of speech, this man's utterance is built as a multimodal semiotic package that incorporates both structure in the stream of speech and two quite different kinds of signs displayed by the body (the deictic point with the hand and the gestural enactment). All of these are embedded within a larger embodied participation framework constituted through the mutual orientation of this man and his interlocutor, who is thus visibly positioned to see what is being displayed through gesture. Moreover, all of this work is in the service of a finely tuned interactive fluency as this man, despite his problems in producing certain kinds of language, moves his utterances and turns smoothly toward completion with minimal delay.

In addition to talk and gesture, this interactive matrix can encompass meaningful structure in the environment. Ramsberger and Menn describe how a speaker who recognizes her problems in producing names organizes a narrative by first getting a piece of paper and establishing in the space it provides a place for each principal character. She then points to these places when identifying characters. Such fields of meaning-making resources can also include objects of various types. This is most vividly demonstrated in Klippi's chapter. The situation she is examining is a meeting in which a therapist and people with different kinds of aphasia come together. One of the men wants to tell the others about his experiences as a prisoner, in Russia during World War II. To tell the others where he was kept as a prisoner, he draws upon a quite extraordinary range of different kinds of resources. Thus, he explicitly uses abilities that others have that he lacks. While he can write, he cannot read. He therefore has another patient read what he has written to see if it makes sense. He also draws upon semiotic structure carried by objects in the environment. The therapist has a small notebook that contains a map. However, using this map successfully requires further creative improvisation. The town where he was kept cannot be found. He therefore takes a pencil, points it at Moscow, and then holds it an angle. One of his co-participants is able to figure out that he is indicating a compass direction from Moscow.

The way in which participants creatively use so many different kinds of resources to work out what they are saying to each other (talk, posture, gesture, maps, pencils to be seen as virtual compass needles, etc.) might seem to pose enormous difficulties for an analyst, who is now faced with a potentially unbounded set of phenomena that must be taken into account. It is important therefore to recognize that what makes a particular, clearly defined subset of phenomena in a setting relevant to the participants, and to the analyst, is the emerging sequential organization of their action. The map and pencil in Klippi's analysis become relevant only when the participants turn to them to try and solve problems that arise in the processes of meaning-making they are engaged in together. The general practices used to organize the production of talk and action in situated interaction make only some features of the environment relevant to the participants and thus to the analyst. It is not necessary to exhaustively inventory everything in a setting, but instead to describe the practices participants use to make just those phenomena that are consequential to their action relevant and salient.

Though different chapters focus on different kinds of phenomena (particular structures in talk, collaborative repair, gesture, posture, tools and artifacts, etc.), what emerges from them as a collection is a demonstration of how a person suffering from language impairment nonetheless continues to use as a point of departure for the construction of relevant meaning and action an environment that contains a rich constellation of powerful semiotic resources. I (2000) describe how fully competent speakers in mundane interaction (for example, girls playing hopscotch) build action by assembling a range of quite different kinds of sign systems in different media (linguistic structure in the stream of speech, prosody, posture, gesture, participation frameworks, sequential organization, the built environment, etc.) to build multi-modal contextual configurations. Rather than being coded entirely in a single semiotic system, meaning and action are constituted through the mutual elaboration of these different kinds of sign systems (e.g., gesture gets its sense from the talk it is tied to, while simultaneously elaborating what is being said in the talk).

Human language is both distinctive and crucial in this process. However, it exists within a larger ecology of sign systems lodged within the primordial site for human action: multiple participants using talk to build action while attending to the distinctive properties of a relevant setting (Goodwin, in press). One of the things that can happen when language impairment occurs is a reorganization of this ecology. For example, talk and the gesture that accompanies it are typically produced by a single individual, the speaker.[3] However, the gestures that Chil produces in chapter 4 are explicated by talk produced by others: his interlocutors trying to work out with him what he wants to tell them. The basic practical, public logic of talk and gesture mutually informing each other remains. However, roles in this process are reallocated as interlocutors take on work typically performed by speakers.

Rather than looking at language development as a process entirely situated within the brain of the individual, it thus becomes possible to investigate creative rearrangements of public practices that adapt, and to some extent compensate for, changes in the abilities of individuals. The practices Chil uses to build meaning and action are not lodged within his body alone, but instead within a unit that includes his interlocutors, the sequential environment, and a semiotically structured material setting. It is here, and not through examination of linguistic output alone, that the ability to constitute meaning within states of talk must be assessed. What we see in a family with an aphasic speaker is a process of development, though one situated within the social group rather than the individual and occurring at the end of the life cycle rather than the beginning.

This raises the question of relationship between work in this volume, which uses the organization of talk-in-interaction to examine aphasic talk, and the long and important research traditions, which have used structural features of the talk produced by aphasics to investigate structures in the brain that make human language possible. The relationship between these approaches can be conceptualized in a number of different ways. First, it is possible to see them as complementary enterprises, one focused on the public organization of human discourse and the other using intricate combinations of formal theories of grammatical organization and actual investigation of particular kinds of damage to the brain to probe the biological infrastructure of language. There is much to be said for this position, especially when one considers the very different kinds of skills and analytic practices required for these different studies.

However, it also possible to see work in these separate domains quite relevant to each other, and indeed this argument is made explicitly by a number of chapters in the collection. Simply put, the organization of utterances, including aspects of their grammatical structure, is shaped by the primordial environment where utterances emerge in the natural world: talk-in-interaction (Schegloff, 1996). In an important article, Kolk and Heeschen (1992) argued that rather than giving a transparent window into processes in the brain, the distinctive grammatical impairments found in the talk of aphasics constituted an adaptation by speakers with limited linguistic abilities to the task of producing meaningful talk for a hearer. In the first part of their chapter here, Heeschen and Schegloff describe a movement from cognitive-experimental to conversation-analytic approaches to the study of aphasia. They note that data for the analysis of aphasic language have typically been obtained in situations that differ in important ways from mundane interaction. Thus, many of the tests used to elicit samples of talk from aphasics are designed to maximize the length of turns at talk by aphasics, something that contrasts quite markedly with preferences for minimization within conversation itself. Such design of the testing situation of course limits the possibility for co-construction by persons with aphasia and their interlocutors found to be so important in many of the other chapters in this volume. In the first part of their, chapter, Heeschen and Schegloff provide quantitative evidence that "telegraphic utterances" characteristic of aphasic speech are far more common in interactive situations than in non-interactive ones and thus constitute a systematic adaptation that is interactionally motivated. The second part of their chapter examines sequences of talk-in-interaction in detail to investigate why such structures might be useful. For example, the nonfinite verbs characteristic of German aphasic speech both occur at the ends of turns, and thus can signal speaker transition, and contain a rich argument structure. Such structure forms the point of departure for interactive unpacking by the aphasic speaker's interlocutor. These utterances are thus adaptive in that they provide resources that facilitate the systematic co-construction of meaning through multi-party interaction. A most important feature of Heeschen and Schegloff's analysis is demonstration of the rich variety of different kinds of activities that can be done through the silences and talk that are typical of aphasic speech, not only by the person with aphasia but also her interlocutor. This variety, and the necessity for nuanced, detailed study of actual sequences, is further demonstrated in Heeschen and Schegloff (1999).

Many of these themes are further developed in the chapter by Wilkinson, Beeke, and Maxim. Their analysis focuses on the extensive use of proterms, such as "do that" or "do it" in the talk of a man who recently suffered a stroke. They argue that rather than directly reflecting processing difficulties in the brain, such use of proterms constitutes a creative solution to the task of producing meaningful, fluent action within the semiotic environment and time constraints created by the context in which such utterances emerge. A primary component of that context is turns at talk occurring within specific sequential positions within conversation. Wilkinson, Beeke, and Maxim provide a quite detailed analysis of this environment and the problems it poses for someone whose language capacities have been impaired. Thus, the inability of an aphasic speaker to produce the appropriate word at the point where it is due both disrupts the flow of the conversation by interrupting the onward progression of his or her turn and makes noticeable a consequential lack of basic competence. Proform utterances nicely avoid these problems by proceeding smoothly toward completion while using structure in the local context (e.g., talk by other speakers that the proterms tie to, or visible phenomena in the surround such as gesture) to provide relevant information that the aphasic speaker would find difficult to specify lexically. Not only does this solve the problem of accomplishing reference with limited linguistic resources but the attention of the participants remains focused on what is being talked about, rather than shifting to the competence, or lack of it, of the aphasic speaker. The contextual environment, and the interactive tasks posed in such an environment, thus sheds crucial light on why forms of a particular type occur in the talk of an aphasic speaker.

Many of these same themes arise in a series of chapters here focused on the organization of repair in aphasic conversation. As noted earlier, repair has a particular relevance to the talk of someone whose language ability is impaired since it constitutes a primary set of resources available to parties in conversation for working out the troubles that occur in their talk. Wilkins, Beeke, and Maxim describe a set of practices that enabled a speaker to avoid repair. By way of contrast, Perkins provides extended analysis of some of the contingencies that arise when possibilities for extensive repair do occur. She uses as a point of departure a range of earlier work (Milroy & Perkins, 1992; Perkins, 1995) demonstrating that the organization of repair in aphasic conversation is structurally different from repair in ordinary discourse. Persons with aphasia are not able to rapidly close repair sequences by producing the word(s) that would constitute a successful and appropriate outcome. Such extended repair sequences both disrupt the onward progression of the conversation and draw attention to the distinctive impairments of the person with aphasia. This can lead to a range of subtle but consequential choices as to whether to pursue repair, with its attendant disruption and troubles, and whether a less than entirely adequate outcome will be accepted as sufficient for the purposes at hand. Visible trouble and lack of full understanding may be allowed to pass in order to avoid protracted repair. This deprives the aphasic speaker of the interactive scaffolding demonstrated throughout this volume as necessary for the social accomplishment of meaning. What the aphasic participant is trying to say is not made clear. He or she then becomes something less than a full-fledged participant in the conversation. Repair, understanding, and the constitution of the person with aphasia as a particular kind of social actor are thus intimately linked.

Laakso demonstrates how some of the long, somewhat incoherent utterances characteristic of fluent (Wernicke's) aphasics might emerge interactively from the kinds of choices made during repair sequences. Participants with difficulties in producing appropriate lexical items are affected in different ways at different points in the basic repair trajectory outlined by Schegloff, Jefferson, and Sacks (1977). While *repair outcome* is typically done by producing specific lexical items, and can thus be problematic for aphasics, the *initiation* of repair can be accomplished through operations on emerging units of talk (self-interruption, sound lengthening, etc.) that are not tied to the specifics of particular, potentially problematic, lexical units. Aphasic speakers thus have much more difficulty in successfully accomplishing repair outcome than in initiating repair. Moreover, the different possibilities for action that arise at alternative points in the repair trajectory can aid aphasic speakers in engaging the help of others to work out interactively what they are trying to say, a process documented in most of the chapters in this volume. Thus, when initiating repair, or shortly after this point, speakers having troubling locating a word can solicit the help of others. Indeed, this is done extensively in both normal and aphasic conversation (Goodwin

& Goodwin, 1986; Laakso & Klippi, 1999; Lindsay & Wilkinson, 1999; Oelschaelager and Damcio and most of the other chapters in this volume). However, if interlocutors are unable to or refuse to provide help, the person searching for the word is thrown back upon his or her own resources. For persons suffering from fluent aphasia, this can be especially consequential, since efforts to produce the sought-for lexical item can lead to further problematic lexical items, and thus exponentially extend the length of the repair process. If interlocutors do not join in this process with contributions of their own, what emerges is a very long utterance characterized by extensive efforts to repair and inappropriate lexical items.

Laakso argues that the kind of talk characteristic of Wernicke's aphasics can thus emerge incrementally as the outcome of a series of interactive decisions in the repair process. Interlocutors' failure to participate has the effect of shifting the responsibility for producing the further talk needed to exit from the repair sequence back onto the aphasic speaker alone and of extending that party's utterance. Moreover, Laakso finds that different kinds of interlocutors make significantly different choices when called upon for aid. Spouses help by providing relevant lexical items, and this leads to comparatively short repair sequences. However, therapists may lack the detailed knowledge of the aphasic's life world required to find what is being sought and, moreover, might have a professional commitment to having the aphasic produce as much lexical material on his or her own as possible. Thus, unlike spouses, therapists frequently shift the burden of repair outcome back to the aphasic. General features of the interactive organization of repair thus have strong, situationally variable consequences for the distinctive forms of talk that a person with fluent aphasia produces.

Anward also investigates repair in talk between a fluent aphasic and a therapist. His analysis is in strong agreement with Laakso's that difficulties in lexical retrieval make self-outcome of repair especially difficult for fluent aphasics. However, he explores such issues by taking into account yet another aspect of the interactive organization of the repair process: the footing (Goffman, 1981) or alignment taken up by a speaker and his or her hearers toward visible problems that emerge in talk. When a speaker recognizes that she is making an error, she can use a variety of devices, including laughter and intonation changes, to reframe what is occurring. In Anward's data, when the speaker realizes that she cannot find a necessary word, she frequently produces laughter. Even in the absence of the ability to produce a successful outcome, such reframing demonstrates a basic competence to recognize that what is being said is not right. Despite her hopefully temporary lapse, the speaker lays claim to participation in the larger cognitive and moral order that is visible in competent talk-in-interaction.

Such reframings are consequential for hearers as well as speakers. Jefferson (1979) has demonstrated that laugh tokens can constitute invitations for others to participate in the laughter. Such changes in footing thus constitute an interactive practice for attempting to exit from the repair process without producing a successful outcome. However, this strategy explicitly draws attention to her lapses in competence, and it frequently leads to a request for further repair, with its attendant problems in producing specific lexical items, from the therapist.

A second telling a month later is far more successful in terms of steady progression toward completion, without being sidetracked by extensive repair sequences. The patient is no more successful in word retrieval, but the footing changes that she makes when difficulties arise do not focus attention on her lapses of competence as a speaker. In light of the extensive problems faced by this patient in her retellings, Anward examines the standard story that is being used as a stimulus to elicit talk from the patient. He finds that its complicated temporal organization poses particular problems for the aphasic speaker who systematically gets into trouble when she attempts to integrate temporally distinct episodes within a single syntactic unit.

Oelschlaeger and Damico focus on how participants constitute themselves as competent social actors through the details of how they participate in word search sequences. Unlike the aphasic speakers investigated by Laakso and Anward, the aphasic speaker in this study suffers from nonfluent rather than fluent aphasia, and all of the sequences examined occur between him and wife. However, the basic architecture for repair is the same. Like speakers without any brain impairment, the aphasic speaker uses standard repair initiators to display to others he is having difficulty finding a word. Oelschlaeger and Damico look in detail at how different kinds of choices for participating in this activity constitute the competence and authority of the person with aphasia. It is clear that in many, but by no means all, cases the spouse can be reasonably certain that her solution to the word search task is accurate (e.g., they have participated in the event being described together). However, rather than rushing in immediately when he first displays trouble, and thus interrupting her aphasic husband's attempts to find the word being sought on his own, the wife waits until he signals that he is requesting help. She then offers a candidate solution to the search as a guess, for example, by speaking it with rising intonation, rather than as definitive statement on her part. She thus publicly displays that ultimate authority for what will count as a correct and appropriate solution to the word search continues to reside with the aphasic speaker, despite his visible difficulties in producing the word being sought on his own. This position is ratified when he marks her choice as correct by saying it without uncertainty, with falling intonation. His action also demonstrates his ability to produce the word correctly. Variations on this process, including alternative guess sequences, demonstrate the visible competence of the aphasic speaker.

When this analysis is compared with others in this volume, it becomes clear that within repair sequences the competence and status of the aphasic speaker can be constituted in a range of quite different and very consequential ways. Thus, unlike the speaker here, Chil in chapter 4 did not have the ability to produce a word being sought correctly even after others spoke it. However, like the speaker here, he was treated as the ultimate authority for what would count as an adequate outcome to the search, and indeed he insisted that others pursue quite extended sequences to reach that point. By way of contrast, some of the aphasic speakers in Perkins's analysis are treated as something less than full-fledged co-participants whose talk must be taken into account by the way in which their interlocutors refuse to do the work required to adequately determine what the aphasic speaker is trying to say. In a quite different fashion, some of the fluent aphasics in Laakso's chapter are put in the position of producing long, rather incoherent utterances when their interlocutors fail to take visible opportunities to help specify the lexical items the aphasic speaker is searching for. Anward finds that repair becomes a crucial locus for consequential shifts in footing. Perhaps because of its pervasiveness and centrality to the interactive constitution of adequate meaning and shared understanding, the repair process provides central resources for formulating the social and intellectual standing of an aphasic participant.

Ramsberger and Menn tie many of the themes in this volume together. First, they explicitly contrast a medical model of aphasia, focused on the individual, with the social perspective visible in all of the chapters in this volume. They also explicitly address the question of how these different frameworks might mutually inform and complement each other. Given the authors' long and distinguished backgrounds in basic aphasia research, and the study of what might constitute effective therapeutic help for people suffering language impairment because of brain damage, their efforts are especially important.

Second, many of the chapters here explore how the abilities of aphasic speakers become fully visible only when they can draw upon an interactive matrix that includes the talk of others and frequently phenomena in their environment. Such settings are sometimes contrasted, implicitly or explicitly, with the medical and therapeutic settings where most assessment of aphasia occurs. Traditionally, tests used to measure the capacities of an aphasic speaker try to control their results by systematically minimizing talk by other participants, which might aid the aphasic speaker in the performance of the test. In an important effort to expand the power of researchers to assess the full, socially enabled communicative abilities of aphasics, Ramsberger and Menn developed a procedure to measure success in talk-in-interaction within a clinic setting. Aphasic speakers were encouraged to use the full resources of talk-in-interaction and co-participation with their interlocutors to make themselves understood as they told the story of what happened on an engrossing television show to someone who had not seen it. With this task, Ramsberger and Menn are able to show statistically reliable differences in communicative success in interaction.

Third, such quantitative differences pose the question, of how a conversational exchange succeeds or fails. To begin to answer this question, Ramsberger and Menn look in detail at the patterns of interaction that occurred between an aphasic speaker and her partner in one telling. The aphasic speaker used creative combinations of bits of talk, gesture, and artifacts to provide information about the story, but rarely expressed complete ideas. Instead, she relied upon the ability of her partner to go beyond what was actually said through processes of inference. This required that the aphasic speaker perform as an active cognitive actor by engaging in continuous monitoring of how she was being understood.

What Ramsberger and Menn find is quite consistent with themes developed in the other chapters in this volume. They note that such a social and interactive framework can be important not only theoretically but may also have real consequences for people's lives. There seems to be a very limited time frame after damage to the brain for recovery of actual linguistic ability. Social practices for building meaning and action within interaction are thus most important for both the assessment, and the treatment, of the chronic consequences of language impairment.

The chapters here thus explore new analytic frameworks, situated within the analysis of talk-in-interaction, for investigating both the language and the meaning-making practices of speakers suffering from language impairment because of damage to the brain. In addition to expanding our understanding of aphasia, by investigating in detail a series of tragic natural experiments, these chapters also aid our understanding of basic practices structuring the use of language to engage in human interaction.

Finally, the phenomena described in these chapters have implications for how social actors are to be conceptualized. The participants whose language capacities have been impaired are all deeply dependent upon others for their ability to function as consequential linguistic, cognitive, and social actors. Their ability to say something relevant requires the collaboration of others. Moreover, the injury to the brain that impairs language frequently leaves the body damaged in other ways as well. It is not uncommon for someone suffering aphasia after a stroke to be also left with partial or complete paralysis on one side of the body. A person in such a situation requires the help of others for not only economic support but also for such basic body needs as bathing, dressing, and going from place to place. The lives of not only the patient but of spouses and other close companions are forever changed. However, most theories of the basic human competence for language, of the social contracts argued to form the basis for the moral and ethical structure of human society, and of social justice take as their point of departure a self-contained actor fully endowed with all that is necessary to produce language and construct action, what Nussbaum (2001) refers to as "the fiction of competent adulthood." These chapters are consistent with recent work that challenges such an assumption (see, for example, Kittay, 1999). Though lacking the ability to produce fully fluent speech, many of the aphasics examined here display remarkable creativity in finding ways to manipulate language, not as something locked inside the individual but instead as socially distributed ecology of public sign systems, in order to produce, in concert with others, consequential meaning and action. They are able to do what they do precisely because they are not isolated actors but participants within a larger social and cognitive world being structured through ongoing processes of human interaction. John Donne (1923/1624, Devotion XVIII) argued that "[n]o man is an island, entire of himself; every man is a piece of the continent, a part of the main." Recognition that human actors are not self-sufficient agents illuminates basic human capacities. While acknowledging the terrible consequences and real limitations of impaired language ability, what emerges from these chapters is not a study of how such actors are defective but instead a subtle and detailed picture of their very real competencies and strengths. It is my own hope that, in addition to the theoretical contributions and therapeutic relevance of what these chapters report, they might also help in some small way to change how people with aphasia are perceived and treated in society.

Notes

1. Schegloff's (1968) formulation of *conditional relevance* provides an early but very clear exposition of how each utterance, as a form of action, creates a framework that shapes both the production and interpretation of the actions (and other events) that occur after it (see also Heritage's [1984: 18] discussion of how utterances in conversation are simultaneously *context shaped* and *context renewing*). The most powerful general treatment of how sequential organization is relevant to the organization of talk-in-interaction can be found in the model for turn-taking developed by Sacks, Schegloff, and Jefferson (1974). It is, however, a pervasive theme in most research by conversation analysts (for example, the extensive lectures on conversation by the late Harvey Sacks [1995/1992]).

2. Vygotsky's (1962; see also Cole, 1985) notion of a zone of proximal development in which the development of children's cognitive abilities is shaped through processes of interaction with more skilled adults provides a model of this process at the opposite end of the life cycle.

3. This had led to very interesting models of how talk and gesture might be complementary manifestations of a single underlying psychological process (McNeill, 1992).

References

Cole, M. (1985). The Zone of Proximal Development: Where Culture and Cognition Create Each Other. In J. Wertsch (Ed.), *Culture, Communication, and Cognition: Vygotskian Perspectives* (pp. 146–161). Cambridge: Cambridge University Press.

Donne, J. (1923 [1624]). *Devotions upon Emergent Occasions*. John Sparrow, ed. Cambridge: Cambridge University Press.

Goffman, E. (1981). Footing. In E. Goffman (Ed.), *Forms of Talk* (pp. 124–159). Philadelphia: University of Pennsylvania Press.

Goodwin, C. (1981). *Conversational Organization: Interaction Between Speakers and Hearers.* New York: Academic Press.

Goodwin, C. (1984). Notes on Story Structure and the Organization of Participation. In M. Atkinson & J. Heritage (Eds.), *Structures of Social Action* (pp. 225–246). Cambridge: Cambridge University Press.

Goodwin, C. (1995). Co-Constructing Meaning in Conversations with an Aphasic Man. *Research on Language and Social Interaction, 28*(3), 233–260.

Goodwin, C. (2000). Action and Embodiment Within Situated Human Interaction. *Journal of Pragmatics, 32,* 1489–1522.

Goodwin, C. (in press). Pointing as Situated Practice. In S. Kita (Ed.), *Pointing: Where Language, Culture and Cognition Meet.* Hillsdale, NJ: Erlbaum.

Goodwin, C., & M. H. Goodwin. (1987). Concurrent Operations on Talk: Notes on the Interactive Organization of Assessments. *IPrA Papers in Pragmatics*, *1*(1), 1–52.

Goodwin, C., & M. H. Goodwin. (1992). Context, Activity and Participation. In P. Auer & A. di Luzio (Eds.), *The Contextualization of Language* (pp. 77–99). Amsterdam: Benjamins.

Goodwin, M. H. (1990). *He-Said-She-Said: Talk as Social Organization among Black Children*. Bloomington: Indiana University Press.

Goodwin, M. H. (1997). By-Play: Negotiating Evaluation in Story-telling. In Gregory R. Guy, Crawford Feagin, Deborah Schriffin, & John Baugh (Eds.), *Towards a Social Science of Language: Papers in Honor of William Labov 2: Social Interaction and Discourse Structures* (pp. 77–102). Amsterdam: John Benjamins.

Goodwin, M. H., & C. Goodwin. (1986). Gesture and Coparticipation in the Activity of Searching for a Word. *Semiotica*, *62*(1/2), 51–75.

Goodwin, M. H., & C. Goodwin. (2000). Emotion within Situated Activity. In N. Budwig, I. C. Uzgiris, J. V. Wertsch (Eds.), *Communication: An Arena of Development* (pp. 33–54). Stamford, CT: Ablex Publishing.

Heeschen, C., & E. A. Schegloff. (1999). Agrammatism, Adaptation Theory, Conversation Analysis: On the Role of So-Called Telegraphic Style in Talk-in-Interaction. *Aphasiology*, *13*(4/5), 365–405.

Heritage, J. (1984). *Garfinkel and Ethnomethodology*. Cambridge: Polity Press.

Holland, A. (1982). Observing Functional Communication of Aphasic Adults. *Journal of Speech and Hearing Disorders*, *47*, 50–56.

Holland, A. L. (1977). Comment on Spouses' Understanding of the Communication Disabilities of Aphasic Patients. *Journal of Speech and Hearing Disorders*, *42*, 307–308.

Holland, A. L. (1991). Pragmatic Aspects of Intervention in Aphasia. *Journal of Neurolinguistics*, *6*(2), 197–211.

Jefferson, G. (1974). Error Correction as an Interactional Resource. *Language in Society*, *2*, 181–199.

Jefferson, G. (1979). A Technique for Inviting Laughter and Its Subsequent Acceptance/Declination. In G. Psathas (Ed.), *Everyday Language: Studies in Ethnomethodology* (pp. 79–96). New York: Irvington Publishers.

Jefferson, G. (1987). Exposed and Embedded Corrections. In G. Button & J. R. E. Lee (Eds.), *Talk and Social Organisation* (pp. 86–100). Clevedon, England: Multilingual Matters Ltd.

Kittay, E. F. (1999). *Love's Labor: Essays on Women, Equality, and Dependency*. New York: Routledge.

Klippi, A. (1996). *Conversation as an Achievement in Aphasics*. Helsinki: Studia Fennica Linguistica 6.

Kolk, H., & C. Heeschen. (1992). Agrammatism, Paragrammatism and the Management of Language. *Language and Cognitive Processes*, *7*(2), 89–129.

Laakso, M., & A. Klippi. (1999). A Closer Look at the "Hint and Guess" Sequences in Aphasic Conversations. *Aphasiology*, *13*(4/5), 345–364.

Lesser, R., & L. Milroy. (1993). *Linguistics and Aphasia*. London: Longman.

Levinson, S. C. (1983) *Pragmatics*. Cambridge: Cambridge University Press.

Lindsay, J., & R. Wilkinson. (1999). Repair Sequences in Aphasic Talk: A Comparison of Aphasic-Speech and Language Therapist and Aphasic-Spouse Conversations. *Aphasiology*, *13*(4/5), 305–326.

McNeill, D. (1992). *Hand & Mind: What Gestures Reveal about Thought*. Chicago: University of Chicago Press.

Milroy, L., & L. Perkins. (1992). Repair Strategies in Aphasic Discourse; Towards a Collaborative Model. *Clinical Linguistics & Phonetics*, 6(1 & 2), 27–40.

Nussbaum, M. (2001). Disabled Lives Who Cares? *New York Review of Books* (January 11).

Perkins, L. (1995). Applying Conversation Analysis to Aphasia: Clinical Implications and Analytic issues. *European Journal of Disorders of Communication*, 30, 371–383.

Sacks, H. (1995 [1992]). *Lectures on Conversation: Volumes I & II*. G. Jefferson, ed. Introduction by E. A. Schegloff. Oxford: Basil Blackwell.

Sacks, H., E. A. Schegloff, & G. Jefferson. (1974). A Simplest Systematics for the Organization of Turn-Taking for Conversation. *Language*, 50, 696–735.

Schegloff, E. A. (1968). Sequencing in Conversational Openings. *American Anthropologist*, 70, 1075–1095.

Schegloff, E. A. (1987). Recycled Turn Beginnings: A Precise Repair Mechanism in Conversation's Turn-Taking Organisation. In G. Button & J. R. E. Lee (Eds.), *Talk and Social Organisation* (pp. 70–85). Clevedon, England: Multilingual Matters, Ltd.

Schegloff, E. A. (1992). Repair After Next Turn: The Last Structurally Provided Defense of Intersubjectivity in Conversation. *American Journal of Sociology*, 97(5), 1295–1345.

Schegloff, E. A. (1996). Turn Organization: One Intersection of Grammar and Interaction. In E. Ochs, E. A. Schegloff, & S. Thompson (Eds.), *Interaction and Grammar* (pp. 52–133). Cambridge: Cambridge University Press.

Schegloff, E. A., G. Jefferson, & H. Sacks. (1977). The Preference for Self-Correction in the Organization of Repair in Conversation. *Language*, 53, 361–382.

Vygotsky, L. S. (1962). *Thought and Language*. Translated by Eugenia Hanfmann and Gertrude Vaker. Cambridge, MA: MIT Press.

2

EMANUEL A. SCHEGLOFF

Conversation Analysis and Communication Disorders

Ancient history

My own interest in the possible bearing of conversation-analytic work on talk vernacularly taken to be problematic or odd or compromised and professionally understood to be pathological in some respect, whether psychiatric or neurological, goes back quite a long time, to before a distinct field recognizable as conversation analysis began. So did Sacks's. Both of us worked very early—in the early 1960s—on materials with an overtly psychiatric pedigree—he on calls to a suicide prevention center and recordings of group therapy sessions with adolescents, I with psychiatric and neurologic assessments of state detainees both criminal (persons pleading insanity as a defense to criminal charges) and civil (persons held for psychiatric examination to see if they should be committed to a mental hospital because they constituted a threat to themselves or others). Both of us worked as well on the psychiatric theorizing that was brought to bear by professionals in the field on those materials, taking it as additional grist for our mill, rather than as a collegial resource.[1]

In the late 1960s, Julius Laffal's book *Pathological and Normal Language* (1965) offered material provocative to many of us trying to come to terms with talk-in-interaction as practical action, or, put another way, as action understood in part by way of the practices (or procedures or methods) for its production. For many of us, the literatures of logic and linguistics—as well as those of psychology—offered versions of such practices that seemed in fundamental ways misconceived, and Laffal (inadvertently, I suspect) provided engaging material. For example, he described a feature observed in some "schizophrenic speech"—the practice of inverting positive

21

and negative. Asked if he was feeling all right, the patient would answer "no" when he was and "yes" when he was not. Laffal reported an effort to see how far this would go, which involved two psychiatrists engaging the patient, one of them a pipesmoker. The other asks the patient, "Is my colleague, Dr. Jones here, smoking his pipe?" "No," says the patient. More of the exchange is reported, but it quickly becomes impossible to keep track of. Here is a two-valued logic with a simple operation—reversal of values; it should not be hard to track, to compensate for the reversal, and "decode" what is actually going on. Yet it proved to be virtually impossible. Clearly, that kind of algorithmic organization of talking in interaction seemed implausible (and, clearly, not on these grounds alone).

Later, after reading Roman Jakobson on aphasia (e.g., Jakobson, 1964, 1966, 1971 inter alia) in the mid-1970s, it seemed clear that whether or not his way of going about the problem worked, we ought to be able to contribute something. An opportunity to do so presented itself in the early 1980s.[2]

My colleague Vicki Fromkin mentioned to me a colleague on campus (Dr. Dianna Van Lancker) who had just returned from a "post-doc" in the midwest where she had worked on prosopagnosia—the vulnerability of some who have incurred trauma to the right hemisphere to experience problems in recognizing familiar faces. Now she was extending her work on such patients to explore problems in recognizing familiar voices. "Really?!" I exclaimed; I've worked on recognizing familiar voices. And so I called Dianna Van Lancker, and we agreed to have lunch and talk about mutual interests.

Well, it turned out (of course) that pretty much all that our interests had in common was the phrase "recognizing familiar voices." Dianna's voices were "familiar" in the sense of being celebrity voices, voices from the common culture: Winston Churchill, Bob Hope, John F. Kennedy, and so on. And "recognizing" them meant being exposed to extremely short taperecorded bits of them and identifying them to a tester, if possible (see inter alia, Van Lancker & Canter, 1982; Van Lancker, Cummings, Kreiman, & Dobkin, 1988). In *my* work (e.g., Schegloff, 1979, 1986), the "familiar voices" were those of persons one knew well—close family and friends, co-workers. And the "recognizing" that was at issue was that made relevant and accountable at the first bit of talk by a caller on the telephone, which might often be, and *normatively* be, not a self-identification by the caller but a brief voice sample, often only "Hi," or "Hello, Jim?" which in differing degrees permitted or demanded the giving of evidence by the answerer that she or he had recognized the caller, with consequent implications if she or he had not. These voices mattered more on the face of it in people's ordinary lives; the recognitions—or rather the failures to recognize—were potentially rather more consequential than the voices and failures to recognize with which Dianna was dealing. And yet those voices, and recognizing them under controlled and standardized conditions, did appear indicative of particular neurological impairments.

Here was a marvelous opportunity to combine naturalistic with experimental research. We planned to secure permission to tape the bedside telephones of recent victims of right hemisphere brain insults and hear how they dealt with the first moments of calls in which friends' and intimates' voices would "naturally" be presented for possible recognition. The patients for the study could be selected according to any experimental protocol that seemed desirable; my collaborator could do the formal testing using snippets of tape from famous people that supported her own research program. I had no objection to the experimental framework for this research, for it left uncompromised the naturalistic auspices of the data with which *my* analysis would have to come to terms. We could then, we thought, compare recognition of familiar/intimate voices with recognition of familiar/celebrity voices, recognition in experimental test situations with recognition as part of an ordinary, naturally occurring, interactional context of the society, and begin to explicate the ways in which our understanding of brain function could be specified and our understanding of the artifacts of experimentation in this area illumined.

It was not to be. Although most referees at the agencies to which we turned for funding thought the proposal worth support, just enough were so committed to purely experimental work that they could not appreciate the naturalistic component and its juxtaposition with the experimental and thus could not support it. So there was no funding, or, as the mythical letter from research support agencies is said to go, "We have nothing but admiration for your proposal!"

I should mention another benefit of this undertaking though, even if it did not come to fruition, and that is the reading of some of the clinical literature in the field. I thought at the time (this was early to mid-80s) that the literature might serve conversation-analytic interests in a fashion similar to the ways in which Goffman drew on the literature of physical handicap and disfigurement—both obtrusive and veiled— in work like his *Stigma* (1963). Goffman found in the exigencies of these "special populations" illumination of problems of interaction, which he went on to argue are confronted in some degree by everyone—problems of the management of appearance and of information, the contingencies of being discredited or discreditable, with the full moral weight carried by those terms.

Although these issues must surely be faced by those with compromised neurological resources as well, it is not this that struck me in the clinical literature. Rather it was the way in which certain neurological "impairments" were seen to affect interactional viability, and the ways in which interactional capacities that one would not have thought were at all related might nonetheless be regularly affected together. Let me offer one case in point of the former, from a neurologist at the University of Texas, some 20 years ago (Ross & Mesulam, 1979). It concerns the reported impairment of the capacity to detect and to display emotion,—to "do emotion," we might say—with trauma to the right hemisphere

A junior high school teacher in her thirties suffered a relatively mild cerebrovascular accident (CVA) to the right hemisphere. After a brief hospital stay and period of recuperation, she returned to work. She lasted less than a week. Teaching boys and girls on the cusp of adolescence, she recurrently had to face incipient disruption of classroom discipline and decorum. When she tried to do so, the consequences of problems in "doing emotion" quickly became apparent. She would respond to the beginnings of some disruption with an admonition, in a prosodically flat voice, "That will be enough of that." If after a few minutes the problem was present still or again, she would say again, "That will be enough of that" (in the same flat voice). And in the face of continued breaches of decorum, she would say again, "That will be enough of that," still in the same flat voice.

The point is that each resaying would ordinarily be delivered in a prosody that displayed upgrade—increased severity, irritation, intolerance of continuation. But these all involve affective displays—doing emotion. In its absence, the kids would not, *did* not, take her seriously. Unable to maintain order in the classroom, she was unable to continue her professional career (at least as of the time of writing the case report). When I teach in my courses on ordinary talk-in-interaction about emotion and affect as being, for purposes of interactional analysis, not *states* but *actions*—outcomes that have to be done, achieved, accomplished—material of that sort allows me to make the case appear not one of academic nitpicking, not one of didactic exaggeration, not one of metaphoric license, but one of virtually literal description.

In the last half dozen years, I have in fact been able to do some limited work in this area with real, empirical materials. It has turned out that I have no materials of my own, but I have been able to work with Claus Heeschen on videotapes collected in home environments of German-speaking aphasics (Heeschen & Schegloff, 1999; chapter 10), and I have had the opportunity to examine some videotapes of commissurotomy patients with whom Eran Zaidel, a neuropsychologist at UCLA, has been working for a number of years. What follows is based on this latter work (and see also Schegloff, 1999).

What follows is divided into three parts, each somewhat truncated so as to accommodate the others. The first part is a brief excursion into the ways in which past CA work can illuminate a stretch of conduct—quite reduced conduct—of a neurologically affected interactional participant. The second part briefly examines one way in which starting with a fragment of interaction involving a neurologically affected participant can lead to exploration of a phenomenon whose interactional provenance is hardly limited to this population. Here, then, is one bit of moving from neurologically defined "stuff" to more general CA concerns. Finally, I would like to mention a few considerations that I think those committed to this intersection of CA with problematized talk need to reflect on in pursuing their work. How is one to think about the characteristics of the data—at what point, and how, does its specifically "neurological" or "problematic" character become relevant? How can one organize an individual worklife and a collective disciplinary community that can contribute both to the concerns of problematized data and to conversation-analytic work more generally? How does this work bear on the more general issue, sure to be increasingly prominent in years to come, of the relationship and intersection of neuroscience and conduct in interaction?

The present inquiry

The project from which I am drawing began with the juxtaposition of some empirical observations with one view about the localization of various aspects of linguistic functioning in the brain.[3]

Roughly, the view held at the time these observations were made (some 15 years ago), and very likely still widely held (but see Perkins, 1998: 307; Zaidel, 1998; Zaidel, Zaidel, & Bogen, 1998), was that, whereas much of the neurological substrate of language—for phonology, syntax, the lexicon, and semantics—is localized in the *left* hemisphere (among the naturally right-handed, etc.), the so-called discourse-organizational and pragmatic functions are situated in the *right* hemisphere. Various sorts of evidence were held to support this view, drawing almost entirely on clinical and testing observations regarding various "pragmatic deficits" attendant upon cerebro-vascular insults to the right hemisphere.

What exactly should count as "pragmatics" or "discourse" has never been thoroughly clarified,[4] let alone become a matter of consensus, and there is at present no compelling reason to think that all the preoccupations that are treated as belonging to "discourse" or "pragmatics" form some sort of unified or coherent domain. But among the deficits included in the discussion of the consequences of disruption in the right hemisphere were counted an impaired capacity to enact and recognize emotional expression; trouble in the use and recognition of non-literal uses of language, such as irony, metaphor, humor, and, most important, indirection; and the compromising of other operations understood to be associated with the use of language in organized undertakings such as interaction—including turn-taking, the doing of particular actions of the "commissive" type, such as commands and requests; and the range of conventional norms we ordinarily term "etiquette" or "politeness."[5]

My skepticism about this unilateral location of the pragmatic and discourse organizational components of language, based in large measure on "testing" of various sorts, led me to want to look at some ordinary specimens of talk-in-interaction involving those with right-hemispheric damage. Through the cooperation of the neuropsychologist Eran Zaidel and the philosopher Asa Kasher, I gained access to videotapes of several testing sessions with commisurotomy patients whom Zaidel has been studying for quite a long time.[6] Although not exactly "right-hemisphere *damaged*," persons who have had commisurotomies have undergone surgery that severed the *corpus callosum*, the pathway through which the two hemispheres of the brain "communicate." However intact the right hemisphere itself may be in these persons, the left hemisphere presumably has no access to its operations and products—at least according to the dominant version of brain function as I understand it.[7] In such persons we should see most clearly the effects of depriving the rest of the language faculty—what is thought of in contemporary linguistics as the very *core* of the language faculty—of the robust operation of its pragmatic and discourse components.

Examining videotapes made of ongoing psycho- and neurolinguistic testing sessions with several such subjects, we observed—sometimes in the course of the testing itself, sometimes in apparent interactional time-outs occupied either with sociability or with ecological adjustments to facilitate the testing—an order of linguistic functioning at prima facie odds with the pragmatic localization view.[8]

However discrete the organization of *syntax* and the other core language components may appear from anything else in human cognitive capacity and practice (as much in the current linguistic cannon holds), *pragmatics* and *discourse organization* seem much less plausibly so. Discourse organization encompasses not only elements of grammatical structure, prosody, and the like but also units whose organization seems to fall outside even a generous drawing of the boundaries of the language faculty. For example, "narrative" is a central kind of discourse structure. It can have a seemingly direct bearing on classically linguistic aspects of language use—for example, on the selection of such grammatical features as verb tense or aspect, or forms of person reference, by reference to the relationship of the sentence under construction to story structure, such as foreground (or "story line") versus background. But the embeddedness of a "narrative" in the interactively organized structure of "a story-telling sequence" in conversation requires—as part and parcel of the discourse organization's operation—recognition of where the story is "not yet over" and "when the story is possibly complete," because different forms of response are incumbent upon hearers at those respective places and different implementations in the talk itself are required of the teller (see Goodwin, 1984; Jefferson, 1978; Lerner, 1992; Sacks, 1974; Schegloff, 1992a, inter alia). But discriminating "the crux" or "the possible completion" of a story is not among what we ordinarily think of as *linguistic* capacities.

Similarly with "pragmatics." It is common in mainline contemporary psycholinguistic work to start accounts of the so-called speech-production process with some "intention" (as it tends to be called)—whether to articulate a proposition or to perform an action. That kernel of "intention" or "action" undergoes a series of operations and transformations until it "comes out" as an utterance (e.g., Levelt, 1989). If this is so, then "pragmatics"—which includes among other things what language is used to do—is the very *fons et origo* (as they used to say), the very first step of the language faculty. But shall we imagine that the organized capacity "to do things with words" (as John Austin, 1962, put it) is entirely separate from the capacity to do things in interaction in other ways? For surely in interaction things are continuously being done in words *and* in *other*-than-words, and the two are intermixed, and, most important, what is being done in words is partially *constituted* by what is being done in *other*-than-words. If the pragmatics is separated from "the rest," can the rest issue in recognizable, coherent, and effective linguistic products? If there are such products, can the pragmatics possibly *be* cut off from the rest of the speech production process?

There are common alternatives to this way of approaching data from commissurotomied patients, common ways of neutralizing such conclusions. For example, if even a few strands of the *corpus callosum* have remained intact, interhemispheric communication may still be possible. Or even though the pragmatic and discourse functions are localized in the right hemisphere, rudimentary capacities remain in the left hemisphere, capacities that are activated, developed, and exploited with the attenuation of interhemispheric communication. There are undoubtedly others (see note 7).

Nonetheless, it may be useful to present here several of the observations that we made on these subjects for two reasons. First, to the degree that the lines of argument outlined in the preceding paragraphs remain unresolved, these observations may have a bearing on claims concerning hemisperic specialization. Second, these observations offer a kind of evidence not previously brought to bear in this area, whether understood as neurolinguistics or as the neurobiology of behavior.[9] At the end, I will offer grounds for proposing that data of this sort will in the long run prove indispensable in achieving the goal of providing a neurobiological account of at least some human behavior.

If we mean to ground these inquiries empirically, we need to consider what forms of data ought to be taken into account. Until now, the key data on which claims have been based have been drawn from testing. There is much to said about the sort of data that testing produces and how it is to be interpreted, but this is not the occasion for it, nor is there the time for it.

Let me just say that *I* wish to bring to bear on the analysis of pragmatics in these split-brain individuals *naturalistic* observations of conduct in interaction, even if the interaction examined was a testing session. From that point of view, the conduct of tester and subject can be treated as constituting just another genre of interaction, whose premises an observer must respect and study but not necessarily assume or subscribe to (see, e.g., Marlaire & Maynard, 1990). Let us note, then, that the sustaining of a testing occasion is itself an interactional achievement. The patient/subject must recognize the auspices under which the tester's utterances are produced, under what auspices responses are to be given, how such responses will be treated upon receipt, and the like. All of this, of course, is a special "frame" (Bateson, 1955/1972; Goffman, 1974) sustained within an *environing* interaction, much as "a game" (such as a card game or a board game) can occupy a special frame within the interaction in which it is played (see "Fun in games," in Goffman, 1961). Some utterances are understood as "within the frame" ("moves" in games; "test items and responses" in experiments and testing situations), and others are recognized as "outside the frame," to be understood and dealt with differently (utterances such as "Are you tired?" "Would you like to take a break?"). Subjects, testers, and often even investigators ordinarily all conspire to disattend the events outside the testing frame and to treat them as "not material or relevant to what the test or experiment is about" (even, "not part of the science"). But we need to recognize that the very capacity to sustain with a professional a testing interaction from start to finish within the larger interactional occasion itself involves quite substantial pragmatic competencies, whatever the results arrived at by assessing the responses to the test items *within* the testing frame. And our subjects appear to have at least that capacity, else they would not still be tested after all these years.

Why, then, these split-brain subjects? For one thing, if the right hemisphere is damaged, or, worse, if it cannot communicate with the left, then we should see in the affected party a massive impairment of the "pragmatic" capacity to conduct interaction in a competent fashion, not only *in* the test materials but in the testing situation that makes the administration of the test materials possible in the first place. That they are still being tested thus provides prima facie grounds for skepticism about the wholesale subversion of the pragmatic component of the language faculty.

One last matter before turning to a few fragments of these interactions, and that concerns what is meant here by "pragmatics." Among the tropes that figure most prominently in the literature on "pragmatic deficit" (as noted earlier) are various forms of "non-literal" speech—including forms such as metaphor, irony, indirection, ellipsis, and humor or laughter. (Although these last do not always involve the non-literal, their involvement in the present inquiry is doubly motivated, the other motivation being the claimed pragmatic deficit in recognizing and expressing emotion.) A variant often given special attention is the doing and recognition of "indirect speech acts," which are taken to reflect a disparity between what their implementing utterances *literally* implicate as actions and what they "*actually*" (and, in this view, "*non-literally*") are taken to implicate.

Aside from these features, other components included in claims about compromised "pragmatics" include implicature, deixis, gesture, rules and practices of politeness and etiquette, and, as pragmatics blends imperceptibly into discourse structure and discourse analysis, those forms of organization that underlie the orderly conduct of talk itself, such as turn-taking, sequence organization, topic organization, and the like. Although there may be other proper components of pragmatics and discourse structure that I have not included, these are surely common, in many instances central, and are more than enough aspects to examine in the talk in interaction of our target population.

Analysis I: From Conversation Analysis
to "neurologically compromised" data

First of all, I would like to engage in a brief exercise in what might be called "applied conversation analysis," or at least one form of it. Here resources developed in past CA work—work addressed to quite different and diverse interests and problems—is brought to bear on data involving participants with putative communication disorders. One object of such an exercise is to render data that may be opaque or recalcitrant to vernacular understanding by virtue of the disorder (or by virtue of its ordinariness and consequent transparent invisibility) more accessible to informed observation and to bring the results of such examination to bear on claims about the disorder or the behavioral mechanisms involved in it.

The fragment, which lasts no more than a few seconds, occurs in the middle of a testing session with a man whom I will call Alvin.[10] Although Alvin does not talk in this exchange (he has been asked by the research assistant to talk as little as possible),[11] the episode displays his capacity to parse and to grasp the talk of an interlocutor and to respond effectively in interaction. For us here, the point is to see the access we get to this brief exchange with the analytic resources of "formal" conversation-analytic treatments of turn-taking and sequence organization.

The research assistant, Dan, has been administering the tests, while the principal investigator, Ezra, is operating the camera in an adjacent room, shooting through the doorway. As the sequence on which we will focus begins (at #1 in the transcript that follows), Alvin is sitting almost motionless, watching the assistant take out and examine the next set of stimulus cards (fig. 2.1).

My examination of this exchange will be organized around the numbers above the lines of transcript. Each marks the locus of some observations about the sequence to that point and the import of those observations, the first of which is the gloss of the state of the interaction at the onset of this sequence just provided.

FIGURE 2.1

Example 1 Ezra and Alvin

```
        #1              #2                          #3
EZ: Alvin, can yo[u come a bit closer to the [ta:ble=
                 [AA turning               [AA leans
                   to EZ                     forward,
                                             head down
              #4            #5
      =may [be even the [re?=
           [AA eyes    [AA grasps chair,
              up          eyes down
                                                        #6
AA: =((slides chair forward one substantial measure, then looks up to EZ))
          #7
EZ: That's [good.=
           [((AA slides forward another small increment))
AA: = ((lips part, head turns back to table, puts left hand to
          #8            #9
      mouth and coughs, [left hand adjusts glasses))
                        [
DG:                     [Oh:   :  :kay, ((puts first new stimulus card
                                       on table in front of AA))
```

Let us note first, at #2, Alvin's prompt coordinated response to Ezra's use of his name as an address term; he looks to Ezra directly after Ezra has spoken his name, aligning himself as a recipient for the turn-in-progress (Goodwin, 1981). That he has analyzed his name—"Alvin"—as an addressing is itself, of course, an achievement. Taken as an object for "on-line" parsing and analysis in real time, "Alvin" can be understood in either of two ways. One is as an address term or vocative; the other is as the subject of a clause/sentence. On the former analysis, Alvin would be the addressee and, potentially,[12] the selected next speaker (the prior request that he minimize speaking to the contrary notwithstanding). On the latter analysis, the utterance would be understood as *about* Alvin, but addressed to the testing assistant, Dan.

Not until the word "you" is there grammatical evidence an utterance along the first of these lines is in progress. But by the time "you" is articulated, Alvin is already turning his head toward Ezra, so that by the time "come a bit" is being said, Alvin is already fully oriented toward him as an aligned recipient (see fig. 2.2).

Since Alvin and Dan are sitting side by side, the loudness of the utterance does not differentiate them as intended recipients. Alvin has analyzed the talk for its displayed target, has recognized its first element as indicative of that, and has produced an appropriate response when he finds himself to be that target—an initial indication of discourse/pragmatic capacity, with respect both to turn-taking and sequence organizational features of the talk; for the design of this bit of talk serves to (potentially) select Alvin to occupy the next turn position and involves constraints on what

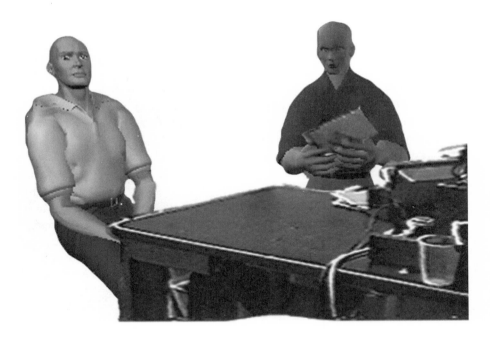

FIGURE 2.2

should be done there as well—a response to the summons, which he here realizes by gaze redirection, in compliance with the earlier instruction to minimize talking.[13]

By #3, Alvin has begun withdrawing his gaze and initiating a compliant response at the word "table," which is projectable as the incipient possible completion of Ezra's turn (see fig. 2.3). Note then that there are at least two orders of discourse/pragmatic competence involved here. The first of these is Alvin's analysis of the turn-in-progress for its imminent possible completion, displayed by his incipient gaze withdrawal— a turn-taking matter.

A second competence displayed here regards the turn's sequence-organizational status; Alvin displays an analysis of Ezra's utterance as making relevant some sort of responsive turn or action next, and "next" means "now." In particular, Alvin begins to display an analysis of Ezra's turn as a *request*, and a request for an *action*, by initiating an action seeable and analyzable (by Ezra) as *compliance* with the request.

Furthermore, the request is in the form that many varieties of conventional speech-act theory would term "indirect." The form *"can you* come a bit closer" in this view literally asks a question about ability or capacity. The "request for action" has to be analyzed out of this utterance as the indirect speech act being enacted. This is just the sort of speech act, just the sort of non-literal usage, which—in the com-

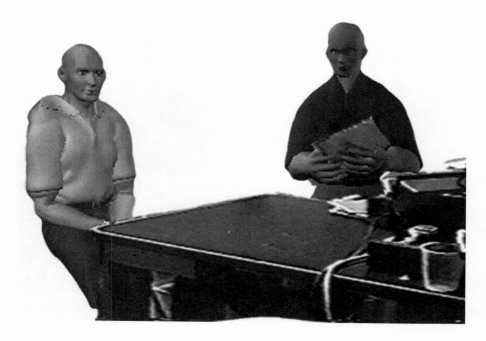

FIGURE 2.3

mon view—persons with a discourse/pragmatic deficit would be expected to have trouble with.[14]

Directly following "table," with the hearable continuation of talk (the "may" of "maybe"), at #4, Alvin apparently registers that the turn may be extended *past* its projectable point of possible completion, and his eyes begin to return to the speaker Ezra (see fig. 2.4)—again turn-taking competence of a detailed sort.

At #5, Alvin hears in the talk that the extension of the turn past its initial possible completion is not "generative," that is, not a whole new unit of talk but additional elements to the prior turn-constructional unit. The previous analysis of upcoming possible completion appears then to be reinstituted; Alvin again withdraws his gaze and continues the previously initiated action, which, with the grasping of the chair, now shows itself transparently to be a compliance with the request (see fig. 2.5); Alvin now slides his chair closer to the table by a substantial increment. Again, then, both turn-taking and sequence-organizational constraints are being grasped and met.

At #6, at the possible completion of the action designed as compliance with Ezra's request, Alvin looks to Ezra (see fig. 2.6). Sequence-structurally this is a third position, a position in which the initiator of a sequence (especially a sequence like a request sequence) regularly makes some assessment of, or other reaction to, whatever

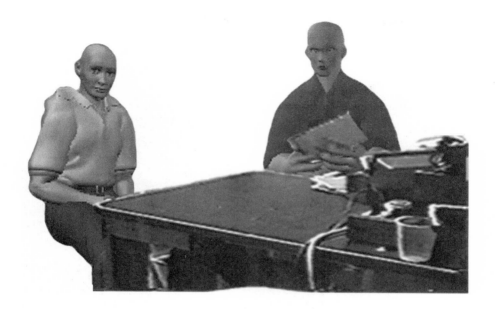

FIGURE 2.4

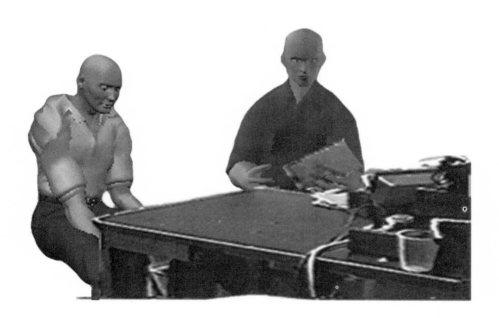

FIGURE 2.5

FIGURE 2.6

was done as a response to the sequence initiation (i.e., in second position). Here, then, is a place at which orientation to sequence structure can warrant "anticipation" of a sequence-structural third position (Schegloff, 1995, in press) uptake—a place for Alvin to look to Ezra for an assessment of the adequacy of his "move"; has he moved "close enough."

Note that here, unlike the first observation earlier, it can *not* be by virtue of Ezra being a speaker or a source of sound that Alvin looks to him. Although Ezra does indeed deliver the type of utterance that "belongs" in third position ("That's good"), Alvin glances toward him *before* this utterance is begun. Note again that the posture in figure 2.6 is captured just before Ezra's assessment, "That's good." This is a gaze direction warranted by *sequence structure* (in particular, request/compliance sequence structure),[15] a relevance structure to which Alvin, by his glance, shows himself to be oriented and attentive. Indeed, his turn to Ezra, aligning himself as recipient, may serve to prompt the assessment utterance that is then forthcoming.

Although we lack the data here, we can venture a guess that as Alvin looks to him, Ezra is neither smiling nor nodding and that his evaluation of the adequacy of Alvin's compliance move is not clear until his utterance. In the absence of "approval," Alvin may read the possible *in*adequacy of his response, and, *as* Ezra is saying "That's good," at #7, Alvin is already executing a move to add another increment of compliance to what he had done before. In the video of this episode, one can see an additional small increment of sliding the chair forward during "That's good," as if in response to the absence of validation of the previously designed compliant action. We have here not merely discourse/pragmatic competence but a kind of sensitive micro-tuning and adjustment of conduct to interactional contingencies in a request/ compliance sequence.

Upon completion of the added increment of moving closer and Ezra's assessment, it appears that Alvin has analyzed Ezra's "That's good" as *both* the end of a turn *and* the end of a sequence. He shows this in several ways. First, he turns his head back to the table and away from Ezra; second, he adjusts his glasses (at #9; see fig. 2.7 top right)—which is for him a "work-related" gesture, regularly used with new or difficult stimulus tasks; third, these movements are well coordinated with the testing assistant, Dan, such that the adjustment of the glasses coincides with Dan's "Okay" and placement of the new stimulus on the table (see fig. 2.7 bottom).

This amounts, then, to Alvin's recognition, and *collaborative constitution* with Ezra and Dan, of this little sequence as a "side sequence" (Jefferson, 1972) interpolated into a larger, ongoing activity, *from* which it created a temporary departure and *to* which there should be a return on its completion. There is then the recognition and joint construction of a *hierarchical* structuring of activities and sequences of activities.

Finally, at just the juncture between the end of the side sequence and the resumption of the "work" activity, Alvin puts his hand to his mouth and coughs (at #8), or to put it in terms of the etiquette with which he shows himself to be in compliance,

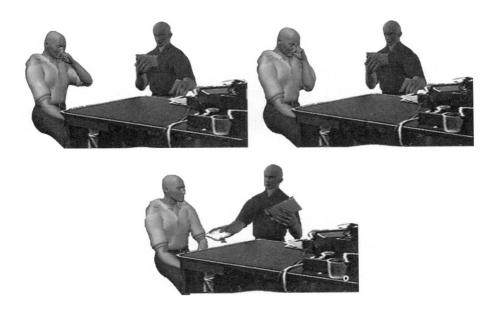

FIGURE 2.7

he "covers his mouth while coughing" (see fig. 2.7 top left). And by placing the cough in the no-man's land between sequences (note, it comes *after* the gaze withdrawal and *before* the adjustment of glasses marking task resumption), he puts it at a relatively non-sensitive moment, when no one is an active interactional co-participant, into whose interactional space this ritually marked body adjustment is thrust. And etiquette is, of course, arguably *another* of the components of pragmatics.

About this whole episode, with its robust and exquisitely detailed attention to compliance with an indirect request, it remains only to remark that, later on, it turned out that (according to the results of formal testing procedures) Alvin "did not perform well on tests related to commands and indirect requests." What is to be made of this sharp contrast in the results of different modes of inquiry requires more careful and sustained treatment than can be given it here, but perhaps the issue can be given an initial, tentative, formulation.[16]

If it is the case that the organizations of practice for doing talk-in-interaction are designed in the first instance for talk *among* recurrent others *about* recurrent others— that is, among a limited circle of interlocutors who, for the most part, know each other and know, for the most part, the world they share in common with each other—then talk among those who do not know each other and do not share a social world and mutually frequented environment represents an extension of the organization of interaction to a second order tier of social and physical reality. If those at neurological risk have the robustness or impairment of their neurological capacity assessed on materials and in settings largely disengaged from their familiar, taken-for-granted, idiosyncratically relevant *lebenswelt*, if their deployment of linguistic resources is assessed in settings shorn of the right to invoke what they know their interlocutor to know, to be routinely able to not have to tell interlocutors everything but to exploit their already knowing it, then what is being assessed is not the first order set of resources for talk-in-interaction. And that is what happens when assessments are based on exchanges only with testers and therapists and not on exchanges with family members, friends, and work associates; when it explores invented and imagined worlds in constructed vignettes and experimental stimuli, in the retelling of test material pictures and cartoons, and the like (Heeschen and Schegloff, chap. 10). Whatever the ostensible objects of measurement are taken to be, it is responses to test stimuli that are being measured, not naturally occurring actions in interaction, engendered by the indigenous exigencies of courses of action pursued in interaction— except for the course of action called "testing." This is not to deny that real things are being assessed by such testing—things that may be indicative of structural and functional properties of the brain and their associated cognitive capacities. It is, however, to call into question the specific features being assessed by instruments not targeted at the likely constitution of the resources for talk-in-interaction and to invite exploration of alternatives—such as assessments conducted on specimens of language use drawn from prima facie first order sites of language use—talk with familiars, about familiars' matters, in familiar contexts.

The little episode examined here is thoroughly unremarkable. How do we find its texture, its structure, what is going on in it? How does one go to work on it? I submit that in order to understand the physical movements that constitute the whole of Alvin's participation in this episode—indeed to come to "see" them at all, in an analytic sense—we need to appreciate (we *have* appreciated) their status as social actions. Compliance, responsive attention deployment, approval solicitation, and the like—that is what they are. By them, Alvin displays his orientation to the relevant organizational dimensions within which this interaction is being realized and on which it is being scaffolded. The timing of his moves displays Alvin's grasp—*in its detailed course*—of the developmental structure of Ezra's talk, as composing a turn constructional unit, which is progressing toward possible completion, at which point it may be for *him* to respond, and as constituting an action that will shape the *terms* of his response within a jointly oriented-to sequence structure. These movements embody and display, in this setting's situated details, Alvin's and Ezra's collaborative orientation to the resources, constraints, and practices of turn-taking and sequence organization as formal organizational frameworks for their concerted participation, through whose deployment the import of what is going on here is materialized, is fabricated, jointly, *by* the parties, *for* the parties.

But how is all that made available to *us*, external observers? We do not encounter it in the same fashion as the participants do—micro-moment by micro-moment forward in real time, subject to the contingencies and exigencies of responding and the interactional import of *non*-response. Here is where the resources of formal accounts of such structures of practice come into play. For that is what conversation-analytic work such as the turn-taking article (Sacks, Schegloff, & Jefferson, 1974) and accounts of adjacency pairs and their expansions (Schegloff, 1995, in press) are designed in part to do.

Surely they are designed to elucidate the elegant formal structure and efficacious design of the organizations of interactional practice as objects of interest in their own right. But their payoff finally rests in their capacity to illuminate actual episodes of interaction, to serve as tools in the understanding of what is going on there for the parties and how it is getting done—tools such as "possible turn completion," "transition-relevance of possible completion," "the conditional relevance brought into play by a first pair part," and so on. Formal analysis is, then, not an *alternative* to "substantive," or "content-ful," or "meaningful" or "setting-specific" treatment of ordinary talk-in-interaction; it is an *instrument* for its *implementation*. It serves us well as professional analysts to the degree that it has accurately depicted the formal character of how ordinary participants in talk-in-interaction co-construct those episodes and understand them in their course, and for that very reason. And its efficacy, it turns out, is not limited to that sense of "ordinary participants" that excludes those with compromised neurological resources; they too participate in ordinary conversation and by reference to the same organizations of practice, even if, of necessity, implemented in somewhat different ways.

Analysis II: From the "neurologically impaired" to Conversation Analysis

The second segment I would like to examine briefly involves the research assistant Dan and another commisurotomy patient/subject, Larry. In this episode I will focus not so much on the general robustness of Larry's pragmatic capacities with turn-taking and sequence organization, but rather on something more specific. I want to focus on an utterance of Larry's in the course of some interactional manipulation by the tester/ researcher and ask: what is this utterance being used to do, what action or actions is it accomplishing? And what practices of talk-in-interaction underlie the production of that action?

These are questions we put to bits of conduct in *anyone's* interaction. So here, although I am not drawing on already accomplished work in the field, I am going about the work in a not uncharacteristic fashion. But in asking "what is going on here? and how?" I am seeking not (or not only) to bring evidence from actual conduct in interaction to bear on an assessment of the robustness of Larry's pragmatic and discursive capacities. I am seeking as well to advance our understanding of talk-in-interaction by going to work on a piece of data from a person diagnosed as having a communication disorder as a possible exemplar of an as-yet undescribed action in interaction.

After about twenty minutes of testing, Dan proposes to Larry that they play cards, specifically the game of "War."[17] After several cards have been played, Dan begins purposely "fooling around."[18] First, he takes a trick in which he had had the *lower* value card; Larry spots the maneuver and reclaims the trick, saying "eh *eh*:::," displaying the card values, and maybe (his talk is obscured at this point) ending with "nice try."[19] A few moments later Dan "fools around" in a different fashion, simply delaying the play of his card after Larry has played his. After a few seconds, Larry calls Dan's attention to the state of play by saying, "I played my nine; whenever you're ready." Shortly thereafter, Dan "cheats" again, again by taking a trick in which his card had the lower value.

Example 2 Dan and Larry
```
    |.....................((L plays his card of next trick))
L:   How long d'you wanna do this for.
            |................((D plays his card of next trick))
    ((D reaches for and takes trick, tamping it on the table and depositing it in his pile.
    At start of D's "taking"action, L starts and aborts a "taking" move of his own.
    As D deposits trick on his pile, L speaks)):
L:   Nice try.                                                    <<— #1
    (0.2)    ((D looks at L.))
    |.........((3–4 lateral head shakes by L))
L:   Nice try.=                                                   <<— #2
D:   =What.=
L:   =My six,=your two=                                           <<— #3
```

```
D:   =So?
     (0.5)
L:   En:: so you took it.                                    <<— #4
     (·)
D:   So?
L:   You shouldn've.                                         <<— #5
     (0.2)
D:   So?
                | . . . . ((L points to his pile, then D's))
L:   't should be on this deck, not that.=                   <<— #6
D:   =So?
     (0.8)
                | . . . . . . . . ((L tilts head, like shrug))
L:   Okay. I pass. I c'n afford to lose those cards.         <<— #7
     (0.8)
L:   I'm winning anyhow.
```

My examination of this very rich sequence will focus only on a single object—
"Nice try" at arrows 1 and 2. To get at what is getting done in this twice-deployed
turn, we will need some analytic resources concerning one of its components, the
use of the term "try," in "nice try."

The term "try" is regularly used when an "effort" has *failed*. This is especially
clear when the verb is used in the first-person past tense. In utterances such as "I
tried to call you" (or "ring you") or "I tried to open the window," one hears that (in
the first case) the call did not get through or wasn't answered, and, in the second,
that the window is still closed. Of course, when one *has* reached someone by phone
or succeeded in opening the window, one has also "tried"; but we don't say we "tried"
when we succeeded; we say the name of what we succeeded at doing—or we don't
say anything at all, because that success will have carried its own information.

"Nice try" is a form related to this usage of "try." It is, in the first instance, an
assessment, which, when its target is the recipient, can embody a compliment, a compliment that can serve as a consolation to one who has "failed," as, for example, the
utterance "That was a good try " at the end of an exchange taken from an episode of
girls playing the game of hopscotch:

Example 3 Hopscotch (from M. Goodwin, 1998, 12:10:42–12:10:55)
```
   Linsey:   ((throws stone and hits line))
     Liz:    Oh! Good job Linsey!
             You got it all the way [on the seven.
Kendrick:                           [((shaking head)) That's-
             I think that's sort of on the line though.
     Liz:    Uh- your foot's in the wr(hhh)ong- [sp(hh)ot.
Kendrick:                                       [Sorry.
             That was a good try.                            <<—1
```

Used this way, through its use to do this action, "Nice try," then, marks what has preceded as "*over*," or *completed*, and as a failed attempt to do whatever "target action" was being done (for example, "trying to win," or "trying to cheat"). I say that it is a form for "consolation," but for certain speaker/hearer combinations, and in the aftermath of certain kinds of events, it can be done and heard as "ironic."

In particular, after a suspected effort to cheat, "nice try," said by the targeted victim, *may* be seen as ironic—as the "cool" or "self- possessed" or "superior" alternative to doing an overt challenge, "outrage," or quitting. And, in complimenting the perpetrator, it can be heard as an *accusation* of sorts—albeit a veiled one, treating the "violation" as *designed* (hence, potentially, "cheating"), rather than as an error or slip, or pretending to do so—a mock or teasing accusation.

In the *first* round of "fooling around" that precedes this (see note 19), Dan takes a trick in which he had the *lower* value card; Larry spots the sleight of hand and *re-claims* the trick, does "disapproving/warning" by saying "eh eh:::," displaying the card values, and possibly then remarking, after about a two-second pause following Dan's acknowledgment "Oh," "Nice try." *This* "Nice try"—if that is what is said—comes after Larry has moved to interdict Dan's play, has detailed the components of the "error," has rectified the situation, and has gotten in return from Dan the acknowledgment (or "change-of-state token," as Heritage, 1984, calls it), "Oh." This "Oh" acknowledges the facticity of Larry's demonstration and registers it as "news" (hence, presumably *not* designed by its agent), but offers no account, no apology, or other acknowledgment of having erred. There is a gap of silence following the "Oh," in which Larry appears to await such an acknowledgment. In this episode, then, "Nice try" comes 1) after an otherwise-possibly-complete-but-for-one-slot sequence, 2) after a position for apology, or error-acknowledgment has passed unfilled, and 3) as a potential alternative account for the already acknowledged misplay, namely, "attempted cheating."

In example 2, directly after Dan wrongly takes the trick, Larry says "Nice try." Here, unlike the response to the earlier bit of "teasing" by Dan with an "in-progress" interpolation of "eh eh:::", "Nice try" is the *initial* response by Larry, one which, first, claims that some event or designed course of action is *over*, and, second, that it has *failed*. Now *what* is just over and failed? Not the game of War; not the round of play in the game. Larry's utterance *presupposes*, and invokes an orientation to, the "*move*" or the "action" as the unit that it describes as a failure, and ironically "compliments." That is, here "Nice try" plays on and invokes *its recipient's guilty knowledge* for its very understanding; that is the sense in which it is—or *does*—a *veiled* accusation. For Dan to "understand" Larry's utterance—that is, to *display understanding* of it as an *interactional* event—is to allow that he "recognizes" what event has just ended and ended in failure, and that is, in effect, to *confess*, for Larry's utterance is predicated on recognizing the "ruse" or the "*cheat*" as what is being referred to. The main tactic for avoiding this outcome is to invoke or claim *non*-comprehension.[20] (Note just in passing how indirection and irony centrally figure in the account I have just offered, and, if the account is correct, in the sophisticated line of action Larry is executing here, and recall the claims about impairments to non-literal and indirect uses of language in the standard account of compromised right-hemispheric functioning.)

Dan does indeed take the tack of non-comprehension—*first* after arrow #1 by looking blankly ("uncomprehendingly" as we say) at Larry; *second* after arrow #2 by the repair initiator or so-called clarification request "what" (Drew, 1997; Schegloff, Jefferson, & Sacks, 1977); and *third*, after Larry's response explicating the card combination that made *him* rather than Dan the winner of the trick, by reiterations of "So?" that claim *non-understanding of relevance* (which here take the place of the "Oh" in the prior go-round).

The relevance, of course, is (within the context understood as "the card game") that the trick should be returned. In the previous episode, Larry reached out and took back the trick in question himself. Here he makes relevant its return *by Dan* with what is, in effect, a pre-request or complaint, or a series of them. If Dan took the trick wrongly or in error, then he should right the wrong and return it. And this is exactly what the researchers say they were trying to elicit from Larry—a request for return of the trick—to *exemplify his pragmatic competence.* Dan's recurrently offered "So?" is meant (within the context understood as "the testing situation") as a prompt to *elicit* the articulation of this request, but it seems to be heard by Larry, with ample grounds (in the context understood as the interaction surrounding the card game), as a willful refusal to understand and respond to the upshot that had been analyzably provided for at arrows 2 and 3. Such a withholding of understanding would ordinarily be understood—*outside* the frame of a testing experiment, that is—as adumbrating, projecting, or even embodying a rejection, a dis-aligning stance toward the action that has been made relevant (Sacks, 1987; Schegloff, 1988a, 1995, in press). Dan's claims not to see the relevance are understood by Larry as unwillingness to return the trick, indeed, as a way of doing/showing "rejection," "refusal," or even "defiance," and hence as an indication of the probable fate of an overt request, were it to be tendered.

Now the practices of ordinary talk-in-interaction are designed to *avoid dis*preferred responses such as rejection. Specifically, "preliminary" moves are used to "test the waters," with no "plunge" if they are unfavorable. So what Larry does here shows quite a robust "pragmatic" capacity, well attuned to ordinary interaction. If the prospect is that a request will be rejected, regularly the request is withheld,[21] as it is here.

Surely here we find pragmatic competence of a level requisite to ordinary conduct, strikingly embodied in Larry's persistent resistance to the efforts of the experimenter to elicit a request as evidence of that pragmatic competence. Indeed, the very "So" that *discourages* Larry's production of a request could easily be taken as evidence for a hypothesis concerning an incapacity to formulate requests, and even as a metric for the extent of his *pragmatic deficit* in this regard. The more that prodding failed to produce a request, the greater the evidence of pragmatic deficit. Framed in the world of testing and experimentation, under the interpretive framework of a theory of pragmatic deficit, this may appear plausible, even compelling. Framed in the world of ordinary interaction, it invites a quite different understanding—one not of compromised pragmatic capacity but of interactional sensitivity. This vignette can therefore serve as an instructive resource explaining contrasting results of naturalistically observed conduct, on the one hand, and the outcomes of testing and other investigator-induced conduct, on the other.

The analysis to this point speaks to the robustness, even sophistication, of Larry's pragmatic competence,[22] but not yet as fully as it might to a payoff for CA. We have begun to pick apart Larry's particular move and how it works, but to derive a more general payoff for a grasp of the interactional phenomenon here, we need more. Do we have in "Nice try" one exemplar of a *type* of action accomplishable through a describable practice of talking in interaction? If so, are our observations about "Nice try" *generic to that action type and that practice*? Or do they instead bear on the *realization* of that action type in a manner fitted to the particulars of this *moment-in-context*? Or are they more obliquely related to the type of action being accomplished and more directly related to what that action is responding to?

So let us look briefly at another instance to join "Nice try" as two instances of a kind of practice for a type of action. In example 4 Carney had sat down on her husband Gary's lap at this backyard picnic recorded in early 1970s Ohio and had fallen off onto the ground. Example 4 comes from the flurry of sequences produced in response to this "accident."

Example 4 Auto Discussion, 3 (simplified)

```
Carney:      [Thank heaven the camera was ['n o(h)o(h)o(h)n
  Curt:                                    [Ehh hu:h huh! ·hhh
  Curt:   [(I don'know I think it's-)]
  Gary:   [ Y o u    r e a l   i z e ] I c'd'v broke my ba:ck,
Carney:   (°eh-k-heh)/(0.3)
  Curt:   W-well that's a'least a'her worries, sh-[she's always got me tuh=
  Gary:                                            [Uh-hu:h,
  Curt:   = (    [          [          )  eh-huh
  Gary:          [u h! u h! [uh! uh!  [uh!=
Carney:                     [A  (h) [  (      )=
  Curt:                             [=eh hu [::h
  ???:                                      = [°(is yer leg all right?)
  Gary:   Yer her cousi[n.
  Curt:                [eh hheh!
Carney:   No:,[just my a:rm,
  Curt:       [That's ruh- It's all in the fam'ly,
          (0.2)
Carney:   Thanks hon,                                            <<— #1
          (0.1)
```

Carney: W'make a good couple.
Gary: ME::,   <<— #2
         (0.2)
Gary: Yer the one thet did it!   <<— #3
         (0.7)
Gary: hhOh my G o:d.hhhh I've got my, sacroiliac twisted all the way arou:n

Carney's "Thanks hon" addressed to her husband (at arrow #1) is the target here, the utterance I propose to consider together with "Nice try." Let me simply mention a few observations about the *two* of them:

1. Both are self-positioning seconds, or reactions—though not "second pair parts." In this respect they are like laughter—irremediably responsive, and as a default, locating the just-preceding (on some granularity scale) as what they are reactive to.
2. Both are "indirect" comments on what another has done, "carried by" an action directed to that other on its completion. "Nice try" is an assessment that carries a compliment as well as a consolation; "Thanks hon" is an appreciation, or rather an "appreciator"—something that expresses or "does" appreciation; and the following, "W'make a good couple" adds the self-congratulatory version of a compliment. That said, we can note that "Nice try" is also an appreciator and that one thing some assessments can be used to do is appreciation. So both combine appreciation and compliment.
3. Both are ironic, in that they convey or articulate an assessment of what they are reacting to, and one with a positive valence ("nice" in "nice try," and "thanks" [i.e., a response to something appreciated] + "hon" (i.e., term of endearment)], though that event in both cases otherwise is being given, or arguably makes relevant, a *negative* assessment.
4. Both are indexical and trade on guilty knowledge. They require their recipients to "solve" what is being complimented or thanked for (or "*blamed* for," once irony is admitted as part of the analysis). Any response other than repair initiation betrays understanding of the indexical reference.
5. Both imply agency, intentionality, and responsibility. (Note: these are vernacular terms here, not analytic ones.) And indeed Gary's response to "Thanks hon"—"*ME*:: Yer the one that *did* it!"—addresses (and disputes) precisely the issue of agency and responsibility.
6. There are also some apparent *turn*-constructional features of these two utterances—for example, that they are both lexical or phrasal— "designedly terse," one might almost say. Compare "Nice try" with the version offered in the hopscotch game: "That was a good try."

Note, by the way, that none of the earlier observations about "try" (pp. 39–41) has any direct application here, once we are trying to explicate the *type* of practice and *type* of action of which these *two* utterances might be *co*-instances—once, that is, we try to develop a more *formal* analysis of the *type* of action being implemented and the practices for implementing it. Different "layers" of practice are involved in describing the type of action and in describing a particular realization of one.

Of course, this is all quite tentative. We have not yet established or grounded the claim that we do indeed have a *type of action* or a *type of practice* here. I have introduced "Thanks hon" to try to exemplify a bit of the analytic procedure of *entertaining or nominating a phenomenon*, a kind of formal analysis of which much CA work is composed, here launched from an episode featuring a participant with putatively compromised pragmatic capacities.[23] By doing so, we can quickly enter a line of inquiry about a type of action in interaction—not communication disorder or specific impairments. Here then we are travelling in the opposite direction from episode #1—from the domain of problematic talk to a more general contribution to conversation analysis.

Reflections on the interface

But isn't something wrong here? Larry does not really seem compromised at all. Indeed, he looks to be quite intact, even sophisticated. So haven't I cheated? Well, yes and no. "Yes" in the sense that I have not in this latter exercise taken a characteristic exemplar of *what is disordered* in those with a communication disorder and shown how to use *it* in building more general CA contributions. I do not really have the data with which to do that, having access only to this commissurotomy material (at least in my native tongue). But I mean to make virtue of necessity. For there is an important point to be derived from what I have actually done, and with this I move into the last part of my remarks. I offer a few reflections on doing CA work with "communication disorders."

In work on "speech disorders," professionals commonly write and talk about "aphasics," about "Brocas" and "Wernickes," meaning by those terms not bearers of those names but bearers of brains "insulted" (as the term goes) in those areas, about "autistics," "Downs," and so on. These then become categories of membership in the society (Sacks, 1972a, 1972b) by reference to which we formulate these parties to interaction, and by reference to which we understand what they could be up to. One of the most invisible and devastating consequences of basing our understanding of these folks on testing situations is that, in them, these folks get to be little else *but* aphasics, Downs, or Brocas. They become mere "language users," as the phrase goes, and ones with problems in that regard, rather than actors with things to do, lives to live, things to give and to request and to tell and to promise, memories to share and call upon in getting their interactional business done, with language among the resources with which to do those things.

When we can address ourselves to the conduct of these folks in their common life settings, we get to see what and who else they are—or if I can put it this way, "who and what they do the being of," and how they do it. It surely must be a policy of inquiry that it remains an open question *what* about a person with Brocas aphasia is aphasic, and what not. I re-invoke a point I wrote about several years ago (Schegloff, 1991), because it seems directly relevant here.

It is only slightly less problematic nowadays than it has been for most of human history to give close disciplined attention to the details of ordinary daily life. What was the point in studying what everyone already knew? One needed a license for close looking, and the two most common licenses (poetic license aside) were the faultedness of what was to be looked at, with the promise of finding ways of ameliorating the fault, and the promise of making intendedly profitable or consequential undertakings *more* profitable or happier in their outcome—undertakings such as negotiation, salesmanship, and the like.

The auspices of this volume are supplied by the former banner. One of its past vulnerabilities has been to attribute to the auspices of the inquiry whatever was found out as a *result* of the inquiry, indeed to formulate the problems of the inquiry by reference to its auspices. But, to cite an older example, not everything that schizophrenics say or think is "schizzy," and some of the things that *are* are not schizzy in principle, only in mode or degree of realization.

So my first reflection here is that we would do well at least some of the time to start by treating the producers of what appears to be disordered talk or other conduct in interaction like other co-participants about whose conduct we ask: what was it doing? How was it doing it? How was it understood (by co-participants)? How did it come to be understood that way? What is the evidence for any of this? We should introduce into the analyses that try to answer these questions the materials and categories of aphasiology, speech pathology and therapy, neuropsychology and neurolinguistics, for example, only as the materials we are examining mandate and require it of us.

There is a consequence of this stance for the professional lives of investigators and for the communities of practice and inquiry that they seek to construct and sustain, and that is the second reflection I would like to share with you. One is more likely to make progress in this specialty only if one is also a generalist. That is, in order to understand well the ostensibly *dis*ordered talk of the affected populations, investigators need to address also the study of ordinary talk by ordinary folks in ordinary (for them) settings.

There is a direct parallel here to colleagues who study talk in "institutional settings," that is, work settings with distinctive practices of talking-in-interaction such as courtrooms in session, broadcast news interviews, classrooms in session, medical consultations, and the like. I hope that it is increasingly understood that these "contexts" cannot be taken as unproblematically relevant. Not everything that occurs in the surgery is medical and needing to be understood by reference to such categories of participant as "doctor" and "patient," nor is everything that occurs in a room in which instruction is intermittently taking place "classroom interaction." Because there are, or can always imminently be, episodes of quite *un*professional conduct in these professional settings, because even the professional talk there is informed by quite vernacular practices of talk in interaction, it is hard to imagine analysis of depth and cogency not being facilitated, and even enabled, by routine participation in analysis of non-specialized materials. Both for the commonalities it allows to be recognized and for the contrasts it allows to be specified, the most penetrating of our colleagues who work on institutional talk also work on "ordinary conversation." And the most effective work often plays back and forth between some type of action or practice in a specialized setting and its occasional or occasioned deployment in ordinary interaction.

I think this is the way workers on communication disorders should organize *their* work life as well. In order to bring past CA work to bear on problematized talk, analysts need to control the CA resources not just from reading them but from deploying them on the materials they inhabit by default. That means practicing them in materials where no systematic contingencies of disability are present as tempting accounts. And those who aspire to derive from their work with problematized materials and from affected participants contributions to the core corpus of CA's understanding of talk-in-interaction will themselves best know how to bring the observations from one domain into the other. But that means being up to speed in the other as well, and that means having an ongoing work life with the materials of ordinary *non*-suspect talk-in-interaction.

Let us not forget where this road leads, and this is the third and last reflection I would like to share.

In the burgeoning preoccupation with the so-called neurobiology of behavior, two tasks will need to be addressed to enable the linkage named by the rubric. One task is the discovery and description of the structure and functioning of the neurological apparatus, and that is the mandate of the neurosciences. The other is the discovery and description of the behavior whose neurobiological grounds are to be elucidated.

Central here will be conduct in interaction, because this species has evolved as a *social* species, and the central site of a social species in the conduct of conspecifics is interaction with one another. It seems fair to say that no one is better positioned to provide the requisite accounts of the organization of conduct in interaction than are those working along conversation-analytic lines. The organizations, the resources, the practices which are of interest here are those which are demonstrably oriented to by the participants. How else could their neurological equipment be implicated in their production?

This is an undertaking to which all good conversation-analytic work will surely contribute. What special contribution may be made by work on those with neurologically implicated communication disorders remains to be determined and discovered. But almost certainly it will be of a piece with the larger corpus of conversation-analytic work.

So the cultivation of work lives and working communities that sustain a mutual enrichment between CA research generically and CA research with problematized talk will serve not only the viability and gratification of the work lives being affected. It promises results—who knows when—at one of the more exciting growth points of human self-knowledge.

Appendix

As Dan is still putting away the cards he won on the prior trick, Larry plays his card for the next trick. Dan hesitates momentarily while playing his card, sees that he has the lower one, then plays the card, withdraws his hand, and then both he and Larry reach for the trick simultaneously. Dan's hand reaches the trick first, and he gathers up the cards as if to take the trick. As Dan taps them on the table to align them before adding them to his pile of won cards, Larry speaks.

```
A   Dan and Larry, Fooling around #1
                    | . . . . ((L starts lateral head shake))
L:   Eh eh. EH eh. Eh eh.                                                <<— #1
                    | . . . ((D looks to L after "depositing" cards))
L:   ((Reaches to D's card pile; as he picks up prior trick, he speaks))
L:   My ten.                                                             <<— #2
     (0.8)   ((L turns over cards of prior trick to reveal their face))
L:   Your three.                                                         <<— #3
D:   So,                                                                 <<— #4
     (0.5)
L:   (°So.)
     (2.0)
D:   ((tamps down his card pile three times))
L:   Nice try.<I'll give you an E for effort, ((while playing next card))  <<— #5
```

Dan undertakes to administer a questionnaire to Larry.

```
B   Dan and Larry, Fooling around #3

1   D:   Where d'you live.
2        (0.5)
3   L:   In a house,        ((smile voice))
4        (0.5)
5   D:   Where.
6   L:   On a stree:t,      ((smile voice))
7   D:   Where,
8   L:   In a city,         ((smile voice))
9        (0.8)
10  D:   Okay=(which part of it.)
```

```
11          (0.8)
12   L:     't's on the north side of the city,
13   D:     On the north side of the city,
14          (0.8)
15   D:     ('cause) this is a real big city=
16          =[I guess there's only one house on the north,=
17   L:     =[(yeah)
18   D:     =one house in the south  [ (      heh heh)
19   L:                              [ (               house. )
20   D:     .hh D'you like it there?
21   L:     It's okay:,
22          (1.0)
23   L:     EHH! hah [ hah hah hah hah hah
24   D:              [ ( ( 4–5 lateral head shakes) )
25   D:     D'you miss being tested.
26          (0.8)
27   L:     Occasionally,
28          (2.0)
29   D:     A:nd d'you miss working.
30   L:     No: ((one lateral head shake))
31   D:     Not at all.
32   D:     No.
33          (1.0)
34   D:     ·hh How many people live in your home usually.=
35   L:     =Too many.
36   D:     ₁heh heh
37   L:     ⌈ heh
38   L:     Three.
39          (0.5)
40   L:     My dad, my wife and I.
41          (2.5)
42   D:     uh How many hours d'you usually spend (0.2) here.
43          (0.2)
44   L:     Not very many.
45          (0.5)
46   D:     How many.
47          (0.8)
48   L:     't depends on (how many tests you have).
49          (1.2)
50   D:     'kay:: who- whom do you:: spend most of your time with
51          at home.
52   L:     Myself.
53          (0.2)
54   D:     ( ( raises first one eyebrow, then the other; smiles) )
55          (2.2)      ( (DG looking at "interview schedule") )
```

```
56   L:   Bu' * boy do I have fun!=        ( (* = begins conventional
57         ₁((laughter))                   gesture for masturbation))
58   D:   ⁽((laughter))
59         (5.0)
```

C   Automobile Discussion, 26

```
  Gary:   He don'work weekends'r nothin, (he'd never sign up fer nothin).
          (2.5)
  Gary:   You just ha::d some.                                        <—#1
          (4.0)
  Gary:   (Loogih dat.)Now I don't have nothin tuh drink.=           <—#2
Carney:   =hm-hm heh-heh ·hhh
   Curt:  Hm-hm=
  Mike:   [Hm-hm
Carney:   [Awwwww.                                                    <—#3
  Ryan:   ·hh heh heh!
  Ryan:   Poor li'l baby,                                             <<—#4
          (0.4)
  Ryan:   [hn-heh-heh! ·hhh
   Curt:  [nn-hn hnehhe [h
  Mike:                 [hn-[-hn-hn-hn- [-hn-hn-hn-hn-=
  Ryan:                     [heh!          [
   Curt:                                    [ha-ha-ha-ha-ha-ha-
          [-ha-ha
  Mike:   =[-hn-hn
  Ryan:   [heh-heh- [-heh
  Gary:            [ (       [           [           =
   ???:                   [·hhhh!        [
  Ryan:                                  [·hhh!
  Gary:   = [           ) .
   Curt:  = [Aa: : [ : : =
  Gary:            [hehhe [heh
   Curt:                  [=hha ha hah=
  Ryan:   =heh heh=
   Curt:  =hheh
          (2.0)
```

Notes

Parts of this chapter, or earlier versions of those parts, have previously been presented at The First Rector's Colloquium, Tel Aviv University, May 1991; at The Program for the Assessment and Renewal of the Social Sciences, University of Pennsylvania, Philadelphia, March 1994; at the 80th Annual Meeting of the Speech Communication Association, New Orleans, LA, November 1994; in a plenary address at the Meetings of the American Association for Applied Linguistics, Chicago, IL, March 1996; in a plenary address to the 6th International

Congress, International Association for Dialogue Analysis, Prague, The Czech Republic, April 1996; at a Colloquium of the Language, Interaction and Social Organization Program, University of California, Santa Barbara, Colloquium, May 1996; in the keynote plenary address at the 5th International Conference of the International Pragmatics Association, Mexico City, July 1996; and as a keynote plenary address at the Conference on "Disorder and Order in Talk: Conversation Analysis and Communication Disorders," University College, University of London, June 1997, the last of which is the basis for the present text. A revised version of the International Pragmatics Association presentation has been published in Schegloff, 1999, and as drawn upon in the section entitled "Analysis I." The present texts was written while I was the grateful beneficiary of a Guggenheim Fellowship and a Fellowship in Residence at the Center for Advanced Study in the Behavioral Sciences, Stanford, CA, under support provided to the Center by The National Science Foundation through Grant #SBR-9022192.

1. See, for example, Sacks's discussion (in Sacks, 1992: I: 302–305 et passim) of the opening analysis in Pittenger, Hockett, and Danehy, 1960, or of observations by Frieda Fromm-Reichmann (at ibid., 768–771), and my treatment of psychodynamic theorizing in Schegloff, 1963.

2. Elements of the following paragraphs have been discussed in Schegloff, 1996: 28–29.

3. Parts of the following discussion, including stretches of its text, especially at pp. 28–37, are taken from Schegloff, 1999.

4. A useful discussion of the boundaries of "pragmatics" may be found in chapter 1 of Levinson, 1983.

5. For a review of much of the relevant literature, see Zaidel, 1998; Zaidel, Zaidel, and Bogen, 1998.

6. I would like to thank Asa Kasher and Eran Zaidel for providing access to data from their study of split-brain patients, a study supported by the USA-Israel Binational Science Foundation (grant no. 88-00116/3) and by the Israel Science Foundation (grants nos. 891/96-7 773//92-3 to Asa Kasher, Tel-Aviv University, and Eran Zaidel, UCLA), and by the USPHS NIH (grant no. NS 20187 to Eran Zaidel).

7. Zaidel et al., 1998: 281 suggest four accounts of "normally unified everyday behavior of the patients" in spite of this disconnection.

8. The work of Zaidel and Kasher from which the data being examined are drawn, as I understand it, has been largely focused on issues concerning the modularity of language structure, issues distinct from those of hemispheric localization, however thematically similar. Whatever inferences may be drawn from the analysis sketched in what follows for issues of hemispheric localization are of equivocal import for issues of modularity (though it may be noted that Zaidel [1998: 83] concludes his review of the relevant literature with the assessment that it "argues against a strictly modular view of natural language competence").

9. Zaidel et al., 1998, explicitly register divergences between conduct in ordinary interaction and performance in testing situations ("Long-term personal interaction with the patients reveals a few persisting cognitive lacunae" (280); "In contrast to everyday interactions, lateralized testing . . . reveals" (280); "In general, . . . split-brain patients behave in a coordinated, purposeful, and consistent manner, belying the independent, parallel, usually different and occasionally conflicting processing of the same information from the environment by the two disconnected hemispheres" (283). But detailed analysis focuses on data drawn from testing, not data drawn from repeatably inspectable conduct in ordinary interaction, on which the analysis

to follow is based, on the premise that it too is amenable to rigorous and telling analysis, which can make distinctive contributions in this area, however different in tenor.

For a discussion of a setting that raises related issues, see Schegloff, 1991: 54–57. For a more general discussion of the relationship between naturalistic and experimental research on talk-in-interaction that bears on testing as a mode of inquiry as well, see Schegloff, 1996: 22–30. And see Heeschen and Schegloff, this volume, chapter 10.

10.   I had intended to make available digitized video clips of this interactional episode, so that readers could get direct access to the data while reading its analysis. It has proved impossible to secure informed consent for the use of frame grabs from the videotape of this interaction with which to give the reader some direct visual access to the material addressed in the ensuing account. Accordingly, using the videotape and frame grabs displayed in conference presentations of this material as the target, we used Adobe Photoshop and the Poser program to model the key aspects of the key moments of Alvin's conduct in this strip of interaction. I wish to acknowledge the contributions of Geoff Raymond of the Department of Sociology and Val Poliuto of the Visualization Center, then both at UCLA, in producing these depictions of a virtual character, which nonetheless capture with remarkable fidelity the key elements of the conduct of a very real, embodied person, while retaining his complete anonymity.

11.   This itself is indicative of a special speech exchange system being in operation for the "testing" interaction, one apparently sustained by the "subject" even in this momentary intermission from it.

12.   "Potentially" because addressing an utterance to someone does not, by itself, select him or her as next speaker. Only certain turn types, if addressed to another, select that other as next speaker. The most common such turn types are those that constitute "first pair parts" of adjacency pairs (Sacks, Schegloff, & Jefferson, 1974: 716–717). The turn which ends up being addressed to Alvin here, being a request, *is* such a first pair part and does select him as next, but that has not yet happened at the moment we are examining.

13.   There is, of course, the possibility that Alvin is merely looking in the direction of the current speaker as a sound source, without discriminating that he is the targeted recipient. We will see later that he looks to Ezra when there is no such basis for his doing so.

14.   I am not, of course, endorsing mainline speech act theory here. Au contraire, the utility and relevance of its way of discriminating direct and indirect speech acts in actual talk-in-interaction is called into question here, as it is elsewhere; see Schegloff, 1988a, 1992b: I: xxiv–xxvii. Shoshana Blum-Kulka has pointed out to me (personal communication) that many lines of speech act theory would now consider the form of this utterance as virtually formulaic and as not implicating the sort of analysis to which the text is addressed.

15.   Not, of course, in the sense of Sperber and Wilson, 1986.

16.   After reading a draft of Schegloff, 1999, from which this section of the present chapter is taken, Asa Kasher (one of the principal investigators in the larger study from whose material this episode was drawn) wrote (personal communication) that, in the testing mentioned in my text, "the S did not use a command, under . . . circumstances where normal Ss do use it regularly, and that he did not react properly to non-regular indirect requests, not of the form of 'could you . . .' and the like, which are usual, but rather of unusual forms ('would it be possible for you' and the like)." The upshot of this colleague's comment was to qualify my invocation of the consequentiality of differences in context between performance in tests and in "real life" exchanges, in accord with the difference

between what "Alvin" does in this example (respond to a "usual form" of indirect request) and what he did poorly at in the tests.

Perhaps so, perhaps not. My text does not question the adequacy of the tests in assessing whatever they will turn out to have assessed, only their relevance to what those who have been tested can do—demonstrably *do* do—in real-life circumstances. What the tests are assessing is, of course, precisely what is at issue here—the organization of a "language faculty?" its mapping to, and implication with, the architecture of the brain? the context-sensitivity of practices of talking-in-interaction?

I am reminded of a number of stories I was told by Claus Heeschen, trained as a formal linguist and aphasiologist (and my collaborator in Heeschen and Schegloff, 1999; chapter 10), in describing his own scientific trajectory from testing as the instrument of inquiry into the speech and other conduct of aphasics to detailed examination of naturalistic records of ordinary interaction in mundane settings with friends and relatives. For example, while engaged in testing aphasic patients, he would ordinarily use rest periods, during which patients had coffee, to go and check his mail. One day, he happened to join the patients in the coffee room during the coffee break and was astonished to hear the patients doing things while talking among themselves or with relatives that they had just shown themselves "unable" to do in the preceding testing session. After that experience, he undertook to try out other methods of inquiry in addition to testing, and, eventually, in preference to it (see the first section of Heeschen and Schegloff, chap. 10).

That there may be important differences in capacity and performance between talking in the special frame of "testing interaction" and in ordinary conversation is, then, no idiosyncratic or casual suggestion on my part; indeed, the contrast is reported by one of the principal investigators of this very project (as cited earlier from Zaidel, 1998, and Zaidel et al., 1998). One payoff we may hope for from the intersection of naturalistic with other modes of inquiry is just such a specification as is at issue here of what tests (or other measurement instruments) are tapping, that is, a specification of validity.

17.   For those unfamiliar with the game, a brief description should be sufficient. The game is quite simple. Each player begins with half of a common deck of playing cards; each round of play consists of the two players revealing the top card in his or her half of the deck by turning it over; the one with the higher value card takes the trick and places the winning and losing cards into his or her pile of winnings, which is used to replenish that player's playing deck when it is exhausted. If the cards are of equal value when turned over, "war" is declared; the players each play three cards face down and a fourth card face up, with the one having the higher value winning the lot; if they are of equal value again, the same procedure is used recursively until someone wins the contested pile. In principle, the game continues until one player has won all the cards, but if adults play at all, they rarely continue to that point.

18.   On the researchers' subsequent account, Dan was attempting through this "fooling around" to elicit "requests" from Larry, these being a speech act from a class—"commissives"—of special interest for pragmatics concerns.

19.   The transcript of that segment appears in the appendix as A.

20.   Another episode in which guilty knowledge and non-comprehension are intimately and strategically related, this one involving a child, is examined in Schegloff, 1989.

21.   What Larry may have lost sight of is that Dan is still operating within the "testing" frame rather than in a "naive" game-playing frame, like a teacher asking the time not to know the time, but to know that the pupil can read the clock.

22. This sophisticated competence is well displayed in an episode that follows almost immediately afterward. See B in the appendix. That Larry understands utterances that are designed to be pragmatically disappointing is shown in the mode of his participation in the activity that directly follows cessation of the card game. Here Dan asks Larry a series of questions, to which Larry gives answers constructed to be *acceptable*, and even *correct* syntactically and semantically, but not pragmatically—"pragmatically unsatisfying," we might call them. In this respect, they are constructed specifically as "teases"—like the teasing response to "Do you know what time it is," "Yes, shall I tell you?" or simply "yes." Thus, he answers "Where do you live?" with "In a house," with a cunning smile on his face. Throughout this episode he hovers on the verge of laughter and tries to draw Dan into laughing with him (for example at lines 23–24), including, in the end, by co-implicating him in a *lewd gestural allusion* to masturbation (talk about non-literal usage as evidence of pragmatic competence!). It is as if he had formulated Dan's conduct in the game of "War" as "teasing"—as an intentional claimed failure of understanding designed to draw the other into a form of responsive conduct that in some fashion is disallowed or disapproved to that other. And he shows here that he can give as good as he got.

23. See C in the appendix for another candidate instance, taken from the same backyard picnic in Ohio. A discussion of a mutual acquaintance is being ended in Gary's first turn in this example, and in the 2.5-second silence that follows, Gary's young son, Ryan, picks up and drains his father's drink.

The candidate exemplar of the practice we have been tracking is at arrow #4. Note then that at arrows #1 and #2, Gary complains about his son's action; at arrow #3 Carney (his wife and Ryan's mother) interpolates a mock expression of sympathy, which the boy Ryan then complements with "Poor li'l baby." Although different from the previous specimens in various ways (in them, the target utterance embodied the complaint; here it is in response to a complaint), this instance seems, like the others, designedly terse and ironic (in its role reversal), but I leave further exploration of this possibility to the reader.

References

Austin, J. L. (1962). *How To Do Things with Words*. Cambridge, MA: Harvard University Press.

Bateson, G. (1955). A Theory of Play and Phantasy. *Psychiatric Research Reports*, 2, 39–51. Reprinted in Bateson, G. (1972). *Steps to an Ecology of Mind*. New York: Ballantine Books, pp. 177–93.

Drew, P. (1997). "Open" Class Repair Initiators in Response to Sequential Sources of Troubles in Conversation. *Journal of Pragmatics*, 28, 69–101.

Goffman, E. (1961). *Encounters: Two Studies in the Sociology of Interaction*. Indianapolis: Bobbs-Merrill.

Goffman, E. (1963). *Stigma: Notes on the Management of Spoiled Identity*. New York: Simon and Schuster.

Goffman, E. (1974). *Frame Analysis: An Essay on the Organization of Experience*. New York: Harper and Row.

Goodwin, C. (1981). *Conversational Organization: Interaction Between Speakers and Hearers*. New York: Academic Press.

Goodwin, C. (1984). Notes on Story Structure and the Organization of Participation. In M. Atkinson & J. Heritage (Eds.), *Structures of Social Action* (pp. 225–246). Cambridge: Cambridge University Press.

Goodwin, M. H. (1998). Games of Stance: Conflict and Footing in Hopscotch. In S. Hoyle &
C. T. Adger (Eds.), *Kids' Talk: Strategic Language Use in Later Childhood*
(pp. 23–46). New York: Oxford University Press.

Heeschen, C., & Schegloff, E. A. (1999). Agrammatism, Adaptation Theory, Conversation
Analysis: On the Role of So-Called Telegraphic Style in Talk-in-Interaction. *Aphasiology*,
13(4/5), 365–405.

Heritage, J. (1984). A Change-of-State Token and Aspects of Its Sequential Placement. In
J. M. Atkinson & J. Heritage (Eds.), *Structures of Social Action* (pp. 299–345). Cambridge: Cambridge University Press.

Jakobson, R. (1964). Towards a Linguistic Typology of Aphasic Impairments. In *Disorders
of Language* (pp. 21–46). London: CIBA Foundation Symposium.

Jakobson, R. (1966). Linguistic Types of Aphasia. In E. C. Carterette (Ed.), *Brain Function*.
Berkeley: University of California Press.

Jakobson, R. (1971). *Studies on Child Language and Aphasia*. The Hague: Mouton.

Jefferson, G. (1972). Side Sequences. In D. Sudnow (Ed.), *Studies in Social Interaction*
(pp. 294–338). New York: Free Press.

Jefferson, G. (1978). Sequential Aspects of Storytelling in Conversation. In J. Schenkein (Ed.),
Studies in the Organization of Conversational Interaction (pp. 219–248). New York:
Academic Press.

Laffal, J. (1965). *Pathological and Normal Language*. New York: Atherton Press.

Lerner, G. (1992). Assisted Storytelling: Deploying Shared Knowledge as a Practical Matter. *Qualitative Sociology*, *15*(3), 247–271.

Levelt, W. J. M. (1989). *Speaking: From Intention to Articulation*. Cambridge, MA: MIT
Press.

Levinson, S. C. (1983). *Pragmatics*. Cambridge: Cambridge University Press.

Marlaire, C., & Maynard, D. (1990). Standardized Testing as an Interactional Phenomenon.
Sociology of Education, *63*, 83–101.

Pittenger, R. E., Hockett, C. F., & Danehy, J. J. (1960). *The First Five Minutes*. Ithaca, NY:
Paul Martineau.

Ross, E. D., & Mesulam, M.-M. (1979). Dominant Language Functions of the Right Hemisphere? Prosody and Emotional Gesturing. *Archives of Neurology (Chicago)*, *36*, 144–48.

Sacks, H. (1972a). An Initial Investigation of the Usability of Conversational Materials for
Doing Sociology. In D. N. Sudnow (Ed.), *Studies in Social Interaction* (pp. 31–74). New
York: Free Press.

Sacks, H. (1972b). On the Analyzability of Stories by Children. In J. J. Gumperz & D. Hymes
(Eds.), *Directions in Sociolinguistics: The Ethnography of Communication* (pp. 325–
345). New York: Holt, Rinehart and Winston.

Sacks, H. (1974). An Analysis of the Course of a Joke's Telling in Conversation. In R. Bauman
& J. Sherzer (Eds.), *Explorations in the Ethnography of Speaking* (pp. 337–353). Cambridge: Cambridge University Press.

Sacks, H. (1987 [1973]). On the Preferences for Agreement and Contiguity in Sequences in
Conversation. In G. Button & J. R. E. Lee (Eds.), *Talk and Social Organisation* (pp. 54–
69). Clevedon, England: Multilingual Matters.

Sacks, H. (1992). *Lectures on Conversation*. Two volumes. Ed. G. Jefferson, with Introductions by E. A. Schegloff. Oxford: Blackwell.

Sacks, H., Schegloff, E. A., & Jefferson, G. (1974). A Simplest Systematics for the Organization of Turn-Taking for Conversation. *Language, 50*, 696–735.

Schegloff, E. A. (1963). Toward a Reading of Psychiatric Theory. *Berkeley Journal of Sociology, 8*, 61–91.

Schegloff, E. A. (1979). Identification and Recognition in Telephone Openings. In G. Psathas (Ed.), *Everyday Language: Studies in Ethnomethodology* (pp. 23–78). New York: Erlbaum.

Schegloff, E. A. (1986). The Routine as Achievement. *Human Studies, 9*, 111–151.

Schegloff, E. A. (1988a). On an Actual Virtual Servo-Mechanism for Guessing Bad News: A Single Case Conjecture. *Social Problems, 35*(4), 442–457.

Schegloff, E. A. (1988b). Presequences and Indirection: Applying Speech Act Theory to Ordinary Conversation. *Journal of Pragmatics, 12*, 55–62.

Schegloff, E. A. (1989). Reflections on Language, Development, and the Interactional Character of Talk-in-Interaction. In M. Bornstein & J. S. Bruner (Eds.), *Interaction in Human Development* (pp. 139–153). Hillsdale, NJ: Erlbaum.

Schegloff, E. A. (1991). Reflections on Talk and Social Structure. In D. Boden & D. H. Zimmerman (Eds.), *Talk and Social Structure* (pp. 44–70). Cambridge: Polity Press.

Schegloff, E. A. (1992a). In Another Context. In A. Duranti & C. Goodwin (Eds.), *Rethinking Context: Language as an Interactive Phenomenon* (pp. 193–227). Cambridge: Cambridge University Press.

Schegloff, E. A. (1992b). Introduction, Volume 1. In G. Jefferson (Ed.), *Harvey Sacks: Lectures on Conversation* (pp. ix–lxii). Oxford: Blackwell.

Schegloff, E. A. (1995). Sequence Organization. Los Angeles: Department of Sociology, UCLA.

Schegloff, E. A. (1996). Issues of Relevance for Discourse Analysis: Contingency in Action, Interaction and Co-Participant Context. In E. H. Hovy & D. Scott (Eds.), *Computational and Conversational Discourse: Burning Issues—An Interdisciplinary Account* (pp. 3–38). Heidelberg: Springer Verlag.

Schegloff, E. A. (1999). Discourse, Pragmatics, Conversation, Analysis. *Discourse Studies, 1*(4), 405–35.

Schegloff, E. A. (in press). *A Primer in Conversation Analysis: Sequence Organization.* Cambridge, England: Cambridge University Press.

Schegloff, E. A., Jefferson, G., & Sacks, H. (1977). The Preference for Self-Correction in the Organization of Repair in Conversation. *Language, 53*(2), 361–382.

Sperber, D., & Wilson, D. (1986). *Relevance: Communication and Cognition.* Cambridge, MA: Harvard University Press.

Van Lancker, D. R., & Canter, G. J. (1982). Impairment of Voice and Face Recognition in Patients with Hemispheric Damage. *Brain and Cognition 1*, 185–95.

Van Lancker, D. R., Cummings, J. L., Kreiman, J., & Dobkin, B. H. (1988). Phonagnosia: A Dissociation Between Familiar and Unfamiliar Voices. *Cortex 24*, 195–209.

Zaidel, E. (1998). Language in the Right Hemisphere Following Callosal Disconnection. In B. Stemmer & H. A. Whitaker (Eds.), *Handbook of Neurolinguistics* (pp. 369–383). San Diego: Academic Press.

Zaidel, E., Zaidel, D., & Bogen, J. E. (1998). Disconnection Syndrome. In J. G. Beaumont, P. M. Kenealy, & M. J. C. Rogers (Eds.), *The Blackwell Dictionary of Neuropsychology* (pp. 279–85). Oxford: Blackwell Publishers.

MAKING MEANING TOGETHER

3

RAY WILKINSON, SUZANNE BEEKE, AND JANE MAXIM

Adapting to Conversation

On the Use of Linguistic Resources by Speakers with Fluent Aphasia in the Construction of Turns at Talk

In aphasiology it is commonly the case that aphasic language structures, such as lexical and grammatical forms, are analyzed and "treated" in relative isolation from, or in parallel to, other, more "functional" aspects of the condition such as the ability to communicate or psychosocial issues. For example, while assessments of aphasic language (e.g., Goodglass & Kaplan, 1983; Kay, Lesser, & Coltheart, 1992) typically focus on lexical, grammatical, or other linguistic structures in relative isolation from their communicative use and psychosocial effects, others focus on communicative abilities (Holland, 1980; Wirz, Skinner, & Dean, 1990) or on psychosocial consequences of aphasia (Code & Muller, 1992) with little or no analysis of the linguistic forms used by the speaker with aphasia under investigation. Within this framework, aphasic language has predominantly been investigated (and treated) using units of analysis such as "word" and "sentence," and assessments of aphasic language have typically adopted methods of data collection that facilitate analysis using these units, such as naming (of objects or pictures), describing (of pictures), or the production of narratives (such as well-known stories) in the form of a monologue.

Linked to this approach to aphasic language, explanations for why people with aphasia display the particular linguistic forms they do have typically been framed in terms of the relationship between these forms, or "symptoms" (Code, 1989), as highlighted by assessments of aphasic language such as those cited here, and the damaged neurological areas or language processing components believed to underlie them (e.g., Caplan, 1987; Ellis & Young, 1996). The extent to which the distinctive patterns of behavior following brain damage, including language behavior, can be treated as a relatively direct reflection of an underlying neurological or neuropsychological impairment has, however, been a subject of continuing debate. Goldstein (1939, 1948), for example, influenced by the work of Jackson (1931), argued that such behavior may reflect not only the underlying damage but also the attempt by the person to adapt or come to terms with that damage. This adaptation was viewed as occurring in relation to the demands of the environment. Thus, as Goldstein (1948: 21) noted in relation to aphasia: "the aphasic patient tries to achieve a condition which allows him to react as well as possible to the tasks arising from his environment."

This view of aphasic language as, at least in part, a result of adaptation has been echoed more recently by aphasiologists such as Penn (1987), Penn and Cleary (1988), and Kolk and Heeschen (1990, 1992, 1996), who have invoked adaptation to account for aspects of aphasic language behavior such as the use of elliptical expressions.

While some of these authors, such as Goldstein, have included in their descriptions a notion of an "environment" to which language may be seen to adapt, there has been little discussion of what the exact nature of such an environment might be or what the environmental demands might be that may motivate speakers to adapt their language in systematic ways. One way in which possible factors motivating adaptation have been discussed is in (neuro)psychological terms; it has been suggested for example that an advantage of speakers adapting their language production may be to "ease the communicative load" (Penn & Cleary, 1988: 10) or to "prevent the computational overload that would result if a complete sentence form were attempted" (Kolk & Heeschen, 1992: 89).

A different and distinctive view of language as adaptation to its environment has emerged from work within conversation analysis (CA) (Ford & Thompson, 1996; Schegloff, 1989, 1991a, 1996a). This approach takes as a primary focus of enquiry and empirical investigation the social structures or organizations of everyday talk-in-interaction, such as the organization of turn-taking, sequences, or repair (Schegloff, 1991b). It is argued that speakers can be seen to orient to these organizations in their talk and in the interpretation of the talk of others, and that it is through their orientations to these social organizations that speakers are able to produce contributions to the interaction which can be seen to be treated by recipients as orderly and understandable (Heritage, 1984).

As Schegloff notes (1989: 140), in this respect conversation analysis differs from some other approaches to talk which view "the mind/brain as the scene of all the action, and the space of interaction as a structureless medium, or at least a medium whose structure is beside the point with respect to what is transmitted through it, as the composition of telephone cable is beside the point for the conversations transmitted through it."

Rather, within a conversation analytic approach, the domain of interaction for which talk is produced is viewed as highly structured and, as such, these structures may be seen as influencing the very form of the talk produced. It is in this way, therefore, that language may be viewed as being adapted to a particular environment:

If the conduct of language as a domain of behavior is biological in character, then we should expect it (like other biological entities) to be adapted to its natural environment. What is the primordial natural environment of language use, within which the shape of linguistic structures such as grammar, have been shaped? Transparently, the natural environment of language use is talk-in-interaction, and originally ordinary conversation. The natural home environment of clauses and sentences is turns-at-talk. Must we not understand the structure of grammar to be in important respects adaptations to the turn-at-talk in a conversational turn-taking system with its interactional contingencies? (Schegloff, 1989: 143–144)

Turn organization has been the focus of a number of CA investigations (e.g., Ford & Thompson, 1996; Sacks, Schegloff, & Jefferson, 1974; Schegloff, 1979, 1996a). Sacks et al. (1974) noted that turns are constructed from components which they termed "turn-constructional units" (TCUs) which could be constituted, in syntactic terms, by a sentence, clause, phrase, or word. Turns are made up of one or more TCUs. The possible completion of a TCU constitutes a "transition-relevance place" (TRP), at which point transition to another speaker becomes relevant, even if the opportunity is not taken up. From this perspective, aspects of language such as grammar and lexis are resources for the production of turn-constructional units and as such are organized with reference to their environment of occurrence. In particular, "one of the main jobs grammar or syntax does is to provide potential construction- and recognition-guides for the realization of the possible completion points of TCUs, and potentially of turns" (Schegloff 1996a: 87). Schegloff (1996a: 55) also notes that turns are different from words or sentences as a unit of analysis in that "talking in turns means talking *in real time, subject to real interactional contingencies*" (italics in original). Turn-constructional units are themselves thus constructed in and for the particular interactional contexts within which they are produced at particular points in time, such as the turn, the sequence within which the turn may occur, and the wider topical and conversational activity to which the utterance contributes.

Recently, such findings from conversation analysis have begun to be applied to the investigation of the forms of language used by speakers with aphasia within interaction. Heeschen and Schegloff (1999), for example, analysed variations in the manifestations of agrammatism evident in the talk of a German-speaking "non-fluent" aphasic, suggesting that the adoption of "telegraphic style" might be an interactional resource which could be used by the speaker to encourage the other participant into collaborating in the construction of the talk. Rönfeldt (1999), also investigating a German-speaking aphasic in conversation, used a combination of conversation analytic and psycholinguistic research findings in order to analyze the production of "paragrammatisms" in talk.

In this chapter we use the methodology and findings of conversation analysis in order to investigate the language used by two speakers with "fluent" aphasia[1] in their conversations. In particular, we focus on different ways in which lexical and grammatical resources are used by these speakers in the construction of turns at talk and the interactional features of these different methods. We focus first on one method used by both speakers which can be seen to involve constructing contributions to conversation using the kind of lexical items and grammatical structures that these speakers might have used before they became aphasic. As we note, this method can regularly be seen to lead to repair and the highlighting of the speakers' linguistic non-competence. We then analyze how, within the same conversations, these speakers also use other methods that appear to be qualitatively or quantitatively different from those they might have used before becoming aphasic. These include the grammatical construction of "fronting" a noun or noun phrase and the use of what we will be calling "general meaning" lexical items such as pronouns, the verb "do," and the noun "thing." We note that an interactional feature of this method of TCU/turn construction is that it can allow these speakers to produce relatively complex contributions to the conversation without repair and the speaker's linguistic non-competence becoming the focus of the conversational activity. As such, these latter methods appear to be ways in which these speakers with aphasia can each be seen to have adapted their language to the environment within which, and for which, it is produced, namely the turn-constructional unit and turn within its conversational context. We conclude the chapter by highlighting some of the possible theoretical and clinical implications of these findings.

The two speakers whose talk is analyzed here, GB and DW, were each recorded in the early stages of recovery following a stroke. GB, who was 43 years old at the time of recording, was a kitchen porter. He became aphasic following a left middle cerebral artery infarct. The data we will be discussing here come from a conversation between GB and his partner, Daniela, at home 11 weeks after GB's stroke. DW, who was 52 years old at the time of recording, was a factory worker who became aphasic following a left middle cerebral artery infarct. The data we will be discussing here come mainly from one conversation between DW and a speech and language therapist in a hospital stroke unit one week after his stroke. One extract (example 6) is taken from DW in conversation with the same therapist seven weeks later.

Constructing turns using "canonical" word order and full form lexical items

One method by which these speakers with aphasia can be seen to attempt to construct their turns at talk in these conversations is by using "canonical" word order (e.g., subject-verb-object)[2] and full form lexical items[3] in a way similar to what might be done by non-aphasic speakers in constructing such utterances. A regular pattern observable in these conversations when this method of turn construction is attempted, however, is that the speaker with aphasia experiences linguistic difficulties, such as the production of linguistic errors or difficulties in word finding/word production, which he or she responds to by initiating repair. Repair as an activity has the potential to take over as the "interactional business" (Jefferson, 1987: 88) of the conversation, replacing whatever action was previously being carried out before the repair was started, and can be accompanied by what Jefferson (1987: 88) terms "accountings," that is activities which are concerned with "addressing lapses in competence and conduct."

In these conversations, when a speaker with aphasia attempts to construct a turn using "canonical" word order and full form lexical items, both these aspects of repair can regularly be seen to occur, often in ways that may particularly highlight the speaker's linguistic non-competence as caused by the aphasia. First, when repair is initiated in non-aphasic talk, speakers regularly orient to the preference for self-repair (Schegloff, Jefferson, & Sacks, 1977) by repairing the trouble source in their talk themselves. In these aphasic conversations, however, the speakers with aphasia, while able to initiate repair, are often unable to achieve the preferred outcome of self-repair because of their linguistic difficulties, and regularly the other participant becomes involved in an attempt to complete the repair (Goodwin, 1995; Laakso & Klippi, 1999; Milroy & Perkins, 1992; Wilkinson, 1995a). Second, while non-aphasic repair is regularly quick and successful (Schegloff et al., 1977), repair in aphasic talk can be long, and can often be abandoned uncompleted (Lock, Wilkinson, & Bryan, 2001). Schegloff (1979: 268–9n.) notes that in conversation there is a "preference for 'progressivity,'" namely a preference "for 'next parts' of structured units (e.g. turns, turn-constructional units like sentences, stories, etc.) to come next." Thus, when a speaker initiates a repair, the preference is for the repair itself to be completed quickly, and by this means to allow the ongoing turn and the action being performed within it (which have themselves been delayed by the repair) to progress to possible completion. A delay in completing repair can therefore be a noticeable and accountable event, leading to participants becoming aware of, and possibly orienting to, possible reasons for the delay, such as linguistic non-competence. As Couper-Kuhlen (1992: 345) notes in relation to repair:

> It may be experienced as a loss of time rather than simply a suspension in time. If so, and if the problem necessitating repair is such that it can be traced back to some personal insufficiency or shortcoming on the part of one of the interactants, then there are important reasons for resolving it as quickly as possible: it has become an 'incident', an event which threatens face and therefore the ritual order. (Goffman 1969)

Therefore, since repair of trouble sources in these conversations may highlight the speaker with aphasia's language abilities (and hence potentially the speaker him- or herself) as "different," "non-competent," or "disordered," it can be seen as having the potential to be a sensitive and embarrassing activity or "incident" (Lindsay & Wilkinson, 1999; Wilkinson, 1995b). That speakers with aphasia may orient to the exposure of their linguistic non-competence in this way can be seen in their reactions in alluding to it, which can include "embarrassed" laughter (Wilkinson,

1995b; Wilkinson, 2002) and evidence of being emotionally upset (Wilkinson, Bryan, Lock, et al., 1998).

We will show here two examples, one from GB's conversation and one from DW's conversation, where the speaker with aphasia's attempt to construct turns using "canonical" word order and full form lexical items leads to linguistic difficulties and repair. In both it will be seen that the speaker with aphasia has difficulty in self-repairing and that the other participant becomes involved in the attempt to complete the repair. Also in both the repair takes several attempts to resolve, with the repair therefore becoming the focus of activity for both participants at this point in the conversation over a number of turns. Finally it will be seen that the speaker with aphasia makes his linguistic non-competence a focus of the activity at these points by alluding to it. In each example, therefore, the action that was being produced in the turn before the repair began can be seen to be replaced by the speaker with aphasia's linguistic non-competence and repair difficulties as the focus of attention and activity.

In example 1, GB and his partner, Daniela, have been making preparations for GB to go to a residential rehabilitation center and GB here is talking about some small cards he is taking with him which have the addresses of friends and family members on them. The difficulties GB has with constructing utterances in the "normal," non-aphasic manner can be seen regularly throughout his talk and is not restricted to the example we are focusing on here, which starts "I haven't got" in line 1. For example, the utterance in line 1 before the one we are focusing on ("one of those little cards with those") projects more to come grammatically, pragmatically, and prosodically (Ford & Thompson, 1996) but, after a pause and a cough is abandoned uncompleted. GB then starts a new utterance, which will be the focus of our attention here. In retrospect it can be seen that the "target utterance" here is something like "I haven't got Theresa's address," an SVO sentence/utterance using full form linguistic items, functioning in the conversation as a sentential turn-constructional unit:

Example 1 (ESRCI: GB4a : 00:12:30)

```
 1  →  GB:        one of those little cards with those, (0.5) ((coughs)) I haven't got /sti/- eh:,
 2  →             (2.0) /trivənz/ tch! kh! (1.6) /trivəz/ (0.5) tch! oh (ged name) there in a
 3  →             minute (.) /trivənz/
 4     Daniela:   ((coughs loudly))
 5     GB:        thank you.
 6     Daniela:   sorry.
 7                (0.8)
 8  →  GB:        eh Steven's (.) dhhhh! /tərivəz/- tch!  ⌈(oh my-)
 9  →  Daniela:                                          ⌊Theresa?
10  →  GB:        Theresa. (.) her ehm (.) her eh name- eh eh ⌈tch!
11  →  Daniela:                                              ⌊her address?
12  →  GB:        a- address. I haven't got it properly anyway so
```

It can be seen that this utterance takes longer for GB to produce (25 seconds) and contains far more failed repair attempts than would be expected with a non-aphasic utterance. The linguistic errors here in the attempt at "Theresa" (his daughter) are paraphasias. In particular it appears that GB's attempts are being affected by his "confusing" his daughter's name with that of his son, Steven (in one case, in line 8, the name "Steven" is produced instead of "Theresa"). He is able to monitor and attempt repair on each of these errors but is unable to complete the repair by producing the name correctly. Similarly his attempt at "address" in line 10 is produced, after some searching, as "name," which again he is unable to repair himself. The extended repair sequence here can be seen to make him vulnerable to other "events" occurring during the repair attempt, thus disrupting and delaying it still further, such as the side sequence (Jefferson, 1972) in lines 4–6, involving Daniela's cough and the reactions to it.[4] This difficulty in achieving self-repair results in Daniela twice (lines 9 and 11) "coming into" GB's turn space and producing a candidate other-repair in the modulated form of a "guess" (Schegloff et al., 1977), thus allowing GB to continue and reach a TRP, and thus potential TCU and turn completion, with "address."[5]

GB's linguistic non-competence, therefore, can be seen to be highlighted in his attempt to produce this utterance using these particular linguistic items in this "canonical" order. First, he has been unable to satisfy the preference for progressivity; the repair sequence itself is extended and involves several failed attempts at self-completion.[6] This therefore also delays the progressivity of the TCU (within which the repair is occurring) towards a TRP and thus possible completion. Second, he has been unable to satisfy the preference for self-repair; it takes Daniela to other-repair on two occasions for the repair attempts on a particular linguistic item to be completed and for the turn to continue. GB can be seen to allude to his linguistic difficulties several times in the sequence by his production of "response cries" (Goffman, 1981a) and comments on his own performance. The former take the form of displays of annoyance such as clicks ("tch!" in lines 2 [twice], 8, 10) and other "exclamatory interjections which are not full-fledged words" (Goffman, 1981a: 99), such as "kh!" (line 2) and "dhhhh!" (line 8). The latter are seen in lines 2–3 ("oh (ged name) there in a minute") and line 8 ("(oh my-)"). Both types of allusion can be seen as "metalinguistic" references by GB, a "shift in footing" (Goffman, 1981b: 152n.) by which he "breaks frame" (Goffman, 1981a) and alludes to his own talk. Goffman (1981a, 1981b) suggests that such verbal behaviors can be seen as an orientation by the speaker to his exposed non-competence by alluding to it and thus displaying that overall he or she is a "competent person" and is able to notice and treat this occurrence as a "lapse," thus "providing evidence to anyone that can hear that our observable plight is not something that should be taken to define us" (Goffman, 1981b: 136). By such behavior GB can be seen to be displaying an orientation toward himself as being noticeably non-competent at this point by alluding to it. At these points in the conversation, therefore, the focus of activity has shifted from *what* GB is saying to *how* he is saying it; it is GB's linguistic non-competence that has itself become the subject of attention and the focus of the conversational activity.

As such, it can be seen that this type of turn construction using "canonical" word order and full forms has, in this case, resulted in the speaker being unable to satisfy some of the preferences which are typically oriented to by speakers in the production of talk, such as achieving progressivity in turn development and, if repair occurs, orienting to the preference for progressivity in completing this repair quickly and also completing it by means of self-repair. Instead, this type of turn has been seen to display some of the features of "dispreferred" turns, such as delays and accounts (Heritage, 1984; Levinson, 1983). Also in this type of turn it has been seen that the speaker's linguistic non-competence may become the focus of the activity.

Similar turn features can be seen to occur in DW's talk when he attempts to construct a sentential TCU using full form lexical items and "canonical" word order. The extract shown in example 2 occurs directly after a very long repair sequence (lasting just over two minutes) not shown here in which DW has been attempting to tell the therapist one of his hobbies. After first telling her that one of them is fishing, he attempts to tell her another one but "perseverates" (Code, 1989), producing the word "fishing" again. Having self-initiated repair on this, he is unable to self-repair, and a long "hint and guess" sequence (Laakso & Klippi, 1999; Lubinski, Duchan, & Weitzner-Lin, 1980) ensues. The repair attempt is eventually abandoned uncompleted by the therapist when she changes the activity by asking DW "what do you normally do in the day" (line 1 in example 2). In response to the therapist's question, DW, after a long delay, is able to produce "work. working" (line 4). In line 11 the therapist asks another question, asking for the name of the place DW worked, which he is unable to provide (line 12). In line 14 he then produces the utterance "I like fishing." It is this utterance and the repair which follows from it that we will focus on here:

Example 2 (PHD: DW1: 00:03:30)

1		Therapist:	what do you normally do in the day.
2			(3.2)
3		Therapist:	( )
4		DW:	⌈ work. work⌈ing.
5		Therapist:	⌊( ) ⌊( )
6		DW:	I worked.
7		Therapist:	>worked<
8		DW:	working.
9		Therapist:	mmhm,
10		DW:	working
11		Therapist:	where do you work?
12		DW:	(0.3) eh:::m (2.0) I—I don't really know what it is yet
13		Therapist:	mm.
14	→	DW:	(0.3) umh (1.5) I like.- I like fishing.

```
15  →  Therapist:    m⌈ mhm
16  →  DW:            ⌊uh- ⌈↓ fishing!
17  →                     ⌊((extended arm gesture))
18  →  Therapist:    >working.<
19  →  DW:            I like, (1.9) ⌈>the other one< (what ⌈ d'(hh)ya hh)      ⌉
20  →                          ⌊((looking at the therapist and smiling while doing   |
                                 "continuation" gesture))                      |
21  →  Therapist:                                  ⌊gh huh huh                 ⌋
22  →  DW:            uh:: (3.8) °yeah I dunno. I ⌈dunno what (it is)°
23  →  Therapist:                                  ⌊so you like working?
24  →  DW:            yeah
25  →  Therapist:    yeah
26  →  DW:            ⌈that's what        ⌈I meant.
27  →                 ⌊((points at therapist))|
28     Therapist:                        ⌊mmhm,
```

Lines 14–27 here involving DW display some similarities to the features described in the conversation involving GB in example 1. First, the trouble source turn here is also a sentential TCU involving full form lexical items and "canonical" sentence structure (in this case, "I like fishing"). In retrospect (lines 16–27) it becomes evident that the target utterance is likely to have been "I like working," but that DW has perseverated here on the utterance "I like fishing," which he produced a couple of minutes earlier in this conversation.

Second, while it is the speaker with aphasia who initiates the repair (with "uh-↓fishing!" in line 16), it is again the other participant, here the therapist, who provides a (possible) completion to the repair. She does this first by producing an explicit other-repair in line 18 which DW appears, from the evidence of his subsequent turns, not to respond to, perhaps either because he did not hear it or because he did not "monitor" it in some way. Second, following DW's displayed inability in lines 19–22 to self-repair, she provides a solution in line 23 by producing the target utterance in the form of a question ("so you like working?"), to which DW agrees ("yeah" and "that's what I meant" in lines 24 and 26 respectively).

A third similarity between examples 1 and 2 is that in both the repair is not completed quickly but rather continues over several turns. In example 2 the target is the lexical item "working"[7]; DW first produces "I like fishing" (line 14) and then fails to respond to the therapist's other-repair in line 18, after which the repair continues over another few turns until lines 23–24.

Fourth, DW can be seen to allude to his linguistic non-competence by joking about it in lines 19–20. Here, he produces the sentence frame "I like," and pauses. He then does what can be seen as (and indeed appears to be interpreted by the therapist as) a joking allusion to his perseveration and inability to repair it himself. He adds (spoken quickly) the phrase "the other one" while smiling at the therapist and producing what can be glossed as a "continuation" gesture, by which he moves his finger several times in a circle in front of his body. The overall meaning here can be interpreted as something like "what was it again, that word I just said earlier?"[8] This is then followed by an utterance and laughter (the utterances being mostly unintelligible on the tape through the laughter). The therapist joins in with this laughter, creating the effect of a shared "joke."[9] Thus, while this allusion is carried out by (joint) laughter rather than displays of annoyance (such as were seen in example 1), it is still the case that at this point in the conversation the focus of activity and joint attention has changed from the content of DW's talk (i.e., talking about his work in lines 1–12) to the fact that he made a linguistic error in line 14 (saying "fishing" instead of "working") and is unable to correct this error himself (lines 16–22).[10]

As such, it can be seen from examples 1 and 2 that there are reasons why speakers with aphasia, such as those discussed here, might be wary of simply trying to construct contributions to talk in the ways they did before the stroke. Even where it might be possible for them to attempt to do so, as was seen earlier, the use of "canonical" grammatical structure and full forms can regularly lead to the occurrence of significant difficulties in progressing the turn, difficulties in achieving self-repair, and thus potentially the highlighting of the speaker's linguistic non-competence and "difference" as a participant in the conversation (Wilkinson, 1995b). Given this situation, it can be seen that speakers may be motivated to adopt other ways of constructing contributions to talk, ways that, while different (in their design or in the quantity with which they are used) from those they used to construct turns before becoming aphasic, might have interactional advantages for them, such as the reduction or removal of the types of repair patterns and exposure of linguistic non-competence that were seen in examples 1 and 2. In the next section we will discuss other methods of constructing turns at talk which can be seen to have been adopted by both these speakers with aphasia and which can have such interactional advantages.

Constructing turns using fronting of noun phrases or using "general meaning" lexical items or both

In the same conversations from which examples 1 and 2 were taken, GB and DW display other methods of turn construction which use a different, "non-canonical", word order pattern or a different "type" of lexical item from that seen in those examples. Example 3 displays these different methods. Here GB and Daniela are discussing the different kitchen knives they each use and how each of them has their own likes and dislikes:

Example 3 (ESRCI: GB4a: 00:40:05)
```
1   Daniela:   you don't like my little knife and I don't like your one.
2   GB:        oh your (.) your kitchen one, (0.3) (I-)
3   Daniela:  ⌈you know the little one
4             ⌊((gestures 'little' with finger and thumb))
```

```
 5                for ⌈paring
 6   GB:          ⌊>yeah yeah< the little ones (.) ⌈the little one ⌉
 7                                                 ⌊((gestures 'little' with finger and thumb))
 8                (.) I can't do it. (.) I can't do it. (.)
 9                but my (0.9) eh (0.8) little- little (waɪl), (.) you don't like it.
10   Daniela:     no I know. (0.6) cos it's the handle is wrong.
11   GB:          oh I ca- I'm all right wi- (0.2) with that I can (1.2) it's also (.) the bit- (.)
12                the ⌈blade on it,
13                    ⌊((mimes ?opening knife))
14   Daniela:     mm.
15   GB:          (1.0) is (.) is a case of (0.5) I wanna, (2.0) (I'm) (1.2) /di/ (1.1) /pɔlɪ/-
16                um (0.3) peeling, (0.8) (on) a, (1.8) (where it's) carro- carrots, (0.8) or
17                even it's (.) potatoes (0.3) it's all right ⌈(.) I can do it.
18                                                          ⌊((mimes peeling/scraping vegetables))
19                ⌈(0.3)
20   GB:          ⌊((GB looks up at Daniela and continues to mime peeling/scraping))
21   Daniela:     ⌈°mm°
22                ⌊((GB looks at Daniela and continues to mime peeling/scraping))
23   GB:          ⌈>(the way I) do it.< (.)
24                ⌊((GB continues to mime peeling/scraping))
25                ⌈you do yours, (0.9) better
26                ⌊((points to Daniela))
27                (0.8)
28                but (.) if you're (0.3) testing (0.2) the /raɪt/ (.) being cooked,
29                ⌈(0.2) (here) you're all right for that                       ⌉
30                ⌊((mimes ?dipping knife in and out of something))⌋
31                (0.5) but ⌈/kulm/ is a different thing.      ⌉
32                          ⌊((GB mimes peeling/scraping))  ⌋
33   Daniela:     ⌈(°huh°)
34                ⌊((GB continues to mime peeling/scraping))
35   GB:          ⌈you can't do                              ⌉ the other one.
36                ⌊((GB continues to mime peeling/scraping))⌋
37   Daniela:     yeah
```

One method of turn construction that GB can be seen to adopt for several of his turns in this example (lines 6–8; line 9; lines 17–23) is a particular grammatical pattern that includes the "fronting" (Quirk, Greenbaum, Leech, & Svartvik, 1985)[11] of a noun/noun phrase followed by a proposition relating to that noun/noun phrase. Grammatically, this kind of construction has been described in terms of "left dislocation" (Duranti & Ochs, 1979; Geluykens, 1992; Kim, 1995; Quirk et al., 1985) and "topicalization" (Duranti & Ochs, 1979), where, as Kim (1995: 247) notes (in a discussion of left dislocation), "the markedness lies in the word order, which deviates from the canonical SVO word order of English." As Geluykens (1992) has noted, part of the distinctiveness of this method of utterance construction is that it is divided typically into three parts: the introduction of the referent by participant A, followed either by a pause or a brief acknowledgement by participant B, then the production by participant A of the proposition concerning the referent. The function of these grammatical constructions has been described in terms of "foregrounding referents" (Ochs & Schieffelin, 1983) or "referent-highlighting" (Geluykens, 1992). The disjoined referent can thus allow the speaker to "set the scene" (Friedman, 1976) or "set out the 'point of departure'" (Quirk et al., 1985: 1417) for the current turn with the "comment" (Li & Thompson, 1976) concerning that referent then following later, usually after a pause or a continuer from the other participant.

Thus, in line 9, GB constructs his contribution here not in the SVO format of "but you don't like my little /waıl/" but rather by first producing a referent, in this case doing object reference ("but my (0.9) eh (0.8) little—little (waıl),"), then, following a short pause, producing an utterance relating to that referent, where the referent's "slot" as a direct object in the grammatical structure is filled by an anaphoric pronoun "it" ("you don't like it.").[12]

A second method GB can be seen to adopt in the construction of his turns in this extract is the use of a large number of what we are calling "general meaning" lexical items, such as pronouns (e.g., "one[s]" in lines 2, 6, and 35),[13] the verb "do" (lines 8, 17, 23, 25, 35), and the noun "thing" (line 31).[14] These are often used together to construct utterances consisting largely of "general meaning" lexical items such as "I can do it." (line 17), "you do yours, (0.9) better" (line 25), and "you can't do the other one." (line 35).

In the remainder of this chapter we will note in passing the regular separate use of these two methods in these conversations involving GB and DW but, for reasons of focus, will concentrate our discussion on utterances where these speakers with aphasia combine both methods, that is, where they construct their turns using a fronted noun/noun phrase followed by a proposition relating to that noun/noun phrase, and where this proposition is constructed largely of "general meaning" lexical items.

Two examples of this pattern can be seen in GB's talk in example 3. In lines 6–8, GB produces the object reference (referring to a knife) "the little ones [.] the little one" and then, after a short pause, says something relating to this reference ("I can't do it. (.) I can't do it."). Similarly in lines 16–23, GB first introduces a reference to specific objects, vegetables ("(where it's) carro—carrots, (0.8) or even it's (.) potatoes"), and then, following a brief pause, produces an utterance relating to that reference ("it's all right (.) I can do it." in line 17, and ">(the way I) do it.<" in line 23).

A similar pattern can be seen elsewhere in GB's talk. It occurs for example in the extract seen in example 4 which takes place a couple of minutes before the extract seen in example 3 and where the topic is again knives.

Example 4 (ESRCI: GB 4a: 00:38:00)

```
1        Daniela:  yeah I'll get her one of those. (0.2) ↑one of those like my kitchen devil
2                  one = ⌈ the double (0.9)      ⌉ double edged one.
3                         ⌊(("twisting" gesture))⌋
```

```
4                    (0.7) cos I mean that- (0.3) look how long I've had that and it's still as
5                    ⌈sharp as          ⌉ any⌈thing
6   →   GB:          ⌊yeah (>well y's-<)⌋   ⌊ with that one, (0.8) even though it:'s: (1.0)
7   →                kit-chen (.) devil (0.5) it's still sharp.
8                    (0.5)
9       Daniela:  yeah (.) ⌈(well)
10  →   GB:               ⌊(what you do) (.) it's (just) that (.) usually now (instead) that one-
11  →                (0.3) my other one, (.) ⌈the big one (0.2) you (ju-)
12  →                                        ⌊((mimes pulling out big knife))
13  →   Daniela:  ⌈°mm°
14  →   GB:       ⌊ and uh ⌈ you just do it
15  →                      ⌊((mimes cutting))
16                   (0.5)
17      Daniela:  yeah it's c- (.) I ⌈ like (.) the reason I like that is ⌉ cos it's got a quite a
18                                    ⌊(("twisting" gesture))             ⌋
19                   flexible (.) ⌈blade
20      GB:                       ⌊yeah
```

In lines 1–5 Daniela is discussing buying a kitchen knife, similar to her own "kitchen devil" knife, as a present for a friend of the couple. In line 6 GB starts his turn (overlapping Daniela's ongoing turn) and produces a reference to this "kitchen devil" knife of Daniela's ("with that one,") which he then goes on to talk about ("even though it:'s: (1.0) kit-chen (.) devil (0.5) it's still sharp . . . (what you do)"). He then (lines 10–11) introduces a reference (again using the pronoun "one" and also, in this case, a short mime) to another knife, his big one ("that one- (0.3) my other one, (.) the big one"), and talks about this (lines 14–15) using an utterance constructed using largely "general meaning" forms ("and uh you just do it") and accompanied by a "cutting" mime.[15]

Why might GB be constructing his turns here and elsewhere in this conversation using these methods? The use of fronted constructions by "non-communication disordered" speakers has been noted as often performing functions concerned with raising alternatives, contrasting, or bringing other members of a previously mentioned set into the conversation (Geluykens, 1992; Ochs & Schieffelin, 1983). This also appears to be at least part of the function of these constructions when used by speakers with aphasia in these conversations. Thus in each of examples 3 and 4 GB uses two fronted constructions, the first to talk about Daniela's knife which she has mentioned in the preceding turn(s), and the second to talk about a different member of the set of objects, his own knife (example 3, lines 6–9; example 4, lines 6–15). A possible advantage for GB here in fronting the noun phrase is that it may make it easier for him to "borrow" linguistic items or constructions recently used by Daniela in order to assist construction of his own turn, perhaps particularly of an element toward the beginning of his turn. Thus in example 3, he fronts the noun phrase "the little ones (.) the little one" (line 6) which was previously used by Daniela in line 3, and in example 4, he uses the phrase "with that one," (line 6), which echoes the use by Daniela of "one" in lines 1 and 2, and "that" in line 4.[16]

It has also been noted that in "normal" conversation, this kind of construction can be used to compete for the conversational floor by, for example, overlapping another speaker's turn. This may also be a useful property of these constructions for speakers with aphasia. In both examples 3 (line 6) and 4 (line 6), GB can be seen to overlap Daniela with turns that start with "yeah" and then use a fronted noun phrase.

There are other features of this construction that can be seen to have possible uses and advantages for speakers with language difficulties, and in particular speakers such as these who have difficulties with word finding and word production. First, this construction allows the speaker to produce a lexical item (or items) in relative isolation from the grammatical constraints that might be present if the item was within, for example, an SVO construction. This potentially makes it more likely that the word will be able to be found and produced. The construction of the proposition element may also be made easier by the fact that an anaphoric pronoun can take the "slot" that might otherwise require a noun/noun phrase. The possible advantage for speakers with aphasia in terms of starting and progressing the turn, therefore, is that they can use the fronted noun/noun phrase to begin an utterance (having perhaps also gained the floor in this way, as noted earlier) and then pause, with little commitment to what form the next part of their turn (the proposition about the noun/noun phrase) will take (see Dik, 1978). The fact that this construction allows the speaker to signal with the production of the fronted noun/noun phrase that the utterance is not yet complete (in grammatical, pragmatic, or prosodic terms: Ford & Thompson, 1996a), may assist him or her in thus "staking a claim" to keep the turn and take the time to construct it up to such a point as it might be hearably complete.

The use of "general meaning" lexical forms can be seen to be potentially useful in that it allows speakers with aphasia to construct these parts of an utterance without having to "access" and produce the kind of full form lexical items that can be particularly difficult for them. As noted earlier, these items can also perform useful indexical functions, allowing the speaker to link to, and build on, other utterances.

Particularly noticeable in these conversations is the fact that the non-semantically specific nature of these lexical items can be a useful resource for these speakers, allowing them, for example, to use the same lexical item with a range of different meanings depending on the context, or to add one of an almost limitless range of possible gestures or mimes in order to make a particular possible meaning by combining gesture and talk together as "mutually contextualizing phenomena" (Goodwin & Goodwin, 1992: 88). An example of the latter can be seen in example 3, lines 17–18, where GB mimes peeling or scraping vegetables while saying "I can do it," thus giving a possible meaning of something like "I can (use this knife to) peel/scrape vegetables," which would likely be difficult or impossible for him to achieve using talk alone.[17] The wide scope of possible lexical meanings provided by this method can be seen from the fact that in lines 14 and 15 in example 4, GB combines a similar linguistic utterance, "you just <u>do</u> it," with a different mime (cutting) to produce a different possible meaning.[18]

By using both methods together in the construction of utterances, speakers with aphasia are thus able to produce a semantically specific noun/noun phrase reference in relative isolation from grammatical considerations, and then produce a more grammatically complex utterance about the referent using "general meaning" lexical items. Crucially, therefore, these methods can be seen to assist them in producing contributions to conversation that, while appearing relatively complex (in that they often include specific reference and sentential constructions) minimize the occurrence of extended repair sequences and the highlighting of the speaker's linguistic noncompetence as the focus of the activity. As such, these methods can be seen to assist speakers with aphasia in constructing contributions to conversation that allow for the speaker to produce actions and activities *by means of* his or her talk, *rather than the (disordered) form of talk itself becoming the focus of the activity* through repair and through participants doing noticings of, and allusions to, the speaker with aphasia's linguistic noncompetence.

With these observations in mind, it is possible to note that DW in the conversation we are examining here uses very similar methods of turn construction to those we have examined in GB's talk. This can be seen in example 5. As this extract starts, the therapist has been asking DW how he has been finding being an in-patient in the hospital ward (near to the stroke unit room where this conversation is taking place) since coming in after his stroke the week before. In particular we will be focusing here on points in the interaction (highlighted by arrows in the margin) where DW uses a combination of a fronted noun/noun phrase and a proposition constructed using "general meaning" forms (and, in some cases, gestures/mime):

Example 5 (PHD: DW1: 00:05:50)
```
 1          Therapist:  made some friends on the ward?
 2                      (1.2)
 3          DW:         (s) y- yeah they're all right, (.) they (.) a bit (1.8) they should
 4                      (2.5) they should do more.
 5                      (0.3)
 6          Therapist:  mm,
 7          DW:         for theirselves.
 8          Therapist:  mmhm?
 9    →     DW:         some are- (.) ⌈I mean (0.3) one (0.4) one of the girls, ⌉
10    →                              ⌊((gestures toward the ward)) ⌋
11    →     Therapist:  ((nods))
12    →     DW:         ⌈she's very very very good.              ⌉
13    →                 ⌊((holds gesture toward the ward)) ⌋
14    →     Therapist:  (.) is she? ⌈mm.
15    →     DW:                     ⌊I-I ⌈mean she can't do ↓nothing. (0.2) ⌉
16    →                                 ⌊((puts hands flat on his legs))      ⌋
```

```
17  →                    (0.3)
18  →                    ⌈↓nothing.                                    ⌉
19  →                    | ((rocks back and forth with hands on legs))|
20  →   Therapist:       ⌊can't                              ⌋ walk. mm.
21      DW:              she don't mind ⌈she don't mind
22      Therapist:                      ⌊mm
23                       that's great ⌈(isn't it)
24  →   DW:                           ⌊but ⌈others,                    ⌉
25  →                                      ⌊((gestures toward the ward)) ⌋
26  →   Therapist:       yeah
27  →   DW:              an::d (0.2) ih-ghh (1.0) ⌈>bhh-<                ⌉
28  →                                            |((does "moaning face"))|
29  →   Therapist:                               ⌊yes                    ⌋
30  →   DW:              they don't- (0.3) they don't do it
31      Therapist:       ⌈mm
32      DW:              ⌊they g- got- you've got to do it. (0.2) you've got to do it.=
33                       =I mean ⌈ I'm (0.2) I'm all right,
34                               ⌊ ((gestures toward himself))
35      Therapist:       mhm
36      DW:              you know but uh (0.3) ⌈I mean she's not >°very well°< ⌉
37                                            ⌊((points toward the ward))      ⌋
38      DW:              =⌈you know I mean you know ⌈she's she- (0.3)         ⌉
39                        ⌊((puts hands on legs))  |((rocks back and forth)) ⌋
40      Therapist:                                 ⌊yes
41      DW:              ⌈she can't do it.          ⌉
42                       ⌊((moves hands on legs))⌋
43      Therapist:       she can't walk whereas you're lucky you- (.)
44      DW:              ex⌈act-
45      Therapist:         ⌊mm.
46      DW:              that's what (.) ⌈I mean
47      Therapist:                       ⌊mhm
48      DW:              yeah ⌈I'm very very (l)ucky
49                           ⌊((gestures toward himself))
50      Therapist:       mm
51      DW:              yeah yeah very ⌈so
52      Therapist:                      ⌊mm
53  →   DW:              but some people
54  →   Therapist:       ⌈mm
55  →                    ⌊they just (thinking) (.) they just don't
56  →   DW:              (.) ⌈woo woo woo woo woo
57  →                        ⌊((does "moaning face"))
58  →   Therapist:       mm
59  →   DW:              they just don't (know) whadda do.
60      Therapist:       yes
61      DW:              °y- ⌈you've got to°.
62      Therapist:           ⌊yes
```

While there are many similarities between some of the turn-constructional methods used by DW in this example and those used by GB in examples 3 and 4, one way in which they are different is that the nouns/noun phrases that DW is fronting in this example are all concerned with the activity of person reference (Sacks & Schegloff, 1979; Schegloff, 1996b), with the persons being referred to here being in the role of grammatical subject in the utterance. In each of the three cases in example 5, we note that DW can use the practice of fronting to first do person reference (and little else) with a noun/noun phrase, and then say something concerning that person using the unmarked form used for doing "locally subsequent reference" in that position, that is, a pronoun (Schegloff, 1996b). This method therefore allows him to construct utterances concerning the previously referred-to person that, although they are often in a sentential format, are produced relatively fluently and without significant repair, in part because they are often constructed using primarily "general meaning" forms, including pronouns for person reference. Thus, after answering the therapist's question about the people on the ward by saying that "they should do more . . . for theirselves" (lines 1–7), DW refers to one particular one with a fronted noun phrase ("I mean (0.3) one (0.4) one of the girls," in line 9), at the same time pointing to the ward. Following a nod from the therapist (line 11), he then (line 12) produces an utterance about her ("she's very very very good.") and, following a brief turn by the therapist (line 14), he produces another utterance about her (line 15) which consists largely of "general meaning" forms including the personal pronoun "she" ("I-I mean she can't do ↓nothing."). This latter utterance is accompanied by a mime which involves him putting his hands flat on his legs and sitting very upright and still, as if in a wheelchair. When there is no immediate response from the therapist, he "upgrades" the utterance by repeating "↓nothing." and rocking back and forth with his hands on his legs, presumably to emphasize the lack of leg movement. The therapist then produces a gloss of DW's "can't do nothing" plus mime as "can't walk" (line 20).[19]

A second example of DW first doing person reference using a noun and then using "general meaning" forms to say something about the person(s) is seen in lines 24–30. Here he uses a fronted noun ("but others," in line 24) plus a gesture of pointing to the ward to produce a contrast with the previously fronted noun phrase "one of the girls," in line 9. After the therapist's continuer in line 26, he first does an utterance including a mime which involves what can be described as a "moaning face" and a "complaining" vocalization, combining to give the impression of people verbally complaining. He then produces the utterance "they don't- (0.3) they don't do it" (line 30), consisting of the personal pronoun "they" and other "general meaning" forms. The utterance in this context appears to be a reference to not trying or not "getting on with it" (see also line 32).

The third example is in lines 53–59 and has a similar format to the previous sequence. Here DW again does person reference using a noun phrase ("but some people" in line 53). Following a continuer from the therapist (line 54), he produces an utterance containing a mime apparently depicting people complaining, then a sentential utterance constructed using "general meaning" forms including the personal pronoun "they" ("they just don't (know) whadda do." in line 59).

As with GB's examples, therefore, these methods of turn construction are used by DW here to highlight different members of a set (here people on the ward). They also display the interactional feature of allowing the speaker with aphasia here to construct turns that were often (for this speaker) relatively complex lexically and grammatically, while managing to avoid extended repair sequences and the consequent highlighting of the speaker's linguistic non-competence.

Discussion and implications

We have analyzed here different methods seen within the same conversations by which two speakers with fluent aphasia used lexical and grammatical resources to construct turns at talk. One method involved the speaker attempting to construct an utterance using similar types of lexical items and a similar word order to that which he might regularly have used before he became aphasic. This often led to repair that was extended, proved difficult for the aphasic speaker to complete himself, and which could lead to the speaker's linguistic non-competence becoming highlighted and alluded to. Different methods involved either a different type of word order, namely the fronting of a noun phrase followed by a proposition, or the use of "general meaning" lexical items. These two methods were regularly combined, such that the speaker produced a fronted noun phrase and then constructed a proposition about it using "general meaning" forms. One interactional feature of these latter methods was that the speakers with aphasia were regularly able to construct contributions through which they were able to achieve various conversational actions, rather than the action shifting to that of repair and of allusions to the linguistic non-competence of the speaker, such as could regularly occur when the first method was used.

A question might then be why one type of turn construction rather than another is used at a certain point in talk. One reason might be that there are certain types of actions in conversation for which certain turn-constructional methods are more useful or relevant. We noted, for example, that the fronting construction was used here for similar purposes as in non-aphasic conversation, such as highlighting different members of a set. While this may be the case, it does not imply that there is necessarily a direct relationship between an action type and the form used to do it. This can be seen in example 6, which is an extract from a later conversation involving DW and the same therapist as in examples 2 and 5. The therapist here, toward the beginning of the session, is asking DW which language items from previous sessions he has been working on since she last saw him:

Example 6 (PHD: DW2: 00:01:35)

1	Therapist:	so what sort of things have you been working on
2		(0.4) ⌈hherm in your speech (0.3) °book°
3		⌊((therapist clears throat; DW puts glasses on and opens book))
4	DW:	⌈ehm:,
5	Therapist:	⌊°( )° we wont go through your book but just ⌈if you can tell me
6	DW:	⌊(not)
7	Therapist:	in your own words ⌈what you've been ⌈what you've been doing
8	DW:	⌊oh just ⌊(/nʊ/-)
9		yeah de- (.) umm (1.2) well I can (.) go through n:ow, (0.2) I- I li- (0.5)
10		°I eh >(what) I can (say like)°< my
11 →		⌈ (0.7) eh Don (.) Don Walker ⌉
12 →		⌊((puts finger onto his name on the front of his exercise book and reads it aloud)) ⌋
13 →	Therapist:	yeah
14 →	DW:	I can do that
15 →	Therapist:	you can say ⌈(all that)
16 →	DW:	⌊(it's pretty) ⌈you know which⌉ I can do that one
17 →	Therapist:	⌊°your name,° ⌋
18	DW:	(.) um I'm (.) trying to do (0.3) my ehm (0.8) (now) (0.8) te-
19		>°/tɛrəmaɪ/ (.) /tɛrəmɪdʒ/°< (.) ehm (0.2) °what d'you call it° eh::m:,
20		(1.6) my ha- my house (0.5) nah ⌈(um-)
21	Therapist:	⌊your address
22	DW:	yeah ⌈I keep on an' on, an' on an' on
23	Therapist:	⌊mm
24	DW:	⌈ I keep doing it then I can't, °an'°
25	Therapist:	⌊(having) to practice it
26	DW:	⌈(you know)
27	Therapist:	⌊yes
28 →	DW:	but others I mean like eh:m: (1.3) eh:: (1.1) °eh° >/dʒrəvə/<- ehm (0.2)
29 →		the months
30 →	Therapist:	yeah,
31 →	DW:	and eh days (0.7)
32 →	Therapist:	((nods))
33 →	DW:	I mean ⌈I- I can- (.) I can do them (.) ⌈them
34 →	Therapist:	⌊mhm ⌊mhm
35	DW:	(0.9) uh >things like that <

What is noticeable here is the methods by which DW attempts to say the items
he has been working on and the different interactional features these methods display. One format in which an answer to the therapist's question in lines 1 and 2 could
be produced is that of a list, and listing is one activity that is often done using a fronting
construction (Geluykens, 1992). It is noticeable here that DW does not, however,
use the fronting construction straight away. In line 11 he does eventually produce
the first item using the type of construction seen in examples 3 to 5, that is, a fronted

noun phrase ("eh Don (.) Don Walker" in line 11), which is followed by a continuer from the therapist ("yeah" in line 13), after which DW produces propositions about the noun phrase constructed using "general meaning" forms ("I can do that . . . (it's pretty) you know which I <u>can</u> do that one" in lines 14–16). This construction, however, is only used after what appears to be a series of attempts to produce an utterance using other formats has failed (lines 8–10).

When he attempts to produce the next piece of information (line 18), while he uses the "general meaning" verb "do," he also uses a canonical SVO format and, as in examples 1 and 2, this type of turn construction results in errors and an extended, and ultimately unsuccessful, series of attempts at self-repair (lines 18–21). As with the two earlier examples, the word search is eventually completed by the other speaker doing an other-repair (that is, "your address" supplied by the therapist in line 21), and, as with these earlier examples, the linguistic non-competence of the speaker with aphasia becomes a topical focus of the talk (that is, "°what d'you call it°" in line 19 and DW's "I keep on an' on, an' on an' on I keep doing it then I <u>can't</u>," in lines 22–24, responded to (in partial overlap) by the therapist with "(having) to practice it" in line 25).

For the third and final piece of information about what he has been working on, DW uses the turn-constructional format of a fronted noun phrase ("but others I mean like eh:m: (1.3) eh:: (1.1) °eh° >/dʒrəvə/<- ehm (0.2) the <u>months</u> . . . and eh <u>days</u>" in lines 28–31), followed by a proposition using "general meaning" forms ("I mean I-I can- (.) I can do <u>them</u> (.) <u>them</u>" in line 33).

What examples such as this suggest is that these methods of fronting and using "general meaning" forms are not simply used "automatically" to do certain actions. Rather they are methods that speakers may "opt" to use (not necessarily with much or any "conscious" awareness) as one way of displaying to a recipient links between the current turn and a prior turn (Kim, 1995) and talking about that linking item. As such, it may be that there are various sequential locations or activities within which a speaker with aphasia might "choose" to use either or both of these methods.[20]

The use of fronting and "general meaning" forms as methods of turn construction can be seen as ways in which both these speakers with aphasia have adapted their language to the environment within which, and for which, it is being employed, that is, the TCU and turn at talk within a particular sequential and topical context in conversation. While these methods are also used in non-aphasic talk, here we see distinctive patterns of use both quantitatively (e.g., the number of "general meaning" forms used both generally and, specifically, with fronted nouns/noun phrases) and qualitatively (e.g., the combination of "general meaning" forms with an iconic gesture to construct particular lexical meanings). An interactional motivation for adopting such methods appears to be that they can provide some functional advantages for turn construction, including the fact that they typically appear to allow for turn/action production without extended repair and highlighting of linguistic non-competence. As such, these methods can be seen as an attempt by speakers with aphasia at a "solution" to the "problem" of turn construction, a solution that different speakers, such as GB and DW here, might arrive at independently.[21]

We might predict that the range and form of possible methods of turn construction by speakers with aphasia might vary depending on a range of factors such as the type and severity of linguistic impairments the speaker has. While the methods discussed here are used in these examples by speakers in the "acute" stages of recovery, such methods are also seen in speakers who are one or more years post-stroke (see Lock et al., 2001). It also appears that we may see that speakers with "non-fluent" aphasia may develop some methods of turn construction that differ from those discussed in the "fluent" aphasic speakers here and that may be seen to take forms that have possible functional advantages given *their* particular linguistic impairments.[22] Particular uses of methods such as fronting or constructions similar to it have been noted in the talk of young children (Ochs, 1979) and in people using American Sign Language (Friedman, 1976), and it may be that such methods can be used by speakers to fulfill certain conversational functions when certain lexical or grammatical resources are not available to them. As such, we might expect that the turn-constructional methods seen in GB and DW here reflect their particular stage of recovery and that different methods, or variations on existing methods, might be used in other stages of the recovery process.

As Schegloff (1996a: 54) notes, conversation "surely appears to be the basic and primordial environment for the use and development (both ontogenetic and phylogenetic) of natural language." What might be visible, at least in part, in the conversation of speakers with aphasia and their conversation partners is the use of methods developed to cope with the functional demands of interaction given the linguistic limitations of one of the participants. In particular, limitations in relation to lexical or grammatical resources might be seen to lead to a reorganization, not just at a neuropsychological level (e.g., Luria, 1966, 1970) but at the social/interactional level of how speakers construct their interactions together. It may be, for example, that participants develop methods that rely on knowledge of the pragmatic or sequential organization of talk-in-interaction to compensate for lexical or grammatical limitations. Thus, while for many people with aphasia it may not be possible to pass or be constituted in social life as "ordinary" (see Sacks, 1984), it is possible to perhaps see in the examples here methods by which they and their co-participants construct new ways of talking that attempt to develop a new "form of life" (Goodwin, 1995, after Wittgenstein, 1953) or way of being and of interacting together.

The analysis here suggests therefore that while concepts such as "word" and "sentence" and the linguistic and psycholinguistic research concerning them have been beneficial in highlighting the nature of linguistic deficits and intact strengths in speakers with aphasia, findings relating to aspects of conversation such as "turn" and "turn-constructional unit" may also be useful, in particular where assessment/analysis of interactional data is concerned. If an aim of aphasiology is to develop explanations of why speakers with aphasia produce the particular language forms they do, it can be argued that such accounts should cover not only the forms elicited within clinical tests but also, and perhaps primarily, the language forms displayed within "spontaneous" language production in talk-in-interaction. Indeed, the data discussed here suggest that without such a focus there is a risk of missing some of the very features that constitute the particular nature of aphasic language. In broadening the focus of these accounts to cover language in interaction it may well be that, as with the data presented here, an account for the language forms displayed will involve not only neurological and neuropsychological factors but also social and interactional ones, such as the use of particular lexical and grammatical forms as resources for the construction of TCUs/turns within a particular sequential and interactional context (see also Heeschen & Schegloff, 1999).

As can be seen from this analysis, the investigation of aphasic talk brings together within the same analytical framework aspects of aphasia that are usually assessed and treated separately. For example, by using the methods and data employed here, it was possible to investigate lexical and grammatical structures not in isolation from their use and effects but rather in their role as resources for the construction of contributions to conversation. As such it was possible to note how the deployment of these resources could lead to repair activity and the exposure of non-competence or could lessen the likelihood of these occurring. Being able to investigate form and function together rather than by using separate assessments can be of possible use in uncovering cause and effect relationships between particular linguistic impairments and everyday functional performance and thus facilitating change in this area.

In most cases, the ultimate aim of intervention targeted at spoken language, auditory comprehension, or functional communication is likely to be to create change in the everyday interactions involving the person with aphasia and their significant others. It has, however, been difficult to prove that lexical or grammatical structures of speakers with aphasia have been changed within spontaneous language use such as conversation following the types of intervention attempted thus far (Lesser & Algar, 1995). In part this difficulty might be linked to the fact that typically the assessment and treatment of aphasic language is carried out in isolation from its role as a resource within interaction, with "generalization" of treated items or structures to conversation left to a later stage. However, such generalization may not be a straightforward process since it appears that producing, for example, a sentential contribution within conversation may involve contextual and temporal factors quite different from those involved in producing a sentence in other types of activity such as within a picture description or monologue.[23] In addition, as seen in examples 1 and 2, attempts by speakers with aphasia to use "canonical" syntactic structure or full form lexical items can take more time and can involve repair, therefore potentially entailing social costs such as being noticeably "different" or "noncompetent" within conversation.[24] Taking such issues into account may be of use in the case of intervention programs that begin by focusing on language structures outside of conversational contexts and subsequently attempt generalization to conversation. At the same time, such considerations highlight the possible usefulness of finding other intervention approaches that attempt to diminish or circumvent the difficulties of generalization and the separation of linguistic and functional concerns. Basing the intervention program, at least in part, on information about the speaker's turn-construction practices in conversation and the language resources used would appear useful for developing valid targets for intervention and for subsequent investigation of whether there is change in conversation following that intervention.

Notes

This research was supported by the Economic and Social Research Council (award reference: R000221841). Earlier versions of parts of this chapter were presented at the International Pragmatics Conference, Mexico City (1996); the conference "Disorder and Order in Talk: Conversation Analysis and Communication Disorders," London (1997); the Symposium on Prosody and Syntax in Interaction, Utrecht (1998); and the Euroconference on the Linguistic Organization of Conversational Activities, in Spa, Belgium (2000). We are grateful to participants at these presentations for their feedback, and also to Shula Chiat and Catrin Rhys and to Charles Goodwin for his valuable and constructive comments at various stages of the chapter's development. Any remaining inadequacies are, of course, our responsibility.

1. There is typically a distinction drawn in aphasiology between "fluent" and "non-fluent" aphasia, where manifestations of fluent aphasia are taken to include anomia, normal or near-normal speech rates, use of a variety of grammatical constructions, use of function words and grammatical inflections, and relatively preserved syntax (Goodglass & Kaplan, 1983; Howard & Hatfield, 1987).

2. The term "canonical" here is simply used for convenience in order to link to previous linguistic and aphasiological work in this area and to provide a contrast to the patterns described in examples 3 to 6; there is work still to be done on which forms of "positionally sensitive grammars" (Schegloff 1996a: 108) might be canonical or "unmarked" for particular actions within particular sequential contexts in conversation.

3. We use this term to draw a contrast between this type of lexical item and the "general meaning" lexical items discussed in this chapter, such as pronouns, the noun "thing," and the verb "do."

4. Since repair itself can be seen as a kind of side sequence (Jefferson, 1972; Couper-Kuhlen, 1992), lines 4–6 here could be seen as a side sequence within a side sequence. This highlights a feature of aphasic talk, namely, that attempts at, for example, repairing a problem can themselves become "diverted" by further problems such as linguistic difficulties. The result is often a kind of "right-branching" pattern to the talk, which may result in the speakers having to do work to "pick up the threads" or even in losing or abandoning the original point (for an example of this kind of pattern over an extended telling sequence see Wilkinson, 1995a).

5. Having reached a potential end of the utterance in line 12 with the production of "address" which has been "given" to him by Daniela, it is noticeable that his next utterance is a "re-doing" of the whole problematic utterance, perhaps as an orientation to the fact that the pragmatic "force" of the utterance may have been lost or distracted from by the extended repair. It is also noticeable that the eventual form here is that of an isolated noun ("address") fol-

lowed by the "re-done" utterance with a pronoun "taking the place" of "her address" (that is, "I haven't got it properly anyway so"). As such, this is a similar pattern of turn construction to the one produced by GB at other points in this conversation, which we will be examining in detail. Here it is produced in the position of "post-other repair" and involves constructing a turn using an item that has been provided by the other participant in the repair.

6. Part of the potential for embarrassment or annoyance here is of course linked to the fact that one of the linguistic items GB is getting wrong and is unable to repair here is the name of his own daughter, which he is being displayed as "confusing" with that of his son.

7. The fact that DW is able to produce this lexical item (after a long delay) in line 4 here but is then apparently unable to do so a few turns later (lines 19–22) is an example of the "variability" of speakers with aphasia that has been noted particularly in relation to performance on clinical assessments such as picture-naming tests (e.g., Howard, Patterson, Franklin, Morton, & Orchard-Lisle, 1984). Observing the phenomenon in conversation allows for other, more "real life" factors to be considered, including for example the "contextual" factors at play in relation to the sequential "slot" within which the searched-for item is due, such as its place in the grammatical development of the turn-thus-far, or the wider action format within which it is relevant (e.g., as an answer to a question).

8. There also appears also to be a humorous element here (signaled perhaps by the movement of gaze to the therapist, the smile, and the gesture which could also have an element of signaling the therapist to speak) of "that word that I can't produce but that you know (and are not telling me)."

9. Alluding to the non-competence by means of a humorous reference to it is thus one way in which speakers with aphasia can both acknowledge the noticeability and existence of the non-competence (and encourage the other participant to acknowledge this too) while displaying that they are coping with it (Wilkinson, 2002). As such, it may contrast with the occurrence of laughter produced by speakers with aphasia in this context that is not accompanied by any obvious attempt at humor, and which the other participant tends not to affiliate with (Wilkinson, 1995b).

10. The possible sensitivity involved in the repair sequence here despite the display of joint laughter is suggested by the therapist's actions in relation to her possible other-repair of DW's error. The other-repair carried out by the therapist in line 18 is noticeable for the lack of "modulation" that these repairs often have; e.g., they are often produced as a "guess" (Schegloff et al., 1977: 378–79) as indeed are those in lines 9 and 11 in example 1. This other-repair is in response to the "third turn repair" initiation (Schegloff, 1996c) by DW in line 16, which follows the start of the therapist's turn in line 15, where by producing the continuer "mmhm," she visibly did *not* either initiate or carry out a repair on DW's error (see Schegloff, 1982). Her subsequent other-repair in line 18, done immediately after DW's repair initiation and displaying confidence about the target (by being done in the form of a statement rather than a guess) can thus be seen as publically displaying that she *had* noticed the error earlier and *could* have carried out repair on it but had chosen at this point to "let it go" (Schegloff, 1992: 1329), producing it only as a "solution" after DW had "noticed" his error but had not corrected it. Having then produced this (delayed) other-repair once and having ignored it, it is evident that she does not produce it again, at least in an "exposed" form. Thus in line 21, she produces not a repair but laughter, despite DW's turn in lines 19–20 making possibly relevant her production of an other-repair next. Again, in line 23, she produces the target ut-

terance in the "embedded repair" (Jefferson, 1987) question format of "so you like working" rather than as an exposed other-repair, such as "working." One advantage of the therapist's turns in both cases here is that it allows her to avoid being seen as repeating her earlier other-repair in line 18 and as thus explicitly "providing again" the solution which DW has at this point in the talk failed to notice she has provided. As such she can be seen to be possibly displaying a sensitivity toward drawing attention to DW's linguistic non-competence as it is displayed here first in the production of his error and then in his failure to pick up her other-repair of this error.

11. See, e.g., Quirk et al. (1985:1377): "fronting is the term we apply to the achievement of marked theme by moving into initial position an item which is otherwise unusual there." We are not here using terms such as "fronting" or "left dislocation" in relation to trans-formational rules (for which see, e.g., Rodman, 1974).

12. While we will be making the point later that this and other methods employed by these speakers have potential functional advantages for them, it is still the case that, at least in some cases, linguistic errors (such as /waɪl/ in this extract) do occur within these constructions, particularly in the fronted noun/non phrase. It seems to be the case, however, that even when these errors do occur, they do not regularly become the source of extended repair sequences or lead to the exposure of the speaker's linguistic non-competence in the ways seen in extracts 1 and 2. Thus in this case, while /waɪl/ can be viewed as a "linguistic error" (involving perhaps a phonemic confusion of "one" and "knife"), it is not treated as a trouble source (see Schegloff et al., 1977 for this distinction) either by GB or (e.g., in line 10) by Daniela.

13. The use of pronouns has long been noted as a feature of fluent aphasia (Bates, Hamby, & Zurif, 1983; Wepman & Jones, 1966), where it has been viewed as, at least in part, a compensatory strategy by speakers with aphasia in response to a problem in the retrieval of nouns (Edwards & Garman, 1989; Lesser & Milroy, 1993). We will be adopting a similarly functional view, while widening our focus to include other types of "general meaning" lexical items, such as "do," and thus concentrating in particular on the process of adaptation at the level of the TCU/turn rather than the individual noun/pronoun. We will also be taking into account the deictic and anaphoric functions of lexical items such as pronouns and "do" as have been highlighted by work within ethnomethodology and conversation analysis (Garfinkel, 1967; Garfinkel and Sacks, 1970; Goodwin, 1996; Sacks, 1992; Schegloff, 1972, 1984, 1989, 1996b; Watson 1987). The usefulness of these items for speakers with aphasia in allowing them to "tie" (Sacks, 1992) their current utterance to others, particularly those of other speakers, has been noted by Wilkinson (1999). While we will be noting that this type of lexical item can have some functional advantages for speakers with aphasia as resources for turn construction, it can also be seen that their lack of semantic specificity has the potential to make it difficult for recipients to work out the possible meaning or pragmatic "force" of the utterance, as is perhaps suggested by some of Daniela's minimal responses in example 3 (e.g., lines 21, 33, 37).

14. Thus, Huddleston (1984: 281), for example, points out that, compared with noun phrases, pronouns have "general meanings." Similarly, Tobin (1993: 30) notes that "'do' is used for general activities in a general or non-specific way or to talk about work," and Quirk et al. (1985: 76–77n.) note that "the items 'do' and 'thing', although they belong to the classes of verb and noun respectively, have semantic functions similar to pro-forms in conveying a

broad and undifferentiated meaning." Crystal (1987: 124) describes language such as this as "semantically 'empty'" and contrasts it with "semantically 'full' lexis."

15. It is unclear here in terms of analysis whether the utterance "you just do it" in line 14 is linked to the reference to GB's knife in lines 10–11 (that is, Daniela cuts with GB's knife) or to the reference to Daniela's knife in lines 6–10 (that is, Daniela cuts with her own knife, perhaps instead of GB's knife). That it may understood by the participants to be the latter is suggested by the fact that in the next turn in lines 17–18 Daniela appears to be displaying, by repeating the same gesture as in lines 2–3, that she is referring here to her own "kitchen devil" knife. (This use of gesture to link, and perhaps disambiguate, reference across turns is also seen in, for instance, example 3, lines 3–4 and 6–7 where, unlike here, it is done by different speakers, and also in the pointing gestures in example 5.) The difficulty for analytic interpretation here may be due in part to the loose grammatical relations between the reference and the following proposition that can occur in this kind of construction (Ochs & Schieffelin, 1983). Importantly, there is no evidence from the data that the participants themselves have any difficulty in understanding the references in this spate of talk.

16. It is also worth noting that the conversation partner may be facilitating this practice as a result of "adapting" his or her own language in ways that make it similar to that of the person with aphasia in order to, for example, assist comprehension or minimize the difference between them. See Heeschen and Schegloff (1999: 396) for a related line of argument.

17. The linguistic difficulties of such an attempt can perhaps be seen in example 3, line 31, where / kulɪŋ/ appears from the context to be a linguistic error resulting from a try at producing a verb such as "peeling" or "scraping."

18. Other examples of "do" plus gesture will be seen in example 5. While traditionally in aphasiology gesture has been assessed and "treated" predominantly in isolation from speech or in its possible role as functioning "in lieu of speech," the analysis here suggests it may be useful also to investigate how speakers combine the two. See also Goodwin (1995, 2000) and Klippi (1996) for investigations of how language and gesture are combined in aphasic talk-in-interaction.

19. DW returns to this description of the girl on the ward a few turns later (lines 38–42) with a similar combination of an utterance consisting largely of "general meaning" forms ("she can't do it." in line 41) and a mime that involves him putting his hands on his legs. Again the therapist provides a gloss (line 43) which here provides an interpretation of this turn by DW and its "point" in relation to earlier turns. Both here and in example 2 (lines 23–27), the therapist can be seen to offer an interpretation of what DW "meant," which can be, and in both cases is, confirmed by DW with "that's what I mean(t)."

20. One sequential context within which fronting (with a proposition using "general meaning" forms) is used in these examples, for instance, is that of delayed progressivity toward achieving self-repair, such as appears to be the case in both example 3 lines 15–16 and example 6 lines 8–11.

21. It is noticeable in this regard that DW's first conversation discussed here (examples 2 and 5) occurs only one week after his stroke, that is, he appears to have developed these methods of talking very quickly in response to linguistic limitations imposed by aphasia and before any systematic therapeutic intervention has begun.

22. See Heeschen & Schegloff (1999). Beeke, Wilkinson, and Maxim (2001), for example, note that the speaker with "non-fluent" aphasia in their data also uses fronting but that what is

regularly being placed in the fronted position in this case is temporal reference (resulting in utterances such as "last week (.) you go out?") rather than the object or person reference seen here in the talk of speakers with "fluent" aphasia. Beeke et al. suggest that this temporal reference may be a method by which the speaker has adapted to limitations in verb production and verb morphology and therefore limitations in displaying tense (cf. Wilkinson, 1995a).

23. See, for example, Goodwin (1979) and Schegloff (1979, 1984, 1996a). Beeke et al. (2001) and Wilkinson (1995a) provide data displaying how the language structures produced by speakers with aphasia on language assessments (such as picture descriptions) may differ from those used by the same speakers within conversation. Such differences are perhaps not surprising since, if as Sacks et al. (1974: 728) suggest, "conversation should be considered the basic form of speech-exchange system with other systems on the array representing a variety of conversation's turn-taking system," these assessments can be seen to involve a very particular type of turn-taking system (see, e.g., Marlaire & Maynard, 1990; Maynard & Marlaire, 1999) which may make relevant the production of quite particular language forms.

24. In a different way, "compensatory strategies" such as the use of gesture, writing, or other low-tech or high-tech communication aids may also be seen by the person with aphasia as drawing attention to their "difference" and, as such, this may be a factor in whether such strategies are used or not in everyday life.

References

Bates, E., Hamby, S., & Zurif, E. (1983). The Effects of Focal Brain Damage on Pragmatic Expression. *Canadian Journal of Psychology*, *37*, 59–84.

Beeke, S., Wilkinson, R., & Maxim, J. (2001). A Case Study of a Non-Fluent Aphasic Speaker: Grammatical Aspects of Conversation and Language Testing Data. *Stem-, Spraak- and Taalpathologie*, *10*(4), 215–232.

Caplan, D. (1987). *Neurolinguistics and Linguistic Aphasiology: An Introduction*. Cambridge: Cambridge University Press.

Code, C. (Ed.) (1989). *The Characteristics of Aphasia*. London: Taylor and Francis.

Code, C., & Muller, D. J. (1992). *The Code-Muller Protocols: Assessing Perceptions of Psychosocial Adjustment to Aphasia and Related Disorders*. Kibworth: Far Communications.

Couper-Kuhlen, E. (1992). Contextualizing Discourse: The Prosody of Interactive Repair. In P. Auer & A. di Luzio (Eds.), *The Contextualization of Language* (pp. 337–364). Amsterdam: John Benjamins.

Crystal, D. (1987). *Clinical Linguistics*. Vienna: Springer-Verlag.

Dik, S. (1978). *Functional Grammar*. Amsterdam: North Holland.

Duranti, A., & Ochs, E. (1979). Left-Dislocation in Italian Conversation. In T. Givon (Ed.), *Syntax and Semantics 12: Discourse and Syntax* (pp. 377–415). New York: Academic Press.

Edwards, S., & Garman, M. (1989). Case Study of a Fluent Aphasic: The Relation between Linguistic Assessment and Therapeutic Intervention. In P. Grunwell & A. James (Eds.), *Functional Evaluation of Language Disorders* (pp. 163–181). London: Croom Helm.

Ellis, A. W., & Young, A. W. (1996). *Human Cognitive Neuropsychology: A Textbook with Readings*. Hove: Psychology Press.

Ford, C. E., & Thompson, S. A. (1996). Interactional Units in Conversation: Syntactic, Intonational, and Pragmatic Resources for the Management of Turns. In E. Ochs, E. A.

Schegloff, & S. A. Thompson (Eds.), *Interaction and Grammar* (pp. 134–184). Cambridge: Cambridge University Press.

Friedman, L. A. (1976). The Manifestation of Subject, Object, and Topic in the American Sign Language. In C. N. Li (Ed.), *Subject and Topic* (pp. 125–148). New York: Academic Press.

Garfinkel, H. (1967). *Studies in Ethnomethodology*. Englewood Cliffs, NJ: Prentice Hall.

Garfinkel, H., & Sacks, H. (1970). On Formal Structures of Practical Actions. In C. McKinney & E. A. Tiryakian (Eds.), *Theoretical Sociology* (pp. 337–366). New York: Appleton-Century-Crofts.

Geluykens, R. (1992). *From Discourse to Grammatical Structure: On Left Dislocation in English*. Amsterdam: John Benjamins.

Goffman, E. (1969). On Face Work: An Analysis of Ritual Elements in Social Interaction. In E. Goffman, *Where the Action Is* (pp. 3–36). London: Penguin.

Goffman, E. (1981a). Response Cries. In E. Goffman, *Forms of Talk* (pp. 78–123). Oxford: Basil Blackwell.

Goffman, E. (1981b). Footing. In E. Goffman, *Forms of Talk* (pp. 124–159). Oxford: Basil Blackwell.

Goldstein, K. (1939). *The Organism: A Holistic Approach to Biology Derived from Pathological Data in Man*. New York: Zone Books.

Goldstein, K. (1948). *Language and Language Disturbances*. New York: Grune and Stratton.

Goodglass, H., & Kaplan, E. (1983). *The Assessment of Aphasia and Related Disorders*. Philadelphia: Lee and Febiger.

Goodwin, C. (1979). The Interactive Construction of a Sentence in Natural Conversation. In G. Psathas (Ed.), *Everyday Language: Studies in Ethnomethodology* (pp. 97–121). New York: Irvington.

Goodwin, C. (1995). Co-Constructing Meaning in Conversations with an Aphasic Man. *Research on Language and Social Interaction, 28*, 233–260.

Goodwin, C. (1996). Transparent Vision. In E. Ochs, E. A. Schegloff, & S. A. Thompson (Eds.), *Interaction and Grammar* (pp. 370–404). Cambridge: Cambridge University Press.

Goodwin, C. (2000). Gesture, Aphasia and Interaction. In D. McNeill (Ed.), *Language and Gesture* (pp. 84–98). Cambridge: Cambridge University Press.

Goodwin, C., & Goodwin, M. H. (1992). Context, Activity and Participation. In P. Auer & A. di Luzio (Eds.), *The Contextualization of Language* (pp. 77–99). Amsterdam: John Benjamins.

Heeschen, C., & Schegloff, E. A. (1999). Agrammatism, Adaptation Theory, Conversation Analysis: On the Role of So-Called Telegraphic Style in Talk-in-Interaction. *Aphasiology, 13*(4/5), 365–405.

Heritage, J. C. (1984). *Garfinkel and Ethnomethdology*. Cambridge: Polity Press.

Holland, A. (1980). *Communicative Abilities in Daily Living*. Baltimore: University Park Press.

Howard, D., & Hatfield, F. M. (1987). *Aphasia Therapy: Historical and Contemporary Issues*. Hove: Lawrence Erlbaum.

Howard, D., Patterson, K., Franklin, S., Morton, J., & Orchard-Lisle, V. (1984). Variability and Consistency in Picture Naming by Aphasic Patients. In F. C. Rose (Ed.), *Progress in Aphasiology* (pp. 263–276). New York: Ram Press

Huddleston, R. (1984). *Introduction to the Grammar of English*. Cambridge: Cambridge University Press.

Jackson. J. H. (1931). *Selected Writings of John Hughlings Jackson* (J. Taylor, Ed.). London: Hodder and Staughton.

Jefferson, G. (1972). Side Sequences. In D. Sudnow (Ed.), *Studies in Social Interaction* (pp. 294–338). New York: Free Press.

Jefferson, G. (1987). Exposed and Embedded Corrections. In G. Button & J. R. E. Lee (Eds.), *Talk and Social Organisation* (pp. 86–100). Clevedon: Multilingual Matters.

Kay, J., Lesser, R., & Coltheart, M. (1992). *Psycholinguistic Assessments of Language Processing in Aphasia.* Hove: Lawrence Erlbaum.

Kim, K. (1995). WH-Clefts and Left-Dislocation in English Conversation. In P. Downing & M. Noonan (Eds.), *Word Order in English* (pp. 247–296). Amsterdam: John Benjamins.

Klippi, A. (1996). *Conversation as an Achievement in Aphasics.* Helsinki: Finnish Literature Society.

Kolk, H., & Heeschen, C. (1990). Adaptation Symptoms and Impairment Symptoms in Broca's Aphasia. *Aphasiology, 4,* 221–232.

Kolk, H., & Heeschen, C. (1992). Agrammatism, Pargrammatism and the Management of Language. *Language and Cognitive Processes, 7,* 89–129.

Kolk, H., & Heeschen, C. (1996). The Malleability of Agrammatic Symptoms: A Reply to Hesketh and Bishop. *Aphasiology, 10,* 81–96.

Laakso, M., & Klippi, A. (1999). A Closer Look at the "Hint and Guess" Sequences in Aphasic Conversation. *Aphasiology, 13*(4/5), 345–364.

Lesser, R., & Algar, L. (1995). Towards Combining the Cognitive Neuropsychological and the Pragmatic in Aphasia Therapy. *Neuropsychological Rehabilitation, 5,* 67–96.

Lesser, R., & Milroy, L. (1993). *Linguistics and Aphasia: Psycholinguistic and Pragmatic Aspects of Intervention.* London: Longman.

Levinson, S. C. (1983). *Pragmatics.* Cambridge: Cambridge University Press.

Li, C. N., & Thompson, S. A. (1976). Subject and Topic: A New Typology of Language. In C. N. Li (Ed.), *Subject and Topic* (pp. 457–489). New York: Academic Press.

Lindsay, J., & Wilkinson, R. (1999). Repair Sequences in Aphasic Talk: A Comparison of Aphasic-Speech and Language Therapist and Aphasic-Spouse Conversations. *Aphasiology, 13*(4/5), 305–326

Lock, S., Wilkinson, R., & Bryan, K. (2001). *SPPARC (Supporting Partners of People with Aphasia in Relationships and Conversation): A Resource Pack.* Bicester: Speechmark.

Lubinski, R., Duchan, D., & Weitzner-Lin, B. (1980). Analysis of Breakdowns and Repairs in Adult Aphasic Conversation. In R. Brookshire (Ed.), *Clinical Aphasiology Conference Proceedings* (pp. 111–116) Minneapolis: BRK Publishers.

Luria, A. R. (1966). *Higher Cortical Functions in Man* (B. Haigh, Trans.). London: Tavistock.

Luria, A. R. (1970). *Traumatic Aphasia.* The Hague: Mouton.

Marlaire, C., & Maynard, D. W. (1990). Standardized Testing as an Interactional Phenomenon. *Sociology of Education, 63,* 83–101.

Maynard, D. W., & Marlaire, C. (1999). Good Reasons for Bad Testing Performance: The Interactional Substrate cf Educational Testing. In D. Kovarsky, J. Duchan, & M. Maxwell (Eds.), *Constructing (In)Competence* (pp. 171–196). Mahwah, NJ: Lawrence Erlbaum.

Milroy, L., & Perkins, L. (1992). Repair Strategies in Aphasic Discourse: Towards a Collaborative Model. *Clinical Linguistics and Phonetics, 6,* 27–40.

Ochs, E. (1979). Planned and Unplanned Discourse. In T. Givon (Ed.). *Syntax and Semantics 12: Discourse and Syntax* (pp. 51–80). New York: Academic Press.

Ochs, E., & Schieffelin, B. (1983). Foregrounding Referents: A Reconsideration of Left Dislocation in Discourse. In E. Ochs & B. Schieffelin, *Acquiring Conversational Competence* (pp. 158–174). London: Routledge and Kegan Paul.

Penn, C. (1987). Compensation and Language Recovery in the Chronic Aphasic Patient. *Aphasiology, 1*, 235–245.

Penn, C., & Cleary, J. (1988). Compensatory Strategies in the Language of Closed Head Injury Patients. *Brain Injury, 2*, 3–17.

Quirk, R., Greenbaum, S., Leech, G., & Svartvik, J. (1985). *A Comprehensive Grammar of the English Language*. London: Longman.

Rodman, R. (1974). On Left Dislocation. *Papers In Linguistics 7*, 437–466.

Rönfeldt, B. (1999). Paragrammatism Reconsidered. *InList 10*, 1–46.

Sacks, H. (1984). On Doing "Being Ordinary." In J. M. Atkinson & J. C.Heritage (Eds.), *Structures of Social Action: Studies in Conversation Analysis* (pp. 413–440). Cambridge: Cambridge University Press.

Sacks, H. (1992). *Lectures on Conversation.* (2 volumes) (G. Jefferson, Ed.). Oxford: Basil Blackwell.

Sacks, H., & Schegloff, E. A. (1979). Two Preferences in the Organization of Reference to Persons in Conversation and Their Interaction. In G. Psathas (Ed.), *Everyday Language: Studies In Ethnomethodology* (pp. 15–21). New York: Irvington.

Sacks, H., Schegloff, E. A., & Jefferson, G. (1974). A Simplest Systematics for the Organization of Turn-Taking in Conversation. *Language 50*(4), 696–735.

Schegloff, E. A. (1972). Notes on a Conversational Practice: Formulating Place. In D. Sudnow (Ed.), *Studies In Social Interaction* (pp. 75–119). New York: Free Press.

Schegloff, E. A. (1979). The Relevance of Repair to Syntax-For-Conversation. In T. Givon (Ed.), *Syntax and Semantics 12: Discourse and Syntax* (pp. 261–286). New York: Academic Press.

Schegloff, E. A. (1982). Discourse as an Interactional Achievement: Some Uses of "Uh Huh" and Other Things That Come between Sentences. In D. Tannen (Ed.), *Georgetown University Roundtable on Languages and Linguistics* (pp. 71–93). Washington, DC: Georgetown University Press.

Schegloff, E. A. (1984). On Some Gestures' Relation to Talk. In J. M. Atkinson & J. C. Heritage (Eds.), *Structures of Social Action: Studies In Conversation Analysis* (pp. 266–296). Cambridge: Cambridge University Press.

Schegloff, E. A. (1989). Reflections on Language, Development, and the Interactional Character of Talk-In-Interaction. In M. C. Bornstein & J. S. Bruner (Eds.), *Interaction in Human Development* (pp. 139–153). Hillsdale, NJ: Lawrence Erlbaum.

Schegloff, E. A. (1991a). Conversation Analysis and Socially Shared Cognition. In L. B. Resnick, J. M. Levine, & S. Teasley (Eds.), *Perspectives on Socially Shared Cognition* (pp. 150–171). Washington, DC: American Psychological Association.

Schegloff, E. A. (1991b). Reflections on Talk and Social Structure. In D. Boden & D. H. Zimmerman (Eds.), *Talk and Social Structure* (pp. 44–70). Cambridge: Polity Press.

Schegloff, E. A. (1992). Repair after Next Turn: The Last Structurally Provided Defense of Intersubjectivity in Conversation. *American Journal of Sociology 97*, 1295–1345.

Schegloff, E. A. (1996a). Turn Organization: One Intersection of Grammar and Interaction. In E. Ochs, E. A. Schegloff, & S. A. Thompson (Eds.), *Interaction and Grammar* (pp. 52–133). Cambridge: Cambridge University Press.

Schegloff, E. A. (1996b). Some Practices for Referring to Persons in Talk-In-Interaction: A Partial Sketch of a Systematics. In B. Fox (Ed.), *Studies in Anaphora* (pp. 437–485). Amsterdam: John Benjamins.

Schegloff, E. A. (1996c). Third Turn Repair. In G. R. Guy, J. Baugh, D. Schiffrin, & C. Feagin (Eds.), *Towards a Social Science of Language—Volume 1: Variation and Change in Language and Society* (pp. 31–40). London: John Benjamins.

Schegloff, E. A., Jefferson, G., & Sacks, H. (1977). The Preference for Self-Correction in the Organization of Repair for Conversation. *Language 53*, 361–382.

Tobin, Y. (1993). *Aspect in the English Verb: Process and Result in Language.* London: Longman.

Watson, D. R. (1987). Interdisciplinary Considerations in the Analysis of Pro-terms. In G. Button & J. R. Lee (Eds.), *Talk and Social Organization* (pp. 261–289). Clevedon: Multilingual Matters.

Wepman, J. M., & Jones, L. V. (1966). Studies in Aphasia: Classification of Aphasic Speech by the Noun-Pronoun Ratio. *British Journal of Disorders of Communication 1*, 46–54.

Wilkinson, R. (1995a). Aphasia: Conversation Analysis of a Non-Fluent Aphasic Person. In M. Perkins & S. Howard (Eds.), *Case Studies in Clinical Linguistics* (pp. 271–292). London: Whurr.

Wilkinson, R. (1995b). Doing "Being Ordinary": Aphasia as a Problem of Interaction. In M. Kersner & S. Peppe (Eds.), *Work In Progress (Volume 5)*. London: Department of Human Communication Science, University College London.

Wilkinson, R. (1999). Sequentiality as a Problem and Resource for Intersubjectivity in Aphasic Conversation: Analysis and Implications for Therapy. *Aphasiology 13*(4/5), 327–343.

Wilkinson, R. (2002). Laughter in response to non-competence in aphasic talk-in-interaction. Manuscript.

Wilkinson, R., Bryan, K., Lock, S., Bayley, K., Maxim, J., Bruce, C., Edmundson, A., & Moir, D. (1998). Therapy Using Conversation Analysis: Helping Couples Adapt to Aphasia in Conversation. *International Journal of Language and Communication Disorders 33* (suppl.), 144–149.

Wirz, S., Skinner, C., & Dean, E. (1990). *The Revised Edinburgh Functional Communication Profile.* Tucson, Arizona: Communication Skill Builders.

Wittgenstein, L. (1953). *Philosophical Investigations.* Translated by G. E. M. Anscombe. Oxford: Basil Blackwell.

4

CHARLES GOODWIN

Conversational Frameworks
for the Accomplishment
of Meaning in Aphasia

Overwhelmingly, research on aphasia focuses on what particular disorders can tell us about how the brain organizes language. However, the problems visible as aphasia have an equally important social life. They shape possibilities for communication and patterns of human interaction in profound and powerful ways. Moreover, when analysis moves beyond the abilities of the isolated individual, we find that the activities of interlocutors, and more generally the organization of talk-in-interaction, provide crucial frameworks that enable someone with severe aphasia nonetheless to construct meaningful action within states of talk. Rather than focusing exclusively on what is distinctive about aphasia, such analysis will also shed light on general practices used by participants in conversation to build action and meaning in concert with each other.[1]

In 1979 Chil, a successful New York lawyer, a man who made his living through his ability to use language, suffered a massive stroke in the left hemisphere of his brain. The right side of his body was paralyzed, and he suffered severe aphasia, losing almost completely the ability to speak meaningful language. He was, however, able to understand what others said to him, to gesture with his one remaining hand, and to use nonsense syllables to produce meaningful intonation melodies. On the advice of the nurse caring for him in the hospital, and against the advice of his neurosurgeons, who insisted that since nothing could be done to repair his brain he would spend the rest of his life in bed in a vegetative state, his family sent him to the Kessler rehabilitation center. After several months of intense work with therapists there, he learned to walk with a brace and to speak three words: *yes, no,* and *and.*[2] For years after the stroke, his wife would dream that he was again able to talk to her.

However, fifteen years later, in 1994 when the videotape that provides the data for this chapter was made, these were still the only three words he could speak.[3]

Of all the words in a language, why these three? Note that all three presuppose links to other talk. *And* ties other units of talk, such as clauses, to each other. *Yes* and *no* are prototypical examples of *second pair parts* (Sacks, 1992b; Sacks, Schegloff, & Jefferson, 1974; Schegloff & Sacks, 1973) used to build a response to something that someone else has said. This vocabulary set presupposes that its user is embedded within a community of other speakers. His talk does not stand alone as a self-contained entity, but emerges from, and is situated within, the talk of others, to which it is inextricably linked. This raises the possibility that despite the extraordinary sparseness of this system, its speaker might nonetheless be able to engage in complicated language games, to say a wide range of different things while performing diverse kinds of action, by using resources provided by the speech of others. In other work (Goodwin 1995a), I have described the organization of sequences in which his crucial moves take the form of *yes* and *no*. Each term can in fact be used to construct a range of different kinds of action through both variation in the way in which it is said, and through its sequential placement. However, because of the necessity of situating each of these words within a proper interpretative framework, he and his co-participants face intricate problems in working out precisely what is being said. What is *no* negating? An item within a set of choices offered by a co-participant or the whole line of action presupposed by an interlocutor's use of such a set in the first place? To work out such issues, Chil and his family use the same conversational structures for accomplishing meaning and action deployed by normal speakers (indeed, Chil has little trouble interacting with strangers as he wanders through the towns around him on an electric scooter doing errands, having frappicinos at Starbuck's, etc.). However, because of Chil's impairments, sequences of talk in which he is a participant are shaped in ways that both make visible his aphasia as a practical and moral issue (e.g., are interlocutors willing to take Chil seriously and perform the work necessary to figure out what he is saying, or will they comfortably ignore him?) and illuminate a range of organizational phenomena that have typically been so taken for granted that they have remained invisible to analysis.

This chapter will focus on Chil's use of gesture, a communicative modality that he uses as extensively as talk. Chil's gestures have none of the syntax, or other language properties, of a sign language. Indeed, like his vocabulary, they seem more sparse and restricted than the gestures of people without brain damage. Despite these very severe restrictions on possibilities for expression through language, he is nonetheless able to engage in complicated conversation. How is this possible? By embedding the semiotic field constituted through his waving hand within the talk and action of his interlocutors, Chil is able to both say something relevant and negotiate its meaning. His gestures do not stand alone, but instead count as meaningful action by functioning as components of a distributed process in which he creatively uses the language produced by others. More generally, these data perspicuously demonstrate how the *transparency* of gesture, that is, the tacit ability of both participants and analysts to easily, indeed spontaneously, find relevant meaning in a speaker's waving hands, is very much a *social accomplishment*, something that participants do in concert with each other through the deployment of both the *sequential organization* of unfolding conversation, and the constitution of relevant *participation frameworks*. By using such resources, human beings are able to embed a moving hand within what Goffman (1964) described as "a single, albeit moving, focus of visual and cognitive attention." Within such a framework, and only within such a framework, gesture as a meaningful act becomes both possible and visible. Simultaneously, participants are provided with the resources they need to work out together what a gesture might relevantly mean, that is, how it might count as an appropriate move in the courses of action they are pursuing together. Such focus on socially organized frameworks for the accomplishment of meaning complements the psychological analysis of gesture found in much other research.[4]

The sequence to be examined

Analysis in this chapter will focus on the use of gesture in a single extended sequence. Chil and his family are planning to go out for dinner. As shown in figure 4.1, Chil is seated in a chair, and his daughter Pat is discussing arrangements with him. Chil's wife, Helen, and Pat's daughter Julia are seated on the couch to Chil's left. The family agrees that all the five members present will eat dinner at six o'clock (lines 1–5 following). The exchange that will be the focus of this analysis then occurs. Chil participates in it by making a series of hand gestures with his left hand (his right hand and arm are paralyzed). In the following transcript, drawings of his handshapes are placed to the right of the talk where they were produced. A downward arrow indicates that Chil is ending his gesture and lowering his arm. To get some sense of the tasks posed for the family here, the reader is strongly encouraged to read through the transcript, while using the changing handshapes to try and figure out what Chil wants to say.

Example 1
1 Pat: So we'll see if they have a table for five.
2 Chil: Ye(h)s.
3 Helen: When? at six a clock?
4 Pat: °mm hmm
5 Chil: Yes.
              • • •
6 Chil: Da da:h.
7 Pat: When we went with Mack and June.
8   We- we sat at a table
9   *just* as we came in the: fr-ont door.

Pat   **Chil**   **Helen**   **Julia**

FIGURE 4.1. The participants

10		*hh We sat with them. (.)	
11		⌐There. ⌐En then we-	
12	Chil:	˪°mmm. ˪*Ni*h *n*ih duh *du*h. Da *du*h.	
13	Pat:	So *five* of us can fit there.	
14		(0.2)	
15	Pat:	*Six* a clock.	
16		(1.0)	
17	Pat:	*Five* people,	
18	Helen	Sure.	
19	Pat:	⌐Its::	
20	Julia:	˪Seven?	
21	Pat:	Seven?	
22		a' clock?	
23		(0.2)	
24	Chil:	No(h).	
25	Pat:	*Six* a clock.	
26		(0.2)	

```
27   Pat:     ┌Seven?
28   Helen:   └°Seven people. Who ┌('d they be)
29   Pat:                         └Five.
30                 (1.0)
31   Helen:   Seven people. ┌Who  are they.
32   Pat:                   └That's six.
33   Julia:   Two?
34   Pat:     ┌Seven?
35   Chil:    └Duh da dah? ((Chil turns and points toward Helen))
36            Ye:s.
37                 (0.2)
38   Pat:     Invite somebody?
39   Chil:    Ye:s.
40                 (0.2)
41   Pat:     Mack en June?
42   Chil:    Yes.
43                 (0.2)
44   Pat:     Oh:.
45                 (2.0)
46   Pat:     Oh:.
```

Situating gestures within activity frames

With hindsight, it is possible to see that Chil wants to invite two additional guests, Mack and June, to dinner. However, it takes intricate, temporally unfolding work for his interlocutors to discover this. Through most of this sequence, Pat interprets any number higher than five as a proposal about the *time* for dinner (lines 15, 21–22, 25, 27), not the number of people who will be going.

Central to this sequence is a debate about the proper use and interpretation of very simple numbers. Numbers provide a prototypical example of universal, abstract, context-free knowledge categories. Moreover, such abstraction is frequently depicted as the clearest and most precise way of knowing something. It is argued that thinking, and the path to knowledge in general, moves from the messy details of particular concrete events to the clarity of context-free, abstract knowledge. In these data, however, the participants have no problems in recognizing that Chil's handshapes represent abstract numbers, such as five. However, establishing that lexical meaning in no way solves the problem of what those numbers mean, either as descriptions of relevant events, or pragmatically, as forms of action, such as a proposal that an invitation be made.

To give Chil's handshapes appropriate meaning, his listeners must embed them within a relevant descriptive frame. The organization of such frames has been an important topic in cognitive science. Indeed, the very activity being planned here, going to a restaurant, has been used as a prototypical example of how context might be coded in a script. These data point to serious problems with such an approach.[5] I want to argue that, rather than being instantiated in autonomous cognitive structures, the crafting of meaning is intrinsically an interactive process, something that people do in collaboration with each other.[6] In line with suggestions by Schegloff (1972), these data support the argument that the really difficult, and crucial, issues in cognition involve not the problem of abstraction but just the reverse: the work of building the particulars of concrete events in locally relevant contexts.

Work on gesture, for example, the analysis of *emblems* (Ekman & Friesen, 1969; Morris, Collet, & O'Shaughnessy, 1979), has frequently assumed that when someone recognizes the lexical affiliate of a gesture, its meaning is known. Not often though, is the issue that simple.[7] To establish the meaning of a term, must one must embed it within a relevant activity, a specific language game (Wittgenstein, 1958: sect. 7). In this very basic task of planning restaurant reservations, numbers play a part in two quite distinct activities: counting the *number of people* who will go the restaurant and establishing the *time* when they will go.[8] In line 12, Chil holds up his hand with all of his fingers stretched apart:

Example 2

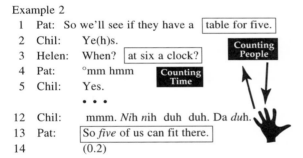

```
 1   Pat:    So we'll see if they have a  | table for five. |
 2   Chil:   Ye(h)s.
 3   Helen:  When?   | at six a clock? |       Counting
                                                People
 4   Pat:    °mm hmm      Counting
 5   Chil:   Yes.           Time
                        • • •
12   Chil:       mmm. Nih nih  duh  duh. Da duh.
13   Pat:    | So five of us can fit there. |
14               (0.2)
```

Pat interprets this (correctly) as counting people and accommodates it to the current line of talk: "So *five* of us can fit there" (line 13), and indeed "five" is the table size agreed upon several seconds earlier.

It is important to recognize that instead of a one-way hierarchical relationship, in which the encompassing activity contextualizes the meaning of the gesture, there is in fact a two-way relationship in which the frame, and the gesture embedded within it, mutually elaborate each other.[9] Thus, Pat can use a specific number that has become identified with a particular activity to locate that activity, that is, to choose the "counting people" frame that currently contains five, rather than other alternatives for the use of numbers also available and relevant in the current environment, such as setting a time for dinner.

Competing frames

In line 14 (fig. 4.2) Chil changes his hand to display two more fingers (since his right side is paralyzed, he has only one hand to gesture with). Pat is now faced with the

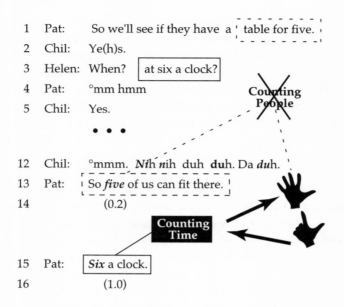

FIGURE 4.2. Competing frames

task of making sense out of this new number. In their earlier talk, any number higher than five referred to the time for dinner, and, though this is not visible in the brief excerpt shown here, there had been negotiation about exactly what time to go, with five, five-thirty, and six all being offered as possibilities. By way of contrast, the number of people who will eat had been treated as a given. Indeed, that number had been arrived at by simply counting everyone in the house. In light of this, Pat is following an entirely appropriate and relevant line of reasoning when she interprets the new number created by the gesturing hand, as a *time reference*.

As the original hand gesture, which provided the five included in Pat's six, is incorporated into this new interpretation, the *counting people* framework is abandoned.[10]

To look at these processes in more detail, I must describe some elements of the grammar Chil uses to organize his gestures. Briefly, I want to argue the unit required for the analysis of gesture here is not the hand in isolation, but instead a multi-party participation unit that encompasses the bodies of both gesturer and addressee, as well as the talk explicating the gesture. This framework is capable of dynamic change as events unfold through time.

The interactive organization of Chil's gestures

Much insightful research has focused on what gesture might reveal about the mental processes of the party producing the gesture (McNeill, 1992). However, for Chil, the accomplishment of meaning through gesture is a thoroughly social process, one that requires the intricate collaboration of others. Analysis will now focus on how his gestures are shaped and organized as interactive processes. Phenomena to be examined will include the detailed articulation of his hand, differentiating groups of related hand movements from each other through systematic use of the arm presenting the gesturing hand, the interactive organization of gesture space, and processes of sequential organization that provide for the display and negotiation of common understanding.

Shaping gestures for recipients

Chil's handshapes are not simply signs for numbers but embodied sequences of movement that must be understood in a specific way by his interlocutors if they are to grasp what he is trying to tell them with these gestures. We will now look at the production of Chil's first two gestures. What the details of his action will reveal is that his gesturing hand is organized not only with reference to the concepts he is trying to express (in the most literal sense particular numbers) but also with an eye toward making crucial features of his handshape salient and understandable to his recipients.

Through almost all of this sequence, Chil's gesture with his thumb and index finger is interpreted correctly as the number *two* (e.g., as an increment to the original five-fingered handshape that identifies the number being worked with as *seven* in lines 20, 21, 27, 28, 31, 33, 34). However, when the gesture first appears, Pat treats it as adding *one* to the original *five*, saying in line 15, "Six a clock." Why is the handshape here treated as exemplifying *one* rather than *two*?

Chil displays the number *two* with his thumb and index finger (D in fig. 4.3). Moving to this new gesture from the initial *five* handshape (A) does not occur instantly, but instead requires a sequence of movement.

First, Chil folds the three fingers that won't be used in the second gesture into his palm (B). As he does this, his thumb also falls into his fist for a very brief moment before being immediately displayed again. The gesture then visible (C) displays two digits, the thumb and index finger. However, with the other three fingers retracted, the index finger is now very prominently positioned as a striking, isolated entity, almost like a lighthouse standing above the landscape formed by the rest of the hand. An interlocutor viewing this sequence of hand movements has grounds for seeing Chil displaying not only a possible *two*, but equally and perhaps more simply, a *one* with his index finger, especially in light of the fact that the number *two* is typically produced in Chil's community not with the thumb but instead with the index and middle finger (insert). The question might arise as to whether the thumb constitutes a counting digit when other fingers are still available.[11]

What happens next provides some evidence that the question of how this shape will be classified is an issue that Chil himself recognizes. He immediately rotates his hand so that the thumb is raised to the same height as the index finger (D). The

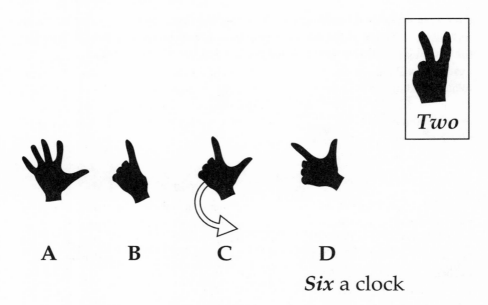

A   B   C   D

Six a clock

FIGURE 4.3. Moving from one handshape to another

handshape now displays a U-shaped figure with two distinct, equally prominent ends. This pattern of hand rotation, sometimes ending with the thumb higher than the index finger, is repeated throughout the rest of the sequence. However, by the time it first occurs at line 15, Pat is already saying "*Six* a clock" and thus treating the handshape as displaying a *one*.

If all that is at issue in the production of Chil's gesture is the outward expression of mental processes, the handshape at C is entirely adequate: holding up two digits constitutes an accurate external representation of the number *two*. The way in which Chil then goes to extra effort to reposition his hand so that both digits are made equally prominent for a viewer provides an example in gesture of what Sacks, Schegloff, and Jefferson (1974: 727) identify as "perhaps the most general principle which particularizes conversational interactions, that of Recipient Design."

Parsing movement into coherent sequences

To count higher than five, Chil, who has the use of only one hand, has to produce a *sequence* of gestures: first a full hand signaling five and then a second handshape displaying additional digits. These hand gestures have to be interpreted not simply as numbers, *but as numbers to be summed together*. This process explicitly contrasts with something else that happens here: *re-doing* the counting sequence. In this activity, another handful of numbers is also displayed. But this is not to be seen as more numbers to be added to the existing sum, but instead as the beginning of another try at getting the meaning of the number right. Thus, at line 17 Pat says not "eleven" (an additional five added to the "six" she produced in line 15) but "*Five*":

Example 3
12   Chil: °mmm. Nih nih da duh Da duh.
13   Pat: So *five* of us can fit there.
14   (0.2)
15   Pat: *Six* a clock.
16   (1.0)

17   Pat: *Five* people,

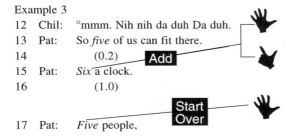

The separate gestures have to be grouped into relevant sequences. Correct parsing has real consequences for subsequent action: to build an appropriate next move, Chil's interlocutor performs different kinds of operations on different sequence types.[12] How are successive hand gestures grouped into relevant sequences? It might seem that this is an interpretive problem posed for the viewer of the gestures, for example, a mental act of classification. However, making visible coherent sequences, and disjunctures between sequences, is intrinsic to the embodied work doing gesture. The visible movements of Chil's body provide Pat with the resources she needs to parse the flow of his gestures into the separate action packages she requires in order to build an appropriate response to them.

The gestures to be summed together are consistently done in a particular way: first, the *five* is produced with all five fingers spread apart. Then, *while holding the hand in approximately the same position in space*, three of the extended fingers are closed. The constant position of the hand in space provides a unifying ground, a framework, within which the successive finger displays emerge as stages in a common activity.

This contrasts quite markedly with what happens when Chil signals that Pat's interpretation is wrong and redoes the gesture. Here, Chil rapidly drops his hand, *thus dismantling the stage for the hand created by the position of the arm in space*, and then raises it again. In essence the stage that provides a framework for the perception of the hand is cleared, and a new stage is created. On such a stage, a hand displaying numbers arrives as a fresh actor, one initiating a new counting sequence, rather than adding to a sequence already in progress.

Why doesn't this new stage signal Pat to move to a new activity or topic? While dropping his hand and then rapidly raising it again, Chil continues to stare intently at his interlocutor. The boundary between successive counting trials is thus embedded within a larger, unbroken framework of sustained focus on a continuing activity with a particular partner.

Rather than standing alone as self-contained units of meaning, Chil's handshapes are systematically informed by a nested set of hierarchical displays created by the rest of his body: first, the movements of his arm that organize individual gestures into separate sequences; and second, his gaze (and the orientation of his upper body) that establishes continuity across the difference counting sequences made visible by his moving arm.[13]

Securing orientation to the gesture

The way in which Chil uses his hand to bracket sequences of gestures is quite consistent with the work of Armstrong, Stokoe, and Wilcox (1995), who argue that the production of gesture involves not just the hand, but many other parts of the body, in particular the arms, moving through time in organized action. However, to analyze these data we have to go beyond the body of the party making the gesture to focus on a multi-party interactively sustained space that provides a framework for common orientation and the production of meaning. The necessity of such a framework can be seen in a number of different ways in this sequence. For example, the place where Chil makes his gesture is organized not only in terms of *his body*, but also with reference to the *position* and changing action *of his addressee*. Thus, Chil places his gesturing hand squarely in Pat's line of sight (fig. 4.4).

Pat   Chil   Helen   Julia

FIGURE 4.4. Multi-party gesture space

If Chil had been talking to Helen, the hand would have been placed quite differently. Gesture space is defined in terms of his interlocutor's body as well as his own.

Moreover, Chil changes the placement of his hand with reference to Pat's orientation. At the beginning of line 12, Pat is looking at Helen (fig. 4.5). Chil, who had been silent, holds up his hand in the *five* shape while producing an intonational tune:

FIGURE 4.5. Securing addressee gaze

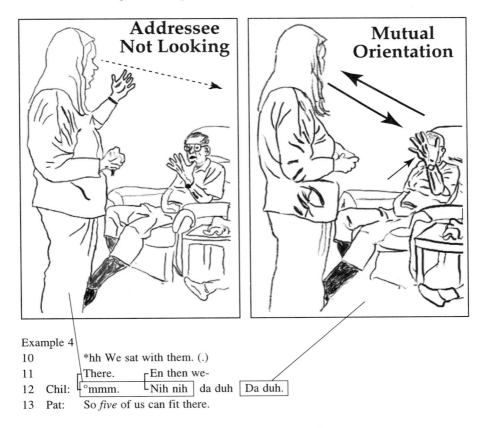

```
Example 4
10              *hh We sat with them. (.)
11              There.        ┌En then we-
12    Chil:  ┌°mmm.     └Nih nih │ da duh │ Da duh. │
13    Pat:     So five of us can fit there.
```

Chil's actions have the effect of drawing Pat's gaze to him.[14] Once she is looking at him, he raises his hand sharply into her line of sight, and this becomes the position used for gesturing throughout the remainder of the sequence. It would appear that his hand, initially in conjunction with his intonation melody, is performing two different, though interrelated actions: first, requesting the orientation of an addressee (by announcing that he has something to say); and second, producing a meaningful utterance, here a sequence of gestures, once his interlocutor is visibly positioned to attend to it. The process that occurs here is structurally analogous to the way in which a state of mutual orientation is negotiated prior to the production of a coherent sentence in conversation. Parties who lack the gaze of a hearer produce phrasal breaks, such as restarts, to request such gaze and speak coherent sentences only after they have the orientation of a hearer (Goodwin 1980, 1981, chap. 2).[15]

In sum, the relevant framework for the analysis of Chil's gesture is not his hand in isolation, or even the entire body of the party performing the gesture, but instead a multi-party participation framework organized so as to constitute a common focus of attention.[16]

Sequential organization

While such a framework provides a stage for working with the gesture, in and of itself it does not provide the resources necessary for the social constitution of what the gesture means. As this sequence demonstrates all too clearly, even within this framework different parties can understand the gesture they are looking at together in quite different ways. What is required in addition are the processes of *sequential organization* that tie Chil's gesture, and Pat's public gloss of it, into a common course of temporally unfolding, meaningful action. Within such a framework, how the gesture is to be understood can be challenged, negotiated, and collaboratively affirmed. Central to this process is a basic sequence in which first Chil produces a gesture and then Pat provides a gloss of it (fig. 4.6).

Within this sequence, the occurrence of a hand gesture by Chil makes it relevant for Pat to provide a gloss showing her current understanding of what he is trying to say. When Pat says "*Six* a clock" in this sequentially defined slot, Chil is able to see that she doesn't understand what he is trying to say.

On hearing Pat's gloss, Chil drops his hand, marking what she has said as in error, and then immediately raises it again. This move once again makes it relevant for Pat to provide a gloss of what he's trying to say (fig. 4.7).

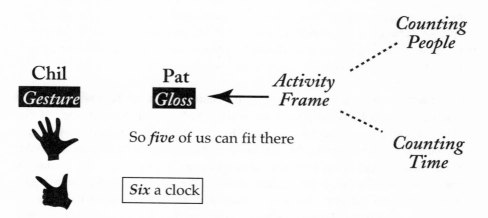

FIGURE 4.6. The sequential organization of Chil's gestures

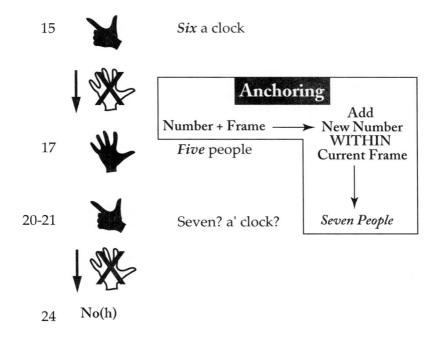

FIGURE 4.7. Anchoring

Starting from scratch, Pat in line 17 says, "*Five* people." It appears that Chil is trying to get Pat to follow a very simple strategy which I'll call *anchoring*. Pat's glosses take the form of a *number plus an activity frame*. By initiating the sequence from scratch, Chil gets Pat to produce a number lodged within the activity frame he wants. His inability to produce more than five fingers at a time now becomes a resource as well as a constraint: he can get Pat to produce a gloss of *five* alone, which embeds it within the *counting people* frame. If she now simply adds a new number within that frame, she'll have the solution he's looking for: "seven people." However, despite the simplicity of this process as a clear, logical procedure, Pat again treats the number as a possible *time* (lines 20–21), though here coloring her answer with greater uncertainty. And indeed other interpretive resources also available in the local environment (for example, the way in which the time they'll eat can be seen to have a negotiable status that the group itself doesn't) are consistent with her choice.

In response, Chil again drops his hand. However, this time, instead of continuing to gaze at Pat, he moves his head away from her and explicitly says "No." Both the withdrawal, which marks a break in the mutual focus that had been sustained with Pat until this point, and the "No" display to his interlocutors that Chil is having serious problems with the interpretive work that Pat is performing.[17] Shortly after this happens, the person who knows him best, his wife, shifts interpretive frames to at last recognize what Chil is trying to say (lines 28, 31).

Example 5

```
24        Chil:    No(h).
25   Pat:    Six a clock.
26              (0.2)
27   Pat:    Seven?
28   ┌Helen:   °Seven people. Who┌('d they be)┐
29   │Pat:                       └Five.
30              (1.0)
31   ┌Helen:   Seven people. ┌Who  are they.┐
32   │Pat:                   └That's six.
33   Julia:   Two?
34   Pat:   ┌Seven?       ((Chil turns and points toward helen))
35   Chil:  └Duh da dah.
36              Ye:s.
37              (0.2)
38   ┌Pat:    Invite somebody?┐
39   └Chil:   Ye:s.
```

Frameworks for constituting meaning through gesture

For normal speakers, gestures typically arrive accompanied by relevant talk. Moreover, the gesture and its lexical affiliate are not only produced by the same person but are deeply intertwined in the development of a common structure of meaning (McNeill, 1992). The accompanying talk not only provides a resource for analysts of gesture, who can investigate in fine detail the precise timing of the unfolding course of the gesture and the words it elaborates (Kendon, 1983, 1994b; McNeill, 1992; Schegloff, 1984), but also for participants, who are easily able to find a relevant meaning in a speaker's moving hand. By way of contrast, the utterances of Chil examined here are done entirely through gesture. Moreover, successful analysis of his gestures has real consequences for subsequent interaction. Within this process, establishing the meaning of a gesture is repetitively posed as a problematic, practical task. The work done to accomplish this task throws into strong relief a range of procedures and resources used to organize gesture as a meaningful, interactively sustained activity.

For descriptive purposes, it can be useful to describe some of these structures in terms of a series of hierarchically embedded organizational frameworks.

1. One can begin with specific handshapes. Rather than being merely expressive, Chil's handshapes are carefully organized to guide specific interpretations by their addressees (see the discussion of his positioning his hand to ensure that *two* rather than a possible *one* is clearly visible).

2. Rather than being static signs, Chil's gestures are constituted through patterns of gestural movement (Armstrong, Stokoe, & Wilcox 1995),

which simultaneously provide information about the operations recipients should perform on the handshapes thus framed. The hand making a display is placed and held in position by an arm. Rather than constituting a constant, amorphous ground to the meaningful figure formed by the hand, the arm is itself an important actor in the organization of Chil's gestures. Its movements delineate the boundaries of relevant sequences of gestures within an extended flow of handshapes. Such parsing of the stream of his visible activity is absolutely central to the successful accomplishment of the tasks his addressees are engaged in, since they must perform alternative types of operations (e.g., summing two numbers together as opposed to starting a count from scratch) on different arrangements of successive handshapes.

3. Locating the lexical affiliate of a gesture does not constitute establishing its meaning. Wittgenstein (1958; Baker & Hacker, 1980) argues that the meaning of a name is not its bearer (e.g., some version of the number *five*), but rather mastery of the practices required to use that sign competently within a relevant language game. Here, multiple language games are at issue: first, the particular activity within which the practice of counting is embedded (e.g., *time* versus *number of people*); second, the larger projects within which an utterance such as *seven people* counts as a relevant move (e.g., a proposal that additional friends be included in the unfolding plans for dinner); and third, the frameworks and procedures that Chil and those around him deploy to make sense out of his gestures in order to accomplish relevant courses of action.

4. The gesture space required for the analysis of what Chil is doing encompasses not only his own body but also that of his addressee. Chil performs special gestural and vocal work to secure her visual focus on his hand and consistently places his hand in her line of sight.

5. Within this framework, one party's talk can gloss and explicate another's gesture. The elements required to assemble the meaning of a gesture are distributed entities, existing in different media (the moving hand and the talk which elaborates it) and, in this case, in the activities of separate participants. The distributed work required to constitute the meaning of a gesture is dramatically visible in Chil's case. However, it is present as well in the talk of parties who are able to speak. Indeed, much recent research on gesture has focused on its close ties to the structure of the talk that accompanies it (Heath, 1992; Kendon, 1994b; McNeill, 1992). McNeill, in his work on growth points, has demonstrated how talk and gesture might emerge from a common source in the production of an utterance. However, quite independent of the psychological origin of such a relationship, the

way in which a gesture and the talk it is tied to mutually elaborate each other constitutes a central arena for social practice in the organization of talk-in-interaction. It provides a key resource for participants faced with the task of making relevant sense out of the field of action embodied in a strip of talk and the co-occurring field of visible behavior within which it is embedded. Though gesture is typically treated as a transparent, seamless package, conversationalists can themselves deconstruct this unity for playful and other purposes. For example, the gestures being made by a speaker can be ridiculed by extracting them from her talk and then re-attaching them to a new, incongruent strip of talk (Goodwin & Goodwin, 1992). Seeing a gesture as a meaningful display characteristically involves not just orientation to someone's moving hand, but rather ongoing synthesis and mutual calibration of quite disparate kinds of information emerging through time within different modalities for expression available to the human body lodged within interaction.[18]

6.   While an interactively sustained, multi-party participation framework provides a stage for the coordinated display of gesture and talk, something more is required to socially constitute its meaning: *sequential organization*. Pat's glosses can be wrong. It is only through temporally unfolding processes of interaction that Pat and Chil establish a common vision of what is being said with the gesture. Here, a range of disparate phenomena, including the talk and the visible body displays of separate people, is integrated into a common course of action.

Conclusion: Some broader implications

The way in which Chil's gestures are deeply embedded within the talk of those around him provides an opportunity to probe basic procedures and frameworks deployed by parties in interaction to constitute meaning together. Chil's use of gesture is by no means the same as that of a person with unimpaired language abilities. Nonetheless, he is able to make himself understood. This is accomplished through systematic transformation of more general resources available for the organization of talk-in-interaction. Thus, in normal conversations, gestures frequently co-occur with talk by the party making the gesture. As this talk carries much (though by no means all) of what is being said, it is possible for hearers on occasion to grasp the substance of an utterance while paying only passing attention to the accompanying gesture, or even ignoring it entirely.[19] By way of contrast, the utterances of Chil being examined here are done entirely through gesture and thus must be attended to by at least one of his addressees.[20] Chil adapts to his gestural utterances one of the basic procedures used by speakers in conversation to obtain the orientation of a hearer to an emerging strip of talk: securing the gaze of an addressee with a preliminary version of the gesture and then redoing the gesture once mutual orientation has been established. As Chil's gestures have the status of full-fledged moves within conversation (e.g., they *do* constitute his turns at talk), it is not at all surprising that resources used more generally to organize participation within the turn are now used to frame his gestures in ways that are not done for the gestures of participants able to speak.

Looking at these same issues from a slightly different perspective, it can be noted that the way in which Chil relies upon the actions of his interlocutors to build meaning and structure that is beyond his own capacities as an isolated individual provides a particularly clear example of what Vygotsky (1962; Cole, 1985) described as the Zone of Proximal Development. However, Vygotsky framed his analysis within a developmental theory: by working with a more experienced partner, the child was increasing his own abilities and competence. This emphasis on an individual's increasing mastery of complex activities has been maintained in more recent work in the Vygotskian tradition (for example Lave and Wenger's [1991] model of learning through peripheral participation within a community of practice). In contrast, Chil has suffered a massive *decline* in his competence, and there is no hope that his linguistic abilities will ever improve. Thus, while Vygotsky's emphasis on the social articulation of knowledge is quite relevant to these data, associated assumptions about an individual's increasing skill and competence that are central to any developmental theory simply do not fit at all. A way out of this impasse can be found by first shifting the unit of analysis from the individual to the social group (see Engeström, 1987; Hutchins, 1995) and, second, by abandoning the notion that evolution is to be equated with cummulative progress (Gould, 1989). Though Chil's abilities as an individual decline catastrophically, the social system within which he is embedded adapts to this crisis and evolves by creatively reshaping frameworks for the organization of interaction so that he is able to continue to function as a viable, indeed central, actor in the courses of collaborative action that make up their lives. Rather than unilinear progress within an individual, development can be seen as a processes embedded within a social matrix that occurs throughout the life cycle. As individuals change or crisis occurs, resources and tasks are redistributed within relevant social units and new forms of practice arise. This process has a micro-historical dimension as well, one that builds upon shared history. Chil is able to tell a story about events that happened fifty years ago by using gesture to get his wife to recall the relevant incident. As she talks, he acts as a co-teller by using gesture and intonation to comment on her talk. If Chil were treated as an individual and isolated from his family, for example, if he were to be put in a nursing home, not only his ability to act by using the resources of relevant others but also much of his memory would be lost as well. The relevant unit for the analysis of Chil's condition is not him as an individual, but rather the frameworks for the production of meaning and action within interaction that link him to the consequential partners who share his life with him.

The particular characteristics of this community have other consequences as well. Despite some moves toward organizing relevant contrasts within a larger system, Chil's gesturing is not in any way comparable to the well-developed sign languages of the deaf,[21] or speaking people prohibited from talking (Kendon, 1988). Thus, his gestures are not organized into elaborate, hierarchically organized structures through syntactic processes. Moreover, unlike communication in a signing community, his interlocutors do not operate under his constraints but instead use the full resources of talk-in-interaction. The work of Singleton, Morford, and Goldin-Meadow (1995) suggests that one very strong constraint inhibiting the elaboration of syntactic relationships between hand movements (i.e., the shift from isolated gestures to a signing system) is the way in which gestures remain parasitic upon the structure of co-occurring spoken language. When speech is present, links between hand movements are provided by the talk and thus do not have to be built into the organization of the gestural stream. Of course, in Chil's case the issue is complicated by the question of whether damage to his brain would make syntax impossible under any circumstances. Nonetheless the work of Singleton and her colleagues leads to the interesting possibility that the hybrid speech community that some stroke victims create with their interlocutors (e.g., one party using gestures and limited speech but tying that to the fully articulated language of others) might itself inhibit the elaboration of more syntactic organization in a stroke victim's gesturing system. Other social factors are at play here as well. Though half a million people suffer strokes in America each year, and three million continue to live with disability because of such trauma, most strokes (over 70%) occur in people over 65 years of age (Leary, 1995). Unlike the situation with the deaf where concerted political action has led to the formation of viable communities and relevant educational institutions, victims of stroke typically live out their lives disconnected from others in a similar state.[22] Thus, instead of an active, well-developed speech community using a language like American Sign Language (ASL) together, and passing it on from generation to generation, the communication of stroke patients develops within thousands of small, isolated pockets, and the special adaptations each family creates die with the person who suffered the stroke.

The processes being investigated here are relevant to a range of other issues as well. First, under the influence of Wittgenstein (1958; Baker & Hacker, 1985), renewed attention has been focused on the question of how people themselves use rules as visible, socially recognized phenomena to organize the activities they are pursuing. To make himself understood, Chil relies upon Pat following a set of public, rule-governed discursive practices embedded in the use of language, for example, counting and adding numbers in a systematic fashion and stating the products of such work in particular linguistic formats. Indeed, if Chil can get Pat to follow *five people* with *seven people*, he will organize the production of a syntactic unit that he is unable to speak (and possibly construct) himself. Rather than taking the form of hidden mental structures that require the ingenuity of a social scientist to explicate, the rule use visible in Pat's talk constitutes a public calculus, one that Chil uses as a resource for the organization of his own action. Though the operations that Pat performs upon Chil's gestures to make sense out of them are completely appropriate, logical, and correct, initially she is unable to grasp what he is trying to say because she embeds his numbers within the wrong activity frame. This does not mean that the procedures she is using to analyze what he is telling her are in some sense defective or need better formulation so that a correct solution is always found. Such a search for bomb-proof criteria for the use of rules is fundamentally misguided. By relying upon each other to systematically use appropriate procedures for making sense out of the activities they are collaboratively pursuing together, Chil and Pat *do* eventually establish what they are trying to say to each other. Similarly, the real presence of multiple possibilities for construing which of several possible rules is to be applied at a specific juncture does not mean that the signs being worked with (such as Chil's handshapes) represent fuzzy concepts. Despite the presence of competing criteria provided by the different interpretative resources available to Pat, both participants recognize the sharp contrast between correct and incorrect solutions and work hard to remedy visible problems. The systematic constitution of meaning is a situated, contingent accomplishment, but one that can be successfully worked out through processes of action embedded within the architectures for intersubjectivity provided by the organization of human interaction (Heritage, 1984; Schegloff, Jefferson, & Sacks, 1977).

Second, gesture figures prominently in a number of recent hypotheses about how human beings might have developed language. In a very interesting series of arguments, Armstrong, Stokoe, and Wilcox (1994, 1995) note that a single gesture, such as one hand moving to *catch* something represented by the other hand, can constitute "a complete transitive sentence. It has a subject, a verb and a direct object, or, in semantic terms, an agent, action, and patient" (1995: 22). While this is certainly true, it nonetheless leaves unresolved the crucial question of how multiple parties—not only the person making the gesture but also his or her interlocutors—are able to understand it in the same way. Chil's handshapes are simpler and even more iconic than the examples given by Armstrong, Stokoe, and Wilcox; moreover, their possible meanings are heavily constrained by being embedded within a recognized activity organized in concert with his interlocutor. However, even under such ideal conditions, figuring out what the handshapes mean emerges as a difficult, problematic task for Chil's addressees. Indeed, though not examined in this chapter, even locating the target of a single pointing finger can take an extraordinary amount of work (see Goodwin, in press, and Haviland, 1998). Within an evolutionary framework, any proposed change in the structure of an organism must have consequences that extend beyond the individual; the development of a private language is not sufficient (such issues apply as well to Bickerton's [1990] hypotheses about mutations for syntax). What is required is a matrix of action within which the symbolic possibilities of gesture and talk can be organized as social phenomena. According to Armstrong, Stokoe, and Wilcox (1995: 218) "the primary problem for any speculative theory about the development of hominid social structure is to explain the origin of the family as the principal unit of social organization." It can be argued instead that the primary form of human social organization—indeed, what defines us as a species—is language itself. Goffman (1964) argued that talk is itself a form of human social organization, a system that requires the systematic, organized collaboration of multiple parties. This has been amply demonstrated by research in the field of conversation analysis, with detailed study of the social organization of a host of phenomena, including turn-taking (Jefferson, 1973; Sacks, Schegloff, & Jefferson, 1974), repair (Schegloff, Jefferson, & Sacks, 1977), sentence construction (Goodwin, 1979, 1981), the social use of syntax by separate parties who collaboratively build single sentences (Lerner, 1987; Sacks, 1992a) and activities within sentences (Goodwin & Goodwin, 1987). As an elementary form of human social organization, talk-in-interaction insinuates itself into the core activities of most other institutions, from the family to decision making in the offices of presidents, the conduct of law courts and educational institutions, and so on. Within the frameworks for collaborative action, and the public, consequential constitution of meaning provided by sequential organization, the symbolic possibilities of both gesture and talk can flourish. In brief, the development of basic structures for the constitution of meaning and action within temporally unfolding processes of human interaction, such as sequential organization, would seem to be a prerequisite for the elaboration of the representational systems now found in both gesture and spoken language. Crucial questions about the origins of language become inaccessible if language is defined only as a symbolic calculus, rather than as a core human institution that constitutes a primordial form of social organization in its own right.

Throughout each day of their lives members of this family face, as an ongoing practical problem, the task of how to constitute shared meaning so that the courses of coordinated action that make up their life world can be accomplished. Such a task, which mobilizes language, gesture, and social organization for the accomplishment of action within consequential settings, sits at the very center of what it means to be human. This chapter has tried to demonstrate that it is precisely the flexible possibilities provided by the changing textures of relevancies invoked through emergent sequential organization, and the interactive organization of relevant participation frameworks, that makes it possible for an actor such as Chil to use gesture to build socially meaningful action. Drawing attention to the wide and important range of pragmatic competence he uses to make himself understood is not meant to suggest that he has the full communicational abilities of someone who can speak. If he could have said as simple a phrase as "seven people," all of the work examined here would have been unnecessary. However, the events investigated here do call into question traditional assessments of competence based purely on the ability to produce language.

Immediately after his stroke, Chil's doctors, focused entirely on the trauma within his brain, said that any therapy would be merely cosmetic and a waste of time, for the underlying brain injury could not be remedied. Nothing could have been farther from the truth, and medical advice based on such a view of the problem can cause irrepa-rable harm to patients such as Chil and their families. As an injury, aphasia does reside within the skull. However, as a form of life, a way of being and acting in the world in concert with others, its proper locus is an endogenous, distributed, multi-party system, within which language functions as a socially organized matrix of public practice.

Notes

I am most deeply indebted to Chil, and his family, for allowing me access to their lives. My understanding of what is happening in these data has been greatly helped by comments from Lisa Capps, David Goode, Cathryn Houghton, Sally Jacoby, Elinor Ochs, Kersten Priest, Curtis Renoe, Emanuel Schegloff, Jennifer Schlegel, Elizabeth Teas-Heaster, and most especially Candy Goodwin.

1. A more limited analysis of the data examined here, focused on gesture rather than sequential organization, appeared as "Gesture, Aphasia and Interaction," pp. 84-98 in *Language and Gesture: Window into Thought and Action*, edited by David McNeill, Cambridge University Press, 2000.

2. Initially therapists tried to teach Chil a wide range of communicative strategies, and at some point he could speak one or two other words ("wine," for example). However, his vocabulary eventually stabilized on "yes," "no," and "and." These three words are central to the sequences of interaction through which meaning and understanding are negotiated in his family. I am using the word "choice" to frame as sharply as possible the issue of functional selection from a larger set of possibilities, not to indicate that there was some single moment when Chil decided which words he would learn, and which he would ignore. From another perspective, it is clear that his vocabulary in fact contains far more than "three words." As this chapter demonstrates, the terms "yes" and "no" encompass a broad range of functionally differentiated forms of action and meaning. Moreover, some of his intonation melodies (e.g., "*duh* duh *duh* duh *duh*" spoken with a characteristic pattern of pitch and stress) are used regularly and systematically to communicate specific stances and responses in much the way that "yes" and "no" are.

In this chapter, only Chil's use of "yes" and "no" will be investigated.

3. His medical records at discharge in 1981 report "severe expressive and moderate receptive aphasia, moderate dysarthria and verbal apraxia." There was never any improve-ment in his condition.

4. See, for example, the exemplary work of McNeill (1992) and his colleagues. The social and interactive organization of gesture has long been emphasized by Kendon (1997). A num-ber of contemporary scholars are now investigating in most interesting ways how gesture is organized with reference to the environment within which it emerges (Hutchins & Palen, 1997; LeBaron & Streeck, 2000; Ochs, Gonzales, & Jacoby, 1996; Streeck, 1996).

5. For a comparison of script-based and sequential approaches to the study of the cog-nitive processes implicated in the organization of action, see Wootton (1997).

6. Though not developed in analysis of the present data, a considerable body of research demonstrates how such situated cognition also uses the tools and resources provided the en-vironment within which action occurs (Goodwin, 1994, 1995b, 1997; Hutchins, 1995; Lynch,

1993; Suchman, 1987). Unlike earlier work studying cognition from the perspective of artificial intelligence, Gutierrez, Rymes, and Larson (1995) investigate scripts as interactively sustained frameworks in a way that is quite consistent withthe analysis developed here.

7. Indeed, as noted by Kendon (personal communication), not all gestures have lexical affiliates.

8. The use of a common counting system across multiple activities is itself a historically shaped process (Nicolopoulou, 1989). Patricia Mason (personal communication) has told me that in Quechua, Spanish numerals are used to count time, while Quechua numerals are used in other domains. Telling time with a numeric clock was a practice introduced by the conquest.

9. In defining the notion of frame, Fillmore (1982: 111) writes that "I have in mind any system of concepts related in such a way that to understand any one of them you have to understand the whole structure in which it fits; when one of the things in such a structure is introduced into a text, or into a conversation, all of the others are automatically made available. " For more extended discussion of how bits of talk invoke a relevant context for their proper understanding, see Duranti (1992), Garfinkel (1967), Goodwin (1996), Goodwin and Duranti (1992), Gumperz (1992), Heritage (1984), Sacks (1992a, 1992b) and Schegloff (1972).

10. For other analysis of how a category and the phenomena to which it is being applied mutually elaborate each other, see Goodwin (1994, 1996). The way in which Chil's five-fingered hand gesture repetitively flips between a time and person reference for Pat in this sequence brings to mind Wittgenstein's (1958: 194) famous use of the gestalt psychologists' "duck-rabbit" to demonstrate how the aspect from which we view something structures our perception of what we see there.

11. Other features of this sequence might also prime Pat to see *seven* as an unlikely number. Thus, once she is using *time* to make sense out of the number, seven o'clock might seem so much later than what they'd already agreed upon that repeating the earlier "six o'clock" would seem to be the most sensible choice for making sense out of his gesture.

12. In line 33, after being unable to find the meaning of *seven*, Julia does raise the possibility that the current handshape should instead be glossed as a *two*, that it should *not* be added to the gesture before it.

13. Kendon (1990) has stressed the importance of seeing the body as a locus for hierarchical displays of orientation. Armstrong, Stokoe, and Wilcox (1995) call attention to the importance of seeing both gesture and spoken language as 1) providing "words," (e.g., rich concepts), and 2) syntax, (e.g., procedures for establishing systematic relationships between concepts). It is clear that Chil lacks syntax in spoken language and, probably does not possess it for gesture either. However, as this sequence demonstrates, he is able to link separate gestures into larger patterns. This suggests that a variety of structures can be used to organize gestural units into larger wholes, but that only some of these constitute *syntax* in the linguistic sense.

14. For other analysis of how parties making gestures both work to focus the gaze of their recipients on the hand(s) making the gesture, and redesign the gesture after its addressee visibly misunderstands it, see Streeck (1993, 1994). For discussion of research pertaining to the question of whether gestures in conversation are in fact communicative (a position that has been challenged by some psychologists), see Kendon (1994b).

15. It is interesting to note that in both situations the item used to solicit orientation is an incomplete version of the utterance or gesture that will constitute the substance of the proposed turn.

16. See Hibbitts (1995) for an analysis of the importance of multi-party participation frameworks for the organization of gesture in the legal system.

17. For related analysis of how such a withdrawal cues others to shift the frame they are using to make sense out of Chil's talk, see Goodwin (1995a).

18. The web of meaning implicated in the organization of gesture does not stop at the actors' skins but encompasses as well features of their environment and historically structured representations of many different kinds (maps, images, graphs, computer screens providing access to worlds beyond the immediate situation, etc.), which give meaning to gesture in a variety of different ways. See, for example, C. Goodwin (1994, 1995b), M. H. Goodwin (1995), Heath (1992), Heath and Luff (1992), Hutchins (1995, 1997), LeBaron and Streeck (2000), and Ochs, Jacoby, and Gonzales (1994).

19. This does not, however, mean, as some psychologists have suggested, that participants in ordinary conversation entirely ignore gesture. For analysis of how speakers reshape emerging action to take into account displays made through gesture, see M. H. Goodwin (1980) and Kendon (1994a).

20. Helen, the person who at last figures out that *seven* is counting people, never turns her head to look at Chil's hand. It is possible that she relies upon Pat's talk alone for access to Chil's gestures.

21. For especially interesting analysis of the development of syntax in a sign language system, and the way in which such a system differs radically from not only gesture but also more primitive signing systems, see Kegl, Senghas, and Coppola (1999).

22. In many cases, including Chil's, stroke victims are able to draw upon the resources of their families, especially their partners. While absolutely central to constituting a relevant and meaningful life world, this situation can place an extraordinary burden on those closest to the stroke victim, who are aging themselves.

References

Armstrong, D. F., Stokoe, W. C., & Wilcox, S. E. (1994). Signs and the Origin of Syntax. *Current Anthropology, 25*(4): 349–368.

Armstrong, D. F., Stokoe, W. C., & Wilcox, S. E. (1995). *Gesture and the Nature of Language*. Cambridge: Cambridge University Press.

Baker, G. P., & Hacker, P. M. S. (1980). *Wittgenstein: Understanding and Meaning*. Chicago: University of Chicago Press.

Baker, G. P., & Hacker, P. M. S. (1985). *Wittgenstein: Rules, Grammar, and Necessity*. Oxford: Blackwell.

Bickerton, D. (1990). *Language & Species*. Chicago: University of Chicago Press.

Cole, M. (1985). The Zone of Proximal Development: Where Culture and Cognition Create Each Other. In J. Wertsch (Ed.), *Culture, Communication, and Cognition: Vygotskian Perspectives* (pp. 146–161). Cambridge: Cambridge University Press.

Duranti, A. (1992). Language in Context and Language as Context: The Samoan Respect Vocabulary. In A. Duranti & C. Goodwin (Eds.), *Rethinking Context: Language as an Interactive Phenomenon* (pp. 77–99). Cambridge: Cambridge University Press.

Ekman, P., & Friesen, W. V. (1969). The Repertoire of Nonverbal Behavior: Categories, Origins, Usage, and Coding. *Semiotica*, 1, 49–98.

Engeström, Y. (1987). *Learning by Expanding: An Activity-Theoretical Approach to Developmental Research.* Helsinki: Orienta-Konsultit Oy.

Fillmore, C. J. (1982). Frame Semantics. In Linguistic Society of Korea (Ed.), *Linguistics in the Morning Calm* (pp. 111–137). Seoul: Hanshin Publishing Co.

Garfinkel, H. (1967). *Studies in Ethnomethodology.* Englewood Cliffs, NJ: Prentice-Hall.

Goffman, E. (1964). The Neglected Situation. In J. J. Gumperz & D. Hymes (Eds.), *The Ethnography of Communication. American Anthropologist,* 66, 6 (pt. II), 133–136.

Goodwin, C. (1979). The Interactive Construction of a Sentence in Natural Conversation. In G. Psathas (Ed.), *Everyday Language: Studies in Ethnomethodology* (pp. 97–121). New York: Irvington Publishers.

Goodwin, C. (1980a). Restarts, Pauses, and the Achievement of Mutual Gaze at Turn-Beginning. *Sociological Inquiry,* 50(3–4), 272–302.

Goodwin, C. (1981). *Conversational Organization: Interaction Between Speakers and Hearers.* New York: Academic Press.

Goodwin, C. (1994). Professional Vision. *American Anthropologist,* 96(3), 606–633.

Goodwin, C. (1995a). Co-Constructing Meaning in Conversations with an Aphasic Man. *Research on Language and Social Interaction,* 28(3), 233–260.

Goodwin, C. (1995b). Seeing in Depth. *Social Studies of Science,* 25, 237–274.

Goodwin, C. (1996). Transparent Vision. In E. Ochs, E. A. Schegloff, & S. Thompson (Eds.), *Interaction and Grammar* (pp. 370–404). Cambridge: Cambridge University Press.

Goodwin, C. (1997). The Blackness of Black: Color Categories as Situated Practice. In L. B. Resnick, R. Säljö, C. Pontecorvo, & B. Burge (Eds.), *Discourse, Tools and Reasonsing: Essays on Situated Cognition* (pp. 111–140). Berlin: Springer.

Goodwin, C. (in press). Pointing as Situated Practice. In S. Kita (Ed.), *Pointing: Where Language, Culture and Cognition Meet.* Hillsdale, NJ: Erlbaum.

Goodwin, C., & Duranti, A. (1992). Rethinking Context: An Introduction. In A. Duranti & C. Goodwin (Eds.), *Rethinking Context: Language as an Interactive Phenomenon* (pp. 1–42). Cambridge: Cambridge University Press.

Goodwin, C., & Goodwin, M. H. (1987). Concurrent Operations on Talk: Notes on the Interactive Organization of Assessments. *IPrA Papers in Pragmatics,* 1(1), 1–52.

Goodwin, C., & Goodwin, M. H. (1992). Context, Activity and Participation. In P. Auer & A. di Luzio (Eds.), *The Contextualization of Language* (pp. 77–99). Amsterdam: Benjamins.

Goodwin, M. H. (1980). Processes of Mutual Monitoring Implicated in the Production of Description Sequences. *Sociological Inquiry,* 50, 303–317.

Goodwin, M. H. (1995). Co-Construction in Girls' Hopscotch. *Research on Language and Social Interaction,* 28(3), 261–282.

Gould, S. J. (1989). *Wonderful Life: The Burgess Shale and the Nature of History.* New York: Norton.

Gumperz, J. (1992). Contextualization and Understanding. In A. Duranti & C. Goodwin (Eds.), *Rethinking Context: Language as an Interactive Phenomenon* (pp. 229–252). Cambridge: Cambridge University Press.

Gutierrez, K. D., Rymes, B., & Larson, J. (1995). Script, Counterscript, and Underlife in the Classroom: James Brown versus Brown v. Board of Education. *Harvard Educational Review,* 65(3), 445–471.

Haviland, J. (1998). Early Pointing Gestures in Zincantán. *Journal of Linguistic Anthropology,* 8(2), 162–196.

Heath, C. (1992). Gesture's Discrete Tasks: Multiple Relevancies in Visual Conduct and in the Contextualization of Language. In P. Auer & A. di Luzio (Eds.), *The Contextualization of Language* (pp. 101–127). Amsterdam: John Benjamins.

Heath, C. C., & Luff, P. K. (1992). Crisis and Control: Collaborative Work in London Underground Control Rooms. *Journal of Computer Supported Cooperative Work, 1*(1), 24–48.

Heritage, J. (1984). *Garfinkel and Ethnomethodology.* Cambridge: Polity Press.

Hibbitts, B. J. (1995). Making Motions: The Embodiment of Law in Gesture. *Journal of Contemporary Legal Issues, 6,* 51–82.

Hutchins, E. (1995). *Cognition in the Wild.* Cambridge, MA: MIT Press.

Hutchins, E., & Palen, L. (1997). Constructing Meaning from Space, Gesture, and Speech. In L. Resnick, R. Säljö, C. Pontecorvo, & B. Burge (Eds.), *Discourse, Tools and Reasoning: Essays on Situated Cognition* (pp. 23–40). Springer.

Jefferson, G. (1973). A Case of Precision Timing in Ordinary Conversation: Overlapped Tag-Positioned Address Terms in Closing Sequences. *Semiotica, 9,* 47–96.

Kegl, J., Senghas, A., & Coppola, M. (1999). Creation Through Contact: Sign Language Emergence & Sign Language Change in Nicaragua. In M. DeGraff (Ed.), *Language Creation and Language Change: Creolization, Diachrony and Development.* Cambridge, MA: MIT Press.

Kendon, A. (1983). Gesture and Speech: How They Interact. In J. M. Wiemann & R. Harrison (Eds.), *Nonverbal Interaction (Sage Annual Reviews of Communication,* Vol. 11). (pp. 13–46). Beverly Hills, CA: Sage Publications.

Kendon, A. (1988). *Sign Languages of Aboriginal Australia: Cultural, Semiotic and Communicative Perspectives.* Cambridge: Cambridge University Press.

Kendon, A. (1990). *Conducting Interaction: Patterns of Behavior in Focused Encounters.* Cambridge: Cambridge University Press.

Kendon, A. (1994a). Do Gestures Communicate?: A Review. *Research on Language and Social Interaction, 27*(3), 275–200.

Kendon, A. (1994b). Introduction to the Special Issue: Gesture and Understanding in Social Interaction. *Research on Language and Social Interaction, 27*(3), 171–174.

Kendon, A. (1997). Gesture. *Annual Review of Anthropology, 26,* 109–128.

Lave, J., & Wenger, E. (1991). *Situated Learning: Legitimate Peripheral Participation.* Cambridge: Cambridge University Press.

Leary, W. E. (1995). Rehabilitation Focus Urged in Stroke Cases. *New York Times* May 28 1995, p. 9.

LeBaron, C. D., & Streeck, J. (2000). Gestures, Knowledge, and the World. In D. McNeill (Ed.), *Gestures in Action, Language, and Culture.* Cambridge: Cambridge University Press.

Lerner, G. H. (1987). Collaborative Turn Sequences: Sentence Construction and Social Action. Unpublished doctoral dissertation, Psychology, University of California at Irvine.

Lynch, M. (1993). *Scientific Practice and Ordinary Action: Ethnomethodology and Social Studies of Science.* Cambridge: Cambridge University Press.

McNeill, D. (1992). *Hand & Mind: What Gestures Reveal about Thought.* Chicago: University of Chicago Press.

Morris, D., Marsh, P., Collet, P., & O'Shaughnessy, M. (1979). *Gestures: Their Origins and Distribution.* New York: Stein & Day.

Nicolopoulou, A. (1989). The Invention of Writing and the Development of Numerical Concepts in Sumeria: Some Implications for Developmental Psychology. *Quarterly Newsletter of the Laboratory of Comparative Human Cognition, 11*(4), 114–124.

Ochs, E., Gonzales, P., & Jacoby, S. (1996). "When I Come Down, I'm in a Domain State": Grammar and Graphic Representation in the Interpretive Activity of Physicists. In E. Ochs, E. A. Schegloff, & S. Thompson (Eds.), *Interaction and Grammar* (pp. 328–369). Cambridge: Cambridge University Press.

Ochs, E., Jacoby, S., & Gonzales, P. (1994). Interpretive Journeys: How Physicists Talk and Travel through Graphic Space. *Configurations, 2*(1), 151–171.

Sacks, H. (1992a). *Lectures on Conversation: Volume 1.* Ed. G, Jefferson. Introduction by E. A. Schegloff. Oxford: Basil Blackwell.

Sacks, H. (1992b). *Lectures on Conversation: Volume 2.* Ed. G. Jefferson. Introduction by E. A. Schegloff. Oxford: Basil Blackwell.

Sacks, H., Schegloff, E. A., & Jefferson, G. (1974). A Simplest Systematics for the Organization of Turn-Taking for Conversation. *Language, 50,* 696–735.

Schegloff, E. A. (1972). Notes on a Conversational Practice: Formulating Place. In D. Sudnow (Ed.), *Studies in Social Interaction* (pp. 75–119). New York: Free Press.

Schegloff, E. A. (1984). On Some Gestures' Relation to Talk. In J. M. Atkinson & J. Heritage (Eds.), *Structures of Social Action: Studies in Conversation Analysis* (pp. 266–296). Cambridge: Cambridge University Press.

Schegloff, E. A., Jefferson, G., & Sacks, H. (1977). The Preference for Self-Correction in the Organization of Repair in Conversation. *Language, 53,* 361–382.

Schegloff, E. A., & Sacks, H. (1973). Opening Up Closings. *Semiotica, 8,* 289–327.

Singleton, J., Morford, J., & Goldin-Meadow, S. (1995). The Generation of Standards of Form Within Communication Systems over Different Timespans. *Journal of Contemporary Legal Issues, 6,* 481–500.

Streeck, J. (1993). Gesture as Communication I: Its Coordination with Gaze and Speech. *Communication Monographs, 60*(4), 275–299.

Streeck, J. (1994). Gestures as Communication II: The Audience as Co-Author. *Research on Language and Social Interaction, 27*(3), 223–238.

Streeck, J. (1996). *Vis-à-vis an Embodied Mind.* Paper presented to the panel "Between Cognitive Science and Anthropology: A Re-Emerging Dialogue." Annual Meetings of the American Anthropological Association, San Francisco, CA, November 21, 1996.

Suchman, L. A. (1987). *Plans and Situated Actions: The Problem of Human Machine Communication.* Cambridge: Cambridge University Press.

Vygotsky, L. S. (1962). *Thought and Language.* Translated by Eugenia Hanfmann and Gertrude Vaker. Cambridge, MA: MIT Press.

Wittgenstein, L. (1958). *Philosophical Investigations.* 2nd ed. Ed. by G. E. M. Anscombe & R. Rhees. Translated by G. E. M. Anscombe. Oxford: Blackwell.

Wootton, A. (1997). *Interaction and the Development of Mind.* Cambridge: Cambridge University Press.

5

ANU KLIPPI

Collaborating in Aphasic Group Conversation

Striving for Mutual Understanding

Speech therapists and aphasiologists are increasingly aware that more information is needed about interaction in aphasia so as to establish newer, effective therapies to help aphasic speakers communicate. Clinical observations and recent studies indicate that aphasic conversations proceed differently from those of normal speakers (Ferguson, 1994; Goodwin, 1995; Klippi, 1992, 1996; Laakso, 1992, 1997; Milroy & Perkins, 1992; Perkins, 1993; Wilkinson, 1995). The main problems in aphasia are ineffective linguistic processing and limited access to linguistic resources. Aphasia affects these processes and resources in variable ways, devastating some systems, leaving others intact. Different types of semantic and syntactic problems, as well as phonological problems, lead to diverse difficulties in conversation. This means that aphasia affects not only linguistic behavior, but patterns of interaction, regardless of the nature of the disruption.

Apart from these difficulties, aphasic speakers may show sensitivity to the addressee's need for more information. Aphasic speakers frequently retain their status as creative and powerful cognitive actors, who attempt to compensate for the loss of linguistic resources by appealing to other semiotic resources. Aphasics may develop adaptive practices to overcome troubles in conversation. These can involve structure in their talk as well as the ability to draw upon both the linguistic abilities of others and structure in their environment. For researchers, this poses the task of looking not simply at what happens within the stream of speech, but rather at the range of meaning-making practices that aphasics and their co-participants use to construct conversation. These include not only language itself but also an array of semiotic resources—variable ability to produce different kinds of structures within the stream of speech, the ability to understand talk, numbers, writing, drawing, and semiotic structure in the environment, and so on. The aim of this chapter is to analyze the systematic conversational practices used to resolve communicative troubles in aphasic group discussions with specific attention to strategies that enhance group members' mutual understanding.

Until now, only one comprehensive study has been published from the perspective of multi-party conversation in an aphasic group (Klippi, 1996). The data used in this chapter is a conversational sequence of an authentic aphasia group. In past clinical practices, several aphasia group approaches have been applied (e.g., Johannsen-Horbach, Wentz, Funfgeld, Herrmann, & Wallesch, 1993; Kagan & Gailey, 1993; Kearns 1986; Pachalska 1993). Prior to the 1990s, the understanding of the structural basis of aphasic interaction was not well known; hence, the theoretical basis for the group approach was not always clear and sound. As our knowledge of this area has increased, however, the group therapy approach is no longer seen merely as a general stimulating technique but as a theoretically based intervention designed to help the aphasic person take an active role when interacting with others. However, further study is needed of the complex structures and practices in aphasia group interaction.

Aphasic group interaction is extremely interesting, because it gives people with complementary deficits and strengths an opportunity to pool their distinctive abilities as they attempt to make meaning together. This chapter will examine how speakers with aphasia build meanings cooperatively by creatively using the resources available in their social context and present in their environment. With the help of the following conversational sequence, I will present characteristic features of aphasia group conversations and show how conversation proceeds in an aphasia group. In addition, I demonstrate the importance of analyzing aphasia within its full social matrix.

The specific questions and objectives of my analysis follow:

1. What are the collaborative processes used to constitute meaning together in an aphasia group? In other words, how do the participants systematically engage in conversational practices to cope with problems of speaking and comprehension and subsequently arrive at mutual understanding?
2. How do people with different linguistic resources help each other to accomplish such understanding?
3. How do the participants use their physical surroundings and their gestures as semiotic resources for conversation?

The aphasia group

The sequence presented in this chapter is extracted from a group session in which four aphasics and a speech therapist (t) were conversing. The participants included three women (Maija, Elina, and the speech therapist) and two men (Jaakko and Paavo). Table 5.1 gives some general data on the aphasic speakers and Table 5.2 provides the scores in the Western Aphasia Battery (WAB, unstandardized Finnish version; Lehtihalmes, Klippi, & Lempinen, 1986). It is followed by a brief description of the history and abilities of each of the aphasics.

Jaakko was a 54-year-old right-handed man who became aphasic after a right hemisphere brain infarction. Immediately after the onset of aphasia, Jaakko's major symptom was jargon speech and he had left-sided dyspractic paralysis. After becoming aware of his speech problems, he stopped communicating verbally and only gradually began speaking very slowly and haltingly. Jaakko had severe problems in formulating propositions and in word finding. His speech was hesitant, repetitive, and marked by several pauses within a short utterance. The following excerpt illustrates Jaakko's difficulties in speech (see appendix 1 and appendix 2 for explanations of transcription and glossing):

Example 1
1   Jaakko: . . . (1.3) ö-men I i I n, (0.7) tonne tonne
                     go-PST-1   there+to there+to
             .. (1.3)er I went, (0.7)there there
2   hh. (1.2) kato I s, .hh (0.5) Valmeti I lle. (0.7) *
                       look-CLI   company name-ALL
             hh.(1.2)look,.hh (0.5) to Valmet.(0.7) *
3   Valmeti I lle. (0.7)* *[*Valmeti I lle*
             company name-ALL   company name-ALL
             to Valmet.(0.7)* *[*to Valmet*
             2 taps on the table*[*taps on the table

TABLE 5.1. General Information on the Aphasic Participants

Speaker	Sex	Age	Diagnosis	Lesion	Duration of illness (years:mo)	Aphasia type
Jaakko	M	54	stroke	CT: lesion in the right temporo-parietal area	1:6	Broca
Maija	F	42	stroke	EEG: left-sided irritative theta activity	12:00	Broca
Elina	F	45	S.A.H.	CT: subarachnoidal haemorrhage, status post ligaturam ophthalmic artery, posterior cer. artery and middle cer. artery	3:4	Anomic
Paavo	M	49	stroke	CT: left-sided temp. lobe; (old) right-sided fronto-temp. lobe	2:5	Anomic; dysarthria

CT = computerized tomography.
EEG = electroencephalography.
S.A.H. = subarachnoidal haemorrhage.

TABLE 5.2. Aphasic Participants' Scores in the Western Aphasia Battery

Speaker	AQ max. 100	Spont. sp. max. 20	Compreh. max. 10	Repetition max. 10	Naming max. 10	LQ max. 100
Jaakko	68.9	13	7.85	6.7	6.9	52.9
Maija	75.0	13	8.7	7.2	8.6	73.7
Elina	92.2	18	9.9	9.9	8.3	95.6
Paavo	85.2	15	10	8.2	9.4	92.4

Jaakko had total agraphia and had difficulty writing even single letters. He was able to write his name and some ideographs (such as the names of the former presidents of Finland), but he could not write words even for the most ordinary objects. He could, however, write numerical information, such as dates, times, and numbers of amounts, although he was not always quite sure whether he had written the number correctly. Jaakko also had alexia. He could name only some letters in the alphabet, although he could combine some pictures of ordinary objects and the written names of them, for instance *kuppi* (a cup), *kynä* (a pencil), and *kampa* (a comb). By the time the aphasia group was established one and a half years after his illness, Jaakko had received individual speech therapy periodically.

Maija was a 42-year-old right-handed woman who became globally aphasic due to a complication during an operation. She also suffered mild right-sided paralysis of the upper limb. In the early stages of aphasia, her speech was extremely slow and laborious with severe agrammatism. She also had word-finding difficulty. Maija could read and write sentences, although very slowly and inaccurately. To alleviate these problems, she received speech therapy periodically for several years. When Maija joined the aphasic group, she had been suffering from aphasia for 12 years. Maija had constant morphological and syntactic problems in her speech as the following example shows:

Example 2
1   Maija: hmm.(.) ede. (0.4) minä edisTYY?=
                            | progress-3
                 mm. progr, (0.4) I progress
2   Therapist: =nii-I?=
                 =mm.hm?=
3   Maija: =edisTYY?
                 progress-3
                 progress?
4   Therapist: =nii-I?
                 = mm-hm?=
5   Maija: =kaksitoista vuotta, (.) edisTYY. (1.0) mm.
                            twelve year+PAR progress-3
                 =twelve years, (.) progRESS. (1.0) mm.

Paavo was a 49-year-old right-handed man who had suffered a left-sided brain infarction after which he became moderately aphasic. With some transient motor symptoms on his right side, his hand movements were slow and inaccurate in the apraxia test. He also had dysarthria, which made his articulation blurred. To remedy his problems, he received speech therapy for some months after the onset of the aphasia. Paavo joined the aphasia group two and half years after his illness, a time when his aphasic problems were rather mild. He had some problems in formulating propositions and minor difficulties with naming. However, his ability to communicate was complicated by the fact that he had dysarthria. Because of this, his articulation was slow and slurred, which sometimes made his speech difficult to understand (see the following excerpt). Paavo's reading and writing abilities, however, were good.

Example 3
1   Therapist: ketkä, (.) ketkä oli mukana.
                 who-PL   who PL be-PST with
                 who, (.) who were with (them).
    (1.6)
2   Paavo: Jaakko oli.
                 1name M be-PST
                 Jaakko was.
    (0.3)
3   X: (—)
    (3.8)
4   Paavo: muita oli, (0.6) *tuurin* piirtein neljäkymmentä, (0.7)°ol I i mukana.°
                 other-PL-PAR be-PST   approximately   forty   be-PST with
                 there were others, (0.6) {approximately} forty, (0.7)°were with (them).°

Elina was a 45-year-old right-handed woman who suffered a subarachnoidal haemorrhage but had no paralysis. Immediately after the onset of her illness, she spoke nothing but jargon. She then received speech therapy periodically, and she recovered extremely well. When the aphasia group started, Elina only had slight aphasic speech problems, such as occasional word-finding problems in conversation. According to the WAB test, her reading and writing abilities were good. She joined the aphasia group three years and four months after her illness. Here is an excerpt from Elina's speech:

Example 4
1   Elina: se loppujen lopuksi oli,.(0.6) mitä nyt on kuullu noista
           it   in the end   be-PST   what-PAR now is hear-PPC those-ELA
           it was after all, (0.6) now what I have heard about those
2   puheista niin aika kallis. (0.4) ku+ottaa huomioon että se
           talk-PL-ELA so   quite expensive PRT+take-3   consideration-ILL PRT it
           talks well rather expensive.(0.4) if one takes into consideration that

3   on (1.3) ↑eläkeläisten   [tai
         is   pensioner-PL-GEN or
         it is (1.3) ↑pensioners' [or
4 Maija: [mm
5 Elina: se oli [makso viissataa ja, (1.0) °olik+se
         it be-PST cost-PST five hundred and be-PST-Q-it
         it was [costs fivehundred and, (1.0) °well was
6 Kalle: [(RYKÄISEE) mm
         [(Clears throat) mm
7 Elina: nyt°kolmekymppii. (0.8) tai jotain.°=
         now   thirty   or something
         it °thirty. (0.8) or something. °=

The time since the onset of aphasia and the severity of aphasia varied among participants. For example, Maija had been aphasic for 12 years, whereas the others had become aphasic later. Jaakko and Maija were regarded to have at least moderate aphasic problems, but Paavo and Elina had only mild aphasic difficulties.

The group sessions, which brought together these people with quite different abilities and language problems, contained a number of group exercises and conversations, usually following a given theme. The beginning and the end of each meeting were reserved for free conversation. The thematic conversations covered different topics including illness, previous work, and so forth. A sequence extracted from a thematic conversation dealing with the participants' previous work served as the data for this chapter.

Data

This excerpt, analyzed here, is a typical example of an extended repair sequence in aphasia group data. The speakers are seated around a table during the conversation. Figure 5.1 illustrates their seating arrangements. Jaakko sits at the end of the table, and Elina and Paavo are facing Maija and the therapist.

The group conversation concerned Jaakko's former work in Russia. This sequence was initiated with Jaakko's agrammatic turn with word-finding difficulty. Two problems arose in this sequence: the first difficulty concerned a new item that Jaakko introduced in the conversation but that later turned out to be the name of a place where Jaakko had worked previously; the second problem dealt with the geographical location of this workplace.

Seeking the referent for the name *Sarja*

This sequence begins in line 1 when Jaakko uses the expression "Sarja is" to abruptly introduce a new topic into the conversation. As the sequence unfolds, it will eventu-

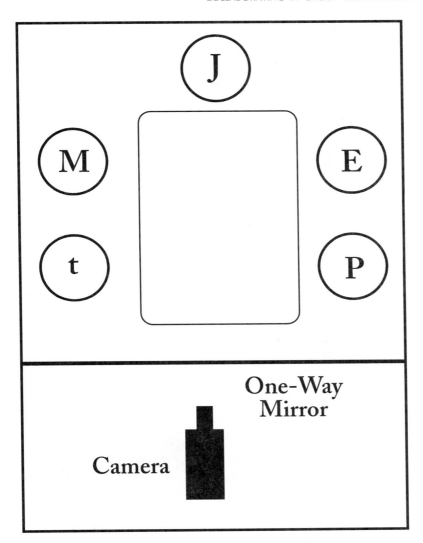

FIGURE 5.1. How the participants are seated

ally become clear that "Sarja" is the name of a place where Jaako worked. However *sarja* is a meaningful word in Finnish (*sarja* = series). Jaakko lacks the linguistic ability to construct a fluent expression that would immediately disambiguate these two possibilities and instruct his addressees to ignore the "series" possibility and treat what he is saying as a place name. The situation is made more difficult by the fact that sequentially a new topic is being introduced, so that the participants cannot rely upon the contextual framing of prior talk to easily see a place name in the current use of the term. However, Jaakko appears to recognize these difficulties and to design a turn that, while agrammatic, provides his hearers with specific resources that can help them hear what he saying as being about a place. To do this, he frames the expression "Sarja" with two different kinds of signs: linguistically he follows "Sarja" with two locative deictic terms *there* (*sinneh*) while nonvocally he uses the pen he is holding to point diagonally in a specific direction (see fig. 5.2).

Example 5

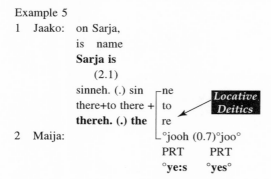

1   Jaako: on   Sarja,
             is   name
             Sarja is
                (2.1)
             sinneh. (.) sin ⌐ne
             there+to there + | to   *Locative*
             thereh. (.) the | re   *Deitics*
2   Maija: └ °jooh (0.7)°joo°
                                 PRT   PRT
                                 °**ye:s** °**yes**°

Though the problematic term "Sarja" is framed both linguistically and gesturally with signs that have a strong locative component, Jaakko's addressees do not provide strong displays that they in fact understand what he is trying to say or recognize that "Sarja" is naming a relevant place. Maija's softly spoken repeated "yes" in line 2

FIGURE 5.2. Pointing with pen

may function more as a display of continuing attentiveness than as a claim of adequate understanding. If they are to successfully continue the conversation, Jaakko's co-participants face two tasks: first, seeking the referent for the name "Sarja" and second, specifying its location. A range of phenomena including Maija's intense orientation toward Jaakko, the incompleteness of what Jaakko has said so far, and the nature of Maija's responses, demonstrates that Jaakko is being urged to continue the "Sarja" issue.

Example 6
3   Jaako: hhh.
            ((*Writes for 7.2 seconds then shows paper to Maija*))
            on I k I s   oikein (2.3) Sae-Sarja
            be-Q-CLI right   name
            is it all right (2.3)   Sae-Sarja
4   Marja: ((*gazes toward paper*))

In line 3, Jaakko sighs loudly and begins to write down the word "Sarja" while looking at the paper (fig. 5.3). When he finishes writing the word, Jaakko turns his gaze to Maija, and asks "is it all right (2.3) Sae-Sarja." Aphasia selectively damages the semiotic abilities of those who suffer from it. While Jaakko can write, he can't read well enough to check his own spelling. However, Maija can read. His request vividly demonstrates how the social group, which contains an array of semiotic resources greater than what might be found within a single individual, can make it

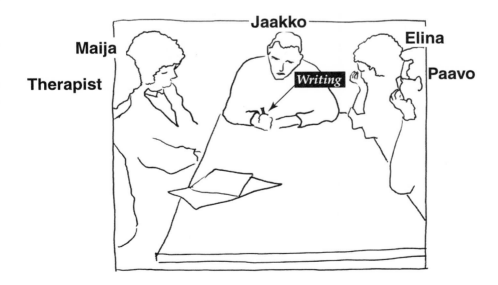

FIGURE 5.3. Writing

possible for participants to accomplish meaning in collaboration with each other that would be beyond their abilities as isolated individuals. The request begins a repair sequence concerning the word "Sarja," especially referring to its written form. The sequence clearly demonstrates the cooperation between Jaakko and Maija. the way in which Jaakko used another participant with different abilities to check out his competence in writing something meaningful. However, it seems that Maija's focus was still on the meaning of the word "Sarja" and not on the written form of it, because while she gazes and points to the paper, she does not give a verbal acceptance.

Jaakko's use of the locative term "there" and his pointing gesture in line 1 may have given a much-needed hint for Paavo, who proposes explicitly that "Sarja" is a place name:

Example 7
        ((*Gazes toward Maija and then therapist*))
  5 Paavo: se paika I n se [nime I ltä] Sarja
             it   place-GEN it name-ELA name
             it of the place [called] Sarja
                 ((*Gazes toward Paavo*))
  6 Maija: [joo]
                              [yes]
  7 Elina: *nods head*
  8 Therapist: **hmm**
  9 Jaakko: *t [änne]*
             here+to
             ***the[re]**
             points diagonally toward left with pen *
                 ((*Gazes toward Paavo*))
 10 Maija: [°Sarja°]
                  name
                  [°Sarja°]
                 ((*Gazes toward Maija*))
 11 Jaakko: juuh=
             ye:ah=
 12 Therapist: =ahaa=
                 =I see=
                 nods head*
                 ((*Gazes toward paper*))
 13 Maija: =joo
             =yes
             nods head*

The contributions of a range of different participants publicly establish and ratify that "Sarja" is a place name. After Paavo displays his understanding of "Sarja" as the name of a place where Jaakko had been (line 5), Elina, Maija, and the therapist produce acknowledgment tokens. These acknowledgments served as confirmations for Jaakko that the participants now understand what "Sarja" is indicating.

Jaakko returns to the task of establishing where "Sarja" is. In line 9 he again points to the left while uttering a deictic proadverb "there." However, Maija repeats "Sarja" with whisper voice and Jaakko accepts this. In response, the therapist gives an acknowledgment "ahaa" (I see), which indicates that she now understands something that she hadn't earlier, and this is followed by another acknowledgment token "joo" (yes) and nods from Maija. These acknowledgment tokens close the conversation with the word "Sarja." The interactive sequence of turns made by multiple parties have publicly established the meaning for it—it has became clear that this is a name of the place.

Several characteristic features are visible in this first subsequence. Jaakko's opening turn "Sarja is, (2.1) thereh. (.) there," demonstrated his restricted verbal behavior with lexical and syntactic problems typical for him. As the participants received two obviously insufficient formulations to decipher, they had a choice: either to gloss over Jaakko's contribution or to begin repair work. As a result of the unclear message, collaboration began, and in line 3, Jaakko wrote down the name "Sarja."

Why did Jaakko change the mode of communication from oral expression to writing? We may also ask, in a Vygotskian sense, what made him choose writing as a tool for communication (Vygotsky 1982/1931)? I maintain that this simple action had important consequences for the conversation. Jaakko's first turn (line 1) was clearly problematic because it introduced two different issues—the name of the place and the direction of the place—to the conversation whose referents were not evident to the participants. By repeating the word "Sarja," Jaakko could force the participants to focus on the first issue. But this interpretation does not explain why he wanted to write this word. As we notice from line 3, Jaakko hesitated when he produced the word "Sarja." He may have been unsure as to whether he had expressed it correctly, and thus he wanted to clarify the word by repeating it and writing it down.

Hence, Jaakko's act can be regarded as *an externalizing strategy*; by using the physical contextual resources, a pen and a paper, he was able to write the word "Sarja." It provided his adressees with new possibilities for evaluating and figuring out what he was saying. As "Sarja" was permanently reproduced on paper, the participants could compare his verbal and written production. In fact, his actions in line 3 can be regarded as a request for confirmation, with the latter part an attempt at explicit acknowledgment that his oral and written expression were equivalent. At this point, his contribution focused on Maija, who responded only by moving her hand to the paper and by gazing at it. Paavo then introduced his candidate understanding, suggesting that "Sarja" was a place. My second argument is that Paavo based his understanding on Jaakko's locative term "there" with a pointing gesture. His interpretation served as the resolution for the current problem. As Schegloff, Jefferson, and Sacks (1977) have suggested, a candidate understanding is the strongest technique for other-repair initiations, leading to the quickest and the most efficient resolution. This case is therefore seen as a confirmation of Schegloff et al.'s finding.

The geographical location of Sarja

Jaakko had already used gestures and locatives to focus on the place where Sarja was located in his first turn (line 1). After the acceptance of the name of the place, Jaakko returned to the issue of specifying the geographical location of Sarja. Figure 5.4 is an example of Jaakko's pointing gesture during the turn in line 14:

Example 8
```
14   Jaakko:  *tonne.(.) tonne.*(2.4)              [hhhhh.3.8]
                  there+to there+to
              *over there. (.) over there.* (2.4) [hhhhh.3.8]
              *points to the left with pen two times *
15   Therapist:              [*takes a map*]
                             ((Gazes toward Jaakko))
16   Paavo:                  [ei  se  löyd I y sieltä. =]
                             NEG it find-REF there+from
                             [cannot find there.=]
17   Therapist: =ei löyd I y.=
                  NEG find+REF
                  =cannot find.=
                  ((Gazes toward map))
18   Paavo:   =ei varmasti. [°e I m+mä us (—)°]
                  NEG for sure  NEG-1 +I
                  =surely not. [°I don't beli(—)°]
19   Therapist:              [löyty I y I kö suunta kuitenki.]
                             find-REF-Q   direction anyway
                             [is the direction found at least.]
                             ((Gazes toward map))
20   Jaakko:   kato I ta I an.
                  look-PASS-4
                  let's look.
                  *stretches his hand toward the map*
```

In line 14 Jaakko points to the same direction as in line 1—diagonally left with his pen—and, unable to explicate the point with rich language, he repeats the proadverbs "over there. (.) over there." while sighing again loudly. Jaakko's frustration and expressive difficulties are obvious, and his loud sighing invites others to help him. The participants are once more involved in a task for giving meaning to Jaakko's turn with two minimal verbal expressions and a gesture that already occurred earlier in the conversation and reappears at this point. His turn's linguistic

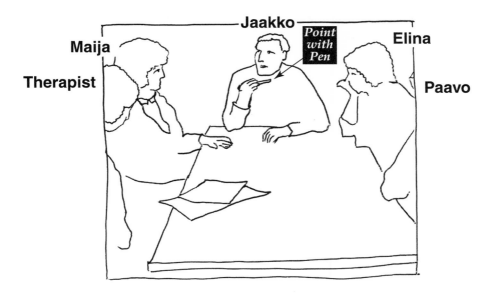

FIGURE 5.4. Pointing with pen again

formulation "over there (tuo+lla)" and his gesture indicate that he wants to specify the geographical location of Sarja. At this moment, the therapist takes a calendar with a map, which she kept on hand in the sessions. This nonverbal act can be interpreted as an other-repair initiation, as an act of again resorting to an external aid in conversation. Jaakko wants to take a look at the map and, the therapist passes the calendar to him.

Example 9
21 Therapist: missä PÄin suurin piirtein. &täs+on niin& täs+on to:ta,(.)
                where   roughly   here+is so   here+is PRT
                which direction approximately.&it's so& it's well,(.)
22   on siinä Neuvostoliitto [mut+se on tommose | na pienelnä=
                  is there Soviet Union   but+it is like that-ESS little-ESS
                  there is Soviet Union [but it's such a small=
23   [*_Jaakko takes a map_*
24 Therapist: =läntti | nä siinä että (.) mutta että suuntah,
                spot-ESS   there PRT but PRT direction
                =area there that(.) but the direction,
25 Jaakko: hh.
26 Therapist: onk+se Euroopan puoleisessa osassa vai
                is-Q+it Europe-GEN side-INE part-INE or
                is it in European or

27   Aasian puoleisessa osassa.
            Asia-GEN side-INE   part-INE
            Asian side.
28   <u>Jaakko: *asettaa silmälasit*</u> just (1.0) just (7.9) (hhhh. 1.1)
                   PRT   PRT
     <u>puts his glasses on</u> **just (1.0) just (7.9) (hhhh. 1.1)**
     ((*Gmap*))
29   Elina: onko lähellä Tsernob/
            be-Q near place name
            is it near Tsernob/
     (1.1)
            ((*Gazes toward map*))
30   Jaakko: * . hh ei . *=
             NEG
             .hh no.=
             <u>shakes head</u>
             ((*Gazes toward map*))
31   Elina: =ei
            NEG
            =no

The therapist subsequently contributes to the conversation with two requests for clarification. The first question is general (line 21), but after noticing that the map was very small, she clarifies her question by asking whether it (Sarja) was on the European or on the Asian side of the Soviet Union (lines 26–27). Jaakko puts on his glasses (line 28) and concentrates on examining the map. His turn displays how focusing on the map requires a different type of embodied practice than merely talking. Jaakko is able to show others explicitly that he is concentrating on the search and needs time for it. He has a pen in his hand, and he puts the point of his pen on the map while uttering "just (1.0) just," and gazing intensively at the map. A pause (7.9-second) follows, during which all participants lean forward toward the map and gaze intently at it. At last, Jaakko sighs, which evidently shows that he had not been successful with his search for the place. Goodwin and Goodwin (1986) describe how recipients use changes in the embodied displays of a party engaged in a word search to determine that a new stage, in which their help is being solicited, is being entered. Elina appears to analyze Jaakko's display of frustration in this way; she immediately makes the next request for clarification, "is it near Tsernob" (line 29) which, however, Jaakko rejects.

Here the immediate activity centers on the small map and Jaakko's pen movements on the map. The question-answer pairs initiated by the therapist and Elina reflect the collaborative nature of the conversation. The last adjacency pair explicitly shows that the searching has to continue because Jaakko does not give an affirmative reply to Elina's question (lines 29–31). Charles Goodwin (1995) has analysed an aphasic conversation where simple question-answer adjacency pairs are used in such a way that a healthy speaker poses questions (guesses) concerning the topic and an aphasic speaker gives "yes" or "no" answers. An aphasic speaker's "yes" answer provides an exit from the guessing sequence, whereas a "no" answer leads to the recycling of another round with a new guess. Lubinski, Dunchan, and Weitzner-Lin (1980) have used the term "hint and guess" sequence for such an exchange (see also Laakso & Klippi, 1999). The following sequence (fig. 5.5) shows that Jaakko is finally able to locate *Sarja*.

Example 10
32   therapist: *°mun täytyy ihan tulla katsomaan kans.°*
              I-GEN   must   quite   come-INF look-INF-ILL too
              °I have to come and look too.°
              __*goes behind J*__

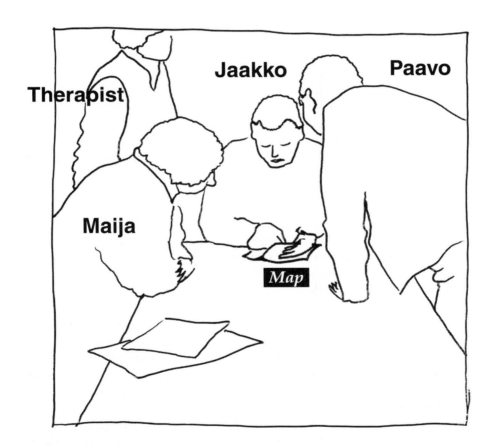

FIGURE 5.5. Map

           ((Gazes toward map))
33   Jaakko: *tässä.*
            here
            here.
            __*points toward map*__
      (3.0)
           ((Gazes toward map))
34   Elina: °ahaa.°
            PRT
            °aha.°
      (2.4)
           ((Gazes toward map))
35   Jaakko: *tässä.*
            here
            here.
            __*points toward map*__
      (0.6)
             ((Gazes toward map))
36   therapist: näytäppä tolle Paavollekin.
              show-CL that-ADE 1name M-CLI
              please show also to Paavo.
37   Jaakko: *tuossa.* (1.5) suurin piirtein.
            there   roughly
            there. (1.5) approximately.
           __*points toward map.*__
           ((Gazes toward map))
38   Paavo: joo joo.
            PRT PRT
            yes yes.
39   Maija: **[mm.]**.

The participants in this sequence concentrated on the searching activity so completely that even the therapist moved from her place near the foot of the table to have a look at the map. In the end, Jaakko found the approximate location of the place (line 33), and while gazing and pointing at the map, he showed it by saying "here." Elina gave an acknowledgment token, "aha (*oh.*)," displaying receipt of new knowledge (cf. Hakulinen & Sorjonen, 1986; Heritage, 1984). After a while, Jaakko repeated the contribution "here" (line 35), again pointing to the map (see fig. 5.5). The turn that follows, which was contributed by the therapist, requests Jaakko to show the place to Paavo. Jaakko then repeats "there (1.5) approximately," for the third time and Paavo acknowledges it.

The collaborative nature of the conversation is again evident through the acknowledging activity after the place has been found. Elina provides the first acknowledgment token (line 34), marking the new knowledge with a dialogue particle "aha." A longish pause then follows without other acknowledgments. Owing to the long negotiation in which all interlocutors had contributed, Jaakko treats Elina's acknowledgment as insufficient, and thus he repeats his previous contribution (line 35). It seems that Jaakko actively intends to keep the sequence open at the point where it could have come to a closing point. The therapist's next turn (line 36) can be regarded both as an acknowledgment token and as a request for Jaakko to again show where the place is, especially to Paavo, who also adds a double acknowledgment token (line 38). After this, Maija also adds another short acknowledgment token. Thus, all the participants produce acknowledgment tokens indicating that they have reached an understanding that is adequate for "current purposes."

The distance of Sarja from Moscow

After this extended attempt at conversing, the issue was still not yet quite clear. The therapist's next question (line 40), "how far from Moscow." referred anaphorically to the preceding conversation ("it" instead of "Sarja"), and can thus be regarded as a request for clarification referring back to earlier talk rather than an attempt to introduce a new topic. This question (line 40) formed the first part of an adjacency pair and thus created an expectation for an answer in the next turn. The sigh at the beginning of Jaakko's turn indicates that he is in trouble again. He then turns his gaze to the therapist and tries to provide an answer, but it is beyond his verbal abilities. He again turns to resources other than talk to help build an answer. While uttering, "look.(.) there" (line 41), he turns his gaze to the paper and points to the numeral 800, which he had previously written down.

Example 11
40   Therapist: [mi] ten pitkä matka Moskovasta.
                how   long way   Moscow-ELA
                [ho]w far from Moskow.
        (1.5)
                ((*Gazes toward therapist and then toward paper*))
41   Jaakko: (hhh. 4.3) ö-ö (1.6) *kato. (.) tossa. *=
                            look   there
                (hhh. 4.3) uh-uh (1.6)*look. (.) there. *=
                points toward paper
42   Maija: =°kaheksan kymmentä°=
                eight   ten-PAR
                =°eighty°=
                ((*Gazes toward map*))
43   Therapist: =kaheksan sataa.=
                eight   hundred
                =eight hundred.=

```
                ((Gazes toward map))
44  Maija: =    [joo]
        =       [yes]
45  Elina:      [°kaheksan sataa°]
                eight   hundred
                [ °eight hundred° ]
                ((Gazes toward therapist))
46  Jaakko: jooh [joh]
        ye:s  [yes]
47  Therapist:  [ kah ] eksansataa kilometriä Mosko [vasta.
                eighthundred       kilometer-PAR Moscow-ELA
                [ei]ght hundred kilometers from Mos[cow.
48  Maija:      [mm
49  Jaakko:     [jooh
                [ye:s
```

Here, Jaakko relies repeatedly on an external aid and points to the paper on the table where he had previously written numbers. At this point a typical incident occurred in the conversation: Maija read the numeral aloud, but incorrectly, whispering "eighty" instead of "800." In response, the therapist makes an immediate correction "eight hundred," which Maija, Elina, and Jaakko accept in overlap with each other. The therapist then continues to make yet another request for confirmation to make sure that it was indeed 800 kilometers from Moscow, which Jaakko and Maija both confirm.

This third subsequence focuses on the distance from Sarja to Moscow and is initiated by the therapist with a wh-question. Once again an external aid was needed, the paper and the numbers on it, before the participants understood the reply. The use of this externalization strategy was initiated by Jaakko.

The direction of Sarja's location

The fourth and the last subsequence concerns the direction of Sarja's location.

Example 12
```
                ((Gazes toward Jaakko))
50  Therapist: hmm-mm. (0.4) elikkä se (0.8) olik+se*       sinne   POHjoseen
                               that means it     be-PST-Q+it there+to north-ILL
                hmm-mm. (0.4) in other words it (0.8) was it*to the North
                *points upward*
51              #päin vai. #*
                wards or
                #wards or.#*
       (0.8)
                ((Gazes toward map))
```

52   Jaakko: ei kun,=
            NEG PRT
            no but,=
            points toward map
53   Therapist: =eei
            NEG
            no:
54   Paavo: itään.[et(—)]
            east-ILL
            to the east. [sou (—)]
55   Jaakko: [***moves his pen showing diagonally toward right***
            (0.7)
56   Therapist: *HETkinen.*
            moment
            just a MOment.
            moves her hand showing diagonally toward right
            ((*Gazes toward therapist*))
57   Jaakko: *ylös.*
            up+to
            up.
            shows diagonally toward right
            (1.5)
58   Therapist: *koilliseen.*
            north-east-ILL
            north-east.
            shows diagonally toward right
            ((*Gazes toward map*))
59   Jaakko: [joo]
            [yes]
            ((*Gazes toward Jaakko*))
60   Paavo: [hmm.]
            [hmm.]
61   Therapist: *koillise | en.*
            north-east-ILL
            north-east.
            shows diagonally toward right

The therapist in lines 50–51 begins by using the expression "in other words" to initiate a repair sequence by offering a gloss of what Jaakko has been saying, "was it to the NOrth#wards or," which he can confirm or deny. Jaakko rejects this while pointing toward the map. Paavo responds to this rejection suggesting "to the east," but later interrupting himself. Next, Jaakko begins searching for the direction by turning his pen to the right with a pointing motion. It seems that he uses his pen to represent points on an imaginary compass, an image that seems to be in front of his eyes. The therapist subsequently says "just a moment" and raises her right hand, imitating Jaakko's gesture.

In figure 5.6, Jaakko himself presents the contribution "up" (line 57), pointing his pen diagonally upward to the right. Looking from the perspective of the imaginary compass in front of him, he then shows the northeast direction. This gesture and the therapist's imitation of it seem to at last clarify the direction, and she offers her understanding by saying "to the north-east" (line 58), which both Jaakko and Paavo simultaneously accept with acknowledgment tokens. The therapist's talk has provided an appropriate frame for the proper seeing and understanding of Jaakko's gesture. The sequence closes only after the therapist repeats her accepted interpretation and points to the northeast. A 5.6-second pause follows. The participants had agreed earlier to interview Jaakko, and his subsequent contribution is oriented to this as he says "and then."

The fourth and last subsequence deals with the direction of place. The earlier conversation revealed that Moscow could be regarded as an orientation focus to use in searching for location of Sarja. The therapist's first candidate understanding, "was it to the NOrth#wards or.#," was accompanied by a gesture. This indicates that the therapist had considered the role of the gesture to be very significant in this sequence. This was clearly not only a sign of the direction, but also *a facilitation strategy* for understanding the direction of the compass (northward) to Jaakko. Paavo's candidate under-

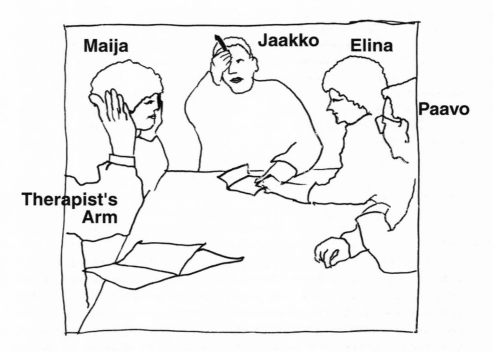

FIGURE 5.6. Northeast

standing "to the east.sou (-)" made Jaakko again resort to gesture, and he then responded with a nonverbal act, changing the tip of his pen to point northeastward. Hence, he again employed *the gestural strategy* to overcome his speech problems and to be able to show the direction. At the end of this sequence, the therapist verbalizes Jaakko's meaning, simultaneously imitating Jaakko's previous gesture.

Discussion

By analyzing this sequence, my aim has been to demonstrate the extended and com-plex nature of an aphasic group conversation. Thus, I have focused on the sequence structure as well as on how participants use their physical surroundings and their gestures as a resource in conversation. This analysis focuses on the aphasic conver-sational participants' use of systematic practices to resolve the problems in conver-sation. Several noteworthy points arose in this sequence.

When a trouble-turn is introduced in aphasic conversation, such as a turn with a word finding difficulty or a very verbally limited turn, the first question is how to treat it. First it is not obvious that the trouble will be taken up. For instance, Lubinski et al. (1980) compared the breakdowns and repairs of an aphasic conversation in three different speech contexts: conversations between an aphasic and a spouse, between an aphasic and a speech therapist, and a segment of a treatment session with a speech therapist. The results revealed differences in the contexts with respect to repairs. One important finding was that in converstions between the aphasic and the speech thera-pist, the speech therapist did not respond to the difficulties of the aphasic speaker by doing repair work, but instead glossed over the breakdowns, whereas in the conver-sation with the spouse, the interlocutors worked together to resolve the breakdowns. Laakso (1992) also reported a similar tendency in her analysis of conversations be-tween aphasics and therapists. It could be that uninstitutionalized conversations, for instance, peer group or aphasic-spouse conversations, are more open to begin repair work than are conversations conducted in institutional settings.

Second, as disordered linguistic resources are among the main problems in apha-sia, "quasi- and nonlexical" elements (Heritage 1989) become extremely important in aphasic conversation. When discussing the notion of context, Goodwin and Duranti (1992) suggest the term *focal event* to identify the phenomenon being contextualized, pointing out that a context is by no means restricted to talk; thus, for instance, non-vocal behavior can create context for talk. I have chosen the previous sequence as a demonstration of the systematic activities based on the integration of verbal behav-ior and the different kinds of semiotic materials used to resolve the recurrent troubles in aphasic conversation. The prominent and the most systematic feature in this con-versation is that Jaakko, being unable to express his meanings by verbal means, used other semiotic resources to externalize his meaning, and these materials served as a point of departure for further operations by his co-participants.

Very little research has focused on nonverbal context renewal activities in disordered conversations. Empirical observations do, however, suggest that the externalized nonverbal acts are very influential context-renewing contributions. In these examples of word-finding difficulties or other expressive problems, these contributions offered additional information. The recipients, especially Jaakko, systematically exploited a wide range of semiotic contextual resources, including compensatory gestures, as well as using concrete objects such as a paper, a pen, and a map. This sequence provides an excellent example of the way in which physical context is combined with activity and how meanings are socially constructed (e.g., Lave, 1993). Thus, this example shows vividly how speech can be replaced by other activities.

Nevertheless, these nonvocal actions were not in themselves sufficient to give meaning to ongoing talk. The nonverbal actions were embedded within the talk of other participants, and the interaction between the participants constituted the meaning for these actions and made them comprehensible for the participants (see Goodwin, 1995). The previous examples indicate that when Jaakko produces a turn with writing or with a gesture, the other participants provide a contribution, for instance, a candidate understanding, showing the current understanding of what he wants to say. The most fascinating issue in this sequence is that everyone, including the aphasic speakers in the group, participated in this collaboration by offering repair initiations. This finding is extremely important because very little knowledge is currently available about aphasic speakers' repair initiations (see however Klippi, 1996).

Goodwin (1995) has analyzed a conversational sequence between the aphasic person, his wife, and a nurse to examine the co-constructing of meaning in conversation. The organizational principles of the sequence were clear. First, unlike many problematic negotiations, the interlocutors assumed that there was a correct answer to the word search and that the aphasic party knew that answer. Second, there was a strong division of labor in the conversation. The participants performed different kinds of action so that the interlocutors provided relevant guesses for the aphasic speaker, who accepted or rejected proposals. Third, the interlocutors engaged in systematic work to formulate new guesses. Finally, the organization of the activity located the aphasic interactant as the central participant. These principles also clearly materialized in this sequence.

The aim of this chapter has been to show the complexity of aphasia group interaction. The more we know about the aphasic interaction, the more we are also able to develop therapeutic interventions to rehabilitate the interactional problems caused by aphasia. We also need knowledge of aphasic interaction and conversation in different contexts. It may be that further detailed analysis of different conversational and linguistic characteristics in different contexts would allow us to develop more refined hypotheses about the relationships between context, conversation, and aphasia.

Appendix 1

Transcript notation

The transcription symbols used are principally the same as in conversation analytic transcriptions (e.g., Atkinson & Heritage, 1984; Button & Lee, 1987; Levinson, 1983; also the Finnish versions Seppänen, 1997).

1. Overlap and Pauses
   [ ]   beginning and end of overlap
   (.)   micropause (less than 0.2 seconds)
  (1.2)   measured pause (1.2 seconds)
   =   two turns connected to each other without any pause

2. Intonation Contour
   .   falling
   ,   slightly falling
  ,.   steady
  ?   rising

3. Laughter
he he   transcribed from particle to particle if possible
 $ $ laughing voice

4. Breathing
.hhh   discernible inhalation
hhh.   discernible exhalation
 .yes   inspiratory articulation

5. Speech Rate and Emphasis
we::l   prolongation of part of a word
JUST   emphasized word or emphasized part of one
  ° °   silent voice

6. Others
      +   legato articulation (siel+on)
   (--)   inaudible word
  (—)   inaudible longer segment
  # #   creaky voice
    /   glottal stop
  puo-   incomplete word
 sirontaa   inaccurately articulated word or unrecognized word
{*follow up*}   hypothesized target of the word in English translation
  {?}   unrecognized word

7. Gestures

* *	beginning and end of gestures in conversational turns
O	refers to the movement of head, e.g. shake/nod
H	refers to the movement of hand
RH	refers to the movement of right hand
LH	refers to the movement of left hand
B	refers to the movement of body
E	ear
EYB	eyebrows
↓	gesture downward
↑	gesture upward
->	forward
<-	backward
D	point to
DR	point to the right
DL	point to the left
T	turn to

8. Gaze

GJ	gaze toward J
GJ . . .	gaze toward speaker J
G,,,J	speaker turns her or his gaze to speaker J
GxxJ	mutual gaze between speaker and J

Appendix 2

Glossing Symbols
(Modified from M.-L. Sorjonen, 1996)

The morphemes have been separated from each other with a vertical line. The following forms have been treated as unmarked forms, not indicated in the glossing:

- nominative case
- singular
- 3rd person singular (except when there are special reasons for indicating it)
- active voice
- present tense
- 2nd person singular imperative

Different infinitives and participal forms have not been specified.

Abbreviations Used in Glossing:

1   1st person ending
2   2nd person ending

3   3rd person ending
4   passive person ending

Case Endings:

Case	Abbreviation	Approximate meaning
nominative	NOM	subject
accusative	ACC	object
genitive	GEN	possession
partitive	PAR	partitiveness
inessive	INE	"in"
elative	ELA	"out of"
illative	ILL	"into"
adessive	ADE	"at, on"
ablative	ABL	"from"
allative	ALL	"to"
essive	ESS	"as"
translative	TRA	"to," "becoming"
abessive	ABE	"without"
instructive	INS	(various)
comitative	COM	"with"

Other Abbreviations:

CLI	clitic	POS	possessive suffix
COM	comparative	PPC	past participle
CON	conditional	PPPC	passive past participle
CNJ	conjunction	PRT	particle
FRE	frequentative	PST	past tense
IMP	imperative	Q	interrogative
INF	infinitive	REF	reflexive
NEG	negation	SG	singular
ORD	ordinal number morpheme	SUP	superlative
PASS	passive	1nameF	1st name, female
PC	participle	1nameM	1st name, male
PL	plural		

References

Atkinson, J. M., & Heritage, J. (eds.). (1984). *Structures of Social Action. Studies in Conversation Analysis*. Cambridge: Cambridge University Press.

Button, G., & Lee, J. R. (1987). *Talk and Social Organization*. Clevedon: Multilingual Matters.

Ferguson, A. (1994). The Influence of Aphasia, Familiarity and Activity on Conversational Repair. *Aphasiology*, 8, 143–157.

Goodwin, C. (1995). Co-constructing Meaning in Conversations with an Aphasic Man. *Research on Language and Social Interaction*, 28, 233–260.

Goodwin, C. & Duranti, A. (1992). Rethinking Context: An Introduction. In A. Duranti &

C. Goodwin (Eds.), *Rethinking Context. Language as an Interactive Phenomenon* (pp. 1–42). Cambridge: Cambridge University Press.

Goodwin, M. H., & Goodwin, C. (1986). Gesture and Coparticipation in the Activity of Searching for a Word. *Semiotica, 62*, 51–75.

Hakulinen, A., & Sorjonen, M.-L. (1986). Palautteen asema diskurssissa. In P. Leino & J. Kalliokoski (Eds.), *Kieli 1* (pp. 39–72). Helsinki: University of Helsinki, Department of Finnish Language.

Heritage, J. (1984). *Garfinkel and Ethnomethodology*. Oxford: Polity Press.

Heritage, J. (1989). Current Developments in Conversation Analysis. In D. Roger & P. Bull (Eds.), *Conversation* (pp. 19–47). Clevedon: Multilingual Matters.

Johannsen-Horbach, H., Wentz, C., Funfgeld, M., Herrmann, M., & Wallesch, C.-W. (1993). Psychosocial Aspects on the Treatment of Adult Aphasics and Their Families: A Group Approach in Germany. In A. Holland & M. Forbes (Eds.), *Aphasia Treatment. Word Perspectives* (pp. 319–334). San Diego: Singular Publishing Group.

Kagan, A., & Gailey, G. (1993). Functional Is Not Enough: Training Conversational Partners for Aphasic Adults. In A. Holland & M. Forbes (Eds.), *Aphasia Treatment. Word Perspectives* (pp. 199–227). San Diego: Singular Publishing Group.

Kearns, K. D. (1986). Group Therapy for Aphasia: Theoretical and Practical Considerations. In R. Chapey (Ed.), *Language Intervention Strategies in Adult Aphasia* (2nd ed., pp. 304–318). Baltimore: Williams & Wilkins.

Klippi, A. (1992). Reaching Towards Mutual Understanding in Aphasic Conversation. Aphasics as Contributors in Conversation. In R. Aulanko & M. Lehtihalmes (Eds.), *Studies in Logopedics and Phonetics, 3*(4), 54–67.

Klippi, A. (1996). *Conversation as an Achievement in Aphasics. Studia Fennica Linguistica, 6.*

Laakso, M. (1992). Interactional Features of Aphasia Therapy Conversation. In R. Aulanko & M. Lehtihalmes (Eds.), *Studies in Logopedics and Phonetics, 3*(4), 69–90.

Laakso, M. (1997). *Self-Initiated Repair by Fluent Aphasic Speakers in Conversation. Studia Fennica Linguistica, 8.*

Laakso, M., & Klippi, A. (1999). A Closer Look at the "Hint-and-Guess"—Sequences in Aphasic Conversation. *Aphasiology: Special Issue on Conversation Analysis, 4–5*, 345–363.

Lave, J. (1993). The Practice of Learning. In S. Chaiklin & J. Lave, (Eds.), *Understanding Practice. Perspectives on Activity and Context* (pp. 3–32). Cambridge: Cambridge University Press.

Lehtihalmes, M., Klippi, A., & Lempinen, M. (1986). Western Aphasia Battery. Unstandardized Finnish version for research purposes.

Lubinski, R., Dunchan, J., & Weitzner-Lin, B. (1980). Analysis of Breakdowns and Repairs in Aphasic Adult Communication. In R. Brookshire (Ed.), *Clinical Aphasiology Conference Proceedings* (pp. 111–116). Minnesota: BRK Publishers.

Milroy, L., & Perkins, L. (1992). Repair Strategies in Aphasic Discourse; Towards a Collaborative Model. *Clinical Linguistics & Phonetics, 6*, 27–40.

Pachalska, M. (1993). The Concept of Holistic Rehabilitiation of Persons with Aphasia. In A. Holland & M. Forbes (Eds.), *Aphasia Treatment. Word Perspectives* (pp. 145–174). San Diego: Singular Publishing Group.

Perkins, L. (1993). The Impact of Cognitive Neuropsychological Impairments in Conversational Ability in Aphasia. Unpublished Ph.D.-thesis. University of Newcastle upon Tyne.

Schegloff, E., Jefferson, G., & Sacks, H. (1977). The Preference of Self-Correction in the Organisation of Repair in Conversation. *Language, 53*, 361–382.

Seppänen (1997). Vuorovaikutus paperilla (Interaction on Paper). In L. Tainio (Ed.), Keskustelunanalyysin perusteet (pp. 18–31). Tampere: Vastapaino.

Sorjonen, M.-L. (1996). On Repeats and Responses in Finnish Conversations. In E. Ochs, E. A. Schegloff, & S. A. Thompson (Eds.), *Interaction and Grammar*. Cambridge: Cambridge University Press.

Vygotsky, L. (1982 [1931]). *Ajattelu Ja Kieli* (Thought and Language). Espoo: Weilin & Göös.

Wilkinson, R. (1995). Aphasia: Conversation Analysis of a Non-Fluent Aphasic Person. In M. Perkins & S. Howard (Eds.), *Case-Studies in Clinical Linguistics* (pp. 271–292). London: Whurr.

PART III

REPAIR

6

LISA PERKINS

Negotiating Repair in
Aphasic Conversation

Interactional Issues

Conversation Analysis has a major contribution to make to the analysis of pragmatics in aphasia. Building on previous work concerning repair in aphasic discourse (Milroy & Perkins, 1992), this chapter considers the negotiation in two particular features of repair organization in aphasic conversation involving (1) the preference for fast resolution of repair work and (2) the orientation to repair as socially sensitive. The analysis of dyadic aphasic conversation presented highlights the collaborative nature of conversation. Pragmatic difficulties can be viewed within a collaborative framework as residing in the interaction to be dealt with by the sequential, collaborative problem solving of both interlocutors.

The application of pragmatics to aphasia

The importance of the application of pragmatics to aphasia has long been recognized and a variety of different theoretical approaches have been applied to pragmatic analyses of aphasia including speech act theory (e.g., Holland, 1980; Wirz, Skinner, & Dean, 1990), Gricean implicatures (e.g., Ahlsen, 1993; Hawkins, 1989) and text analysis (see Huber, 1990, for a review). It has been suggested (Milroy & Perkins, 1992, 1997; Lesser & Milroy, 1993) that the data-driven approach of conversation analysis has a number of features valuable to the analysis of aphasic interaction but not offered by the theory-driven pragmatic approaches of philosophy and linguistics.

A major strength of CA is that it provides procedures for analyzing real interaction, thus allowing the characterization of aphasic interaction without prior problematic assumptions of how this relates to normal interaction. Perkins (1995) stresses that use of normal conversation as the benchmark for aphasic discourse is unsatisfactory. The unique demands of aphasia necessitate that it be treated autonomously to achieve a clear insight into its management.

In fact, CA is the only approach to pragmatics that takes account of the minutiae of conversation, such as the interactional consequences of filled and unfilled pauses, overlaps, and repairs. Such phenomena are particularly common in aphasic discourse as a consequence of linguistic impairments. Thus, CA addresses the level of pragmatic impairment typically found in aphasia (i.e., pragmatic difficulties as a consequence of linguistic impairments in phonological, semantic, and syntactic processing; Perkins, 1993: 27). CA does not stress the separateness of pragmatic and other linguistic impairment but provides instead the tools for describing the observable interactional consequences of particular impairments.

A further strength of CA is that it treats conversations as a collaborative achievement (Schegloff, 1982); thus, aphasic interaction is seen as the joint achievement of both the participant with aphasia and his or her conversational partner. Instead of simply identifying pragmatic failures, CA focuses on what and how interaction is achieved, thus highlighting the abilities of the person with aphasia to use the sequential and collaborative construction of discourse to communicate.

Conversation involves more than the effective transmission and receipt of information. It is "a vehicle through which selves, relationships and situations are socially constructed" (Schiffrin, 1988: 272). Schegloff (1992) stresses its role as a primordial site of sociality. Because the ability to use this social vehicle depends on language, aphasia results in a compromised ability to engage in social life. Organizational features of conversation do, however, provide devices that allow conversationalists to negotiate some of the consequences of aphasia. This chapter explores the use of repair in aphasic interaction, focusing on the collaborative negotiation of its usage between people with aphasia and their conversational partners.

The sequential organization of conversation and the role of repair

Conversation is sequential, with each turn built in relation to the prior turn. Schegloff (1979) refers to this as the sequential implicativeness of a turn and proposes that this property provides for the routine display of participants' understanding of each other's turns (Schegloff, 1992). An immense variety of trouble sources can, however, arise in interaction, which obstruct the production of a sequentially implicated next turn. The organization of repair provides a mechanism to deal with such trouble sources. The organization of repair is the self-righting mechanism for the organization of language use in social interaction. This mechanism is particularly pertinent in aphasic interaction, where language abilities are impaired.

Schegloff Jefferson, and Sacks (1977) propose a distinction between the initiation of a repair and its outcome. These phases can be carried out by different people. Thus, repair can be initiated by the speaker of the trouble source (self-initiated repair) or by another party (other-initiated repair). In either case, the carrying out of the repair can be done by either self or other. Thus, repair sequences can take a number of forms whose respective structural placements are ordered relative to each other. Other-initiation is nearly invariably held back until the trouble source turn's possible completion. In addition, self- and other-initiation have different courses. Self-initiation of repair can be, and usually is, combined with a candidate repair. In contrast, other-initiation often locates the trouble source to yield self-repair in the next turn. Thus, the organization of repair provides centrally for self-repair, which can be arrived at by the alternative routes of self-initiation and other-initiation, routes which themselves are organized to favor self-initiation. The different forms of repair are not, therefore, structurally equivalent or equipotential. The participants' opportunities to carry out repair lead to a preference for self-repair and self-initiation.

The preference for self-repair can be seen to relate to the orientation, in the organization of conversation, to sequential implicativeness. When other-initiated repair occurs, it results in the sequential implicativeness of current turn being displaced for at least one turn (Schegloff, 1979). The repair work becomes the interactional business, with current business suspended until it is resolved.

Analysis has demonstrated that interlocutors orient to repair work as socially sensitive. If the problem necessitating repair can be traced back to some personal insufficiency, it becomes an event that threatens face (Goffman, 1955; Couper Kuhlen, 1992). Jefferson (1987) demonstrates that a characteristic of other repair is an accounting of lapses in conduct that have given rise to repair work. Furthermore, repair initiation can be used for the display and potential deflection of disagreement (Schegloff, 1982).

Repair organization deals rapidly with trouble sources. In normal interaction, it is overwhelmingly carried out within the turn in which the trouble source appears (self-initiated self-repair), with less preferred forms of repair (other-initiated and other repair) overwhelmingly resolved within two further turns (although see Schegloff, 1987, 1992, on third and fourth position repairs). As outlined later, however, in aphasic interaction, rapid repair work is often not achieved, giving rise to different interactional issues for the interlocutors to negotiate.

Repair in aphasic conversation

Repair organization is a particularly important device in aphasic discourse, given the variety of potential trouble sources that may impede the progression of conversation. Milroy and Perkins (1992) propose that repair in aphasic discourse has a complex organization that appears to be structurally different in several respects from repair organization in normal discourse. For the person with aphasia, linguistic impairments necessitate greater use of repair work. The same linguistic impairments, however, limit his or her ability to execute self-repair within the turn of the trouble source. As a consequence, the fast resolution of repair seen in normal conversation is not accomplished and successful repair outcomes can be described as collaboratively achieved rather than completed by self or other.

Milroy and Perkins propose that Clark and Schaefer's (1987, 1989) CA-motivated model of conversational contributions provides a useful framework to capture the complexity of aphasic repair organization. The model stresses the collaborative nature of conversation, with contributions to conversation having two constituents: the *presentation phase*, where an utterance is presented by the contributor (interlocutor A); and the *acceptance phase*, which is initiated by the listener (interlocutor B) but which involves both interlocutors working to establish that B has reached an understanding of A's presentation sufficient for current purposes. This phase may constitute either positive evidence of understanding (in the form of acknowledgment tokens or moving on to the next relevant contribution) or initiation of repair work.

Central to the model is the *principle of least collaborative effort*, whereby participants strive to minimize the total effort spent on a contribution in both the presentation and acceptance phases. There is generally a trade-off in effort between initiating a presentation and refashioning it, in that the greater the effort expended on designing a presentation, the less is needed for acceptance. However, a number of factors may give rise to presentations that require collaborative repair work to achieve completion of the acceptance phase. Milroy and Perkins suggest that the principle of collaborative effort operates in aphasic conversations in that less overall collaborative effort is required if the unimpaired conversational partner contributes to the repair work to achieve acceptance of a presentation than if the aphasic partner works in isolation to design an immediately acceptable presentation (a task that may be beyond his or her linguistic abilities).

In accordance with the principle of least collaborative effort, initiation of the acceptance phase should precisely reflect the state of understanding reached, enabling repair work to be focused as precisely as possible. As each acceptance phase initiator is, in itself, a presentation that requires acceptance, contributions may be hierarchically structured, with presentations embedded within higher level acceptance phases. Every acceptance phase must ultimately end with a speaker presupposing acceptance by moving on to the next relevant contribution, thus preventing the recursive process spinning out indefinitely.

Data presented in Milroy and Perkins (1992) demonstrate the ability of Clark and Schaefer's model to capture the often complex nature of aphasic repair sequences, with embedded acceptance phases employing a variety of acceptance phase initiators to build toward completion. It captures the collaborative construction between the person with aphasia and his or her conversational partner of an understanding sufficient for current purposes.

Work on repair in normal conversation suggests that repair is socially delicate, with potential threat to the face of the perpetrator of the trouble source. Wilkinson (1995) has addressed this issue in aphasic conversation. In relation to Sacks's (1984) proposal that deviations from "being ordinary" are accountable and require inter-actional work to avoid potentially negative interactional incidents, Wilkinson pro-poses that displays of non-competence in aphasia are interactionally delicate, bringing to the conversational surface the issue of the person with aphasia as a "non-ordinary" interactant. He identifies a sequential pattern around trouble sources in conversations between therapists and patients. The patient laughs and often makes some form of account for the lapse in competence. In the next turn, the therapist resists affiliating with the laughter and does not comment verbally on the lapse. Parallels can be drawn between this pattern and that seen in tellings of troubles (Jefferson, 1984), in which the troubles-teller uses laughter as a resource to display that he or she is coping with the trouble and the troubles-recipient exhibits concern about the trouble. Because laughter can be viewed as treating the trouble lightly, the troubles-recipient does not affiliate with the laughter. Wilkinson suggests that the therapist, by withholding laugh-ter, is attempting to keep the non-ordinary identity off the conversational surface.

Given the sensitivity of protracted repair in exposing failures in competence, an option open to interlocutors is to opt for a non-repair of a trouble source. Depending on the form of trouble source, a number of options are possible, including passing over a trouble source altogether (Heritage & Atkinson, 1984) and embedded correc-tion as an alternative formulation (Jefferson, 1987).

Repair in aphasic interaction is interactionally delicate and complex. I will use data to examine how repair is negotiated in dyadic conversations of three people with aphasia with both a relative and with the researcher. All conversations were recorded in the aphasic people's homes. Further details of data collection methods and the nature of linguistic impairments can be found in Perkins (1993, 1995).

Negotiating whether to repair

As noted, one option open to interlocutors is to pass over potential trouble sources. It is well established that hearable errors do not necessarily yield repair in normal conversation (Schegloff et al., 1977). In Clark and Schaefer's model, this can be seen to relate to the purpose of a presentation being to achieve an understanding suffi-cient for current purposes. An error need not interfere with this and in this case will not need to be treated as something requiring repair work. This is illustrated in ex-ample 1[1] in which an aphasic man, AD, is talking to the researcher:

Example 1
I   AD: y'see and I had three years in the [am] y'know as well
2   LP: was that when the war was on
3   AD: inthewar

The phonological error for the word "army" does not interfere with LP reaching an understanding sufficient for current purposes, as demonstrated in the production of a next relevant presentation in turn 2 (T2).

In interaction, the notion of what is sufficient for current purposes is negotiable, and interlocutors may opt for lax criteria of what is sufficient to minimize collaborative effort and avoid a protracted repair sequence, as shown in example 2:

Example 2

```
 1   RE:   when do they go away you usually do it when they're away don't
            you well* that's the back Tom
               [
 2   AD:       (1 syllable)
 3   AD:   oh yeah
 4   RE:   mhm
 5   AD:   yeah
           (1.0)
 6   RE:   (I syllable)
            [
 7   AD:   'cause* you think they're going away tomorrow you mean you think
            they're going away
 8   RE:   I'm saying do you know when they're going away
                            [
 9   AD:                              yeah they usuall*y do but I'll get that one done
            before this weekend I shouldn't I'll get that one finished
10   RE:   aha
```

This example is taken from a conversation between an aphasic man, AD, and his adult daughter, RE. They are discussing the cutting of AD's hedges. RE produces a complex turn (TI), which contains a wh-question ("when do they go away"), followed by a clause with a final tag question ("you usually do it when they're away don't you"), followed by a qualifier that specifies who "they" refer to ("well that's the back Tom"). The two questions have made two issues sequentially relevant in the next turn: the provision of the information of when they go away and confirmation or rejection of the information preceding the tag question. In T3, AD produces a sequentially relevant next turn that responds to the tag question. RE accepts this (T4) without reinitiating the first question of her previous turn, which AD has not responded to, and AD produces a further minimal turn ("yeah"). After a lapse in the conversation of one second, AD then initiates repair on RE's T1 with a demonstration of understanding reached in T7 for RE to either confirm or reject. RE's T8 shows that the understanding displayed by AD is not correct, and she redoes the first element of her earlier turn with a different syntactic structure. AD initiates T9 in overlap of RE's repair and this displays that he has again not understood RE's question about when the neighbors are going away. T9 does not display sequential relevance in that a question makes sequentially relevant an answer to it or an account for why an answer is not done (Schegloff, 1972). AD does neither. Although an option open to RE is to initiate further repair work to deal with this, she does not take it. Instead, she provides AD with acceptance of his non-sequential turn, thus allowing the conversation to progress. In relation to the notion of what information might be considered "sufficient for current purposes," the information about when AD's neighbors are going away is not essential to the current purpose of the conversation and, thus, the misunderstanding is allowed to pass.

The displayed misunderstanding in example 2 was not an obstacle that interfered with the progression of the conversation. In some contexts, however, choosing the option of not repairing may have more marked interactional consequences. Consider example 3 from a conversation (in strong local dialect) between a woman with aphasia (EN) and her male cousin (BC):

Example 3
```
1    BC:   Winnie has she shifted yet
2    EN:   no er sh- was she was s- supposed to (I) with her daughter for er
           for s-
                [
3    BC:       go* to go to Fleetwood she's go*ing she's going to Fleetwood
                                                 [
4    EN:                                          oh
     BC:   as well wasn't she
           [
5    EN:   was was she* oh I didn't know she was going to Fleetwood
                                                              [
6    BC:                                                       oh* aye
           she gan to live for at Fleetwood
7    EN:   oh I thought she was living around here
8    BC:   she w- she's living out she was living in Valley View=
9    EN:   =aye
10   BC:   er Letts Way but I don't know what er (.) three weeks since I was
           talking to her and she said well w- I'll be away shortly
11   EN:   aha=
12   BC:   =but I don't know whether she was with her
13   EN:   no (2 syll.) just she was er (1) daughter was waiting for some t-
14   BC:   'cause she's got a house
15   EN:   o:h
16   BC:   down there 'cause he's in the police thing down there now in
           the* in the gaol
           [
17   EN:   a:h
           (1.1)
```

18	BC:	he's got his job er er he's off the buses now he's in the* on the
		[
19	EN:	ah
	BC:	gaols thing now you see and I thought the way she was talking I thought she might've been away about a fortnight
20	EN:	no she was w- she was supposed to er (1) I've forgotten but she was but she was (1.6)
21	BC:	I was talking to her at the butchers down down the bottom and* she was telling us she says oh I'll not be long away I'll not be
		[
22	EN:	mm
	BC:	long before I'm going
		(1.2)
23	EN:	mm
		[
24	BC:	I* says y'gannin for good or what she says I'm not y- it's it's a big house she's I'm going to live with them
25	EN:	aye but er but she (2) eee I don't know what she said
26	BC:	that's what she said to me anyway hinny and I thought maybe you had heard it whether she'd moved or not you see
		[
27	EN:	n*o
28	BC:	'cause I've never been I've never been over there for donkeys 'cause she's never in
29	EN:	no
30	BC:	she's always down at the daughters y'see hen

The example commences with BC asking a yes/no question about whether a mutual friend (Winnie) has moved. EN responds to this with "no" and then continues her turn. Her linguistic impairments are clearly causing her difficulties as marked by numerous self-repair attempts with filled and unfilled pauses and repetitions. She does not manage to complete her turn, and BC comes in with T3 in overlap with EN immediately dropping out. BC does not initiate repair on EN's incomplete T2. In relation to Clark and Schaefer's model, this absence of repair initiation indicates that he has reached an understanding sufficient for current purposes, allowing him to produce a sequentially relevant next turn. Analysis of the sequence as a whole, however, suggests that BC is not reaching an understanding of EN's presentation sufficient for current purposes. This is demonstrated by the repetition of part of T2 in T20 ("no she was w- she was supposed to"). EN's re-presentation of this part of T2 demonstrates that she does not accept that the presentation has indeed achieved an understanding by BC sufficient for current purposes. In T20, EN again runs into difficulties, and BC takes the floor before completion of the turn (similar loss of the floor before completion is also seen in T13).

Reinitiation of her attempted presentation at T2 and T20 is again seen at T25. This turn commences with a clause that, after a two-second unfilled pause, is abandoned with an account for this ("eee I don't know what she said"). In the following turn (T26), BC readdresses the original question of T1 of whether Winnie has moved ("I thought maybe you had heard it whether she'd moved or not you see"). EN responds to this turn with "no." This turn is interesting, given that at other points in the sequence there are clear markers that she did indeed have knowledge about Winnie's move. For example, in T2 she answers BC's question on the topic, not with an account for why she cannot answer the question (e.g. "I don't know" or "I haven't heard") but with an answer ("no"). Furthermore, T13, T20, and T25 all indicate some knowledge on the topic, although linguistic difficulties interfere with completion of the presentations.

The movement from knowing about Winnie's move (T2) to not knowing (T27) has been interactionally negotiated. EN's aphasic difficulties have a significant impact in the sequence, in that while BC is not initiating collaborative repair on her incomplete presentations, EN's repeated attempts at the provision of information about Winnie indicates that she has not accepted that her presentations have been understood to a level sufficient for current purposes. The re-presentations are abandoned in T25 with an account, and thus EN's information does not develop the topic. The display of not knowing in the account in T25 and her denial of knowledge in T27 permit the curtailment of her (not very successful) attempts and thus can be seen as interactional devices to opt out.

In example 3, BC often opts not to initiate repair on potentially problematic turns but instead moves on to the next relevant presentation. This has consequences, however, for EN, who, because of her linguistic impairments, is not able to design a presentation that achieves a level of understanding sufficient for her current purposes (and her re-presentations indicate that she has different criteria in this respect to BC). As a consequence, her attempts to contribute to the development of topic fail, and, across the sequence, EN's status changes from an interactive participant with knowledge to contribute to a non-interactive participant taking a more passive recipient role.

A comparative quantitative analysis of the number of collaborative repair sequences and proportion of major turns produced in 12-minute extracts of dyadic conversations between EN and BC and EN and the researcher (Perkins, 1995) demonstrates that BC rarely employs the resource of collaborative repair. Instead, EN's potentially problematic turns are effectively glossed over. The consequences of this are demonstrated in the proportion of major turns produced by each of the interlocutors, with EN contributing only 30%, with the majority of her turns taking the form of minimal turns (e.g., "aha," "mm"). As a consequence of the lack of collaborative repair work being carried out by BC, EN's presentations do not shape the following interaction, thus giving rise to a passive role in the interaction. This contrasts with her conversation with the researcher and the conversations between two other aphasic people and their relatives. In all of these, collaborative repair is used frequently to achieve acceptance of the aphasic interlocutor's presentations. As a consequence, the proportion of major turns is shared much more equally between the interlocutors.

To conclude, in aphasic conversation, where there is an above average number of potential trouble sources as a consequence of aphasia, one option open to interlocutors is to operate a lax criterion of what constitutes understanding sufficient for current purposes, allowing problems in understanding to pass. This option avoids potentially face-threatening repair work. However, it does have implications for the interactional role of the person with aphasia, whose ability to contribute to the interaction may be severely limited by the absence of collaborative work on his or her contributions.

Negotiating collaborative repair: Accountings and corrections

In line with the principle of least collaborative effort, interlocutors orient to complete repair work as quickly and efficiently as possible. In doing this, they minimize "time out" from the main interactional work being done. Other interactional issues may, however, result in some extension of collaborative repair work. These include the need to do correction and the need to account for lapses in competence. Each of these issues will be addressed in the analysis of example 4, which presents a collaborative repair sequence from a conversation between an aphasic woman, JJ, and the researcher.

Example 4

226	LP:	has he had a job over the summer or
227	JJ:	yeah he's he's (2.1) well he finished er was it a week ago or two weeks no it it'll just be over the week* now erm (1.5) he (0.9) was
		[
228	LP:	right
cont.	JJ:	doing for the (3.5) it's er now then (0.6) the [if] the nuts=
229	LP:	=mm {hehe}
230	JJ:	sorry but I'm trying to (0.6) the
		[
231	LP:	is* it anything to do with his course
232	JJ:	no* nothing at all {hehehheheh} 'hhh er::m (1.8) it's (0.8) er:
		[
233	LP:	no
cont.	JJ:	hospital (1.5)
234	LP:	Queen Elizabeth
235	JJ:	no its over this way

236   LP: Prudhoe
237   JJ: thank you
238   LP: right
239   JJ: I now I cannot get that out do you know that is one of the things* I
                                                                    [
240   LP: yeah
cont. JJ: cannot get it out
                   [
241   LP: yeah* {*hehe*}
242   JJ: what is it again
243   LP: Prudhoe
244   JJ: Prudhoe Prudhoe Prudhoe that's it and erm {cough} he just tried
             'cause he he he just couldn't get anything at all

This example has a similar initial shape to example 3, with the non-aphasic participant asking a yes/no question and the aphasic participant responding to this with a yes/no answer and further elaboration of a turn, which runs into difficulties because of word-finding problems. At this point the extracts take a different shape with an extensive collaborative repair sequence negotiated in contrast to the absence of collaborative repair in example 3. The focus of the collaborative repair is to establish where JJ's son has been working. Both participants use a number of strategies to achieve resolution of the trouble source including questions to obtain information (T231), circumlocutory information ("hospital" in T233, "over this way" in T235), and candidate understandings based on circumlocution (T234 and T236). Each turn builds on the previous one to move closer toward completion of the collaborative repair. Success is marked in T237 by JJ's "thank you." T238 following this can be seen to function to accept both JJ's acceptance of T236 and the original presentation that has been the focus of the collaborative work.

This pair of minimal turns is typical of the negotiated closing down of complex repair described by Milroy and Perkins (1992). In accordance with the principle of least collaborative effort, the main interactional business can now be returned to, and the interaction can progress. This does not happen, however. Instead, JJ in T239 produces a metalinguistic comment on the word-finding difficulty she has been experiencing. This provides an accounting for the lapse in conduct that has given rise to the repair work. LP produces minimal turns in acceptance of this turn in overlap (T240 and T241), but the repair sequence is still not closed down as JJ addresses the issue of correction in T242, asking for a model from LP. This is provided in T243, and JJ repeats this three times. Finally, the current business, which has been suspended by the repair work, continues in the latter part of T244.

Turns 239 to 244 demonstrate that orientation to the principle of least collaborative effort (by minimizing the length of repair work) may in fact be deferred to deal with the socially sensitive occurrence of a display of non-competence. Although the extended collaborative repair sequence differs from that seen in normal conversation in that resolution of the trouble source arises from the joint work of both inter-locutors together rather than carried out by "self" or "other," the end sequence has features typical of the pattern of exposed correction of normal discourse Jefferson described (1987: 88). One of these features is accountings that address the lapses in competence as seen in JJ's T239. Orientation to the lapse is also seen at other points in the repair sequence. In T229 LP produces "mm" with a short laugh. Although turns such as "mm" typically do the work of passing the opportunity to do repair work, thus implicating that repair work is not required (Schegloff, 1982), the following turn indicates that this is not the work being done in this turn. The laughter appears to mark some difficulty in the interaction that JJ orients to in T230 by providing an account of her previous problematic turn ("sorry but I'm trying to"). In T232 JJ rejects LP's attempt in the previous turn to narrow down the sort of job her son is doing and then produces laughter before continuing with the repair work. As described by Wilkinson (1995), the pattern seen in telling troubles is seen here, with LP withholding affiliating laughter, thus keeping the non-ordinary identity off the conversational surface. LP does produce a small sequence of laughter later in the sequence in T241, with her acknowledgment of JJ's account. In her next turn, JJ does not affiliate with this laughter but continues with the repair work.

This brings us to a second feature of this repair sequence, which Jefferson describes as a typical pattern of exposed correction in normal interaction: the following series of turns:

1. A speaker produces some object (x)
2. A subsequent speaker produces an alternative (y)
3. Prior speaker produces the alternative (y)

JJ's word-finding difficulties mean that item 1 of the series is not produced but is oriented to by both interlocutors from T227 to T235. Item 2 of the series is produced by LP in T236 ("Prudhoe"). Item 3 is addressed in T242 and is produced in T244; JJ's aphasic difficulties result in the item taking more than one turn for this to be done. Thus, although the repair work could be seen to be completed by T238 as both interlocutors have reached an understanding sufficient for current purposes, JJ withholds her collaborative contribution to the close-down of the repair until she has produced the correct item. This is a common pattern in aphasic interaction where a specific lexical item is the focus of repair. An example of its usage with a phonological error is seen in example 5:

Example 5
158   AD: . . . . . they put me back into the er (1.2) hospitals and and [ɛ? 'ɛlɪvənts
            'ɛlɪvəns] where you get your not your ['ɛlɪvənts] er you get you (1)
            hhh err: (1.6) [kalf kəl 'kɒlənəns kɒlf kə]

                                                    [
159   LP: con*valescence=

160   AD: =['kɒlvənəns
161   LP: convalescence right
162   AD: and I came there and they took me back. . . .

Item 1 of the series is the repeated phonological attempts in T158. LP produces an alternative (item 2) in T159, and AD produces the alternative (item 3) in T160. This runs into difficulties, however, in that his phonological production difficulties result in a further phonological error. As a consequence, LP produces the correction again in combination with an acknowledgment token, and the repair is closed down as AD moves on to the next relevant contribution in T162, thus allowing the interactional business to progress.

Both illustrate that aphasic interlocutors orient to organizational features of repair, although their linguistic impairments may give rise to further collaborative work with their conversational partners, subsequently resulting in more time out from the main interactional work.

Discussion

The analysis presented in this chapter has highlighted that the organizational phenomenon of repair provides an important resource to deal with the interactional consequences of aphasia. Two specific features of repair organization, however, have further repercussions for aphasic interaction.

First, repair organization embodies a preference for quick repair to minimize disruption to the current interactional business. As a consequence of language-processing impairments, aphasic trouble sources are often not resolved quickly and complex collaborative work is required for resolution. The interlocutors can be seen, however, to orient to the principle of least collaborative effort to complete repair work as efficiently as possible, taking account of the linguistic resources available to the aphasic interlocutor, to allow the progression of the current interactional business.

Second, repair is treated as interactionally delicate; if the trouble source can be traced back to some personal insufficiency, it becomes a socially sensitive event. In aphasic conversation, trouble sources can frequently be traced back to the aphasic participant's personal insufficiency in linguistic processing. This gives rise to interactional work to minimize the threat to face. Thus, repair work, although an invaluable resource in aphasic conversation, also creates potentially delicate interactional issues. Interlocutors have the option not to initiate repair work but to let misunderstandings or even failures in understandings go by. As illustrated in example 3, however, this may have notable interactional consequences for an aphasic interlocutor who requires collaborative repair work to successfully make a contribution to conversation. Thus, the withholding of the collaborative "scaffolding," which can be provided only by the non-impaired conversational partner, may severely limit what that aphasic person is able to achieve interactionally.

Extample 4 shows that repair is oriented to as interactionally delicate, with the originator of the trouble source (the aphasic interlocutor) providing accounts for her lapse (accountings are also seen in example 3). In addition, orientation to the need for the production of the "corrected" item is demonstrated. This production of the correct version does not relate to reaching a mutual understanding sufficient for current purposes but goes beyond it. The consequence of this work is to extend repair work; indeed, the turns involved in this may themselves be affected by aphasia, as seen in example 4. As a consequence, restoration of the suspended interactional business is further delayed.

To conclude, analysis of aphasic discourse highlights the fundamentally collaborative nature of conversation. Pragmatic difficulties should, therefore, perhaps be seen within this collaborative framework as a difficulty residing in the interaction to be dealt with by the sequential problem solving of both interlocutors. This concurs with Goodwin's (1995: 31) statement that "as an injury, aphasia does reside within the skull. However, as a form of life, a way of being and acting in the world in concert with others, its proper locus is a distributed multi-party system." This view has implications for rehabilitation, as problem-solving abilities to deal with aphasia of both the person with aphasia and his or her conversational partners will vary. Conversation analysis provides the aphasia therapist with a tool to identify precisely how interlocutors are negotiating aphasia. Thus, it provides a starting point to discuss whether, through modification of current interactional strategies, the aphasic person's use of conversation as a vehicle through which self, relationships, and situations are socially constructed (Schiffrin, 1988: 272) can be enhanced.

Note

I would like to express my gratitude to the people with aphasia and their families who allowed me to record their conversations for research purposes. I was supported by a grant from the British Economic and Social Research Council (grant reference 000236456) during the preparation of this chapter.

    1. Conventions used in data extracts:
[	Point at which utterances above and below are produced in overlap.
•	Point where overlap ceases.
(0.0)	Pauses or gaps in tenths of seconds.
(.)	Micropause.
(x syll.)	Uncertain passages of transcription with number of syllables.
==	Latched utterances with no gap.
[}	Phonetic transcription following the International Phonetic Association (1989) conventions.
{ }	Laughter.

References

Ahlsen, E. (1993). Conversational Principles and Aphasic Communication. *Journal of Pragmatics*, *19*, 57–70.

Clark, H. H., & E. F. Schaefer. (1987). Collaborating on Contributions to Conversation. *Language and Cognitive Processes*, *2*, 1–23.

Clark, H. H., & E. F. Schaefer (1989). Contributing to Discourse. *Cognitive Science*, *13*, 259–294.

Couper-Kuhlen, E. (1992). Contextualising Discourse: The Prosody of Interactive Repair. In P. Auer & A. Di Luzio (Eds.), *The Contextualisation of Language* (pp. 337–364). Amsterdam: Benjamins.

Goffman, E. (1955). On Face Work. *Psychiatry*, *18*, 213–231.

Goodwin, C. (1994). Co-constructing Meaning in Conversations with an Aphasic Man. Paper presented at The American Association for Applied Linguistics, Baltimore, March 6, 1994.

Hawkins, P. (1989). Discourse Aphasia. In P. Grunwell & Allan James (Eds.), *The Functional Evaluation of Disorders* (pp. 183–199). London: Croom Helm.

Heritage, J., & Atkinson, J. M. (1984). Introduction. In J. M. Atkinson & J. Heritage (Eds.), *Structure of Social Action: Studies in Conversation Analysis* (pp. 1–15). Cambridge: Cambridge University Press.

Holland, A. (1980). *Communicative Abilities in Daily Living: A Test of Functional Communication for Aphasic Adults*. Baltimore: University Park Press.

Huber, W. (1990). Text Comprehension and Production in Aphasia: Analysis in Terms of Micro- and Macrostructure. In Y. Joanette & H. H. Brownell (Eds.), *Discourse Ability and Brain Damage*. New York: Springer-Verlag.

Jefferson, G. (1984). On the Organization of Laughter in the Talk about Troubles. In J. M. Atkinson & John Heritage (Eds.), *Structure of Social Action: Studies in Conversation Analysis* (pp. 346–369. Cambridge: Cambridge University Press.

Jefferson, G., 1987. On Exposed and Embedded Correction in Conversation. In G. Button & J. R. E. Lee (Eds.), *Talk and Social Organization* (pp. 86–100). Clevedon: Multilingual Matters.

Lesser, R., & Milroy, L. (1993). *Linguistics and Aphasia: Psycholinguistic and Pragmatic Aspects of Intervention*. London: Longman.

Milroy, L., & Perkins, L. (1992). Repair in Aphasic Discourse: Towards a Collaborative Model. *Clinical Linguistics and Phonetics*, *6*, 27–40.

Milroy, L., & Perkins, L. (1997). Sharing the Communicative Burden: A Conversation Analytic Account of Aphasic / Non-Aphasic interaction. *Multilingua*, *16*, 199–215.

Perkins, L. (1993). The Impact of Cognitive Neuropsychological Impairments on Conversational Abilities in Aphasia. Doctoral dissertation, University of Newcastle upon Tyne.

Perkins, L. (1993). Pragmatics Applied to Aphasia Rehabilitation. In M. Paradis (Ed.), *Foundations of Aphasia Rehabilitation*. London: Academic Press.

Perkins, L. (1995). Applying Conversation Analysis to Aphasia: Clinical Implications and Analytic Issues. *European Journal of Disorders of Communication*, *30*, 372–383.

Sacks, H. (1984). On Doing "Being Ordinary." In John M. Atkinson & J. Heritage (Eds.), *Structure of Social Action: Studies in Conversation Analysis* (pp. 413–440). Cambridge: Cambridge University Press.

Schegloff, E. A. (1972). Sequencing in Conversational Openings. In J. J. Gumperz & Dell H. Hymes (Eds.), *Directions in Sociolinguistics; The Ethnography of Communication* (pp. 346–380). New York: Holt, Rinehart and Winston.

Schegloff, E. A. (1979). The Relevance of Repair to Syntax-for-Conversation. In T. Givon (Ed.), *Syntax and Semantics 12: Discourse and Syntax* (pp. 261–286). New York: Academic Press.

Schegloff, E. A. (1982). Discourse as an Interactional Achievement: Some Uses of "Uh Huh" and Other Things that Come Between Sentences. In D. Tannen (Ed.), *Georgetown University Roundtable on Language and Linguistics*, *93*, 71–93.

Schegloff, E. A. (1987). Some Sources of Misunderstanding in Talk-in-Interaction. *Linguistics*, *25*, 201–218.

Schegloff, E. A. (1992). Repair after Next Turn: The Last Structurally Provided Defense of Intersubjectivity in Conversation. *American Journal of Sociology*, *97*, 1295–1345.

Schegloff, E. A., Jefferson, G., & Sacks, H. (1977). The Preference for Self-Correction in the Organisation of Repair in Conversation. *Language*, *53*, 361–382.

Schiffrin, D. (1988). Conversation Analysis. In J. Frederick (Ed.), *Linguistics: The Cambridge survey* (pp. 251–276). Cambridge: Cambridge University Press.

Wilkinson, R. (1995). Doing "Being Ordinary": Aphasia as a Problem of Interaction. In M. Kersner & S. Pepe (Eds.), *Work in Progress*, Vol. 5. London: Department of Human Communication Science, UCL.

Wirz, S., Skinner, C., & Dean, E. (1990). *Revised Edinburgh Functional Communication Profile*. Tucson, Arizona: Communication Skill Builders.

7

MINNA LAAKSO

Collaborative Construction of Repair in Aphasic Conversation

An Interactive View on the Extended Speaking Turns of Persons with Wernicke's Aphasia

The typical feature of Wernicke's aphasia is fluent but erroneous speech. Speakers with Wernicke's aphasia make phonemic errors (in Finnish, they say the word *herkku* [delicacy] instead of *serkku* [cousin], for example) and blend semantically close words (in Finnish, *poika* [son] instead of *isä* [father], for example). Thus, although they speak at a quite normal speaking rate, sounds shift and words blend in their speech. Sometimes whole utterances consist of neologisms, non-existing words that sound like but are not words of the speaker's language. Due to the problems with proper content words, they also may adopt a strategy to use very general or less accurate words that are easy to produce without errors. These speech errors, combined with the speech comprehension difficulties typical of Wernicke's aphasia, obviously cause difficulty in conversational interaction.

Wernicke's aphasics typically produce quite long turns at talk. Plentiful speech and extended speaking turns are considered characteristic of Wernicke's aphasia, that is, a symptom of the speaker's linguistic disorder (Goodglass & Kaplan, 1983). Accordingly, the speech of Wernicke's aphasics has been mostly studied from a framework that focuses on phenomena internal to the speaker (e.g., Buckingham, 1990; Butterworth & Howard, 1987; Ellis, Miller, & Sin, 1983; Miller & Ellis, 1987). In contrast to this view, this analysis will show how the extended turns of Wernicke's aphasics are generated in interaction with other people. What appears to be a single long turn is, in fact, a product of interaction in which the interlocutor is a crucial co-participant.

This chapter applies the analysis of repair organization developed by Schegloff, Jefferson, and Sacks (1977) to aphasic conversational data. For Schegloff et al., repair is a conversational activity that deals with recurrent problems in speaking, hearing, or understanding: Various speech errors form potential problems for mutual understanding between participants and are dealt with sequentially through organized repair practices. As the problems of speaking and understanding are definitional of Wernicke's aphasia, the study of repair appears relevant to the study of conversation of Wernicke's aphasic speakers. In particular, I will examine occasions when the aphasic speaker makes an error, tries to self-repair it, and has difficulty in finding the appropriate words to do the actual repair.

When aphasic speakers get into trouble with repairing their speech problems, the interlocutors can either join in the repair activity or withdraw from working out the difficulty. Interlocutors' different responses have consequences for not only the success or failure of the repair but also the structure of the talk produced by the person with aphasia. If the interlocutors do not collaborate, the aphasic speakers must repair the problems alone. Thus, despite the similarity of aphasic speech problems, conversations will take different courses: the problem may be solved collaboratively by the actions of the interlocutor, or the aphasic speaker may extend his or her speaking turns in repeated attempts to resolve the problem. The production of extended speaking turns is thus interactive, rather than a simple manifestation of the underlying cognitive deficit that produced the aphasia.

Database

Conversations of two Finnish aphasic speakers, Akseli and Aarno, were analyzed (see table 7.1). The names of all speakers are invented. To make it easier for the reader, aphasic speakers' names begin with the letter A. The names of the therapists begin with the letter T, and the name of the spouse with the letter S.

TABLE 7.1. The Conversations and Participants

Conversation 1		
Place: a speech therapy room at a hospital		
Duration: 17 minutes		
Participants:		
Akseli	Tero	Saara
Male Wernicke's aphasic	Male speech therapist	Akseli's wife
66 years old	35 years old	In her sixties
Conversation 2		
Place: a speech therapy room at an outpatient rehabilitation clinic		
Duration: 15 minutes		
Participants:		
Aarno	Tarja	
Male Wernicke's aphasic	Female speech therapist	
63 years old	31 years old	

TABLE 7.2. The Information on the Aphasic Speakers' Illness

	Aarno	*Akseli*
Etiology	Cerebral infarct	Cerebral infarct
Lesion location	Large left temporal parietal lesion	Left frontal parietal and parietal-occipital lesion
Duration of illness	2 months	3 months

The conversations were videotaped in speech therapy settings, and they took place in the beginning of a therapy session. Akseli was visiting his speech therapist together with his wife Saara, so there were three participants in the conversation. Aarno was talking with his speech therapist Tarja. In both conversations, the topics discussed were recent events that had occurred after the previous session.

Both aphasic speakers had the aphasia as a result of a cerebral infarct in their posterior left-brain hemisphere (see table 7.2). The posterior location is typical of Wernicke's aphasia (Damasio, 1981; Naeser et al., 1987). Both aphasic speakers were still in the acute stage of their illness: Aarno had suffered the cerebral accident 2 months and Akseli 3 months before.

The two aphasic speakers were identified as Wernicke's aphasics (see table 7.3 for the aphasia test results). According to the performance in the test, Aarno was severely impaired in his speech comprehension skills, whereas Akseli had a less severe comprehension deficit. However, in conversation their comprehension problems did not appear as severe. They both had serious problems in repetition and naming tasks as well. As a whole, Aarno's test results show somewhat more grave impairment than Akseli's results.

Both speakers had erroneous fluent speech typical of Wernicke's aphasia. They made phonemic and semantic speech errors but also used general or less accurate words instead of more informative content words. They produced neologisms mainly as the result of a search for more accurate words. The adoption of a strategy to use general, easy words and the production of neologisms only after several attempts at an appropriate expression suggest that they were aware, at least to some extent, of their speech problems and tried to avoid and repair errors. In fact, fluent aphasic

TABLE 7.3. The Test Performance of the Aphasic Speakers

	Aarno	*Akseli*
Type of aphasia	Wernicke	Wernicke
Overall score (maximum 100)	19.8	45
Comprehension score (maximum 10)	0.6	3.6
Repetition score (maximum 10)	0.8	2.8
Naming score (maximum 10)	0.3	2.0
Severity of aphasia (maximum 5)	1	1

speakers are more aware of their speech difficulties than traditionally has been thought (Laakso, 1997).

Two main excerpts, "the heart beat adjustment" from the conversation between Akseli, Tero, and Saara, and "the means of transportation" from the conversation between Aarno and Tarja, are analyzed here in more detail. The transcripts of the two excerpts in their whole length are in the appendix. In the transcription, the talk of each person is depicted on three lines (see Example 1).

Example 1

```
        T____ , , , looks at his sides              . . . S_____ , , ,
Akseli: ja sit *.h menih- (1.0) * kui mää sanaa osasi *sen ku meni se ruo-*
        and then      go-PST         how  I    word-PAR can-CON it-ACC when go-PST it ?{food}
        and the*n .h it went- (1.0) *how could I word it *when it went that foo-*
               * POINTS TO THE FLOOR *                     * PRODS AT HIS WIFE *
        (T___ = looks at Tero; S___ = looks at Saara; , , , = moves gaze away from a recipient;
        . . . = moves gaze toward a recipient; * = a mark for the beginning and end of a
        gesture)
```

Each chunk of three lines is read as follows: the first line is the original Finnish talk (in bold), the second line is the English word-by-word gloss (in smaller font size), and the third line is the translation into English (in italics). Speaker's gaze toward the recipient is marked with a line above the transcript of the spoken utterance. The notation of gaze follows the transcription convention developed by Goodwin (1981). Gestures are indicated below the three-line transcript. No specific symbols are used in the notation of gestures.

The organization of repair in aphasic conversation

A repair sequence consists of some problem (the trouble source), optionally followed by a repair initiation and a repair (Schegloff et al. [1977]; see fig. 7.1). As can be seen in figure 7.1, repair sequences can take different courses from the initiation to the outcome. Most commonly the speaker immediately initiates repair when the speech problem arises by interrupting their ongoing speech (this is referred to as a self-initiation, see A in fig. 7.1). However, if the speaker does not initiate repair, the recipient can do it in the next turn by making a clarification request (this is called other initiation, see B in fig. 7.1).

According to Schegloff, Jefferson, and Sacks (1977), self-repair is structurally preferred (see the outcome of the repair in A in fig. 7.1). Furthermore, interlocutors usually initiate repair with questions that let the speaker do the actual repair (see the outcome in B). As a whole, in ordinary conversation, the system of repair operates within a few turns in the immediate environment of the trouble source (Schegloff, 1992). Sequences like C and D are less frequent in ordinary conversation between normal

A. SELF-INITIATED SELF-REPAIR
    TURN 1   S: A chair—no, I mean the table.

B. OTHER-INITIATED SELF-REPAIR
    TURN 1   S: A chair. ((points at a table))
    TURN 2   R: What?/A chair?
    TURN 3   S: A table.

SELF-INITIATED OTHER-REPAIR
TURN 1   S: A chair—no, ((points at a table))
TURN 2   R: A table.
TURN 3   S: Yes.

OTHER-INITIATED OTHER-REPAIR
TURN 1   S: A chair. ((points at a table))
TURN 2   R: You mean a table.

FIGURE 7.1. Different types of repair sequences. (S = speaker of the problem turn; R = recipient of the problem turn)

speakers. However, in conversations between native and non-native speakers, interlocutors often repair on the behalf of the less competent speakers (e.g., Juvonen, 1989).

Finnish fluent aphasic speakers use the same means to self-initiate repair as non-aphasic Finnish speakers (Laakso, 1997: 129). In addition to common repair initiators such as a cut-off, a pause, and a sound stretch, Finns use particles *ei* ("no"), *eiku* (approximately "no+but" or "no, I mean"), *tai* ("or") and *siis* (approximately "I mean") (see also Sorjonen, 1997). Example 2 presents self-initiated repairs by a normal and an aphasic Finnish speaker.

Example 2 (/word/ = problematic word; {target} = potential target of the erroneous word)
(NS = normal speaker)
1 NS: **tää oli:↑ (1.4) /Mendels-sonin/ (0.9) >ei↑ku Gustav (.) Gustav Maalerin<**

      this was   2name+GEN   no I mean 1name   1name   2name(Mahler)

      this wa:s ↑ (1.4) /Mendels-son's/ (0.9) >no I mean Gustav (.) Gustav Mahler's<
2   **(.) sinfonia numero yks.**
    (.) symphony number one.
(AS = aphasic speaker)
1 AS: **ei mulla enää   muita   ku /isä/ (0.2) Eiku tuo /poika/ °ei poika**

      NEG I-ALL anymore other-PL-PAR than   father   no+but that son   NEG son

      no I don't have any other than /father/ (0.2) no I mean a /son/ not a son
2   **voi voi (1.9) tää /velä/ (.) veli.**

      oh oh   this {veli=brother} brother

      oh dear (1.9) this {brother} (.) brother.

As can be seen from example 2, the aphasic speaker self-initiates repair and locates an aphasic error as a repairable. She tries to self-repair but has difficulty in completing the repair, in finding a word to replace the aphasic word. Although the practices of initiating repair can be preserved, Wernicke's aphasics have difficulty in accomplishing a proper outcome. The difficulty is obviously due to the aphasic problems in producing appropriate content words. Thus, instead of making an immediate self-repair, Wernicke's aphasics often end up searching for words (about this practice, see Laakso, 1997: 134–135). This problem appears also when the interlocutor makes an other initiation: the aphasic speaker has problems in providing the answer, and thus completing the repair. The situation of aphasics shows that there are in fact consequential differences between the different stages of repair. By initiating repair, the aphasics being examined here show that they recognize that something is wrong, but they frequently lack the more detailed linguistic capacities required to right this wrong.

Furthermore, if the aphasic makes a self-repair, it is often done in an aphasic manner with distorted or general words that may call forth other subsequent repair actions either by the aphasic or by the co-participant(s). As a consequence, repairs are extended from the turn where the problem emerged into several succeeding speaking turns, and the possible outcome to the repair becomes sequentially achieved. Compared to the repairs of non-aphasic speakers that maximally occupy a few turns, repairs in aphasic conversation are longer.

Collaboration in the repair of aphasic errors

In the presence of aphasic difficulty, conversation can be co-constructed by the non-aphasic (Goodwin, 1995; Wilkinson, 1995) or other aphasic (Klippi, 1996) participants. In previous studies, co-construction has been found to occur in connection with non-fluent aphasia. It is suggested that the telegraphic speaking style used by non-fluent aphasics invites the interlocutors to co-construct the talk together with the aphasic speaker (Heeschen & Schegloff, 1999). Non-aphasic interlocutors have also been observed to take part in repairing aphasic word retrieval problems by offering words for aphasics (Ferguson, 1992; Laakso & Klippi, 1999; Milroy & Perkins, 1992; Oelschlaeger, 1999).

Word searches can be constructed in a way that provides a possibility for the recipients of talk to take part in the search. Goodwin and Goodwin (1986) describe a range of practices used by both speakers and recipients to co-construct the activity of searching for a word. Speakers typically withdraw their gaze from the recipient when the search begins and may also show a "thinking face" expression. Recipients interpret the withdrawal as a sign that, though not speaking, the speaker has not relinquished the floor but is engaged in the activity of searching for a word and does not want to be interrupted. On seeing this, recipients begin to attend to the activity of searching in an enhanced way and frequently shift their gaze and orientation to the speaker. On the

Picture 1   Picture 2

FIGURE 7.2 Akseli and Saara in a word-finding problem

other hand, if the speaker gazes at a recipient during a search in progress, this is inter-preted as an invitation to take part in the search. Thus, the actions of the speaker during a word search direct the recipients either to actively help in the search or to allow the speaker time to search the word herself. The recipient's attention, while not trying to claim the floor, is in itself a structured form of participation.

The practice of appealing to a recipient can be seen in the following word search (see example 3). Akseli is telling the speech therapist Tero about his heart beat ad-justment operation (besides his stroke, he has a heart condition) that had taken place a couple of days before the current therapy session. While he is telling the story, he looks at the therapist. But, when he encounters word-finding problems, he first with-draws his gaze from the therapist, looks forward with a thinking face (see frame grab 1), and then turns his gaze to his wife and prods at her (see frame grab 2). Akseli's gaze is marked above and Saara's gaze below Akseli's utterance.

Example 3

          raises head with gaze withdrawn
                    |
          T___, , looks his sides ↓ THINKING FACE . . S_____

1 Akseli: **ja sit *.h menih- (1.0) *kui mää sanaa osasi*sen[>ku meni se ruo-<***
         and then   go-PST   how I word-PAR can-PST it-ACC when go-PST-3 it {food}
         and then .h it went-(1.0) how could I word it >when it went foo-<
            * POINTS TO THE FLOOR *   * PRODS AT HIS WIFE *
                                    [
  _____, , [looks at the floor
2 Saara: **[meniks ne kaikki tuonne**
                                go-PST-Q they all   there
                                [did they all go there
                                [* POINTS TO THE FLOOR *
Note: Akseli and Saara, but not the therapist, are shown in the video clips.

Akseli begins with a continuation to his story: "and then went" (line 1). However, he does not continue smoothly but pauses and motions downward. After that he briefly displays a thinking facial expression (see picture 1 in figure 7.2). With these three actions, the activity of word searching becomes visible to the co-participants. After the pause, he makes the search explicit with a question *kui mää sanaa osasi sen* ("how could I word it," line 1). During the question, he turns his gaze to his wife (see picture 2). This practice of turning toward someone who shares knowledge of what is being searched for is a common practice of ordinary conversation. Goodwin (1987) has noted that in multi-party conversation speakers may withdraw their gaze from one recipient as the search is initiated, but then move it to a 'knowing recipient' who might help in the search. As Saara knows what had happened in the heart beat adjustment, she is a knowing recipient, a person in a position to help recover the next events in the story. Besides gazing at Saara, Akseli also prods her with an index finger (see picture 2), which further intensifies his appeal for her help. Saara reacts immediately to Akseli's appeal: she asks a question ("did they all go there") and also repeats Akseli's gesture of pointing toward the floor. By doing this, she attempts to clarify what Akseli was striving at with his preceding actions. Thus, Saara uses the participation framework provided by Akseli's gaze to her and actively co-participates in the search.

If the aphasic speaker appeals for the co-participation of recipients during a word search, the recipients will likely respond to the appeal by offering an outcome to the search. Like first pair parts, a request for help/co-participation creates a slot where a lack of such help can be discovered as something that Schegloff (1968) has called a noticeable absence. In example 4, Aarno appeals to his speech therapist Tarja as Akseli did to his wife (see picture 4 in fig. 7.3). However, Tarja does not respond to the request for help.

Picture 3   Picture 4

FIGURE 7.3 Aarno and Tarja in conversation

Example 4

7 Aarno: **mutta siin on nyt kyllä että: (0.2) mul on nyt< (0.5)**

       but   there is now indeed that   I-ADE is now

       but it is now really so that: (0.2) now I have< (0.5)

8   **vaimo olla mukana tuolla et me käydään /askelmalla/**

         wife   be-INF along   there   PRT we visit-PAS-4 footstep-ADE

        the wife to be with me over there so we come with the /footstep/

                          3   4->

9 ->   **(0.2) <tai ton (0.8) °bus-°, SIIS ku PÄÄstään tänne,**

               or   that-GEN   ?{bus} PRT   PRT get-PAS-4   here+to

          (0.2) <or that (0.8) °bu-°, I mean as we get over here,

          4

             ((Aarno looks at Tarja during the pause; Tarja looks back))

10 ->   (1.8)   ((Aarno points at Tarja with the right hand and taps table))

11   **°tonne tilaan°, (0.6) ni päästään näkemään missä se on.**

       there+to space-ILL   PRT get-PAS-4 see-INF-ILL where   it be-3

      °to that space°, (0.6) so we get to see where it is.

Tarja is looking at Aarno all the time, and her gaze is not marked in the transcript. In line 9, after trying to accomplish an immediate self-repair, Aarno withdraws his gaze from Tarja and displays a searching activity during the expression "I mean when we get over here" (line 9). During the word "here" he turns back to Tarja and shifts his gaze to her. In addition, the word "here" is not produced with a final falling intonation but with a rising falling intonation, indicating that the utterance is not yet finished. After producing "here," Aarno pauses for 1.8 seconds (line 10). During the pause, he keeps looking at Tarja and also points at her with an index finger while simultaneously tapping the table. However, Tarja does not respond to this appeal, although she keeps looking back at Aarno. Her contribution remains noticeably absent. As a consequence, in line 11, Aarno himself continues the talk.

As can be seen in example 4, recipients do not necessarily respond to an invitation to take part in the search. Of course, the capability of different recipients to figure out what the aphasic speaker is trying to say can vary. The speech therapist obviously does not have a candidate resolution readily at hand. She is not a knowing recipient who has shared background knowledge with the aphasic speaker. However, she could have made a clarification request in the same way as the wife in example 3, or she could have offered alternatives by asking whether he comes by bus/tram/underground/taxi on the basis of common cultural knowledge. However, she takes a more passive role in the conversation. The behavior of the therapist may also reflect traditional speech therapy practices to prompt the aphasic to speak by himself or herself. Nevertheless, the lack of co-participation has quite remarkable consequences for the progression of the repair: the speaking turns of the aphasic speaker tend to extend.

The sequential analysis of repair trajectories: Differences in participation

The following analysis will exemplify how the extended talk of Wernicke's aphasics results from their frequent attempts to repair their errors and find the appropriate word. These repeated attempts emerge when the interlocutor ignores the aphasic speaker's appeals for help and does not take part in the repair activity. Depending on whether interlocutors collaborate or not, repair operations in my database take prototypically two different courses: a course in which the self-repair attempts of the aphasic speaker are pronounced and another in which the interlocutor collaborates in the resolution of the trouble. If the interlocutor takes part in the repair activity, sharing knowledge with the aphasic speaker seems to be crucial for a quick resolution of the problem.

In the following, repair in conversations of Akseli and Aarno will be examined. These two repair trajectories demonstrate common cases of practices in my data. In the first sequence (with Akseli), the wife actively co-participates and has a shared life history with Akseli. As a consequence, the repair resolution is fast. In the second sequence (with Aarno), the therapist does not actively take part in the repair. Characteristic for this interaction is the fact that the therapist does not possess the shared knowledge with the aphasic that would enable him or her to quickly resolve the trouble.

Co-participation and shared knowledge lead to a fast and successful repair

In example 5, repair is made in a cooperative manner and the resolution is fast. Furthermore, the aphasic speaker directly addresses the wife to invite her to take part in the word search. There are three participants—Akseli, his wife Saara, and the speech therapist Tero—in this interaction, but it is the wife who collaborates with the aphasic speaker.

Example 5 ((Akseli is looking at the speech therapist before this turn))

       T___, , looks his sides THINKING FACE . . S_____

1 Akseli: **ja sit *.h menih- (1.0) *kui mää sanaa osasi *sen [>ku meni se ruo-<***

        and then   go-PST   how   I word-PAR can-PST it-ACC   when go-PST-3 it {food}

        and then .h it went-(1.0) how could I word it >when it went foo-<

          * POINTS TO THE FLOOR *   *   PRODS AT HIS WIFE *

                                                     [

       _____, , [looks at the floor

2 Saara: **[meniks ne kaikki tuonne**

   ->   [go-PST-Q they all there

<pre>
                                          [did they all go there
                                          [* POINTS TO THE FLOOR *
          S___, , LOOKS FORWARD   THINKING FACIAL EXPRESSION
3 Akseli: eiku: MIkä se sana ku- (0.8) hrm::m (0[.4) ruokaa juo- .h
          no+but what it word when   food-PAR {juoma=a drink}
          no but WHAt is the word that- (0.8) hrm::m (0.4) food dri- .h
                                                   [
_____[__, , LOOKS FORWARD
4 Saara: [ei kai se ny- ei kai se ny VEri
  ->   NEG PRT it now NEG PRT it now blood
                                           [it sure not now- it sure not now

5   vo[inu olla
          can-PPC be
          couldn't be blood
             [
             [T___,.S__,.T_____
6 Akseli: [VER- *JUST sitä *just.
          {blood} right   that   right
          [BLO- JUST right that.
               *BEATS AIR *BEATS AIR
</pre>

(S___=Akseli's gaze to Saara, T___=Akseli's gaze to Tero, speaker gaze at recipients is marked above the speaker's talk, whereas recipient's (Saara's) gaze at the speaker is under speaker's talk)

Akseli begins with "ja sit meni" ("and then went," line 1) while simultaneously looking at and pointing downward to the floor. However, he pauses as he cannot immediately explicate what it is that "went." Then he comments on his word-finding difficulty ("how could I word it," line 1) and moves his gaze to his wife Saara (line 1). Besides gazing at his wife, Akseli also prods her with an index finger. By doing this, Akseli appeals for her help as a person who knows how the story may go (see example 3 for the details of this). Akseli's wife reacts to his appeal and asks a question ("did they all go there," line 2) and also points in the direction of the floor. Akseli rejects this, shifts his gaze away, and asks a self-directed search question "mikä se sana ku" ("what is the word that," line 3). He continues the search by saying "hrmm" and pausing (line 3). Simultaneously, Saara begins to offer an outcome to the search: "ei kai se ny-" ("it sure not now," line 4). As Akseli does not yet stop talking after the pause but produces some candidate repairs "ruokaa juo-" ("food {drink}"), the wife's utterance becomes overlapped. She, however, starts the overlapped expression again and produces a candidate repair "veri" ("blood," line 4) in a point where Akseli already has cut off his word recovery attempt. Akseli confirms with strong emphatic stress that this is the word he is searching for. Then he turns back to the speech therapist Tero to go on with telling of the story (line 6).

To conclude, here the aphasic speaker actively invites his wife to take part in the word search and the wife joins the search. She is also able to provide the missing word, "blood." This interaction resembles a repair sequence of non-aphasic conversation as the problem is resolved within a few speaking turns.

Lack of co-participation intensifies aphasic speaker's self-repair effort and extends his speaking turns

In this sequence, Aarno, a speaker with Wernicke's aphasia, both self-initiates the repair activity and makes several attempts at self-repairing. The sequence begins with two questions of Tarja, the speech therapist. The first question is how Aarno has managed to travel to the therapy (line 1), and Aarno has no difficulty in answering that he is doing fine with the traveling to the rehabilitation clinic (line 5). The second question concerns the means of transportation Aarno uses when is coming to the clinic (line 3). However, answering this question turns out to be problematic for Aarno, as it requires the usage of a proper noun: he should name the means of transportation he uses. However, he produces either paraphasic or very general words and cannot find a word to explicate the means of transportation by which he arrives at the speech therapy session (lines 8–11). Furthermore, he continues self-repair in the turns that follow.

Example 6a

1 Tarja: **mitenkä sä pääset tänne kulkemaan.**
           how-CLI you get-2   here+to go-INF-ILL
           how do you manage to travel here.

2   (0.8)

3 Tarja: **millä   kulkuneuvolla   tulet.**
           which-ADE means of transportation-ADE come-2
           what means of transportation do you use.

4   (1.3)

5 Aarno: **AI? (0.2) meil menee: yy °hyvin ni aika hyvin°.**
           PRT   we-ADE go-3   uh   well   PRT rather well
           OH? (0.2) we are doing: uh well yeah pretty well.

6   (0.3)

7 Aarno: **mutta siin on nyt kyllä että: (0.2) mul on nyt< (0.5)**
           but   there is now indeed that   I-ADE is now
           but it is now really so that: (0.2) now I have< (0.5)

8   **vaimo olla mukana tuolla et me käydään /askelma/lla**
           wife   be-INF along   there PRT we visit-PAS-4 /footstep/-ADE
           the wife to be with me over there so we come with the /footstep/

9   **(0.2) <tai ton (0.8) °bus-°, SIIS ku PÄÄstään tänne,**
                 or that-GEN ?{bus}   PRT PRT get-PAS-4 here+to
           (0.2) <or that (0.8) °bu-°, I mean as we get over here,

```
           _____ ((Aarno looks at Tarja during the pause; Tarja looks back))
10 =>      (1.8) ((Aarno points at Tarja with his left hand and taps the table))
           ─────────────────────────────────────────────────────────
11 =>      °tonne  tilaan°, (0.6) ni päästään näkemään missä se on.
           there+to space-ILL        PRT get-PAS-4   see-INF-ILL where  it  be-3
           °to that space°, (0.6) so we get to see where it is.
           _____ ((Aarno gazes at Tarja))
12 =>      (0.9)
13 Tarja:  °mjoo:o,°
           PRT
   ->      °myea:h,°
14         (0.5)
           ──────────────────,       · ·─────────────────────────────
15 Aarno:  me on käyty mut mä oon nyt ollu kuitenkin, (0.6) hyvin menny (0.3) läpi.
           we  is visit-PPC but  I   be-1 now  be-PPC anyway       well    go-PPC        through
           we have been to but now I have been anyway, (0.6) has gone well (0.3) through.
           _____ ((Aarno gazes at Tarja))
16 =>      (0.5)
17 Tarja:  joo+o.
           PRT
   ->      yea+ah.
18         (0.4)
           ──────────────────, , ,
19 Aarno:  °/omassuus/ ku    /näs/   /näs/°    nääs    he $Tai tol    al-$ (0.8) alhaal
              ?          when    ?        ?        PRT       or that-ADE  ?-        down-ADE
           °  ?          when {y'see} {y'see}° you see he $or there do-$ (0.8) down
                   · ·──────────────────────
20         siis (0.7) °senhän pitää tuolah.°
           PRT        it-ACC-CLI must  there
           I mean (0.7) °it has to there h.°
           _____ ((Aarno gazes at Tarja))
21         (0.5)
22 Tarja:  joo, mihis     asemalle te        tuutte,
           PRT  where+TO station-ALL you(PL)  come-2–PL
           yes, at which station do you come,
```

(___ = Aarno's gaze toward the therapist; Tarja's gaze is focused on Aarno all the time and has not been marked on the transcript)

After producing the paraphasic word (*askelma*, "a footstep," line 8) Aarno makes a self-repair attempt with the word *bussi* ("a bus") but cuts it off ("bus-," line 9). Then he tries to fix the trouble with a circumlocutory explanation ("I mean when we get here," line 9), to which he then invites Tarja to co-participate (see example 4 for the details of this). However, Tarja does not make the next sequential action invited by Aarno (line 10). At this poin, Tarja maintains Aarno's self-repair by withdrawing co-participation. Aarno makes another try with a silently pronounced place description and pauses. Again, although Aarno keeps gazing at Tarja during the pause (line 11), she doesn't take the next turn, and Aarno continues with a circumlocutory explanation ("so we get to see where it is," line 11) by which he ends his self-repair effort.

Besides not taking part in the word search when it is invited by the aphasic, the non-aphasic co-participant also delays the acknowledgment of the aphasic's turn completion and does not go on by making a sequentially relevant next move. In line 11, Aarno finishes the effort to self-repair: he both completes the turn with a falling intonation and keeps his gaze toward his recipient Tarja (see lines 16 and 21 for a similar practice). In lines 12–13, we can see that Tarja does not give a prompt and confident acknowledgment to Aarno's self-repair. She doesn't either explicitly request clarification or state that she didn't understand what Aarno meant. Furthermore, she does not continue the topic of the talk by producing a full topical turn. Instead, she responds with a considerable delay, producing her acknowledgment *joo* (appr. "yeah," line 13) in an insecure manner with a silent voice. In addition, she stretches the "joo" and produces it with a rising final intonation displaying a request, or more generally, a sign for the speaker to continue. This is also how Aarno interprets it, as he continues the same topic by restating the fact that, in any case, he has been doing well with the transportation (line 15). He treats Tarja's request merely as a sign to continue. At this point, if the interlocutor had been satisfied with it, his turn could have offered a compromise outcome to the troublesome search for the means of transportation. However, this is not the case.

Aarno's restatement about doing well with the transportation is acknowledged by Tarja with the token "joo," but this time with a falling intonation (line 17). Here "joo" treats the previous turn of Aarno as an unproblematic fact and even indicates that this issue is closure-relevant and already dealt with (about strategic usages of "joo," see Sorjonen, 1996). Again, however, Tarja does not use her possibility to produce a full turn at talk. In this way, she steers Aarno back to the track of elaborating the troublesome issue that wasn't resolved yet, that is, how he arrives at therapy (lines 19–20).

The multi-unit speaking turns of Aarno are in fact achieved by the actions (and the withdrawal of particular actions) of the non-aphasic participant (for a similar practice in ordinary conversation, see Schegloff, 1982). The long speaking turns can be due to a certain interactive pattern: the aphasic says something less clear and the interlocutor neither acknowledges it nor continues on the topic of the talk, which leads the aphasic speaker to repair and rephrase what he just had said. This pattern can be a characteristic feature of therapeutic interaction and not appear in everyday conversations with relatives or friends. Indeed, a goal of speech therapy is to get the aphasic speaker to speak and practice his own expression.

There is also a notable change in the therapist's non-verbal feedback pattern as the sequence develops: during Aarno's first answer (lines 5–8), the therapist nods confirmingly both when Aarno mentions that they are doing pretty well and when he says that he comes with his wife. After the self-repairing starts (line 9), the therapist's nodding ceases and does not emerge again in the sequence. The lack of tokens of recipiency may also enhance the aphasic's effort to self-repair: since the recipient does not give any token of understanding, the speaker continues to repair (see also Goodwin, 1980).

As the conversation continues (example 6b, lines 22–35), the therapist adopts a more active role and makes some clarification requests. However, the clarification requests are based on an interpretation that, unfortunately, happens to be wrong. She treats the means of transportation as already determined and asks a question assuming that Aarno uses the underground ("at which station do you come," line 22). It seems that she has interpreted the word *askelma* ("a footstep") as the word *asema* ("a station"). This causes confusion in the aphasic speaker and the clarification attempts fail (lines 24–37). Finally, the aphasic speaker self-completes the repair, although it takes time (lines 39–50).

Example 6b

22 Tarja: **joo, mihis   asemalle te   tuutte,**

PRT   where+TO station-ALL you (PL) come-2-PL

-> *yes, at which station do you come,*

23 (0.8)

---

24 Aarno: **mitäh?**

what h?

25 Tarja: **mihinkä   asemalle te   tulette?**

where+TO-CLI   station-ALL you(PL) come-2-PL

-> *at which station do you come?*

26 (2.7)

27 Aarno: °**<mistä:h(.) siis mistä mää°, se on nytte noin, (0.4)**

where+FROM   PRT where+FROM I   it is now   like that

°*from where(.) I mean from where I°, now it is so, (0.4)*

28 **sehä alkaa sillon+ku (0.2) sillon ku nää on sielä.**

it-CLI begins   then   when   then   when these are there

it y'know begins when (0.2) when these are there.

___, , ((looks first at Tarja and then withdraws gaze))

29 (2.1)

((looks forward with thinking face))

30 Aarno: °**sehä on (1.8) tossa te /soot-tema vuola/° (0.4) siis se on,**

it-CLI is   there+IN you(PL) ?   ?   PRT   it   is

°*y'know it is (1.8) there you / ? ? / ° (0.4) I mean it is,*

31 **(0.8) työaika/la/ (0.3) käydään ä- (.) sielä.**

work time+/?{during}/   go-PAS-4 ?-   there

(0.8) /{during}/ working hours (0.3) we go ?- (.) there.

32 (1.4)

33 Aarno: **ja sit tuun (0.4) kouluun tänne.**
           and then come-1   school-ILL here
           and then I come (0.4) here to school.
           ___ ((looks at Tarja))
34   (1.3)
35 Tarja: **mm, tuutteks   te   tohon Kampin, (1.0) [°asemalle°.**
           PRT come-2PL-Q-CLI you(PL) that+TO place-name-GEN   [station-ALL
->   *mm, do you come to that Kamppi,   (1.0) [°station°.*
                                                           [
           _____ , ,   [
36 Aarno: **[e:j ku (.) täähä on**
                                                    [NEG but   this-CLI is
                                                    [*no: but (.) y'know this is*

37   **(0.8) täähä alkaa sielä,**
                    this-CLI begins there
           (0.8) y'know this begins there,
38   (3.0)
                    ._____,
39 Aarno: **°voi voi on vaikee nyt° me ollaan siellä ihan (2.3) °mä en nyt muista**
           PRT PRT is difficult now   we be-PAS-4 there PRT   I NEG-1 now remember
           °oh it is difficult now° we are right there (2.3) °now I don't remember
41   **tossa noin mitenkä se tuo sanotaan°.**
           there+IN PRT how-CLI it   that say-PAS-4
           over there how do you say that°.
42   (0.5)
           . ._____, , , ((looks forward in the air with a thinking face))
43 Aarno: **.mt mut siis ku: # (2.2) se< (0.9)°/ty-ös/ tyypillinen a- alkaa siis°**
           but PRT when   it   ?   typical   begins PRT
           .mt but I mean when: (2.2) it< (0.9) °?-? typical b- begins I mean°
                      ((turns head forward))
           . . ._____, , , ((looks at the table))
44   **(3.0) °ehä mä muista nyt sit sanoa (.) (kyllä usein on) kyllä oikeen**
                   NEG-CLI I remember now then say-INF   PRT often is PRT   right
           (3.0) °well I don't now remember to say (.) (indeed often is) just right
           ((turns to Tarja))   ((turns face down))
           ((looks forward in the air))   ((looks at his watch))
45   **miten se on (mut sehä on)° <MU↑LLAHA >MEnee siinäh< *(0.7) *<MU↑LLAHA**
           how it is but it-CLI is   I-ADE-CLI   goes   there   I-ADE-CLI
           how it is (but it just is)° <IT↑ TAKES me there y'know (0.7) <TA↑KES y'know
           ((lifts face forward))   *((turns to his watch))*
           ((looks watch)). ._____
46   **melkeen #öö# (0.4) <kas- (.) ö siis TUOL alhaal ku< (0.6) AUTO VIE TUOla**
           almost   uh   ?-   I mean there down-ADE when   car takes
there
           nearly #uh# (0.4)?- (.) uh I mean THERE down when (0.6)a CAR TAKES THEre
           ((points at his watch with the index finger)) ((points at Tarja)) ((moves finger to the left))

——————————————————————————————, , ,

47   **yy (.) mä< ## siis tilaan sen tossa (.) <maksan sitte sen (0.3)**

     I   PRT order-1 it-ACC there+in   pay-1   then   it-ACC

uh (.) *I< ## so I order it there (.) <pay for it then (0.3)

((points behind his shoulder))   ((brings hand to watch and taps it))

((looks at his watch))

48   **siihen aikaan ni (0.5) SE VIE JUStii NOin öö (0.5) KAkskytä: (0.5)**

that-ILL time-ILL PRT   it takes just   about   twenty

at that time so (0.5) IT TAKES JUst ABout uh (0.5) TWEnty: (0.5)

((points at watch;   pointing at watch continued))

. . . ————————————————————————————————

49   **>vähä yli kakskyt minuuttia kö< (0.2) vei (.) tolla: (1.0)**

(a bit)   over twenty   minute-PAR   that   take-PST-3 that-ADE

>a bit over twenty minutes that< (0.2) it took (.) with that: (1.0)

((points at watch))   ((points aside))

50   **ku mä olin   täällä.**

when I   be-PST-1 here

when I was here.

((nods sideward aside))

51   (0.6)

52 Tarja: **mm.**

(_____ = Aarno gazes at his therapist Tarja , , = turns gaze away from the therapist .. = brings the gaze to the therapist)

In line 22, after making a quick acknowledgment with "joo," the therapist does not just stay waiting for the aphasic's contribution but asks a question ("at which station do you come"). However, for Aarno, this is not the resolution of the problem; in fact, it brings about more problems. Aarno displays this by requesting clarification ("what," line 24). After hearing the question again, Aarno produces a very long pause (line 26) and then silently asks himself where he comes from. He doesn't produce the sequentially relevant answer to Tarja's request and name a station. However, neither does he explicitly deny that he comes to a station. In this, his speech comprehension problems may play a role: to contradict Tarja's interpretation, he should be very sure about his own understanding.

Aarno does not acknowledge Tarja's suggestion that he comes to a station but tries to self-repair, again with rather general utterances ("now it is so," "this y'know begins when," "then when these are there," lines 27–28). During the second of these utterances, he shifts his gaze to Tarja, displaying orientation to her. In addition, he uses an expression that appeals to the co-participant, namely, *sehä* (it-CLI, meaning approximately "this you know"). He continues to gaze at Tarja during the pause (line 29). As Tarja does not respond, Aarno goes on with his attempts to self-repair (lines 30–33).

In line 35, after withholding all nodding or verbal acknowledgments and just gazing at Aarno, Tarja finally reacts with "mm" and asks "do you come to that Kamppi (1.0) °station°" now offering herself a candidate underground station as Aarno did not do so. After hearing the name of the station, Aarno instantly rejects the offer. However, he is not able to produce the very word that would immediately clarify the issue. Instead of simply saying "no but you know this is a taxi/tram/etc.," he has to pause ("no but y'know this is" [0.8], line 36). The core problem is that Aarno is not able to produce the crucial nouns that would clarify the issue. Thus, he can't clearly state that the frame is completely wrong: instead of asking questions about the station, the therapist should go back to the means of transportation issue that has not been solved yet (see also Goodwin [1995] for similar problems with frames in connection with non-fluent aphasia).

As the cooperative undertakings of Tarja do not help, the sequence ends in intensified self-repair efforts by Aarno, and the speech therapist withholds participation. Finally, Aarno himself finds a way to describe how he travels to therapy by a car that he orders and pays for (i.e., obviously a taxi) and that it takes him about twenty minutes to travel from home to the clinic (lines 45–48). Note in particular how Aarno raises his voice (both the volume and pitch, line 45) as he finds this way to accomplish his search for the means of transportation. However, Tarja acknowledges this only with a simple "mm" (line 52).

To conclude, in this sequence the efforts of the Wernicke's aphasic speaker to self-repair are pronounced. Orientation toward aphasic's self-management of the aphasic trouble is also maintained by the actions of the speech therapist when she withholds co-participation. What obviously also causes difficulty is that the therapist avoids requesting clarification immediately and does not state her inability to understand explicitly (although it may be displayed in her non-verbal behavior). Neither does she make it explicit that she has made an interpretation about the means of transportation or offer it first as a candidate understanding to ask confirmation for it (i.e., "do you come by underground"). Instead, she directly asks a question concerning the underground station that causes more problems. As a consequence, the resolution of the repair remains based on the aphasic's isolated ability to find a way to complete the repair with talk, gesture, or other devices. The aphasic speaker must then rely entirely on his own resources, instead of creating a situation where he could solicit and use the help of others.

Concluding remarks

In conversation with aphasic persons, collaboration of the non-aphasic participants is needed in order for the conversation to succeed. At least two underlying factors play into how interlocutors collaborate. The first is whether interlocutors use participation frameworks for collaborative management of aphasic problems. This becomes explicit in word searches in particular, as their organization as such makes recipients' collaborative actions possible. Second, recipients also differ in how much they share knowledge with the speaker, so that their ability to help varies. There can be quite different bases for this shared knowledge, including a common cultural knowledge (of places in a city) or a shared life history with the speaker (such as the spouses of aphasics have).

The length and construction of the repair sequence is shaped by the choices the interlocutors make about whether to join in the repair operation. The two sequences analyzed develop in different ways. There are two basic patterns. In the first, the interlocutor joins in solving the problem (example 5). The wife of the aphasic speaker provides the words for him. In the other pattern (example 6), the interlocutor orientates toward the self-repair of the aphasic speaker. This pattern may be due to an institutional practice, as the interlocutor is a speech and language therapist.

However, several reasons may account for the difference between examples 5 and 6. First, the wife in example 6 knows more about the recent experiences of her husband than the speech therapist in example 5 about his client. Second, the speech therapist acts differently: she withdraws co-participation and does not offer candidate solutions or ask clarification.

The two aphasic speakers whose conversations were analyzed have similar difficulties with finding content words. Due to these problems, their interlocutors cannot easily understand what they are trying to say. The repair efforts focus on searching replacements for too general, erroneous, or missing expressions. In this respect, aphasic conversations differ from ordinary conversations where repairs are essentially used in social-interactive functions (see Arminen, 1996; Goodwin, 1987).

In these data, the speech problems are the subject of the aphasic speaker's self-repair efforts: the aphasic speakers interrupt their speech after producing aphasic word forms and search for the correct word. This indicates ability to self-monitor one's own speech and a similar preference for self-repair as in ordinary conversation (as in Schegloff et al., 1977). However, the limited number of cases studied here does not imply that repair is always self-initiated by all Wernicke's aphasic speakers, as self-monitoring of one's own speech can sometimes fail, at least in the acute stage of Wernicke's aphasia.

On occasion, the aphasic speakers abandon the attempt to actually produce the crucial word and instead search for other resources that might communicate what they want to say, such as pointing at relevant things and providing talk that might give their addressees cues about the word sought. Thus, despite the inability to produce the critical word, the people with aphasia are doing active cognitive work to communicate what they want to say.

Furthermore, when the self-repair efforts fail, the interlocutors are invited to take part in the repair activity. Most often, this is done by shifting gaze toward or by pointing at the interlocutor. However, interlocutors such as speech therapists do not necessarily co-participate in the repair activity, even though they are invited to do so.

This finding contrasts with previous observations that interactions with competent and less competent speakers endorse other-repair as the resolution of the repair process (e.g., Milroy & Perkins, 1992; Norrick, 1991).

According to the observations just presented, the long speaking turns of the fluent aphasic speaker, as well as the complex repair sequences that arise, are not a constitutive feature of aphasic conversation as such but are brought about through practices of therapeutic interaction. It may be that the therapeutic practices are inclined to encourage patients to work out their speech problems on their own. Similarly, in second language instruction, repair activities tend to become long and complex when the focus is on teaching the language, not on sharing the substance of conversation (see Juvonen, 1989). However, one may discuss what would be a productive way to interact with an aphasic speaker and what should be the role of the therapist. Instead of eliciting speech, could therapy offer opportunities and practice in joint production of the ideas the aphasic speaker wants to communicate?

Appendix

"The means of transportation"; Aarno (aphasic)
and Tarja (speech therapist)

1 Tarja: mitenkä sä pääset tänne kulkemaan.
           how-CLI you get-2   here+to go-INF-ILL
           how do you manage to travel here.
2   (0.8)
3 Tarja: millä   kulkuneuvolla   tulet.
           which-ADE means of transportation-ADE come-2
           what means of transportation do you use.
4   (1.3)
                                    · ·_____
5 Aarno: AI? (0.2) meil menee: yy °hyvin ni aika hyvin°.
           PRT   we-ADE go-3   uh   well PRT rather well
           OH? (0.2) we are doing: uh well yeah pretty well.
6   (0.3)
7 Aarno: mutta siin on nyt kyllä että: (0.2) mul on nyt< (0.5)
           but   there is now indeed that   I-ADE is now
           but it is now really so that: (0.2) now I have< (0.5)
           ·_____
8   vaimo olla mukana tuolla et me käydään   askelmalla
           wife   be-INF along   there PRT we visit-PAS-4   footstep-ADE
           the wife to be with me over there so we come with the footstep
           _____, ,   · ·_____
9   (0.2) <tai ton (0.8) °bus-°, SIIS ku PÄÄstään tänne,
                   or that-GEN   ?{bus}   PRT PRT get-PAS-4 here+to

(0.2) <or that (0.8) °bu-°, I mean as we get over here,
_____ ((Aarno gazes at Tarja during the pause))
10   (1.8)   ((Aarno points at Tarja with his left hand and taps the table
with his right hand))

---

11   °tonne tilaan°, (0.6) ni päästään näkemään missä se on.
       there+to space-ILL   PRT get-PAS-4   see-INF-ILL where it   be-3
       °to that space°, (0.6) so we get to see   where it is.
12   (0.9)
13 Tarja: °mjoo:o,°
            PRT
            °myea:h,°
14   (0.5)
       _____,   · ·_____
15 Aarno: me on käyty mut mä oon nyt ollu kuitenkin, (0.6) hyvin menny (0.3) läpi.
            we is visit-PPPC but I be-1 now be-PPC anyway   well   go-PPC through
            we have been to but now I have been anyway, (0.6) has gone well (0.3) through.
16   (0.5)
17 Tarja: joo+o.
            PRT
            yea+ah.
18   (0.4)
       _____,,,
19 Aarno: °omassuus ku näs   näs° nääs   he $Tai tol al-$ (0.8) alhaal
            ?   when ?   ?   PRT   PRT that-ADE ?-   down-ADE
            ° ?   when {y'see} {y'see}° you see he $or there do-$ (0.8) down
       · ·_____
20   siis (0.7) °senhän   pitää tuolah.°
       PRT   it-ACC-CLI must there
       I mean (0.7) °it has to there h.°
21   (0.5)
22 Tarja: joo, mihis asemalle te   tuutte,
            PRT where+TO station-ALL you(PL) come-2-PL
            yes, at which station do you come,
23   (0.8)
       _____
24 Aarno: mitäh?
            what h?
25 Tarja: mihinkä   asemalle te   tulette?
            where+TO-CLI station-ALL you(PL) come-2-PL
            at which station do you come?
26   (2.7)
27 Aarno: °<mistä:h (.) siis mistä mää°, se on nytte noin, (0.4)
            where+FROM PRT where+FROM I it is now   like that
            °from where(.) I mean from where I°, now it is so, (0.4)

· ·———————————————————

28   sehä alkaa sillon+ku (0.2) sillon ku nää   on sielä.
      it-CLI begins then   when   then   when these   are there
      it y'know begins when (0.2) when these are there.
      __, , ((looks first at Tarja and then withdraws gaze))
29   (2.1)
      LOOKS FORWARD WITH THINKING FACE
30 Aarno: °sehä on (1.8) tossa te *soot-tema vuola*° (0.4) siis se on,
          it-CLI is   there+IN you(PL) ?   ?   PRT it is
          °y'know it is (1.8) there you ? ? ° (0.4) I mean it is,
31   (0.8) työaikala (0.3) käydään ä- (.) sielä.
                work time+?   go-PAS-4 ?-   there
          (0.8) {during} working hours (0.3) we go ?- (.) there.
32   (1.4)

· ·———————————————————

33 Aarno: ja sit tuun (0.4) kouluun tänne.
          and then come-1   school-ILL here
          and then (I) come (0.4) here to school.
34   (1.3)
35 Tarja: mm, tuutteks   te   tohon Kampin, (1.0)[°asemalle°.
          PRT come-2PL-Q-CLI you(PL) that+TO place-name-GEN [station-ALL
          mm, do you come to that Kamppi,   (1.0) [°station.°
                                                       [
36 Aarno: [e:j ku (.) täähä on
                                                       [NEG but   this-CLI is
                                                       [no: but (.) y'know this is
37   (0.8) täähä alkaa sielä,
                this-CLI begins there
          (0.8) y'know this begins there,
38   (3.0)

                                   ·————————,

39 Aarno: °voi voi on vaikee nyt° <me ollaan siellä ihan (2.3) °mä en nyt muista
          PRT PRT is difficult now   we be-PAS-4 there PRT   I NEG-1 now remember
          °oh no is difficult now° <we are right there (2.3) °now I don't remember
41   tossa noin mitenkä se tuo sanotaan°.
          there+IN PRT how-CLI   it   that say-PAS-4
          over there how do you say that°.
42   (0.5)
          · ·——————————, , ,LOOKS FORWARD IN THE AIR WITH CONCENTRATING FACIAL
          EXPRESSION . . .
43 Aarno: .mt mut <u>siis</u> ku: # (2.2) <u>se</u>< (0.9)°<u>ty</u>-ös <u>tyy</u>pillinen a- alkaa <u>siis</u>°(3.0)
                  but PRT when   it   ?   typical   begins PRT
          .mt but I mean when: (2.2) it< (0.9) °?-? typical b- begins I mean°(3.0)
                  TURNS HEAD FORWARD   TURNS a
          ———————————————————, , , LOOKS AT THE TABLE

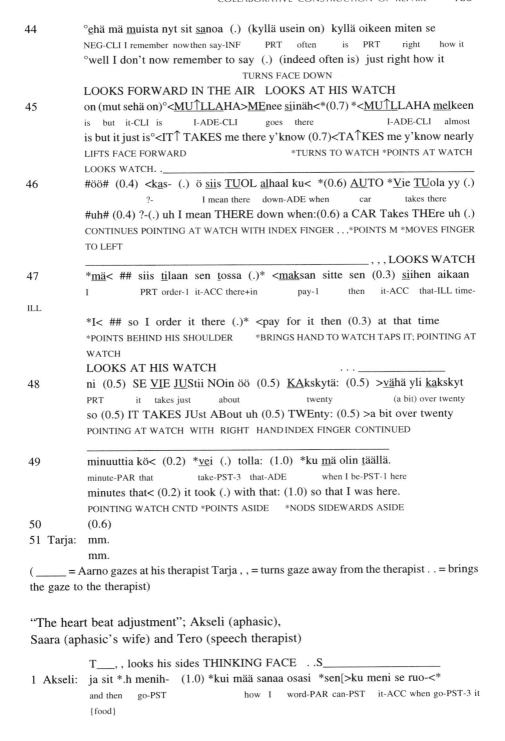

44   °ehä mä muista nyt sit sanoa (.) (kyllä usein on) kyllä oikeen miten se
NEG-CLI I remember now then say-INF   PRT   often   is   PRT   right   how it
°well I don't now remember to say (.) (indeed often is) just right how it
                                TURNS FACE DOWN
    LOOKS FORWARD IN THE AIR   LOOKS AT HIS WATCH

45   on (mut sehä on)°<MU↑LLAHA>MEnee siinäh<*(0.7) *<MU↑LLAHA melkeen
is but it-CLI is   I-ADE-CLI   goes there   I-ADE-CLI   almost
is but it just is°<IT↑ TAKES me there y'know (0.7)<TA↑KES me y'know nearly
LIFTS FACE FORWARD   *TURNS TO WATCH *POINTS AT WATCH
LOOKS WATCH. ._____

46   #öö# (0.4) <kas- (.) ö siis TUOL alhaal ku< *(0.6) AUTO *Vie TUola yy (.)
                 ?-   I mean there   down-ADE when   car   takes there
#uh# (0.4) ?-(.) uh I mean THERE down when:(0.6) a CAR Takes THEre uh (.)
CONTINUES POINTING AT WATCH WITH INDEX FINGER , , ,*POINTS M *MOVES FINGER
TO LEFT
_____ , , , LOOKS WATCH

47   *mä< ## siis tilaan sen tossa (.)* <maksan sitte sen (0.3) siihen aikaan
      I   PRT order-1 it-ACC there+in   pay-1   then   it-ACC that-ILL time-
ILL
    I< ## so I order it there (.) <pay for it then (0.3) at that time
    *POINTS BEHIND HIS SHOULDER   *BRINGS HAND TO WATCH TAPS IT; POINTING AT
    WATCH
    LOOKS AT HIS WATCH   . . . _____

48   ni (0.5) SE VIE JUStii NOin öö (0.5) KAkskytä: (0.5) >vähä yli kakskyt
    PRT   it takes just   about   (0.5) twenty   (a bit) over twenty
    so (0.5) IT TAKES JUst ABout uh (0.5) TWEnty: (0.5) >a bit over twenty
    POINTING AT WATCH WITH RIGHT HAND INDEX FINGER CONTINUED

_____
49   minuuttia kö< (0.2) *vei (.) tolla: (1.0) *ku mä olin täällä.
    minute-PAR that   take-PST-3 that-ADE   when I be-PST-1 here
    minutes that< (0.2) it took (.) with that: (1.0) so that I was here.
    POINTING WATCH CNTD *POINTS ASIDE   *NODS SIDEWARDS ASIDE
50   (0.6)
51 Tarja: mm.
          mm.
(_____ = Aarno gazes at his therapist Tarja , , = turns gaze away from the therapist . . = brings
the gaze to the therapist)

"The heart beat adjustment"; Akseli (aphasic),
Saara (aphasic's wife) and Tero (speech therapist)

       T___, , looks his sides THINKING FACE . .S_____
1 Akseli: ja sit *.h menih- (1.0) *kui mää sanaa osasi *sen[>ku meni se ruo-<*
         and then   go-PST   how I   word-PAR can-PST it-ACC when go-PST-3 it
         {food}

and then .h it went-(1.0) how could I word it >when it went foo-<
      * POINTS DOWNWARDS *   * PRODS AT HIS WIFE *

           [

_____, , [looks at the floor

2 Saara: [meniks ne kaikki tuonne

  ->   [go-PST-Q they all there

           [did they all go there

           [* POINTS TO THE FLOOR *

S___, , LOOKS FORWARD THINKING FACIAL EXPRESSION

3 Akseli: eiku: MIkä se sana ku- (0.8) hrm::m (0 [.4)ruokaa juo- .h

        no+but it word when   food-PAR {juoma=a drink}

        no but WHAt is the word that- (0.8) hrm: :m (0.4) food dri- .h

           [

_____[__, , LOOKS FORWARD

4 Saara: [ei kai se ny- ei kai se ny VEri

  ->   NEG PRT it   now NEG PRT it now blood

           [it sure not now- it sure not now

5   vo [inu olla

          can-PPC be

          couldn't be blood

          [

          [T___, .S__, .T_____

6 Akseli: [VER- *JUST sitä *just.

        {blood} right   that right

        [BLO- JUST right that.

           *BEATS AIR *BEATS AIR

(S___ = Akseli's gaze to Saara, T___ = Akseli's gaze to Tero, speaker gaze at recipients is marked above the speaker's talk, whereas recipient's (Saara's) gaze at the speaker is under speaker's talk)

Note

I am deeply grateful to Professor Charles Goodwin for his valuable comments on the manuscript of this chapter. This study was financially supported by the Research Council for Culture and Society of the Academy of Finland (project number 49250).

References

Arminen, I. (1996). On the Moral and Interactional Relevancy of Self-Repairs for Life Stories of Members of Alcoholics Anonymous. *Text*, *16*(4), 449–480.

Buckingham, H. (1990). Abstruse Neologisms, Retrieval Deficits and the Random Generator. *Journal of Neurolinguistics*, 5, 215–235.

Butterworth, B, & Howard, D. (1987). Paragrammatisms. *Cognition*, *26*, 1–37.

Damasio, H. (1981). The Cerebral Localization of the Aphasias. In M. T. Sarno (Ed.), *Acquired Aphasia* (pp. 27–50). New York: Academic Press.

Ellis, A., Miller, D., & Sin, G. (1983). Wernicke's Aphasia and Normal Language Processing: A Case Study in Cognitive Neuropsychology. *Cognition*, *15*, 111–144.

Ferguson, A. (1992). Conversational Repair of Word Finding Difficulty. In M. Lemme (Ed.), *Clinical Aphasiology* 21 (pp. 299–310). Austin, Texas: Pro-Ed.

Goodglass, H., & Kaplan, E. (1983). *The Assessment of Aphasia and Related Disorders*. 2nd ed. Philadelphia: Lea & Febiger.

Goodwin, C. (1981). *Conversational Organization*. New York: Academic Press.

Goodwin, C. (1987). Forgetfulness as an Interactive Resource. *Social Psychology Quarterly*, *50*, 115–131.

Goodwin, C. (1995). Co-Constructing Meaning in Conversations with an Aphasic Man. *Research on Language and Social Interaction*, *28*(3), 233–260.

Goodwin, M. H. (1980). Processes of Mutual Monitoring Implicated in the Production of Description Sequences. *Sociological Inquiry*, *50*(3–4), 303–317.

Goodwin, M. H., & Goodwin, C. (1986). Gesture and Co-Participation in the Activity of Searching for the Word. *Semiotica*, *62*(1/2), 51–75.

Heeschen, C., & Schegloff, E. (1999). Agrammatism, Adaptation Theory, Conversation Analysis. On the Role of the So-Called Telegraphic Style in Conversation. *Aphasiology*, *13*(4–5), 365–405.

Juvonen, P. (1989). Repair in Second-Language Instruction. *Nordic Journal of Linguistics*, *12*, 183–204.

Klippi, A. (1996). *Conversation as an Achievement by Aphasics*. Helsinki: Finnish Literature Society.

Laakso, M. (1997). *Self-Initiated Repair by Fluent Aphasic Speakers in Conversation*. Helsinki: Finnish Literature Society.

Laakso, M., & Klippi, A. (1999). A Closer Look at the Hint and Guess—Sequences in Aphasic Conversation. *Aphasiology*, *13*(4–5), 345–363.

Miller, D., & Ellis, A. (1987). Speech and Writing Errors in Neologistic Jargon Aphasia: A Lexical Activation Hypothesis. In M. Coltheart, G. Sartori, & R. Job (Eds.), *The Cognitive Neuropsychology of Language*. London: Erlbaum.

Milroy, L., & Perkins, L. (1992). Repair Strategies in Aphasic Discourse; Towards a Collaborative Model. *Clinical Linguistics & Phonetics*, *6*, 27–40.

Naeser, M., Helm-Estabrooks, N., Haas, G., Auerbach, S., & Srinivasan, M. (1987). Relationship Between Lesion Extent in Wernicke's Area on Computed Tomographic Scan and Predicting Recovery of Comprehension in Wernicke's Aphasia. *Archives of Neurology*, *44*, 73–82.

Norrick, N. (1991). On the Organization of Corrective Exchanges in Conversation. *Journal of Pragmatics*, *16*, 59–83.

Oelschlaeger, M. (1999). Participation of a Conversational Partner in the Word Searches of a Person with Aphasia. *American Journal of Speech-Language Pathology*, *8*, 62–71.

Schegloff, E. (1968). Sequencing in Conversational Openings. *American Anthropologist*, *70*, 1075–1095.

Schegloff, E. (1982). Discourse as an Interactional Achievement: Some Uses of "uh huh" and Other Things that Come Between Sentences. In D. Tannen (Ed.), *Georgetown University Roundtable on Languages and Linguistics* (pp. 71–93). Washington, DC: Georgetown University Press.

Schegloff, E. (1992). Repair After Next Turn: The Last Structurally Provided Defense of Intersubjectivity in Cconversation. *American Journal of Sociology*, *97*(5), 1295–1345.

Schegloff, E., Jefferson, G., & Sacks, H. (1977). The Preference for Self-Correction in the Organization of Repair in Conversation. *Language*, *53*, 361–382.

Sorjonen, M-L. (1996). On Repeats and Responses in Finnish Conversations. In E. Ochs, E. A. Schegloff, & S. A. Thompson (Eds.), *Interaction and Grammar* (pp. 277–327). Cambridge: Cambridge University Press.

Sorjonen, M-L. (1997). KorjausjäSennys. [Repair Organization]. In L. Tainio (Ed.), *Keskustelunanalyysin Perusteet* (pp. 111–137). Vastapaino: Tampere.

Wilkinson, R. (1995). Aphasia: Conversation Analysis of a Non-Fluent Aphasic Person. In M. Perkins & S. Howard (Eds.), *Case Studies in Clinical Linguistics* (pp. 271–292). London: Whurr.

8

JAN ANWARD

Own Words

On Achieving Normality through Paraphasias

Oh no, I've said too much
I haven't said enough

    R.E.M, "Losing My Religion"

As Harvey Sacks never tired of pointing out,[1] ordinary conversation holds its own measure of poetic language, in the sense of Jakobson (1960). Of course, this is pleasing to our self-esteem as practicing conversationalists, for poetic talk, unlike normal talk, is regarded as a fine achievement, something laudable and hard to come by. However, we should actually be as pleased with our capacity to produce pedestrian "normal" talk. As more than thirty years of Conversation Analysis have shown, normal talk is as much of an achievement as is out-and-out poetic talk.

Ordinary conversation can, in fact, become too poetic. If talk strays too far from the received stocks of linguistic resources on which normal talk about familiar topics in familiar activities typically relies, if "people begin to toss around old words in new senses, to throw in the occasional neologism, and thus to hammer out a new idiom," as Rorty (1991: 88) puts it, then words begin to stand out as words and meaning becomes problematic, for words thereby lose their character as transparent vehicles of meanings, which allow us to "hear meanings" in an almost unmediated fashion.

Compare, for instance, the standard greeting in example 1a, with the version of it in example 1b, to be found at the very beginning of the sixth chapter of James Joyce's *Finnegans Wake*.

Example 1
a. How do you do tonight, ladies and gentlemen?
b. Who do you no tonigh, lazy and gentleman?

Heard in the right kind of context, 1a would attract no attention at all, would be completely transparent to an immediately assimible meaning, and would get its work done in a swift and hardly noticeable way; 1b, in contrast, would attract attention to itself, its meaning would be a problem, and it would not get any practical work done, in almost any kind of context.

Thus, a balanced measure of normality needs to be achieved in conversation.

In this chapter, I will focus on a kind of aphasia that has precisely the effect of making people too poetic, making them toss around old words in new senses and throw in neologisms all the time. For such people, normality is particularly hard to come by. The purpose of this chapter is to compare two closely similar conversations, one in which normality is not achieved and one in which it is, to discern by which methods such people can, against tough odds, achieve a working normality.

A case in point

A woman in her seventies—call her Bernardina Höglund—who has suffered a hemorrhage in the left hemisphere of her brain and as a result has developed an aphasic condition, meets her speech therapist—call her Marianne—for a training session. As part of the training, Bernardina is asked to read a short story aloud and then retell it. However, the retelling does not go well and it ends on a note of failure:

Example 2 Bernardina I

Marianne:	hur gick de på slute då
Bernardina:	ja de va att han hade ramla me huv:et °först°
	((laughs)) nämen kan [du fatta
Marianne:	[ska vi ge oss då
Bernardina:	ja läste ju utan vidare då ju

(Marianne:	how did it end then
Bernardina:	yes it was that he fell with his head °first°
	((laughs)) no but can [you understand
Marianne:	[shall we stop it then
Bernardina:	I read without problems then you know)

A month later, Bernardina and Marianne meet again, and Bernardina is again asked to read the story aloud and then retell it. This time, the retelling is successful and is followed by a fairly elaborate and mutually reinforcing closing sequence:[2]

Example 3 Bernardina II

Bernardina:	äm ja i alla fall blev pojken ähh djupt skadad
	och:: de e klart de va en s en ban en bali otäck skola
	för pojken hade ramlat med huvet före
Marianne:	(pp)
	ja just de
Bernardina:	va de nå mer ((laughs))
Marianne:	[nä de va väl de va]

Bernardina:	[((laughs))]
Marianne:	[tyckte du att du fick me alltihopa]
Bernardina:	[((laughs))]
	va skadad
	de va ju kul på sätt å s också
	å de va ju nå rolit ju
Marianne:	ja de va en poäng där
Bernardina:	javisst de fanns en poäng ((lau[ghs))]
Marianne:	[((laug]hs))
	visst gjorde re de
(Bernardina:	ehm yes in any case the boy was ehh deeply injured
	and:: it is clear it was a s a ban a bali nasty school
	for the boy had fallen with his head first
Marianne:	(pp)
	that's right
Bernardina:	was there anything else ((laughs))
Marianne:	[no that was it]
Bernardina:	[((laughs))]
Marianne:	[do you think you got it all]
Bernardina:	[((laughs))]
	how injured
	it was nice in a way too
	and there was something funny
Marianne:	yes there was a point there
Bernardina:	sure there was a point ((lau[ghs))]
Marianne:	[((laug]hs))
	certainly there was

A tough case

The story that Bernardina is asked to read aloud and retell is reproduced in example 4. The story takes the form of a reported dialogue between a boy and a farmer, and thus consists of a number of units with the format of "X says Y."

> Example 4
> En pojke kom en dag inspringande på en bondgård
> och frågade om han kunde få låna en spade.
> När bonden undrade vad han skulle ha den till
> svarade pojken att hans bror hade ramlat i ett träsk
> och att han måste gräva upp honom.
> Hur djupt har han ramlat i, frågade bonden.
> Upp till vristerna, blev svaret.
> Men då kan han väl gå därifrån utan din hjälp,
> då behöver du väl ingen spade.

Pojken såg förtvivlad ut och sa:
Ja, men ni förstår han ramlade med huvudet först

(A severe fall / A tough case
A boy came one day running into a farm
and asked if he could borrow a shovel.
When the farmer wondered what he would use it for
the boy replied that his brother had fallen into a swamp
and that he had to dig him up.
How deep has he fallen into [the swamp], the farmer asked.
Up to the ankles, was the answer.
But then he surely can walk away from there without your help;
then you'll need no shovel.
The boy looked unhappy and said:
Yes, but you see he fell with his head first.)

A problematic start

In the first session, Bernardina reads the story aloud and then volunteers her name.

Example 5 Bernardina I
I1. Bernardina: de e [Bernardina Höradson]
I2. Marianne: [mm va fint] ja
I3. Bernardina: ((laughs)) tå blir de

(I1. Bernardina: it is [Bernardina Höradson]
I2. Marianne: [mm how fine yes]
I3. Bernardina: ((laughs)) so goes it)

Then, Marianne asks Bernardina to retell the story from memory, and Bernardina starts doing so, after some negotiation:

Example 6 Bernardina I
I4. Marianne: ska vi se om du kan berätta re där nurå
I5. Bernardina: så ska ja spela de utan
                 å de ska du ha på papper också
I6. Marianne: (pp) a vi prövar
                 (p) mm
I7. Bernardina: jaa (p) de va en otäck (p) skog (p) sega som skogale
                 ((lau[ghs))]
I8. Marianne: [((laug]hs))
                 va vare de handlade om

(I4. Marianne: let's see if you can tell that now
I5. Bernardina: so I'll play it without
                 and that you'll have on paper too

I6. Marianne: (pp) ok let's try
                   (p) mm
I7. Bernardina: weell (p) it was a nasty (p) forest (p) sega that skogale
                   ((lau[ghs))]
I8. Marianne: [(((laug]hs))
                   what was it it was about)

However, the retelling almost immediately crashes. The reason for this is not hard to
see. Let us look at I7 again, breaking it down more carefully into its parts:

Example 7   Bernardina I
I7. Bernardina: jaa (p)
                   de va en otäck (p)
                   skog (p)
                   sega som skogale .
                   ((laughs))

(I7. Bernardina: well (p)
                   it was a nasty (p)
                   forest (p)
                   sega that skogale.
                   ((laughs)))

After a normal, run-of-the-mill opening, consisting of a planning or hesitation marker
("jaa"),[3] followed by a routine presentational format ("de va en __"; ["it was a __"])
and a contextually reasonable adjective, "otäck" (nasty), fitted into that format, I7
becomes progressively more and more incomprehensible.

The next item is the noun "skog" (forest), which does not figure at all in the story,
but of course has some connection with the place nouns that do figure in the story,
"bondgård" (farm) and "träsk" (swamp). However, its combination with "otäck" is
quite unexpected, because it is the events, not the setting, of the story that can reasonably be glossed as nasty.

The final part of I7, "sega som skogale," is completely incomprehensible. The
word form "sega" exists in Swedish; it is the singular definite or plural form of the
adjective "seg" (tough). However, in I7, sega is used as a noun, as evidenced by the
relative clause opening (som) that follows it. In Swedish, adjectives can be used as
nouns, provided that a "real" noun can be inferred from the context, as in example 8.

Example 8 (Speaking of candy)
         De sega smakar bättre än de mjuka
         (the tough tastes better than the soft)
         ("The tough ones taste better than the soft ones")

In I7, however, no plural noun can be inferred, so sega can only be interpreted as a
nonsense noun, homonymous to a form of the adjective seg.

The relative clause in the final part of I7 comes out even worse. After som, one would expect a finite verb, but skogale is not a Swedish verb form. There is no verb "skoga" in Swedish, and there are no Swedish verb forms ending in -ale. It would actually be possible to coin a verb skoga (meaning "to forest") in Swedish, which would have the past tense form "skogade"—with *d* instead of *l*—but it is not easy to figure out what sense something like "forested" would make in the context.

It is highly probable—but impossible to demonstrate conclusively—that sega som skogale is an attempted repair of "otäck skog." Both expressions are noun phrases and the format ("de va en"; "it was a __") allows just one noun phrase to fill its variable slot.

Bernardina ends skogale on a falling intonation, thus marking it as a self-contained unit. Then she starts laughing. As Marianne picks up the laughter, and then lets it develop into a request for a repair, it is not unreasonable to hear Bernardina's laughter as a kind of comment on the strange way in which I7 came out.

This anlysis is further supported by the similar ending of the name sequence in example 5, where Bernardina's failure, in I1, to pronounce her own name correctly is followed in I3 not only by a laughter but also by an explicit comment on the way she just pronounced her own name.

Wernicke problems

Bernardina's problem in I7 is best understood as an inability to complete the presentation format ("de va en __") with a received and relevant content word.

Bernardina shares this problem of not being able to fit a received and relevant word or phrase into a chosen frame with other people who have suffered insults to Wernicke's area in the left hemisphere of their brain and as a result have acquired aphasia.

No content words

At one extreme, this kind of aphasia results in speech completely lacking in content words. In example 8, for example, Sonja (S) is using the format "di skulle __"—a not uncommon format for reporting on previous treatment—but fails to fit anything more specific than the auxiliary verb "göra" (do) and the pronouns "de" (neuter it, that) and "den" (non-neuter it, that) into that format.

Example 9 Vislund
V1. Therapist: va (p) va gjorde ni för någonting
V2. Sonja: jaa hon gick (p) ää di skulle ju göra (p) eeh (p) me själva
                 [de]
                 [((points to right leg))]
V3. Therapist: benet?

V4. Sonja:	net (p) på mej
V5. Therapist:	mm
V6. Sonja:	å så själva (p)
	[den]
	[((points to right arm))]
V7. Therapist:	armen ja han
V8. Sonja:	alla gånger vet du ff

(V1. Therapist:	what (p) what did you do
V2. Sonja:	well she went (p) eeh they.were.going.to do (p) eeh (p) with the very
	[that]
	[((points to right leg))]
V3. Therapist:	the leg?
V4. Sonja:	eg (p) on me
V5. Therapist:	mm
V6. Sonja:	and then the very (p)
	[that]
	[((points to right arm))]
V7. Therapist:	the arm yes he
V8. Sonja:	all times you know ff)

However, Sonja compensates for her unspecific words by pointing first to her right leg and then to her right arm, thus inducing her speech therapist to engage in supporting other-repairs, in V3 and V7, of a kind analyzed in detail by Charles Goodwin (1995).

Such repairs typically involve the following steps:

1. Aphasic says something, s
2. Other proposes a more specific formulation of s, s'
3. Aphasic accepts or rejects s'

These repairs amount to the co-construction of a turn that in the end is heard as being meant by the aphasic. Thus, through V6, V7, and V8, Sonja is heard as having meant "and then the arm."[4]

Paraphasias

At the other extreme, we find aphasics such as Bernardina, who produce fluent speech with what appears to be a normal measure of content words. However, a surprising number of these content words are "strange": either neologisms, such as skogale in I7 or contextually inappropriate received words, such as skog in I7.

Such strange words are known as *paraphasias* in the aphasiological literature. Lesser (1978: 187) contains a well-known classification of paraphasias. Lesser's first distinction is between "dictionary words" and "not dictionary words," that is, between word forms that "belong" to the language used and word forms that do not belong to that language. In B7, skog is a dictionary word, and skogale is not. The classification of sega is slightly problematic, but as I argued, sega is best understood as a word not in the dictionary but homonymous to a dictionary word.

Lesser's second distinction is between "target word identifiable" and "no target word identifiable." A target word is a form that the analyst assumes the speaker would have produced instead of a strange word, had he or she had access to it. A target word is inferrable from an actual word form if it is sufficiently similar to the actual word form phonologically, morphologically, or semantically. If the actual word is not a dictionary word, only phonological similarity is held to be relevant.

Skog, sega, and skogale all belong to the category of "no target word identifiable." There are no obvious sound-alikes or mean-alikes that could be substituted for skog, sega, and skogale in B7 and "rescue" the sense of that turn.

An instance of "target word identifiable" can be found in example 10.

Example 10   Petra I
PI1. Petra: javisst ja (p)
                 de där en d<u>a</u>r [också]
PI2. Therapist: [d<u>är</u> är] också en ja

(PI1. Petra: right (p)
                 there this one 'th<u>a</u>re' [too]
PI2. Therapist: [th<u>ere</u> is] one too yes)

The speech therapist's response to Petra, in P2, is cast in a normal echo format, which allows us to identify Petra's utterance "de där en dar också" as a slightly distorted version of "de är en där också."

In contrast to skog, sega, and skogale, där and dar are thus words from which target words can be inferred: they are phonological distortions of är and där, respectively.

When we combine Lesser's two distinctions, we get four basic types of paraphasia, as shown in table 8.1.

Dictionary words from which target words can be inferred are instances of *verbal paraphasia*, while dictionary words from which target words cannot be inferred, such as skog, are instances of *semantic jargon*. Words that are not dictionary words, but from which target words can be inferred, such as dar, are instances of *phonemic paraphasia*, while words that are not dictionary words and from which no target words can be inferred, such as skogale, are instances of *neologistic jargon*.

TABLE 8.1. Four Basic Types of Paraphasia

Paraphasia	Dictionary word	Not dictionary word
Target word identifiable	VERBAL PARAPHASIA	PHONEMIC PARAPHASIA
No target word identifiable	SEMANTIC JARGON	NEOLOGISTIC JARGON

Verbal paraphasia is then further subdivided into formal verbal paraphasia and semantic verbal paraphasia, depending on whether inference of a target word is based on formal similarity (e.g., dar → där) or semantic similarity (e.g., no → yes or boy → girl).

Repair

Wernicke's aphasics of Bernardina's type are not necessarily helped by repairs.[5] Unlike aphasics of Sonja's type, who fail to make their turns specific enough, thus flouting Grice's First Maxim of Quantity (Grice, 1975), Bernardina and people like her say too little and too much at the same time. They produce all the time repairable content words, with unclear meanings, but attempted repairs of such words may result only in other equally repairable content words. This holds both for self-repair, as I7 shows, and for other-repair, as can be seen from PI13 in example 11, where Petra, instead of accepting the therapist's word *blåbär* (blueberry), substitutes the eminently repairable nonce-word *pölsul* for it.

Example 11 Petra II

PII1. Petra:	och (p) det här är
PII2. Therapist:	blåbär tycker ja de ser ut so[m::]
PII3. Petra:	[ja] (p)
	pölsul ette ja
PII4. Therapist:	mm
PII5. Petra:	mm (p) mm (p) [ja]
PII6. Therapist:	[ja]

(PII1. Petra:	and (p) this is
PII2. Therapist:	blueberries I think it looks a[s::
PII3. Petra:	[yes (p)
	pölsul it is yes
PII4. Therapist:	mm
PII5. Petra:	mm (p) mm (p) [yes]
PII6. Therapist:	[yes])

Reframing

Repair also fits into a wider context, where speakers' competence and self-image are at stake. In his study "Radio Talk," Erving Goffman (1981) points out that everyday activities typically are carried out on the presumption that the people involved in these activities share certain basic competences. One such activity is, of course, ordinary talk. Thus, when people contribute to a round of talk, they not only add something to the topics at hand; they also project themselves as ordinary competent speakers.

This means that lapses in talking (and in other everyday activities) must be dealt with in such a way that they do not call into question a person's basic competences.

As Goffman shows, there are several techniques for doing that. One such technique is repair. A lapse can be constructed as something temporary and contingent, if it is adequately repaired at the first possible occasion by the one who produced it. Hence, we have the preference for self-repair in roughly egalitarian contexts (Schegloff, Jefferson, & Sacks, 1977). A second technique is to redefine the speaker's and the other participants' relation to a stretch of talk where a lapse occurs, to do what Goffman calls a change in footing. Through such a change in footing, the stretch of talk where a lapse (or some other conversational problem) occurs is reframed and normal expectations of it are lifted.

Reframing can be done in several ways, which can be combined. A basic means of reframing a stretch of activity is laughter (Freud, 1992/1905; Goodwin, 1990, chap. 5; Sacks, 1992, vol. II: 207). As Sacks (1992, vol. II: 207) shows, laughter works both proactively, before the fact, as a way of preparing the scene for something problematic, and retroactively, after the fact, as a way of reframing something that has alrady occurred. Other displays of emotion, such as moaning or sighing, can have the same function. A further means of reframing is a change in voice or accent (Anward, 1993). Finally, as Goffman (1981) discussed at length, explicit comments, both proactive and retroactive, puns, and jokes are frequent means of doing reframing.

In sum, by laughing (or moaning) about it, by producing it in a different voice or accent, by commenting on it, punning on it, or joking about it, a speaker can mark a stretch of talk as something out of the ordinary, displaying in this way her or his knowledge of normal expectations, thus blocking any doubts about competence.

A constant dilemma

Aphasics of Bernardina's type seem very reluctant to abstain from content words and be reduced to the same competence level as aphasics of Sonja's type. This puts them in a constant dilemma. To the extent that they are aware of their own words,[6] they need to relate to their paraphasias in as competent a way as possible.

Of the techniques we have reviewed for preserving competence in the face of lapses, I have already suggested that repair is of limited use to this category of speakers. This leaves change in footing. And of the various means to do a change in footing, proactive measures and puns appear to be beyond their capacity. Thus, retroactive laughter or comments, precisely what Bernardina is using in I3 and I7, seem, along with change of voice, to be the means by which aphasics of this type can project their competence.

The cards that are dealt Bernardina are then a severe inability to find received and relevant content words; a reluctance to abstain from content words, because of the self-image such an abstinence would project; and a limited repertoire of competence-projecting devices. Let us now turn to how Bernardina plays this hand in the two retellings.

Sequential structure of the first retelling

We return to the first retelling. After Bernardina's story has crashed in I7 and Marianne has requested a repair in I8, Bernardina repairs I7 in I9.

Example 12 Bernardina I

I7. Bernardina:	jaa (p) de va en otäck (p) sk<u>o</u>g (p) sega som sk<u>o</u>gale
	((lau[ghs))]
I8. Marianne:	[((laug]hs))
	va vare de h<u>a</u>ndlade om
I9. Bernardina:	de va en en oturlig o <u>o</u>lycka kan vi säja ((laughs))
I10. Marianne:	aa
(I7. Bernardina:	well (p) it was a nasty (p) f<u>o</u>rest (p) sega that sk<u>o</u>gale
	((lau[ghs))]
I8. Marianne:	[((laug]hs))
	what was it it was ab<u>ou</u>t
I9. Bernardina:	it was an unfortunate a <u>a</u>ccident we can say ((laughs))
I10. Marianne:	yes)

The repair is immediately reframed by an explicit comment on its approximateness ("we can say") and a unilateral laughter, which can be heard as indicating that this may do for now, although it may be some distance away from the headline she is trying to reproduce. Marianne accepts this, and Beranrdina then moves on.

Example 13   Bernardina I

I7. Bernardina:	jaa (p) de va en otäck (p) sk<u>o</u>g (p) sega som sk<u>o</u>gale
	((lau[ghs))]
I8. Marianne:	[((laug]hs))
	va vare de h<u>a</u>ndlade om
I9. Bernardina:	de va en en oturlig o <u>o</u>lycka kan vi säja ((laughs))
I10. Marianne:	aa
I11. Bernardina:	blann barnen (pp)
	att den ena kom in till en b<u>o</u>nde å sa att (p)
	fråga om han fick låna en: en sp<u>a</u>de (p)
	efter honom så han kunde hjälpa mm ssk
	nä ja k<u>a</u>n inte
I12. Marianne:	joodå
I13. Bernardina:	ja k<u>u</u>nde förut ((laughs))
	ja k<u>a</u>n inte nu
	han-ehm han ba å få låt ett en sp<u>a</u>der å hjälpa å få upp
	%frun sin% ·hh
I14. Marianne:	va skulle han få <u>u</u>pp
I15. Bernardina:	·hhh nä ja h<u>ö</u>r inte hhh
I16. Marianne:	va vare han skulle få <u>u</u>pp för nånting
	[va skulle han gräva <u>u</u>pp]

I17. Bernardina:	[han]skulle få upp brodern som kom ur ur ur laget
	ja men om han bar om han löser s:e se s s hälarna så
	nä nu kan jat inte (p)
	·hnä
I18. Marianne:	hur gick de på slute då
I19. Bernardina:	ja de va att han hade ramla me huv:et °först°
	((laughs))
	nämen kan [du fatta]
I20. Marianne:	[ska vi ge oss då]
I121.Bernardina:	ja läste ju utan vidare då ju

(I7. Bernardina:	well (p) it was a nasty (p) forest (p) sega that skogale
	((lau[ghs))]
I8. Marianne:	[((laug]hs))
	what was it it was about
I9. Bernardina:	it was an unfortunate a accident we can say ((laughs))
I10. Marianne:	yes
I11. Bernardina:	among the children (pp)
	that the one came in to a farmer and said that (p)
	asked if he could borrow a a shovel (p)
	after him so he could help mm ssk
	no I can't
I12. Marianne:	yes you can
I13. Bernardina:	I could before ((laughs))
	I can't now
	he-ehm he ask to bollow a a spades and help to get up %wife his%
I14. Marianne:	what would he get up
I15. Bernardina:	hhh no I don't hear hhh
I16. Marianne:	what was it he would get up for something
	[what would he dig up]
II7. Bernardina:	[he] would get up the brother who came out-of out-of out-of
	the team
	yes but if he jus if he loosens s:e se s s the heels then
	no now I can't (p)
	·hno
I18. Marianne:	how did it end then
I19. Bernardina:	yes it was that he fell with his head °first°
	((laughs)) no but can [you understand]
I20. Marianne:	[shall we stop it then]
I21. Bernardina:	I read without problems then you know)

In I11, Bernardina first produces three complete syntactic units without any paraphasias in them, successfully reproducing the beginning of the story. However, when
she is unable to finish the fourth such unit (in the fourth line of I11; "hjälpa" [help]
requires an object), she breaks off the retelling, changes footing, and explicitly states
her inability to go on with the retelling. After a reaffirming response from Marianne

(I12), Bernardina elaborates on her current situation, contrasting her former ability (first line of I13) to her present inability (second line of I13).

Then she backs up to the unit of the third line of I11, repeats it in a slightly worse version (the third line of I13),[7] and produces a new version of the unit that was interrupted in the fourth line of I11. This time, Bernardina manages to provide "help" with an object. and thus completes the unit. However, she cannot find the right wording of the object, and she seems to recognize that also, because she speaks the object phrase in a different, very flat voice, which it is natural to interpret as a framing device.

In response to that, Marianne requests a repair (in I14). We can see a pattern emerging here. The repairs so far are all self-repairs. In two cases, they are other-initiated, and there seems to be a recurring context for such other-initiation. Not all paraphasias that Bernardina produces are followed by a request for repair. Other-initiations seem cued by the way Bernardina relates to her own choice of words. Only when Bernardina frames a token of paraphasia as problematic, by means of a laughter, as in I7, or by means of a change in voice, as in I13, does Marianne request a repair of Bernardina. Notice also that this does not happen in I3 or I11, where paraphasia or breakdown is reframed by an explicit reflexive comment by Bernardina. The context for other-initiation of repair is thus the occurrence of something that Bernardina treats as a problem but takes no explicit stand on.

Yet Bernardina does not accept Marianne's request for repair and instead does another footing change, this time formulating her inability as an even more fundamental inability, as an inability to hear.[8] Marianne then repeats her request twice, with raised voice, before Bernardina finally, overlapping with Marianne's second request, produces a third version of the unit that was interrupted in I11 and is able to move forward again. She expands the "get up"-unit with a relative clause, which contains an instance of paraphasia, and then starts a conditional sentence, left unfinished (the second line of I17).

At this point, Bernardina does yet another change in footing, this time stating her inability to go on in more final terms (the third line of I17), and underlining her statement with a following inhaled "no." This makes Marianne change her strategy. Instead of requesting yet another repair, she simply prompts Bernardina to wrap up the story (I18), which Bernaridna finally is able to do, in I19.

After that, both Marianne and Bernardina break frame, and Bernardina once more contrasts her present inability to her former ability.

Sequential structure of the second retelling

The second retelling starts in II19, again after some negotiation. Bernardina reproduces the beginning of the story successfully, but then interrupts herself (the seventh line of II19; the verb "prova" [try] needs a complement), just as in the first retelling. However, this time, Bernardina does not attempt to repair the interrupted unit but just moves on. Even though she produces paraphasia in each unit from then on, she is able to cover two more turns of the story dialogue and get positive feedback from Marianne, before she comes to a unit she is unable to finish (the first line of II21). The change in footing that follows this breakdown takes the form of an explicit comment (the second line of II21). However, this time she does not ascribe inability to herself but simply notes that it is harder to retell the story from memory than it is to read it aloud. Marianne then encourages Bernardina to go on, which she does in II23. She connects back to II19, invokes the headline, producing paraphasia in both these units, and is finally able to bring the story to an appropriate end.

Example 14   Bernardina II

II14. Marianne:	sen Bernardina så skulle ja faktiskt vilja att vi fortsatte med att
	du försökte berätta den där historien (p)
	utan att titta på
II15. Bernardina:	den där pojken
II16. Marianne:	på texten
III7. Bernardina:	jaa
II18. Marianne:	du kan försöka berätta va re va re handla om
II19. Bernardina:	jaa
	de va två pojkar dom va bröder fick man (p) vadevarå
	han va (p)
	han va ute ute på lande på lande som han inte kände till
	å då gick a in till en bonde och frågade honom
	om han kunde få låna e p spade rå (p) till honom (p)
	å prova åv
	jaa sas sa: bonden buev han mycke skadad då
	jaa han stog me f me me f s sedena uppåt sa grabben
	jaa ((laughs))
II20. Marianne:	mm
II21. Bernardina:	( ) grabben mhm grabben va fedi för (p)
	nää de går inte alls lika bra när man inte har nåt läshäfte
II22. Marianne:	jamen de går ju jättebra
	du har ju berätta nästan alltihopa redan
II23. Bernardina:	äm ja i alla fall blev pojken ähh djupt skadad
	och:: de e klart de va en s en ban en bali otäck skola
	för pojken hade ramlat med huvet före
II24. Marianne:	(pp)
	ja just de
(II14. Marianne:	then Bernardina I would actually want that we continued with
	your trying to tell that story (p)
	without looking at
II15. Bernardina:	that boy
II16. Marianne:	at the text
III7. Bernardina:	yees

II18. Marianne:	you can try telling what it was it was about
II19. Bernardina:	yees

it was two boys they were brothers you got (p) what-it-was
he was (p)
he was out out in the country in the country that he didn't know
and then he went in to a farmer and asked him
if he could borrow a p shovel then (p) to him (p)
and try and
yes saids said the farmer weas he very injured then
yes he stood with f with with f s sedena up said the guy
yes ((laughs))

II20. Marianne:	mm
II21. Bernardina:	( ) the guy mhm the guy was fedi for (p)

noo it doesn't work at all as good when you don't have any text

II22. Marianne:	yes but it is working very good

you have told almost all of it already

II23. Bernardina:	ehm yes in any case the boy was ehh deeply injured

and:: it is clear it was a s a ban a bali nasty school
for the boy had fallen with his head first

II24. Marianne:	(pp)

that's right)

In keeping with the whole atmosphere of the second retelling, the comments after it (cf. example 3) do not at all concern Bernardina or her abilities but concentrate on the quality of the story retold.

No doubt, the second retelling is more successful than the first one, but not because the second retelling is somehow a "better" retelling than the first one. The original story does not come across in comprehensible form in either of the two retellings. Moreover, there is no significant difference in the number of paraphasias in the two retellings. Rather, what seems to be happening in the second retelling is that Bernardina manages to mobilize her resources in such a way that she does not feel compelled to raise the issue of her own competence at every step. Hence, she need not engage in repair, which, just as we suspected earlier, turns out not to be a very helpful strategy for Bernardina. Furthermore, she need not continuously reframe stretches of her retelling, by means of laughter, changed voice, or explicit comment.

To understand how Bernardina manages to mobilize her resources in such a benign way in the second retelling, we must take a closer look at the story she is retelling, in particular, the passages where Bernardina gets into trouble.

The story

"A Severe Fall," repeated in example 15, is a popular story in Swedish speech therapy. One can wonder, though, whether anyone has ever reflected on its semantic structure and its suitability for use with people having language problems. The story actually has a fairly complicated structure.

Example 15 Ett svårt fall
1a.   En pojke kom en dag inspringande på en bondgård
1b.   och frågade om han kunde få låna en spade.
2a.   När bonden undrade vad han skulle ha den till
2b.   svarade pojken att hans bror hade ramlat i ett träsk
2c.   och att han måste gräva upp honom.
3.   Hur djupt har han ramlat i, frågade bonden.
4.   Upp till vristerna, blev svaret.
5a.   Men då kan han väl gå därifrån utan din hjälp,
5b.   då behöver du väl ingen spade.
6a.   Pojken såg förtvivlad ut och sa:
6b.   Ja, men ni förstår han ramlade med huvudet först

(A Severe Fall / A Tough Case

1a.   A boy came one day running into a farm
1b.   and asked if he could borrow a shovel.
2a.   When the farmer wondered what he would use it for
2b.   the boy replied that his brother had fallen into a swamp
2c.   and that he had to dig him up.
3.   How deep has he fallen into [the swamp], the farmer asked.
4.   Up to the ankles, was the answer.
5a.   But then he surely can walk away from there without your help;
5b.   then you'll need no shovel.
6a.   The boy looked unhappy and said:
6b.   Yes, but you see he fell with his head first.)

At one level, the story reflects a straightforward sequence of past events, a scene-setting event (1a) followed by a dialogue consisting of seven turns, all but one glossed by a speech act term: the boy asked (1b)—the farmer wondered (2a)—the boy replied (2b, 2c)—the farmer asked (3)—[the boy] answered (4)—[the farmer] (5)—the boy said (6).

However, the structure of the dialogue is not entirely straightforward.[9] The initial request for a shovel in 1 does not get a direct answer. Instead, the farmer questions the request by asking two successive questions (in 2 and 3) and using the boy's answers (in 2 and 4) to conclude that the boy does not really need a shovel, a conclusion challenged by the boy's final turn (6).

At the level of what the boy and the farmer talk about, the story is even more complicated. After the dialogue situation has been introduced in 1, the farmer's question in 2a introduces yet another situation, a future, projected event, where the boy uses the borrowed shovel. In 2b and 2c, then, this question in 2 is answered by a combination of a flashback to a past event, the boy's brother falling into a swamp, and a further specification of the projected event, the boy digging up his brother.

Sentences 3 and 4, question and answer, constitute another flashback, adding to the past event line, by specifiying futher details of the brother's fall.

Then, in 5, a further complication is introduced. The farmer proposes an alternative projected line of events, where the brother walks away from the swamp on his own accord, and the farmer does not have to lend his precious shovel to the boy.

In 6, the story reverts to the dialogue situation, zooming in on the look and emotional state of the boy, before proceeding to the climax, another flashback, where the farmer's alternative line of events is completely demolished by the boy's further specification of the past event line.

In summary, the story moves between the four situations involved, as shown in table 8.2.

Trouble spots

Given the analysis of "A Severe Fall" in example 16, we see that Bernardina gets into trouble when she attempts to integrate two temporally distinct episodes within one syntactic unit, when she attempts to cover a radical temporal shift within the confines of one syntactic unit.

In the first retelling, the entire sequence from the fourth line of I11 to the first line of I17 is spent on an attempted retelling of 2b and 2c, which, however, never comes out right. Bernardina's narrative strategy here differs from that of the original story, in that Bernardina skips 2a and joins 2c directly to 1b, leaving 2b to be appended to 2c as a relative clause modifying "brodern" (as in the first line of I17). This makes the story less jumpy timewise, but still Bernardina does not manage to retell 2 correctly. The first time Bernardina attempts to move from 1b to 2c, she is unable to finish the syntatic

TABLE 8.2 Story Situation

| | | Projected event | |
Past event	Dialogue situation	Boy's version	Farmer's version
	1		
	2a	2a	2a
2b	2b		
		2c	
3	3		
4	4		
			5
	6a		
6b			

unit she has started. The second time she attempts this move, she completes the unit but ends it with a paraphasia marked by a changed voice. The third time, after heavy soliciting from Marianne, Bernardina gets 2c right and manages to move on to 2b, which she ends with a paraphasia that she, however, lets go.

Then—in the second line of I17—Bernardina attempts a move from 4 to 5, something along the lines of "yes but if he just loosens his heels, then [he can walk away by himself]," and is again unable to finish the syntactic unit she has started.

In the second retelling, just as in the first retelling, Bernardina is unable to finish the syntatic unit she has started when she attempts to move on from 1b to 2c, in the seventh line of II19. However, as we have already seen, this time she simply gives up the attempt to retell 2 and moves on to 3 and 4, in the eighth and ninth lines of II19. Both her version of 3 and her version of 4 contain paraphasias, but they are passed over without reframing of any kind. After that, she skips 5, and moves directly to 6, in II21.

At this point, Bernardina gets into trouble again, in trying to move from 6a to 6b. There is a paraphasia in the counterpart of 6a, and when she moves into 6b, she is unable to finish the unit she has started.

After having explicitly acknowledged this trouble, Bernardina reconnects to 4 in II23, elaborating on the last two lines of II19 (and keeping the same paraphasia), and then she moves on again, this time skipping 6a. Instead, she brings in a version of the headline, with a paraphasia that is passed over, in the second line of II23, and then finally moves on to 6b, in the last line of II23.

Bernardina's progress

In the first retelling Marianne and Bernardina aim at hi-fi quality, a faithful reproduction of the written story. This is quite evident from the questions Marianne asks:

Example 16   Bernardina I

I4. Marianne:	ska vi se om du kan berätta re där nurå
. . .	
I8. Marianne:	((laughs))
	va vare de handlade om
. . .	
I14. Marianne:	va skulle han få upp
. . .	
I16. Marianne:	va vare han skulle få upp för nånting
	va skulle han gräva upp
. . .	
I18. Marianne:	hur gick de på slute då
(I4. Marianne:	let's see if you can tell that now

. . .

| I8. Marianne: | ((laughs)) |
| | what was it it was ab<u>ou</u>t |

. . .

| I14. Marianne: | what would he get <u>up</u> |

. . .

| I16. Marianne: | what was it he would get <u>up</u> for something |
| | what would he dig <u>up</u> |

. . .

| I18. Marianne: | how did it <u>e</u>nd then) |

First, when Marianne asks Bernardina to retell the story, Marianne explicitly raises the issue of competence ("see if you can"). In the subsequent questions, Marianne focuses on specific points of the written story. Moreover, the past tense of these questions suggests that these points have already been intersubjectively established, that they are old information. Finally, two of these questions—I8 and I16 first line— use a very specific Swedish construction, the cleft WH construction, which implies that the person who asks the question actually knows the answer but has temporally forgotten it. However, in classrooms and in speech therapy, where the knowledge of the teacher/speech therapist is not at issue, such questions have the force of reminding students/patients of things they actually know—or at least (should) have learned. Thus, Marianne's questions in the first retelling is very much directed toward making Bernardina reproduce something she has already done, and it is evident from the way Bernardina construes a contrast between her ability before and her inability now in I13 that this is also the way she understands the task at hand.

This kind of situation, where hi-fi reproduction is demanded, is actually about the worst kind of situation for an aphasic of Bernardina's type. First, it requires of the aphasic both a cognitively complex organization of the topic at hand and a specific vocabulary to express it, both extremely difficult tasks for speakers of this category.[10] Second, the context is such that the issue of the aphasic's competence is raised at every step of the interaction, necessitating extensive competence work, in addition to the already demanding reproductive tasks.

In the second retelling, in contrast, Marianne demands less of Bernardina, just asking her to try and tell the story, to "try and tell what it was it was about" (notice again the cleft WH construction, which, however, in this case is radically softened by the "try"), and when Bernardina gets into an impasse, Marianne just encourages her to go on, without demanding anything specific of her. In general, the atmosphere in the second retelling is much more relaxed. Marianne even seems slightly absent-minded. There is a rather long pause after II23 before Marianne acknowledges (realizes?) that Bernardina has just produced the last line of the story.

This kind of situation gives Bernardina room to construct a story she can actually tell. As we have seen, in the second retelling Bernardina picks bits and pieces of the written story, skipping those she cannot manage, keeping the others, and making a story out of them that ends on the right line. In this way, she can minimize the cognitive complexity of the topic at hand, but still produce a story.

Bernardina is free to manipulate not only pieces of the story but also the vocabulary used to narrate it. As noted in the previous section, Bernardina lets a number of paraphasias in the second retelling go undealt with. These are listed in example 17.

Example 17
mycke skadad
sedena
djupt skadad
en ban en bali otäck skola

To understand the nature of these expressions, we must first note that Bernardina's access to content words is actually topic-sensitive. While she has grave problems mobilizing content words to narrate the past and projected event lines of the story, she has almost no problems narrating what is happening in the dialogue situation of the story and few problems in talking about her immediate situation together with Marianne and the activities that go on there.[11]

It might not be far-fetched, then, to think that the expressions in example 17 are actually recruited from the immediate situation of Bernardina or based on expressions recruited from that situation. Obvious candidates for such recruited items are "otäck" (nasty), "skada" (injury), and "skola" (school).[12] The words otäck and skada are, of course, immediately relevant to Bernardina's current situation, particularly since the story ends on a line talking about the head, precisely where Bernardina's injury is. The words otäck and skada are also likely to have been triggered by the words "svår" (severe) and "spade" (shovel) in the written story. The word skola may seem surprising in this context, but as Ing-Mari Tallberg has shown (Tallberg, 2001), speech therapy patients, with a wide variety of handicaps, typically associate the speech therapy situation with a situation more well-known to them, the questions and answers pattern of primary school classrooms.

Once this part of the analysis is established, we realize, somewhat startled, that the story Bernardina tells in the second retelling session actually makes sense, not as a retelling of the written story in example 2, but as a semi-personal story in its own right, as a story about how one person tells another, sympathetic person about the head injury of a third person. In other words, in the second retelling session, Bernardina constructs a story that is both tellable and meaningful in the current situation, from bits and pieces of the written story and the cognitive and linguistic resources available to her in her immediate situation.

Notes

The material in this chapter was presented at a conference on Order and Disorder in Talk in London, June 1997, at seminars at the University of Stockholm in 1998 and 1999, and at a meeting with members of the Swedish Psychoanalytical Society in May 2000. I thank the audiences at these occasions for valuable comments and suggestions. In particular, I am indebted to Lars Fant for useful discussion. I have discussed the material several times with Päivi Juvonen, whose help and comments I gratefully acknowledge. A special thanks to Ing-Mari Tallberg, who made the material available to me, and to Chuck Goodwin, but for whose patience and encouragement ever since we first came to discuss aphasia, over lunch a hot day in Albuquerque in the summer of 1995, this chapter would never have seen the light of day. Moreover, Chuck's perceptive and constructive comments on the antepenultimate version of the chapter made it significantly better.

I wish to dedicate this chapter to the memory of Gunnel Källgren, dear colleague and Swedish pioneer in the study of aphasia and interaction (see Källgren, 1985).

1. See the references under "poetry" in the index to volume 1 and the references under "'poetics' of ordinary talk" in the index to volume 2 of Sacks (1992).

2. Transcription conventions follow the system of Gail Jefferson, as modified by Ochs (1979). Overlaps are within [ ]. An underlined vowel indicates primary stress (sentence accent). A period (.) indicates a terminal fall. (p) inidcates a pause. %X% indicates that X is spoken in a different voice.

Swedish vowels are long before at most a single consonant, short otherwise. The quality of the vowels can be glimpsed by the folowing rough correspondences: *a* is pronounced as the vowel in *park* (long), *hut* (short), *å* as in *long*, *ä* as in *well* (except in the hesitation words *ähh*, *äm*, where it is pronounced as the vowel in *can*), *e* as in *well*, *i* as in *seen* or *sing*, *o* as in *cool*, and *ö* as in *bird*. The vowel *y* has no English equivalent, but corresponds roughly to German *ü*. The vowel *u* in Swedish is a central, high, rounded vowel, with few equivalents outside of Scandinavia. Swedish consonants are fairly straightforward. The combination of r and a consonant is, however, pronounced as a retroflex version of the consonant following r.

3. The vowel in "jaa" is not lengthened, but reduplicated.

4. For more extended discussion of the use of deictics to produce a description or narrative by pointing to a body part, see Wilkinson, Beeke, and Maxim (chap. 3).

5. For an extensive study of self-repair in Wernicke aphasics, see Laakso (1997).

6. Which might be more often than is sometimes thought; see again Laakso (1997).

7. There are two paraphasias in the third line of I13: "låt" (a nonce-word) instead of "låna" (borrow) and "spader" (spades) instead of "spade" (shovel).

8. This response might even be interpreted as resistance, in the psychoanalytic sense. See Green (2000:1) for a similar example.

9. As Chuck Goodwin suggests (personal communication), the entire story can be analyzed as an initial request followed by an extended insertion sequence.

10. As well as for other speakers with various types of language handicaps. See Tallberg (2001).

11. Of the 19 paraphasias on content words (excluding proper names) produced by Bernardina in the two retellings, 12 (63%) occurred in units recounting past or projected events of the story. In contrast, of the 84 content words (again excluding proper names) in the two retellings, only 35 (42%) were located in units recounting past or projected events of the story.

12. Note that even in the first retelling, the very first content words that Bernardina uses seem to be based on these words.

References

Anward, J. (1993). How Accents Mean. In *Fonetik 93. Papers from the Seventh Swedish Phonetics* Conference (pp. 77–80). RUUL 23. Uppsala: Uppsala University, Dept. of Linguistics.

Freud, S. (1992 [1905]). *Jokes and Their Relation to the Unconscious*. Harmondsworth: Penguin Books.

Goffman, E. (1981). *Forms of Talk*. New York: Blackwell.

Goodwin, C. (1995). Co-Constructing Meaning in Conversations with an Aphasic Man. *Research on Language and Social Interaction*, *28*(3), 233–260.

Goodwin, M. H. (1990). *He-Said-She-Said: Talk as Social Organization Among Black Children*. Bloomington: Indiana University Press.

Green, A. (2000). The Central Phobic Position: A New Formulation of the Free Association Method. *International Journal of Psychoanalysis*. Available: http:www.ijpa.org

Grice, H. P. (1975). Logic and Converrsation. In P. Cole & J. L. Morgan (Eds.), *Syntax and Semantics 3: Speech Acts* (pp. 41–58). New York: Academic Press.

Jakobson, R. (1960). Linguistics and Poetics. In T. A. Sebeok (Ed.), *Style in Language*. Cambridge, MA: MIT Press.

Källgren, G. (1985). "Nu talar vi om katter." Textanalys av ett samtal mellan en afatiker och en logoped. *ASLA Information*, *11*, 1.

Laakso, M. (1997). *Self-Initiated Repair by Fluent Aphasic Speakers in Conversation*. Helsinki: Finnish Literature Society.

Lesser, R. (1978). *Linguistic Investigations of Aphasia*. London: Arnold.

Ochs, E. (1979). Transcription as Theory. In E. Ochs & B. B. Schieffelin (Eds.), *Developmental Pragmatics* (pp. 43–72). New York: Academic Press.

Rorty, R. (1991). *Essays on Heidegger and Others. Philosophical Papers*, Vol. 2. Cambridge: Cambridge University Press.

Sacks, H. (1992). *Lectures on Conversation*. Vols. I and II. New York: Blackwell.

Schegloff, E. A., Jefferson, G., & Sacks, H. (1977). The Preference for Self-Correction in the Organization of Repair in Conversation. *Language*, *53*, 361–382.

Tallberg, I.-M. (2001). *Semantic Analysis of Irrelevant Speech in Dementia*. Studies in Logopedics and Phoniatrics, No 11. Stockholm: Karolinska Institutet, Huddinge University Hospital.

9

MARY L. OELSCHLAEGER
AND JACK S. DAMICO

Word Searches in Aphasia

A Study of the Collaborative Responses of Communicative Partners

Within the discipline of clinical aphasiology, we are becoming progressively aware of the need to study the communicative ability of persons with aphasia in authentic conversational settings. Based on the work of a number of researchers (Goodwin, 1995; Holland, 1982, 1983; Klippi, 1991; Lyon, 1992; Oelschlaeger & Damico, 1996), we recognize that many persons with aphasia communicate better in natural conversational settings than we would predict, given their performances on traditional test batteries of aphasia. That is, despite significant documented impairments within their neurological systems that lead to extensive linguistic deficits, many persons with aphasia are still able to function relatively well in conversational settings.

Despite these current findings, however, we have not been able to fully demonstrate and explicate the aphasic's ability to use talk-in-interaction. This lack of documented research is primarily due to our assumptions about language as a cognitive system within the mind of the person with aphasia and because of the research methodologies traditionally applied in clinical aphasiology (Damico, 1993; Damico, Simmons-Mackie, & Schweitzer, 1995). We need to employ other assumptions about language and conversation, and we need to use more authentic research stances if we are to understand the pragmatic life of brain-damaged patients.

Recently, there has been increasing interest in investigating aphasia from a more authentic perspective. Studies by Armstrong (1989), Ferguson (1992, 1994, 1996), Goodwin (1995), Simmons-Mackie and Damico (1996a, 1996b), and others (e.g., Copeland, 1989; Klippi, 1991; Penn, 1987) have looked at the communication ability of persons with aphasia by shifting the research paradigm from a traditional to more qualitative, interpretive frames to obtain a more authentic picture of everyday language use. Specifically, a more sociological perspective defines conversation as the primary focus of study and stresses the co-participatory nature of language and conversation.

By studying conversation in persons with aphasia as a socially interactive phenomenon, characterized as "talk-in-progress" "locally managed" by its participants (Sacks, Schegloff, & Jefferson, 1974), we should learn more about the impact of aphasia on interactive social behavior and about how persons with aphasia accomplish interactive activities despite their neurological impairments. Do the systematic properties of the sequential organization of conversation noted in non-brain-damaged persons exist in persons with aphasia? If so, how are they achieved by the participants, given that one of the conversationalists is limited in language ability? If, indeed, conversations with persons with aphasia are systematically and sequentially organized by participants, we may gain greater understanding of the communicative success noted in the "talk" of persons with aphasia.

This chapter relates findings from a long-term investigation of the natural conversations of a person with aphasia and his most frequent conversational partner, his spouse (Oelschlaeger & Damico, 1998a, 1998b). Using videotaped data, we explored a wide range of phenomena relevant to the interactive sequential organization of conversation. This chapter focuses primarily on word searches and the co-participatory strategies that this husband/wife dyad employs to overcome these instances of difficulty in conversation due to the word retrieval deficits common to aphasia.

Methodology

Data collection

Over a two-month period, we videotaped the natural conversations of Ed, a person with aphasia, and his wife M, his primary conversation partner, in their home. Both Ed and M were in their early fifties and had been married for 28 years. Ed had a six-year history of a single left CVA with residual right hemiplegia and aphasia. His aphasia was moderately severe as characterized by an aphasia quotient of 46.6, which derived from the administration of the Western Aphasia Battery (WAB; Kertesz, 1982) (subtest scores for the WAB are presented in appendix 1). Descriptively, Ed understood what was being said to him relatively well and was generally able to follow the topic of conversation. However, when comprehension depended on a single word or when the talk of others was too long or linguistically complex, he would misunderstand. Although he could use many different forms of language and could, almost always, get his main idea across, his spontaneous speech was peppered with instances of word-finding difficulty and grammatical errors. Qualitatively, his language production was slow and effortful.

In total, eight naturally occurring conversations of Ed and M were obtained. Five conversations were between Ed and M only; on three other occasions, two other persons, MO and MG, were present. Information about conversation length and turns-at-talk for all participants is presented in table 9.1.

In the 266 minutes of videorecorded conversation, the combined total of turns-at-talk was 3,561. Despite his moderate aphasia, Ed was an active participant in these conversations, with his total number of turns almost equal to his spouse.

Data analysis

All the videotapes were transcribed and then cyclically reviewed to identify recurring patterns of interaction between Ed and M. This data analysis was conducted in the following stepwise manner:

1. Major patterns of interaction were grossly identified. One specific pattern repeatedly observed was a sequence of interaction that occurred when Ed's conversational turn was incomplete.
2. The focus of this analysis moved to these incomplete turns.
3. Subsequent review of instances of Ed's incomplete turns revealed an even more specific recurring pattern associated with word retrieval difficulty. More specifically, 38 instances were observed when Ed initiated a word search and his spouse, M, joined his speaking effort.
4. These 38 word search sequences were then selected for sequential analysis: the observable verbal and non-verbal behaviors of both Ed and M were detailed on a turn-by-turn basis. Analysis of word search sequences included the turn initiating the search and all subsequent turns until the word search was terminated.
5. From these behavioral analyzes, patterns of organization of the 38-word search sequences were identified. Interpretive analysis of patterns was performed to explicate the meaning and design of their organization.

TABLE 9.1. Turns-at-Talk for Conversational Participants for Each Conversation

Conversation		Ed	M	MG	MO
A	42 min	211	192	197	0
B	28 min	212	213		
C	31 min	169	195	49	173
D	35 min	186	176		
E	44 min	184	336	56	289
F	19 min	64	55		
G	31 min	122	114		
H	36 min	185	183		
Total	266 min	1333	1464	302	462

Focus of data analysis

Selection of conversational sequences characterized by M's participation in Ed's word searches was not an a priori decision but emerged from data analysis. Nonetheless, for several reasons this focus is particularly meaningful to the purpose of this study. First, word retrieval deficits, the assumed basis for Ed's word searches, are characterized as a universal feature of aphasia, regardless of severity and regardless of any assumption of types of aphasia (Brookshire, 1992; Davis, 1993). This universality supports generalization of the findings of this study to other conversations and, potentially, other individuals with aphasia. Second, studies of ordinary speakers have described how participants work both systematically and collaboratively to manage word-finding problems (Goodwin, 1979; Goodwin & Goodwin, 1986; Sacks, 1992). This invites comparison of our findings with those of ordinary speakers. Third, there is a current trend in aphasia therapy to train "communicative partners" (Holland, 1991; Kagan, 1998; Kagan & Gailey, 1993; Lyon, 1989, 1992). The knowledge gained in this study about conversational participants when word-finding problems occur may enhance the clinical meaningfulness of these therapeutic endeavors.

Word retrieval difficulty in conversation

Before discussing the interactive patterns used by this couple, we describe Ed's word-finding difficulty that served as the basis for the focus of this study. Representative incomplete turns Ed produced, thought to be associated with his word retrieval deficit, are illustrated in example 1 a and b. These utterances occurred consecutively in conversation A.[1]

In this conversation, Ed, his wife (M), and a female visitor (MG) were sitting at the kitchen table in Ed and M's home. At this point in the conversation, the topic was Ed's employment before and after his stroke.

Example 1

(a)   x~mid distance gaze————————,,,—gaze down————————————
83   Ed: Well, I was a **(1.0) I'm the- uhm how should I say it? (2.1) I'm:::(1.7)**
              -gaze further down and head down——x
84   **can't think of the name of it.**
(b)
89   Ed: Let me see. I'll put that another word **(2.0)** I like it **(1.0)** but **uh (2.1)** now
              that they said that you can do- engineering but no more.**(1.5)** So okay
              "What do you want me to do?" **(l.5)** and **(5.0) tsk uhm::** about **4**
              months 5 months (1.5) well what do we do next? You know? And says
              uh 'well, I don't know'**(1.6)** so I went down to::: **(1.5) uhm (2.6) uhm (*)**
              no (1.8) hm::::::

Most germane to this study is the characterization of these utterances as reflective of word-finding difficulty in aphasia as they occur in conversation. Research of ordinary speakers has identified a number of verbal, non-verbal, and linguistic phenomena collectively described as word search indicators (Goodwin, 1987; Goodwin & Goodwin, 1986; Shegloff, Jefferson, & Sacks, 1977). These include the following:

> verbal: cutoffs (e.g., glottal stops, breaks in phonation), speech perturbations e.g., uhm, uh), pauses, revisions/restarts, negative tokens (e.g., no), sound stretches

> non-verbal: diversion of gaze from recipient to mid-distance or gaze withdrawal

> linguistic: wh-question (i.e., what was the name of that?) and meta-linguistic comments (e.g., how should I say it; can't think of the name of it).

In example 1 a and b, the word search indicators (indicated by bolded items in the utterance and marking of mid-distance gaze) of Ed's word retrieval difficulty in his conversational turns are the same as those identified in research of ordinary speakers. What is somewhat extraordinary is their frequency and their impact on verbal fluency and total turn length. Ed's turn in example 1 b was 53 seconds. If word search indicators were omitted, the length of utterance would be significantly reduced (e.g., just subtracting pauses would reduce his speaking effort by more than 20 seconds). In addition, the qualitative feature of verbal fluency and subjective judgment of verbal proficiency would be dramatically enhanced. These quantitative and qualitative features serve to differentiate the conversation of a person with aphasia from an ordinary speaker.

Word search sequences

As with ordinary speakers, several types of interactive management strategies or patterns occur in the face of the word retrieval difficulties observed in this interactive aphasic/spouse dyad. Significantly, these patterns rely on extensive collaboration between the individual with aphasia and his wife. Specifically, two types of word search sequences noted in the interactions of non-aphasic dyads were identified: guess sequences and alternative guess sequences. The conversational collaborations needed to negotiate these word search sequences are discussed in the next sections.

Guess sequences

An interactional sequence that frequently occurred when Ed had difficulty saying a word was a guess sequence as illustrated in example 2a and b.

Example 2

(a) In conversation A, the topic was Ed's occupation. MG has just asked Ed what he does for a living and he is responding to her.

```
         x—mid-distance gaze————————————,,,—gaze down————————————
83.  Ed:  Well, I was a (1.0) I'm the- uhm how should I say it? (2.1) I'm::: (1.7)
         -gaze further down and head down——x
84.       can't think of the name of it.
85.  M:   Draftsman?
         ,,,—MG—x
86.  Ed:  Draftsman.
```

(b) In this example (also taken from conversation A), the topic was videotaping. Ed is telling MG about how often he was videotaped by his speech-language pathologist when he was receiving aphasia therapy.

```
         x————————,,,—MG————————————,,,—gaze down————————————x
19.  Ed:  I'd say ten (2.3) uh (1.5) uh (1.8) uhm I can't think of the name of it.
     M:   x————nod x 4—————————————————————————————x
20.  M:   Times?
     Ed:  x-gaze down-x
         ,,,–MG–x
21.  Ed:  Times
```

In both of these examples, Ed initiates a word search and M joins his effort by offering a word to him as a guess. A detailed examination of the organization of the conversational sequence presented as example 2b shows how guess sequences are interactionally accomplished.

In line 19 of example 2b, Ed makes his word finding difficulty visible to M by word search indicators (e.g., pauses, interjections, gaze, and verbalizations).

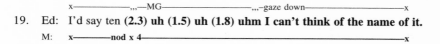

```
         x————————,,,—MG————————————,,,–gaze down————————————x
19.  Ed:  I'd say ten (2.3) uh (1.5) uh (1.8) uhm I can't think of the name of it.
     M:   x————nod x 4—————————————————————————————x
```

That M recognizes that Ed is initiating a word search is seen in her gaze. As shown in bold under line 19, her orientation is heightened; she continuously gazes at him throughout his utterance. Her monitoring of his utterance is also evident in her affirmative head nods. What is interactively important here is that M's nods provide visual feedback to Ed, albeit peripheral to his direct gaze, that his utterance is being understood as he is saying it. It supports his speaking effort (Goodwin, 1979, 1981) and *despite his difficulty speaking*, Ed continues making additional efforts to say the desired word. However, following several unsuccessful attempts, he abandons his search, as shown in his downward gaze and his verbalization that he is unable to say the desired word. These non-verbal and verbal behaviors serve as an indirect invitation for M to join his effort (Oelschlaeger, 1999) which she does in line 20. Here she offers a candidate word as a guess.

```
        x————————-,,,—MG————————————-,,,—gaze down——————————x
```
19.   Ed: I'd say ten (2.3) uh (1.5) uh (1.8) uhm I can't think of the name of it.
20.   M: **Times?**
    Ed: x-gaze down-x

The fact that she offers a guess at this point and that her offer is syntactically and semantically coherent with Ed's utterance shows again how she has been actively monitoring his utterance. It also demonstrates her interactive role as a listener/speaker, accepting the indirect invitation to participate and, simultaneously, making a claim on what will happen next in the conversation. Specifically, her guess provides the organizational structure of a question-answer adjacency pair (Sacks, 1992; Sacks et al., 1974; Schegloff & Sacks, 1973). That is, when a question is asked, an answer is projected. Thus, when M joins Ed's search by offering a word as a guess, she selects Ed to take the next turn in the conversation.

Not only is Ed selected as next speaker, but by asking a question, M defines what he is to say. He shows his understanding of this interactional technique in line 21 when, immediately following M's guess, he repeats her word as an answer.

20.   M: Times?
         ,,,–MG–x
21.   Ed: **Times.**

His answer acknowledges M's contribution and affirms its accuracy. Simultaneously, he returns his direct gaze to the conversational recipient (MG). In this way, Ed indicates that the search is over and that he is going to continue his conversational thrust.

Social identification and participation

The obvious outcome of the guess sequence is the production of the desired word (e.g., termination of the word search) with subsequent continuation of the conversation. However, equally important to recognize is the social action of this sequence, seen in additional analysis of Ed's and M's design of their turns. Relating first to M is the recognition that she designed her contribution to Ed's word search as a guess. This is significant because M could respond to Ed's difficulty in more than one way. Knowing the spousal relationship between these two, one might assume that she often knew what he was trying to say. This experiential knowledge gives her the option of framing her turn differently. For example, in example 2a, an alternative might be to state "draftsman" affirmatively. However, this option would have a different interactional thrust. If she offered her word declaratively, she would essentially finish Ed's as yet incomplete turn. Offering a word to a person who is having difficulty saying it is socially appropriate and is often viewed as "helping." By giving help, M is socially constituted as a "helper." However, it has a less positive social implication relative to the person being helped. The social implication in this instance would be that Ed is incapable of finishing it himself. By finishing his turn for him, M would socially identify Ed as linguistically inferior. As his turn would now be completed, she could continue speaking, co-opting his conversational participation even more. But by offering Ed a candidate word as a guess, M selects him as the next speaker. By providing him with an opportunity to participate, she socially identifies him as a competent speaker. This social identification is additionally supported through her rising intonation. Here again, she treats Ed as conversationally competent, as such use presumes his ability to understand the social action implicated by this prosodic feature.

Complimenting the social action of M is that Ed, through his answer turn, also presents himself as a competent speaker. He demonstrates his competence in a number of ways. First, when M uses the paralinguistic raising intonation of a guess, he offers an answer. In this way, he shows that he understood, through his own monitoring of her talk, that a question was being asked and that the next move in the conversation was his. Second, his answer is a repetition of M's guess, stated with falling intonation. As he produces the desired word in this way, he, in effect, completes the word search that he started, talking for himself rather than letting others talk for him. He regains his position in the conversation and could even continue talking, should he desire. He holds up his end of the conversation *despite aphasia*. Third, in repeating the desired word, he lets the other conversational participants know he is capable of saying it. He could, of course, have designed his answer with a simpler form of agreement such as "uh-huh" or "yes" to show that M's guess was the word he was trying to say. And the conversational outcome would have been the same—the word search would have been terminated and the conversation would move forward. But in this instance, Ed's ability to say the word himself would be open to question. However, when he repeats M's word, the implication is that his word search occurred *not because he couldn't say the desired word at all* but, rather, he couldn't come up with the word he wanted to say *just then*. In this way, he presents his difficulty as a characteristic of the moment, more like the transitory difficulty experienced by ordinary speakers (Goodwin & Goodwin, 1986; Schegloff et al., 1977) than the pervasively present difficulty of a linguistically inferior speaker.

Alternative guess sequence

Not all word searches were as easily and simply resolved as those illustrated in example 2a and b. At times, M's offered guess was inaccurate. This couple then used an alternative guess sequence strategy. Alternative guess sequences are characterized by the same basic question and answer organization of a single guess sequence. One important difference, however, is the greater social impact of multiple inaccurate guesses on a conversation. In this situation, the threat to conversational flow is increased. As noted in research of ordinary speakers, alternative sequences require additional collaboration by participants to work their way through the search and to continue their conversation (Goodwin, 1995). How this is accomplished by Ed and M appears in example 3. Here, the first guess is rejected. Nonetheless, the conversational work continues by both Ed and M, again leading ultimately to communicative success.

Example 3

541. MG: Then they realized, then they put you in the hospital.

542. M: Uh huh.

,,,—looks down—circles hand around head——

543. Ed: Yeah but then they did uh (1.2) the uh (1.9) uh what do you call it (2.1)

——x

544.   the uh

545. M: **MRI?**

gaze down

546. Ed: **No.**

547. M: **Angioplasty?**

gaze down

548. Ed: **No.**

549. MG: EEG?

gazes down-,,,-MG——,,,—gaze down——————————————x

550. Ed: No. The irr . . . no (tsk tsk) **srays.** What do you call it?

(1.0)

551. M: **An x-ray?**

,,,-M & nod-,,,MG——————————————————

552. Ed: X-ray. And he says 'oh look he's got a tra

553. MG: //Look there!

Some of the unique collaborative interactions exemplified in this alternative guess sequence are "no" tokens and the provision of additional information following inaccurate guesses. First, Ed's "no" tokens in lines 546, 548, and 550 show again his competency as a conversational participant. He is monitoring and understanding what is being said and is able to reject offered words. In terms of the immediate needs of the conversation, they function to indicate inaccuracy. From them, M learns the error of her guess. If she is to continue to participate in Ed's search, she must guess again. And without additional information, her subsequent guesses are derived from semantic information of "things that happened when Ed was in the hospital" (line 541).

Second, relating to the provision of additional information is that, following two inaccurate guesses (and a third by MG in line 549), Ed attempts to say the word again.

550. Ed: No. The **irr** . . . no (tsk tsk) **srays.** What do you call it?

Clearly, he recognizes the threat to the flow of conversation and shows his uncertainty about M's ability to provide an accurate answer by renewing his own effort to say the desired word. Even though unsuccessful, his attempt provides additional information about the phonological structure of the word he is searching for. In this way, he keeps the search going and elicits M's participation, again resulting in her offer of a final, accurate guess. That his attempt provided additional information that she could use in her turn appears in the phonological similarity between his word "srays" and her guess "x-ray" (line 551).

Implications of word search sequences to aphasia

Based on our analyses, the collaborative interactions of Ed and M noted in these word search sequences lead to communicative success in ways that positively influence social identities. Additionally, their co-participation is especially adaptive to Ed's aphasia, as seen through additional analysis.

Soliciting and maintaining Ed's participation has special relevance with regard to aphasia. One common clinical complaint and observation, supported by the literature, is the lack of participation and initiation of conversation by persons with aphasia (Armstrong, 1989; Copeland, 1989; Klippi, 1991). By guessing, selecting him as speaker, and treating him as a competent speaker, M supports Ed's participation in conversation generally.

Of course, it is quite possible, as with ordinary speakers, that offering a word as a guess reflects speaker uncertainty. However, Example 4 offers evidence that this is not the case.

Example 4
In this example, Ed is telling MG about the distance he had to travel from his home to work when he was in the military.

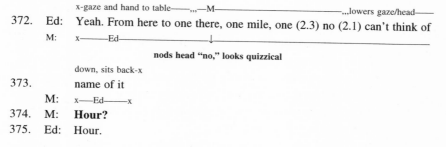

372.   Ed: Yeah. From here to one there, one mile, one (2.3) no (2.1) can't think of

373.   name of it

374.   M: **Hour?**
375.   Ed: Hour.

Here, in line 372, Ed initiates a word search, and during his effort, M nods her head "no" and looks quizzically toward him. These non-verbal behaviors provide feedback to Ed that his efforts are not succeeding. As they signal he is "wrong," they additionally imply that M knows what's "right." That is, she knows the direction of his talk. Even so, when she does participate in the search, her candidate word is a guess. As such, this example supports the interpretation of her contribution as one intended to elicit Ed's participation rather than a reflection of her own uncertainty.

Ed's use of repetition as a way to confirm the accuracy of M's guess is also especially adaptive to his aphasia. As noted previously, he could have responded with a simpler form of agreement (e.g., yes or uh-huh). However, as Jefferson (1973) notes in conversational analysis literature of ordinary speakers, yes/no is a "general acknowledger" and does not "prove understanding." Answering her question with a repetition provides M with more information about how adequately and accurately he has processed her guess. Ed's repetition reduces the question M might have about his auditory comprehension of her talk in a way a yes/no does not. This is an important adaptation because auditory comprehension ability is always at issue generally with aphasia and more specifically with regard to the parameters of Ed's language deficit (see appendix 1).

Evidence to support the interpretation of a repetition as more informative than yes/no is seen in example 5. In this example, M shows her insecurity about his comprehension of her guess as she repeats it when his answer is structured as a yes/no.

Example 5
In a discussion in conversation B of a person at Ed's place of employment, a search for a proper name is in progress:
261.   M: Oh::: its not Gambsy.
262.   Ed: **No, no.**
263.   M: **Tchikowski?**
264.   Ed: **No.**
265.   M: **Jack Tchikowski.** No?

In this guess sequence, Ed rejects M's first guess (line 262). Even though his "no" shows his lack of acceptance of M's offer, it provides her with little information about the basis for rejection. It could be that indeed, "Tchikowski" was not the name he was looking for. But it is also possible, *because of Ed's aphasia*, that he rejected her guess because he did not accurately auditorily process her offer. In light of this ambiguity, she repeats the offer and adds the tag "no" question in line 265. This requires him to process her guess again and confirm his rejection as a means to eliminate her uncertainty about the accuracy of his response.

A final comment on Ed's answer as a repetition relates to its benefit to himself. His repetition of her guess provides him with an opportunity for reauditorization, assisting his linguistic processing of the word and assuring the accuracy of his response (see Oelschlaeger & Damico, 1998b, for a more extensive discussion of repetition in aphasic conversation). Some indication that Ed repeats M's word to permit additional auditory processing occurs in the next example.

Example 6

Ed and M are sitting on their patio in conversation B, discussing work that needs to be done on their RV.

372. Ed: Yeah, I know. Because the the uh the uh the uh wheel no the
373. M: the **tailpipe**?
374. Ed: **Pipe. No no** the- you see
375. M: the b-
376. Ed: //it's lower
377. M: **the bumper**?
378. Ed: **the bumper.** No. Was a uh-
379. M: What was that? Well, one of 'em is the gas can tank.

In each attempt to resolve the word search, Ed repeats M's guess (line 374, 378), which, as noted in previous examples, typically affirms accuracy. However, as noted here, following repetition, he rejects her guesses with a "no" token. Thus, his repetition provides feedback not only to her but to himself. His restatement of her word allows him an additional opportunity to assess its accuracy. He is then able to construct the rest of his utterance, accordingly assuring that the conversation stays on track. His provision of an answer as a repetition can then be seen as a constructive adaptation to his aphasia.

Conclusion

Our analysis of just a few features of the single and alternative guess sequences shows that Ed and M socially organize their conversation. They work together to resolve a word search and keep the conversation moving. They use each other's turns to build their own turn, with their movement through the word search being highly—yet spontaneously—choreographed. They are able to use their mutual knowledge of specific interactional techniques to organize the conversational disruption of a word search. In a systematically organized way, they collaborate to complete Ed's turn and continue their conversation.

Analysis of the utterances of this couple when word retrieval problems occurred in their conversation showed that they "talk" in many ways just like ordinary persons. That is, their conversation is systematically, sequentially organized through their collaborative co-participation. In addition, evidence of specific interactional techniques shows that they accomplish the social organization of their conversation in much the same way as ordinary speakers. Despite Ed's aphasia, they are able to use the procedures ordinary speakers use to produce and understand conversation. They also show their collaborative sophistication in how they dynamically establish and maintain social identities within their conversations.

These findings have direct implications for issues relating to communicative competence and, more specifically, relating to why persons with aphasia are "perceived to talk better than they speak." As the data from this study and from the few others that have examined the interaction of conversational participants (Armstrong, 1993; Ferguson, 1992; Goodwin, 1995; Klippi, 1991; Oelschlaeger, 1999; Oelschlaeger & Damico, 1998a, 1998b; Simmons-Mackie & Damico, 1995, 1996a, 1996b) show, communicative success is not solely a product of an individual's contribution. Rather, it results from the interactive communicative process.

Studies have emphasized the "intactness" of interactional competencies of the person with aphasia. This study certainly supports this observation. But results of this study also emphasize M's competencies in the presence of Ed's aphasia. They are both ordinary and extraordinary speakers. As noted previously, both Ed and M uniquely adapted their conversational collaborations to Ed's language ability. These unique adaptations have important implications both to the experience of communicative success and the social life of this couple. As Kagan and Gailey (1993) have stated, the inability to communicate in conversation jeopardizes the psychosocial well-being of a person with aphasia and their communicative partners. Ed and M, through structuring their interactions in a way that capitalize on Ed's language ability, enhance his conversational participation, their experience of communicative success, and (presumably) their psychosocial well-being. To be sure, they are not able to eliminate the influence of his aphasia, but they are able to co-construct their conversation, despite his linguistic deficit.

Several questions arise from review of the findings of this study. One is whether the adaptations in organizational structure are simply idiosyncratic to this couple, possible only because of Ed's language (dis)ability. Comparison of these findings to those of Goodwin (1995), Simmons (1993), and Simmons-Mackie and Damico (1996b) suggest this is not the case. Goodwin's study involves a severely aphasic man whose language ability was limited essentially to yes/no. In this report, Goodwin describes how family members adapted their questions to this gentleman, posing them in yes/no binary form. Simmons (1993) and Simmons-Mackie and Damico (1996b) note the use of various iterative utterances and gestures by a severely aphasic female to solicit the participation of others in conversation. Study of other couples is needed to provide additional information about interactional competencies.

Other questions arise as to how Ed and M's interactional competencies and the adaptations to them were incorporated into their conversation. Were these same competencies present prior to Ed's stroke or acquired subsequently? Were modifications intuitive or a result of experience? Again, additional research, studying the conversational interactions of couples, especially over time, will provide information relevant to this question.

Besides identifying directions in future research, this study also has implications for aphasia management. Certainly, results support the adoption of a more sociolinguistic perspective in aphasia treatment as seen in programs emphasizing the importance of communicative partners to communicative success (Holland, 1991; Kagan, 1998; Kagan & Gailey, 1993; Lyon, 1989, 1992).

Appendix 1

Western Aphasia Battery scores

Subtest	Subtest score
Spontaneous Speech	
Information Content	9/10
Fluency	9/10
Total	18/20
Comprehension	
Yes/No Questions	60/60
Auditory Word Recognition	57/60
Sequential Commands	50/80
Total	167/200
Repetition	58/100
Naming	
Object Naming	54/60
Word Fluency	8/20
Sentence Completion	10/10
Responsive Speech	10/10
Total	82/100
Aphasia Quotient	46.6
WAB Aphasia Classification	Conduction aphasia

Appendix 2

Talk is transcribed using a simplified version of the Jefferson transcription system (Sacks, Schegloff, & Jefferson, 1974).

1. (#)   : a number in parentheses indicates elapsed time in seconds for pauses 1 second or greater. This device is used between turns at talk between speakers, between two separable parts of a single speaker's talk, and between parts of a single speaker's turn.
2. ? & . : punctuation markers are used for intonation. A question mark indicates rising intonation and a period indicates falling intonation.
3. :   : a colon is used as a sound production marker, indicating that the prior syllable is prolonged.
4. -   : a short dash indicate a "cut off" of the prior word or sound.
5. (*)   : single pairs of parentheses with asterick indicate that transcribers are not sure about the words contained or that the talk was unintelligible.
6. //   : the double oblique indicates the point at which a current speaker's talk is overlapped by the talk of another.

Transcription of gaze and gesture

Gaze and gesture transcription is based on a system described by Goodwin and Goodwin (1986).

1. Gaze of the listener is marked below the turn at talk. A line indicates that the listener is gazing toward the speaker.
2. Gaze of the speaker is marked above the turn at talk. A line indicates that the speaker is gazing toward the listener.
3. x   : marks the beginning and end of the direction of gaze.
4. ,,,   : indicates a shift of gaze from one direction to another.
5. Specific gaze direction is described orthographically through indication of the person or place of the direction of gaze (i.e., mid-distance, away, or initial of person).
6. Gesture of the speaker is described orthographically above the turn at talk.

Note

1. Conversational behaviors of specific interest are in boldface throughout this chapter, with inclusion of transcription markings as necessary for understanding the text. Transcription markings are described in appendix 2.

References

Armstrong, E. M. (1989). Conversational Interaction Between Clinician and Aphasic Client During Treatment Sessions. Paper presented at the American Speech Language Hearing Association, St. Louis, Missouri, November.

Armstrong, E. M. (1993). Aphasia Rehabilitation: A Sociolinguistic Perspective. In A. Holland & M. Forbes (Eds.), *Aphasia Treatment: World Perspectives* (pp. 263–290). San Diego, CA: Singular Publishing Group.

Brookshire, R. (1992). *An Introduction to Neurogenic Communication Disorders* (4th ed.). St. Louis, MO: Mosby-Year Book.

Copeland, M. (1989). An Assessment of Natural Conversation with Broca's Aphasics. *Aphasiology, 3*, 301–306.

Damico, J. S. (1993). Establishing Expertise in Communicative Discourse: Implications for the Speech-Language Pathologist. In D. Kovarsky, M. Maxwell, & J. S. Damico (Eds.), *Language Interaction in Clinical and Educational Settings* (pp. 92–98). ASHA Monographs Vol. 30. Rockville, MD: American Speech-Language Hearing Association.

Damico, J. S., Simmons-Mackie, N. N., & Schweitzer, L. A. (1995). Addressing the Third Law of Gardening: Methodological Alternatives in Aphasiology. In P. Lemme (Ed.), *Clinical Aphasiology, 23*, 83–93. Austin, TX: Pro-Ed.

Davis, G. A. (1993). *A Survey of Adult Aphasia and Related Disorders* (2nd ed.). Englewood Cliffs, New Jersey: Prentice-Hall.

Ferguson, A. (1992). Conversational Repair of Word-Finding Difficulty. In M. Lemme (Ed.), *Clinical Aphasiology: Conference Proceedings, 11*, pp. 299–307. Austin, TX: Pro-Ed.

Ferguson, A. (1994). The Influence of Aphasia, Familiarity and Activity on Conversational Repair. *Aphasiology, 8*, 143–157.

Ferguson, A. (1996). Describing Compentence in Aphasic/Normal Conversation. *Clinical Linguistics and Phonetics, 10*, 55–63.

Goodwin, C. (1979). The Interactive Construction of a Sentence in Natural Conversation. In G. Psathas (Ed.), *Everyday Language: Studies in Ethnomethodology* (pp. 97–121). New York: Irvington Publishers.

Goodwin, C. (1981). *Conversational Organization: Interaction Between Speakers and Hearers.* New York: Academic Press.

Goodwin, C. (1987). Forgetfulness as an Interactive Resource. *Social Psychology Quarterly, 2*, 115–131.

Goodwin, C. (1995). Co-Constructing Meaning in Conversations with an Aphasic Man. *Research on Language and Social Interaction, 28*, 233–260.

Goodwin, M. H., & Goodwin, C. (1986). Gesture and Co-Participation in the Activity of Searching for a Word. *Semiotica, 62*, 51–72.

Holland, A. (1982). Observing Functional Communication of Aphasic Adults. *Journal of Speech and Hearing Research, 47*, 50–56.

Holland, A. (1983). Remarks on Observing Aphasic People. In R. Brookshire (Ed.), *Proceedings of Clinical Aphasiology Conference* (pp. 1–3). Minneapolis, MN: BRK Publishers.

Holland, A. L. (1991). Pragmatic Aspects of Intervention in Aphasia. *Journal of Neurolinguistics, 6*, 197–211.

Jefferson, G. (1973). A Case of Precision Timing in Ordinary Conversation: Overlapped Tag-Positioned Address Terms in Closing Sequences. *Semiotica, 9*, 47–96.

Kagan, A. (1998). Supported Conversation for Adults with Aphasia: Methods and Resources for Training Conversation Partners. *Aphasiology, 13*, 816–832.

Kagan, A., & Gailey, G. (1993). Functional Is Not Enough: Conversation Partners for Aphasic Adults. In A. Holland & M. Forbes (Eds.), *Aphasia Treatment: World Perspectives* (pp. 199–225). San Diego, CA: Singular Publishing Group.

Kertesz, A. (1982). *Western Aphasia Battery.* New York, NY: Grune Stratton.

Klippi, A. (1991). Conversational Dynamic Between Aphasics. *Aphasiology, 5*, 373–378.

Lyon, J. G. (1989). Communicative Partners: Their Value in Reestablishing Communication with Aphasic Adults. In T. Prescott (Ed.), *Clinical Aphasiology* (vol. 18. pp. 11–18). Boston: College-Hill Press.

Lyon, J. G. (1992). Communication Use and Participation in Life for Adults with Aphasia in Natural Settings: The Scope of the Problem. *American Journal of Speech-Language Pathology, 1*, 7–14.

Oelschlaeger, M. L. (1999). Participation of a Conversation Partner in the Word Searches of a Person with Aphasia. *American Journal of Speech-Language Patholog, 8*, 62–71.

Oelschlaeger, M. L., & Damico, J. S. (1996). The Re-Establishment of Communicative Success After Aphasia: Collusional Evidence in Spousal Interactions. Paper presented at the Clinical Aphasiology Conference, Newport, Rhode Island, June.

Oelschlaeger, M., & Damico, J. S. (1998a). Joint Productions as a Conversational Strategy in Aphasia. *Clinical Linguistics and Phonetics, 12*, 459–480.

Oelschlaeger, M., & Damico, J. S. (1998b). Spontaneous Verbal Repetition: A Social Strategy in Aphasic Conversation. *Aphasiology*, *12*, 971–988.

Penn, C. (1987). Compensation and Language Recovery in the Chronic Aphasic Patient. *Aphasiology*, *1*, 235–245.

Sacks, H. (1992). *Lectures on Conversation*. Cambridge: Basil Blackwell.

Sacks, H., Schegloff, E. A., & Jefferson, G. (1974). A Simplest Systematics for the Organization of Turn-Taking for Conversation. *Language*, *50*, 696–735.

Schegloff, E. A., & Sacks, H. (1973). Opening Up Closings. *Semiotica*, *8*, 289–327.

Schegloff, E. A., Jefferson, G., & Sacks, H. (1977). The Preference for Self-Correction in the Organization of Repair in Conversation. *Language*, *53*, 361–382.

Simmons, N. (1993). An Ethnographic Investigation of Compensatory Strategies in Aphasia. Unpublished dissertation, Louisiana State University: Baton Rouge, Louisiana (UMI: Ann Arbor, MI) (9401569).

Simmons-Mackie, N. N., & Damico, J. S. (1995). Communicative Competence in Aphasia: Evidence from Compensatory Strategies. In P. Lemme (Ed.), *Clinical Aphasiology* (vol. 23, pp. 95–105). Austin, TX: Pro-Ed.

Simmons-Mackie, N. N., & Damico, J. S. (1996a). Accounting for Handicaps in Aphasia: Communicative Assessment from an Authentic Social Perspective. *Disability and Rehabilitation*, *18*, 540–549.

Simmons-Mackie, N. N., & Damico, J. S. (1996b). The Contribution of Discourse Markers to Communicative Competence in Aphasia. *American Journal of Speech Language Pathology*, *5*, 37–43.

PART IV

INTERACTION AND ASSESSMENT

10

CLAUS HEESCHEN
AND EMANUEL A. SCHEGLOFF

Aphasic Agrammatism as Interactional Artifact and Achievement

Interaction-oriented approaches to aphasic language use need no special justification and motivation. After all, talk-in-interaction is the place "where the results of brain damage become visible and consequential for people's lives" (Goodwin, 1996). Nevertheless, we will try to show that the meaningfulness—actually the necessity— of a conversation-analytic approach to aphasia can grow out of investigations originally designed and cast in terms of traditional experimental-quantitative methodology and within a cognitivist approach to aphasia. In the first part, we describe a series of investigations dealing with agrammatic speech and strongly suggesting that the concrete way in which the patients express themselves depends on how conversational partners interact with them (and on whether they interact with them at all). Hardly anybody who considers language and language use within an interaction-oriented framework in general, and within a conversation-analytic one in particular, will be surprised by such a suggestion. Actually, if this suggestion is empirically justified, aphasic language use would constitute an exciting and attractive field of observation for conversation analysis. Yet such an outcome would be highly unwelcome for the majority of present-day aphasiologists. Most aphasiologists assume—tacitly or explicitly—that performance data from brain-damaged subjects can be used "as a window into the structure and organization of normal cognitive processes" (Caramazza, 1997: 137). If, however, this performance is the joint product of the brain-damaged subject and his or her concrete interactant in concrete circumstances at concrete occasions, then the "window" is somewhat "dirty," and perhaps quite opaque.[1] Such a state of affairs would not affect Caramazza's carefully formulated methodological position: his concern is the relevance of impairment data for cognitive neuropsychology, for theoretical accounts of and constraints on (cognitive!) theories of normal language processing (Caramazza, 1986, 1992). If data from talk-in-interaction (perhaps not only from interactions between an aphasic and an unimpaired speaker, but interactional data in general) turn out to be opaque with respect to a cognitive model of language processing, then they are simply theoretically irrelevant. This is a consequent and clear position; however, we leave it to the reader to evaluate a cognitive aphasiology for which data from the natural habitat of our language-processing capacities—unimpaired or impaired—are uninteresting.

The first part of this chapter outlines the "way from cognitive-experimental to conversation analytic approaches to aphasia" in the context of the special problem of agrammatism; the second part presents analytic explications of episodes of conversation between an agrammatic patient and unimpaired others and considers how such an analysis might provide answers to questions raised in the first part but also how it engenders new—hopefully fruitful—questions.

From Adaptation Theory to Conversation Analysis

There has been considerable controversy and disagreement about whether agrammatism is a uniform and unitary phenomenon, whether agrammatism is a distinct aphasic syndrome at all, the theoretical perspectives under which agrammatism can be meaningfully described (a linguistic theory or a processing model), and the role of language-specific factors in the manifestation of agrammatism, and so on.[2] For overviews of the state of affairs, see Kean (1995), Kolk (1998), and Jarema (1998). Despite this diversity of views and approaches, global standard characterizations of agrammatic speech output invariantly refer to the same features. For the major European languages, these are (for other languages, see Menn & Obler, 1990):

1. laborious non-fluent speech
2. impoverishment of the available syntactic structures
3. incorrectly constructed sentences and phrases
4. break-offs of sentence or phrase constructions
5. incorrect morphology
6. omission of morphological elements

Both incorrectness (substitutions) and omissions co-occur in agrammatic speech; in terms of Kleist's (1934) highly systematic terminological framework, both paragrammatisms and agrammatisms can be found. This seems to be puzzling, as the term "agrammatism" suggests a preponderance of "absences," of omissions, but agrammatic speech as characterized by a mixture of "a-" and "para-" phenomena has long been known by the old and classical neurologists (see Bleser, 1987, for a review of the old literature) and has been explicitly confirmed by more recent authors (see, among others, Caplan, 1987: 278–279; and see the detailed descriptions in Menn & Obler, 1990).

The following example from patient W illustrates all of the mentioned features. Patient W, age 41, had suffered a trauma ten years before the first author contacted her. She was diagnosed through the Aachen Aphasia Test (AAT; Huber et al., 1983; for an English description of the test, see Huber et al., 1984) as a moderately severe case of Broca's aphasia with marked agrammatism as the central symptom. She had a hemiparesis of the right arm. All fine movements were carried out with her left arm and hand. Her formal education consisted of ten years of elementary schooling. She had never had a profession. Her native and only language is German. She speaks High German, with some usages characteristic of Berlin dialect. Mood was normal. (See appendix 1 for transcription explanations.)

Example 1
((W tells a story depicted on five cartoons. The first cartoon shows a man lying in his bed and hitting a ringing alarm clock; the time on the clock is 7:00. The second shows the man sleeping again and his wife coming in; the time is 8:00 now. The third cartoon shows the man eating his breakfast; his wife points angrily to a clock in the kitchen; the time is 8:30 now. The fourth cartoon shows the man running hastily to work. The fifth shows the man at work with his legs on the desk; the man is sleeping again. The transcript of W's telling is rough because it is the grammatical properties of her speech which are of primary interest here.))

1 W: Der Mann ((disturbances from the outside)) klingelte
       The man ((disturbances from the outside)) rang
2   der   Wecker,   ((again disturbances))
       the-MASC-SG-NOM alarm-clock, ((again disturbances))
3   zur   Arbeit!   ähm (8.0) Die   Frau   schimpft
       to-the work!   ähm (8.0) The-FEM woman rebukes
4   der   Mann, ähm (4.2) der   Mann
       the-MASC-SG-NOM man,   ähm (4.2) the-MASC-SG-NOM man
5   schläft, (4.2)   der   Mann ähm die
       sleeps, (4.2)   the-MASC-SG-NOM man   ähm the-FEM-SG-NOM
6   Frau   (5.1)   acht Uhr   Arbeit gehn! ähm
       woman   (5.1)   eight o'clock work to-go! ähm
7   (2.3) der   Mann (3.5) die
       (2.3) the-MASC-SG-NOM man   (3.5) the-FEM-SG-NOM
8   Frau   (6.4) weckt   (4.2) ((sighs)) uh schwierig!
       (7.4)
       woman (6.4) awakes (4.2) ((sighs)) uh difficult!
       (7.4)
9   ähm (7.4) der   Mann ißt schnell. (4.8)
       ähm (7.4) the-MASC-NOM-SG man   eats fast.   (4.8)
10   ((click, inbreath)) (5.2) der Mann   läuft
       ((click, inbreath)) (5.2) the-MASC-SG-NOM man runs
11   zur   Arbeit, (3.8) der   Mann schläft, ja!
       to-the work, (3.8) the-MASC-SG-NOM man   sleeps, ja!

The features of agrammatic speech are illustrated by the following observable characteristics of this spate of talking:

1. The speech is effortful and halting, as evidenced by the pauses.
2. The repertoire of syntactic structures is reduced to very simple main clauses in canonical word order.
3. "Der Mann klingelte der Wecker"/ the man rang the alarm-clock (lines 1–2) is a misconstruction: the verb "klingeln"/ to-ring cannot take an object; anyway, the case marking for the object "der Wecker"/ the-MASC-SG-NOM alarm-clock would be wrong; it is nominative, but it should be one of the oblique cases.
4. The expression "acht Uhr Arbeit gehn!"/ eight o'clock work to-go! (line 6) looks like reported speech of what the woman said to her husband. Under this reading then, the preceding "der Mann die Frau" (lines 5–6) would be an abandoned construction. Also the construction on lines 7–8 ("die Frau weckt"/ the woman awakes) looks like a break-off; the verb "wecken" requires an object.[3]
5. The article "der" in line 2 was already mentioned as an instance of incorrect morphology (see 3).
6. In the expression "acht Uhr Arbeit gehn" (line 6) a preposition and an article are missing before "Arbeit"; it should be "zur Arbeit"/ to-the work.

Agrammatic speech, for which these descriptions and characterizations hold, is typically obtained by means of elicitation techniques such as picture descriptions (as in Goodglass & Kaplan, 1972), retelling a fairy tale (Menn & Obler, 1990), or a semistandardized interview (as in the AAT by Huber et al., 1983). In all these techniques, the interviewer/tester/experimenter is typically very withholding and gives the patients a long time to produce their utterances.[4] In more technical terms, the interviewer/tester/experimenter aims at *maximizing* the turns of the patients. This is clearly in contrast to the organization of ordinary conversations with its structural bias for turn minimization (Sacks, Schegloff, & Jefferson, 1974; Schegloff, 1981), although it resembles the organization of some interviews, such as broadcast news interviews, which promote expanded response turns (cf. Heritage & Greatbatch, 1991). And it prompts investigation of agrammatic speech in more ordinary interactions. Kolk, Heeschen, and their co-workers have collected and analyzed large samples of agrammatic speech in German and Dutch obtained in more natural and "ordinary" settings, such as informal conversations between patients and aphasiologists during a break in experimental sessions over a cup of coffee (or in comparable circumstances). This situation is frequently referred to in this section of the chapter, and, thus, for convenience, it is named the "baseline condition."[5] The speech of agrammatics in the baseline condition differs radically from the speech obtained under the more formal test-like situations mentioned earlier. Kolk and Heeschen (1992) found that speech from the baseline condition is almost exclusively characterized by omissions of grammatical elements (that is, by "a-phenomena"); almost no substitutions (that is, "para-phenomena") occur. This omission style is usually referred to as *telegraphic style*. The following examples from patients K and W will give the reader an impression of this style. The episode with K (who is not discussed elsewhere in this chapter) is included because it is hard to find another episode in which all properties of telegraphic style are so beautifully exemplified; K offers a textbook case of aphasia.

Patient K was a right-handed male, age 51; etiology was CVA; postonset was 13 years. He was diagnosed and classified by means of the AAT as a moderately severe Broca's aphasic with marked agrammatism. He had a marked paresis in his right arm and hand; all fine movements were carried out with his left arm and hand. His native and only language was German. He spoke High German with occasional Berlin-specific features. His formal education was nine years of elementary schooling. Before the CVA, he was a construction worker. At the time the first author had contact with him, he was living in a half-way house and was working in a sheltered workplace in Berlin-West. Mood was normal, given the circumstances.[6]

Example 2a From a Conversation Between K and the First Author (H)
((The conversation takes place in K's room in the half-way house. K shows H his large collection of audio equipment and of cassettes. Then H takes a sip of coffee; there is silence for 9.4 seconds, then:))

1 H: [inbreath] aber wozu   brauchen Sie dann so viele
              but for-what need   you then so many
              So, why do you need so many radios?
2   Radios?
        radios?
3   (3.1)
4 K: Ja,   ja det äh [inbreath] anjesammelt also.
        Yeah, yeah that äh   collected-PP PRT
        Yeah, yeah, that uh   just piling up
5 H: [((laughs))
6 K: [naja
7 H: (x) hat sich so angesammelt [(xxx)
            has itself so collected
            just kept piling up
8 K: [Ja, teilweise ä
                                    yes, partly   ä
9   teilweise jekriegt   und teilweise gefunden.
        partly   received-PP and partly   found-PP.
10 H: gefunden?
        found-PP?
11 K: Ja.

12 H: Wo   hat (.) wo   findet man denn Radios?
         Where has (.) where finds one PRT radios?
         Where has (.) where do you find radios?
13 K: Ja he
14   (2.0)
15 K: [inbreath] na hier (wieder) gekauft.
                   na here (again) bought-PP.
16 H: Das ham Se   sich   gekauft?
         that have you for-yourself bought-PP?
17 K: äh (1.6) vierhundert und etwas.
         äh (1.6) fourhundred and something.
18 H: hm
19 K: Ja?
20 H: Ja:
21 K: (xxx) ä zwei dreie (.) hab' ik och ä och jekriegt.
                ä two   three (.) have I also ä also received.
22 H: aha
23 K: "(x na x x Mensch /jefut/ Mensch nee, Mensch õna)"
         "(x na x x man   /found/ man   no, man   õna)"
24 H: Aber was meinen Sie denn   mit Sie   haben Radios
         But what mean you-POL PRT by you-POL have radios
         But what do you mean by you found radios?
25   gefunden, wo findet man denn Radios? Doch nicht
         found-PP, where finds one PRT radios? PRT   not
         Where does one find radios—not on the street?
26   auf der Straße?
         on the street?
27 K: Doch.   Papierkorb.
         Well-yes. Waste-paper-basket.
28 H: Radios   in'n   Papierkorb?
         radios into-the waste-paper-basket?
29   (6.0)
30 H: Wer schmeißt denn Radios /ins/   Papierkorb,
         Who throws   PRT radios /into-the/ waste-paper-basket,
         Who throws radios into the waste paper basket,
31   doch nur, wenn sie kaput   sind?
         PRT only, when they broken are?
         only when they are broken?
32 K: nee nee, det nich
         no no, that not
33 H: ganze   Radios schmeißt man einfach so weg?
         working radios throws   one simply so away?
         Who throws away working radios?
34   (2.2)
35 K: ja!

36   (1.5)
37 H: puh! [die Leute ham wohl   zuviel   Geld   dann, nich?
         puh! [people have PRT too-much money then, ne?
38 K: [naõja
39   (1.7)
40 H: und Sie   ham die   denn gefunden?
         and you-POL have them-DEM then found?
         and you found them?
41 K: jaja   in (x) jekuckt   äh, jedesmal   äh=
         yeahyeah into (x) looked-PP äh, every-time äh=
42 H: =aha
43 K: Papierkorb   äh rausbringen wa?
         waste-paper-basket äh to-take-out eh?
44 H: Ja: :
45 K: reingekuckt   wa? (1.7) ä ä Flaschen [Flaschen
         looked-PP-into wa? (1.7) ä ä bottles   bottles
46 H: [aja jaja
47   (2.3)
48 K: leere   Flaschen,
         empty bottles,
49 H: hm hm hm:=
50 K: =Geld   gesucht=
         money looked-PP-for
51 H: naja, Flaschen versteh'   ich
         naja, bottles   understand I
         bottles I can see

Example 2b From a Conversation Between W and the First Author
1   ((H asks W what she did yesterday))
2 W: Gestern? (10.2) " "gestern?" " (1.3) uh
         Yesterday? (10.2) ""yesterday?"" (1.3) uh
3 H: oder [irgend-
         or   some-
4 W: [ah ja
            ah ja
5 H: Ja!
         Yes!
6 W: ä Markt ähm (4.6) eingekauft
         ä market ähm (4.6) shopping-done
7 H: Ja::?
         Yes?
8   (2.8)
9 W: ähm Lebensmittel (4.3) und Obst gekauft
         ähm   food   (4.3) and fruit bought-PP
10 H: hmhm,

11 W: "und"   (2.7) Markt   geguckt
          "and"   (2.7) market looked-PP
12 H: Auf welchem Markt war das denn?
          At   which market was that PRT?
13 W: Karstadt- äh Hermannplatz
              ((*Karstadt is name of a department-store,*
                Hermannplatz the name of a square))
14 H: Is'   da 'n Wochenmarkt?
          Is there a   weekly-market?
15 W: Ja
16 H: Aha!
17 W: Dienstag
          Tuesday
18 H: hm
19 W: Donnerstag und Freitag
          Thursday   and Friday
20 H: aha,   da   haben Sie   eingekauft?
          aha, there have   you-POL shopping-done?
21   (1.0)
22 W: Ja,   mal   gucken
          Yes, PRT to-look-around

The formal core features of telegraphic style are:

1. absence of finite verbs; that is, auxiliaries are omitted (e.g., "Geld gesucht"/ money looked-for-PP instead of the more elaborate "Ich habe Geld gesucht"/ I have looked- for money, line 50 of example 2a; other occurrences of past participles without an auxiliary can be found in lines 4, 9, 15, 41, 45 of example 2a, and lines 6, 9, 11 of example 2b), and inflected main verbs are replaced by the infinitive (e.g., "Papierkorb rausbringen"/ waste-paper-basket to-take-out-INF for the more elaborate "Ich bringe den Papierkorb raus"/ I take the waste-paper-basket to the outside, line 43 of example 2a. An example from W is: "mal gucken"/ PRT to look around, line 22 of example 2b.). Note that the infinitive in German is not a bare stem form, but has a suffix "-en."

2. omission of determiners and articles (e.g., "Papierkorb rausbringen" instead of the more elaborate "den Papierkorb rausbringen," line 43 of example 2a).

3. omission of prepositions (e.g., "doch. Papierkorb"/ well-yes. waste-paper-basket, line 27 in example 2a; note that H indeed understands this bare noun phrase (NP) as a prepositional phrase (PP), as evidenced by his question for confirmation, "Radios in'n Papierkorb"/ radios into the waste-paper- basket?, line 28 of example 2a. An omission of preposition and article made by W can be found in line 6

of example 2b: "Markt eingekauft"/ market shopping-done instead of
the more elaborate "auf dem Markt eingekauft"/ on the market
shopping-done).

4. omission of grammatical subjects in constructions without a finite
   verb. An exception is "det äh [inbreath] anjesammelt also"/ that
   collected-PP PRT in line 4 of example 2a. Otherwise, all constructions
   with a non-finite verb have a null-subject (lines 9, 15, 41, 43, 45, 50
   of example 2a; lines 6, 9, 11, 22 of example 2b). Characteristically,
   the one construction with a finite verb (line 21 of example 2a) does
   have a subject.

It should also be noted that the speech of the patients is a bit less laborious than in
the formal test situation, though still non-fluent. But the patients sound "less vexed."

This list of features by and large fits with the formal-linguistic characterization
of agrammatic speech as resulting from the omission of (higher) "functional heads"
(Cahana-Amitay, 1997; Hagiwara, 1995; Haverkort, 1999; de Roo, 1999).

The most striking feature of telegraphic style, however, is that all the expressions are correct in themselves, and that is not trivial (according to the motto "what
is omitted cannot be wrong"), given complex morphological and word order regularities of German that have to be observed in these telegraphic, subsentential expressions (for details, see Kolk & Heeschen, 1992; and the introductory part of
Heeschen & Schegloff, 1999). And they are correct also with respect to subtle, more
hidden regularities: it is not only that certain elements can be omitted, but sometimes
they even *must* be omitted. Thus, in many expressions in which the finiteness is absent, the grammatical subjects must be omitted as well; otherwise, the "telegram"
would sound straightforwardly incorrect (suppose patient K had added the subject
"ich"/ I to the expression in line 50 of example 2a: "Ich Geld gesucht"/ I money
looked-PP-for—that would make the expression "impaired"). Another instance of
such a "must-be-omitted" regularity is that, absent the finiteness, the reflexive pronoun must also be absent. An example is K's utterance in line 4: "det äh [inbreath]
anjesammelt also"/ that uh just piling up. The German verb for "to keep piling up" is
reflexive, "sich ansammeln"/ literally: to collect oneself. The patient omits the car-
rier of finiteness—the auxiliary—and, consequently, omits the pronoun, too. The
presence of the reflexive pronoun would make the expression sound awful (??? "Det
sich anjesammelt").[7] When resuming K's utterance in line 7, H did produce the reflexive pronoun, but he also produced a finite verb form. Further investigations of
the agrammatics' conversational speech revealed that their "telegrams" are not only
correct but also quite normal insofar as they follow structural patterns of elliptic
expressions used by normals in casual speech designed to be compact (e.g., "Nice
weather today," "Going to miss it?"[8] etc.) (Hofstede, 1992).

It appears that agrammatic patients have an option in the way they express themselves: they either aim at complete sentences but have to "pay" for it with a lot of

errors, as in example 1 and in the example in appendix 2, or they resort to a simplified "register," to subsentential expressions they can produce without errors and with less effort, but in this case they have to "pay" for it because overuse of these expressions—although they are normal with respect to their formal pattern, their structure—is certainly deviant from normal usage, as in examples 2a and 2b. The existence of such an option is the key observation for the adaptation approach to agrammatism as developed by Kolk, Heeschen, and others on the basis of German and Dutch data. Here it is assumed that telegraphic style is not the direct display of the impairment of the cognitive achitecture of language processing underlying agrammatism (which is assumed to consist of limitations on the temporal organization of syntactic processing [Kolk, 1995]), but it is rather the display of an adaptation to the deficit. The patients circumvent, so to speak, their problems in formulating elaborated expressions (such as complete sentences) by simplifying their messages in such a way that they can be just processed by their impaired syntactic formulator. The resulting utterances then are short subsentential expressions, "telegrams" that formally resemble elliptic expressions used by normals as well, although—to repeat—the almost exclusive use of these expressions over a whole episode is certainly somewhat abnormal.[9]

Admittedly, it is fairly loose parlance to speak of "omissions," "telegrams," or "ellipses." These terms used in traditional descriptions of agrammatic speech (and of normal subsentential expressions) suggest that something is missing in these expressions. But this is only so from a normative linguistic perspective, with its emphasis on isolated complete sentences as the analytic primitive. In contrast, the conversation-analytic term "turn constructional unit" (TCU) implies that nothing is missing in a unit to which the participants of an interaction are oriented as a possibly complete turn, be that unit a sentence, a phrase, or a word (Schegloff, 1996b; the matter is discussed in some detail in Heeschen & Schegloff, 1999). The terms, then, are used here for consistency with usage in the traditional literature and in earlier articles. Wherever possible and feasible, in particular in the second part of this chapter, "telegram" and "ellipsis" are replaced by "subsentential expression." Traditional terms appear in scare marks.

It is equally loose and problematic talk to speak of "omitting." This suggests that the speaker of a subsentential unit first designs his utterance as a complete sentence, then decides to omit certain elements, and then reorganizes the grammatical structure according to the rules of his language. Given current models of language production (Levelt, 1989), this is simply nonsensical. Instead, in such a framework one must assume that the design of an utterance as subsentential is located at a very high level of production—in all likelihood already on the level of "intentions." Thus, if a speaker produces "Nice weather today," he never meant to say anything more than just this, certainly not the sentence "Today the weather is nice" or "There is nice weather today," from which he then subtracts some elements at a lower level of production. Again, for consistency with usage we nevertheless use the terms "omitting," "omission," or "omitted elements." Properly understood, these terms mean "absent as compared with a more elaborate expression." The terms are purely descriptive and do not refer to any processing step.

If the patients have an option, a strategic choice[10] to speak like this or like that, then we can ask what factors determine their choice. The cited examples of the differences between speech obtained under formal test conditions and in more ordinary talk-in-interaction suggest that the decisive factor is the presence or absence of ordinary interaction as the oriented-to context. Whereas in the informal conversation (examples 2a and 2b) the aphasiologist interacts with the patients in a more or less ordinary way, the cartoon story tellings (example 1 and example in appendix 2) were elicited in such a way that the patient produces a monologue without any "ordinary" communication. The cartoons were lying open between the patient and the experimenter/tester, so the telling of the stories had no meaningful communicative function. The experimenter/tester had announced that he would not interrupt but also would not help the patient in telling the stories and that the patient had all the time needed for the task. Interventions by the tester/experimenter were reduced to occasional expressions of support, such as encouragements to go on or reassurances that the patient need not feel time pressure. As mentioned, the tester/experimenter does not behave ordinarily here insofar as he or she tries to maximize the patient's turn; furthermore, the discourse the patient produces is not an achievement as in ordinary conversation (Schegloff, 1981) but rather the result of a pact between patient and experimenter signed beforehand. And, finally, the tester's/experimenter's behavior here is an extreme case of conduct described by Jefferson (1984) as "perverse passive."

However, the claim that ordinary interaction makes the difference between the two conditions is still not adequately justified; another factor is confounded with the "interaction" factor. In the "non-interactional" (or, more precisely, "attenuated-interactional") condition, the "content"—the "what has to be said"—is entirely given by the cartoons, whereas in the baseline condition the "what" is more or less up to the patient. And this may also contribute to the determination of linguistic form, that is, the choice between more elaborate expressions and telegraphic style. To assess the possible influence of this confounding factor, we asked four German-speaking and four Dutch-speaking aphasics, all diagnosed as Broca's aphasics with agrammatism by means of the German and Dutch versions of the Aachen Aphasia Test, respectively, to tell four cartoon stories in the formal ("non-interactional") test situation and again (some weeks later) with the following modifications: they had to tell the stories to a confidant (as a rule, a close relative) who did not know the stories and could not see the cartoons. Furthermore, the confidants were free to interfere with the patients' talk by questions or remarks whenever they wanted to do so. The task set for patient and confidant by the experimenter was just "to get the story across." This condition is referred to as "interactional story telling." The four cartoon stories came from the set used by Goodglass, Christiansen, and Gallagher (1993). The wake-up story in example 1 is just one of these simple stories. The two story telling conditions were then compared with the speech obtained in informal conversation (baseline condition).

The results can be found in Heeschen and Kolk (1994). Here, we present the results of only one patient. Patient W is quite representative for the agrammatic group; her talk in a naturalistic conversation with her daughter and her mother will be described and analyzed in part 2 of this chapter. W was almost indefinitely cooperative so that she participated in two additional conditions of cartoon storytelling not presented in Heeschen and Kolk (1994).

Before describing the outcome of the experimental series, we need to discuss three points:

1. The use of telegraphic style is not an all-or-none phenomenon. In a given episode or in a given task, a patient almost never uses telegraphic expressions throughout. Only a certain percentage of utterances are telegraphic. Note in this context that even patient K—who is an extreme telegraphic speaker—produces one fully elaborated expression (line 21 in example 2a). The percentage of subsentential expressions varies from one patient to the other and sometimes even within one patient across various sessions. In non-impaired speakers in casual speech, roughly 10% of all utterances are subsentential (Hofstede, 1992). There is unanimity among experienced aphasiologists if a person produces more than 30% subsentential utterances, he or she is recognizable as using telegraphic style.

2. In order to quantify the extent to which telegraphic style is used in a given situation in a given patient, one needs an operational criterion, a definition of what counts as telegraphic' utterance. There are good theoretical and empirical reasons to introduce the presence or absence of a finite verb form as the defining criterion. Many regularities of telegraphic-elliptic or subsentential expressions in German (and in all likelihood also in Dutch) center on the finite verb or its omission, respectively (Klein, 1985). And as shown by Hofstede (1992), roughly 90% of all omissions of grammatical elements by agrammatic speakers occur in expressions without a finite verb. Hence, the percentage of non-finite expressions is an empirically justified and theoretically motivated variable to characterize the trend of a given patient's telegraphic style.

3. In a quantitative assessment of the telegraphicity of a stretch of speech, it is advisable not to count subsentential expressions as telegraphic that are immediate responses to wh-questions (e.g., Where are you going?—to Berlin). Subsentential expressions in this position are too normal, too canonical (Schegloff, 1996b). Furthermore, in the experimental conditions in which the experimenter reduces his or her interventions to a minimum, no questions are asked. Subsentential utterances as responses to questions have no chance to occur here so

that not counting them makes the various conditions—the interactional and attenuated-interactional ones—more directly comparable.

In table 10.1, the percentages of telegraphic (that is, non-finite) utterances used by patient W, the percentage of finite utterances, and the percentage of "remainders" (that is, not clearly analyzable utterances and fixed formulaic expressions) are presented together with the absolute number of utterances (n) in each of the three conditions described (baseline, "non-interactional," and interactional storytelling).

Samples of W's speech for the baseline condition and for the attenuated-interactional storytelling were already given (Examples 1 and 2a). In example 3 W's way of constructing the wake-up story with her adult daughter (D) is presented.

Example 3 Interactional Storytelling

1	W:	(ähder) Mann, (4.4) weckt,
		(ähthe) man, (4.4) awakens
2		(3.2)
3	D:	Was macht er?
		What does he?
4	W:	Äh klingelt äh /dem/ Wecker, "klingelt"
		Äh rings äh /the-MASC-SG-DAT/ alarm-clock "rings"
5		(2.8)
6	D:	Ja, da ist ein Mann und der Wecker klingelt(?)
		Yes, there is a man and the alarm-clock rings(?)
7		.3)
8	W:	äh aufstehn, acht- sieben Uhr, (3.1)
		äh to-get-up, eight- seven o'clock (3.1)
9		/den/ Wecker klingelt. (6.0) hm=
		/the-MASC-SG-ACC/ alarm-clock rings. 6.0) hm=
10	D:	= Was macht der Mann?
		= What does the man {do}?
11		(0.8)
12	W:	raufäh- raufhauen [((laughter))
		on- to-hit-on ((laughter))
13	D:	[auf'n Wecker?
		on-to-the alarm-clock?

TABLE 10.1 Percentages of Nonfinite (NF), Finite (F), Remaining Utterances (R) and Absolute Number of Utterances (n) for Patient W in Three Conditions

$a1$ = Baseline				$a2$ = "Non-interactional" storytelling				$a3$ = Interactional storytelling			
NF	F	R	(n)	NF	F	R	(n)	NF	F	R	(n)
73	7	20	(30)	24	73	3	(37)	52	30	18	(94)

14 W: Ja, /den/   Wecker
          Yes, / the-MASC-SG-ACC/ alarm-clock
15   rauf- /ran-/ hauen. (1.3) ähm
          on- /at-/   to-hit. (1.3) ähm
16   (6.2)
17 D: Bleibt   er liegen im   Bett oder?
          Continues he to-lie in-the bed or?
18 W: Ja, ja! Acht Uhr   äh schläft- äh weiterschlafen
          Yes, yes! Eight o'clock äh sleeps- äh to-continue-to-sleep
19 D: Hm,   bleibt liegen im   Bett bis   acht [Uhr?
          Hm, continues to-lie in-the bed until eight o'clock?
20 W: [Ja,
                                            Yes,
21   die Frau   ähm (5.3) böse
          the woman ähm (5.3) angry
22 D: Die   ist böse, warum?
          She-DEM is angry, why?
23 W: Ja ähm weiterschlafen   ((laughter))
          Yes ähm to-continue-to-sleep ((laughter))
24 D: Weil   er weiter "geschlafen"
          Because he continued-PP-to-sleep
25 W: Ja ähm (6.7) die Frau   (5.7) guckt auf die Uhr und
          Yes ähm (6.7) the woman (5.7) looks at   the clock and
26   (3.8)
27 D: guckt wie spät es ist oder was?
          looks how late it is or what?
28 W: Ja. äh der Mann ähm beeilt sich
          Yes, äh the man ähm hurries-up
29 D: hm?hm?
30   (5.0)
31 W: auf der Straße, ähm
          on the street, ähm
32 D: Wie auf der Straße? Ist er rausgegangen oder was?
          How on the street? Has he gone-out   or   what?
33 W: (nein) beeilen
          (no)   to-hurry-up
34 D: Mit der Frau?
          With the woman?
35 W: Nee, der der Mann beeilt sich ähm (5.8) auweia
          No, the the man hurries-up ähm (5.8) gee!
36   ((laughter)) hm der   (1.4)
          ((laughter)) hm he-DEM (1.4)
37 D: geht irgendwohin?
          goes somewhere?

38 W: Nee, auf der Arbeit
         No,   at   work
39 D: Hm
40 W: ähä (2.4) der Mann (4.4) ä:h auf'n Stuhl
         ähä (2.4) the man   (4.4) ä:h on-the chair
41   eingeschlafen.
         fallen-to-sleep.
42 D: Der   ist eingeschlafen. [((laughter))
         He-DEM has fallen-to-sleep.
43 W: [((laughter))

Without going into the details, one can easily see that W produces here quite a number of non-finite, subsentential expressions that are not direct responses to wh-questions by D so that they are to be counted as telegraphic or non-finite expressions. A very revealing occurrence is the self-correction in line 18. W starts a finite construction ("acht Uhr schläft"/ eight o'clock sleeps) but cuts it off and provides instead the verb in the infinitive ("weiterschlafen"/ to-continue-to-sleep), a clear example of redesigning her utterance from elaborate to telegraphic.

Each condition of table 10.1 was compared with the other two conditions by means of a chi-square test. As there are three conditions plus two additional ones (described below) so that there are 10 comparisons, the level of significance was fixed at .005. The difference between a1 and a2 was significant: ($\chi^2[2] = 30.61$; $p < .005$) as well as the difference between a2 and a3 ($\chi^2[2] = 21.00$; $p < .005$). There was no significant difference between a1 and a3 ($\chi^2[2] = 6.86$; $p > .005$). That is to say, patient W's strong tendency toward telegraphic style in informal conversation decreases in the "non-interactional" (or more precisely: in the attenuated-interactional) storytelling condition (as expected), but increases in the interactional storytelling, up to almost the same degree as in the baseline condition. It appears that the factor "what has to be said" cannot be responsible for the difference between speech obtained in informal conversation and speech obtained in formal test condition; otherwise, there should also have been a difference between informal conversation and interactional storytelling. As the latter is not the case, the factor "presence vs. absence of ordinary interaction" as responsible for the difference between a1 and a2 seems justifiable. However, again this is a bit premature. Another and hitherto disregarded factor is confounded with "interaction," namely, the person interacting with the patient: in a1, it is an aphasiologist, and in a3 it is a confidant. To check the possible influence of this factor, we introduced an additional non-interactional storytelling condition: some weeks after a3, patient W had to tell the cartoon stories again, this time to her daughter; but the latter was requested "to behave like a tester/experimenter," that is, in the same way as described for the aphasiologist in a2. In this non-interactional storytelling to the daughter (condition a4), patient W showed the following distribution of non-finite, finite, and remaining utterances: NF = 10%, F = 69%, R = 20%, and n = 49. Example 4 shows W's telling of the wake-up story under this condition.

Example 4 "Non-interactional" Storytelling to a Close Relative

1   W: Der Mann haut auf den Wecker.   (13.7) Der Mann
         The man   hits   on   the   alarm-clock. (13.7) The man
2   schläft weiter.   (3.4) Die   Frau   (9.5) spricht
         continues-to-sleep. (3.4) The woman (9.5) speaks
3   mit dem Mann und (8.1) acht Uhr   (7.2) auf die- nee
         with the   man   and (8.1) eight o'clock (7.2) on the- no
4   (16.1)
5   D: Du hast Zeit
         You have time
6   (5.4) das [Früh-
         (5.4) the   break-
7   D: [((clears throat))
8   W: das Frühstück (4.9) und (15.6) auf (14.2) hm (2.8)
         the breakfast   (4.9) and (15.6) on (14.2) hm (2.8)
9   die   Frau sieht auf die Uhr. (5.8) Der Mann °schn-°
         the woman looks at the clock. (5.8) the man   °schn-°
10   (2.8) der Mann (4.4) ißt   schnell. (11.7)
         (2.8) the man   (4.4) eats quickly. (11.7)
11   der Mann beeilt   sich auf auf auf die Arbeit nee
         the man   hurries up to to to the work   no
12   ((sighs)) (1.3) auf auf die Arbeitsstelle zu gehen.
         ((sighs)) (1.3) to to   the workplace   to go.
13   Ach du Schreck, (0.6) der Mann schläft weiter.   Na!
         good gracious, (0.6) the man   continues-to-sleep. Na!

As can be seen, the daughter is quite successful in playing the "perversely passive" professional tester. And as the latter, she elicits elaborate finite non-telegraphic expressions from her mother by acting like this. W's grammatical elaborations are quite remarkable. In line 11–12 she produces a fully correct matrix clause with a fully correct subordinate clause—a rare occurrence in Broca's patients. The elaborations and the correctness of her expressions, however, cost a dramatic amount of time.

The statistical evaluation of the data showed that this condition differed significantly from a1 ($\chi^2[2]$ = 37.78; p < .005) as well as from a3 ($\chi^2[2]$ = 26.73; p < .005), but not from a2 ($\chi^2[2]$ = 7.79; p > .005). Obviously, it does not matter whether the "tester" is a professional as in a2 or a confidant; the decisive factor appears to be the practices adopted for the conduct of interaction.

However, a factor is still confounded with "interaction": some colleagues of the first author have raised the argument that, in talk-in-interaction, the speaker does not only have to attend to his or her own speech but also to the speech of the other so that interaction brings about a higher cognitive load. To check the possible influence of this factor we asked the patient to tell the cartoon stories once more (again, some weeks later), this time as in a2 (formal test condition with an aphasiologist), but the difficulty was enhanced by a dual task arrangement: while telling the stories, a taped voice gave the patient commands to press either a green or a red button as fast as possible. Intervals of these commands were random; the average interval was 20 s. The "wake-up" story under this condition was as follows:

Example 5
((The straight vertical lines stand for the commands to push a button))

1   W: Der Mann schläft (6.9) /morgen/   früh
         The man   sleeps (6.9) /tomorrow/ in-the-morning
2   acht nee sieben Uhr   wecken   (3.4) der Mann |
         eight no seben o'clock to-awake (3.4) the man /
3   (8.5) der Mann (7.3) | (13.9) ach Mensch! (2.3) haut
         (8.5) the man   (7.3) / (13.9) oh man!   (2.3) hits
4   auf'n   Wecker   ((laughter)) | (3.2)
         on-to-the alarm-clock ((laughter)) / (3.2)
5   ach du Schreck! (3.5) der Mann schläft weiter   (2.7)
         oh Lord!   (3.5) the man   continues-to-sleep (2.7)
6   die Frau   schimpft (11.6) acht Uhr   ((sighs))
         the woman scolds   (11.6) eight o'clock ((sighs))
7 | (4.0) der Mann- äh die Frau   schimpft (6.7) oh (3.9)
         / (4.0) the man-   äh the woman scolds   (6.7) oh (3.9)
8   /der/   Frau   die   Frau |
         /the-MASC-SG-NOM/ woman the-FEM-SG-NOM woman /
9   die Frau   (2.8) guckt auf die Uhr.   halb neun
         the woman (2.8) looks at   the clock. half past eight
10   (3.2) die äh Fr- | äh die Frau   äh der Mann
         (3.2) the äh woman | äh the woman äh the man
11   ißt   schneller. (6.5) Der Mann verschlafen. (5.6) Der
         eats faster.   (6.5) The man over-slept-PP. (5.6) The
12   Mann rennt /auf/ die Arbeit ach du Schreck! ((laughter))
         man   runs /to/ the work oh lord!   ((laughter))
13 | (6.1) der Mann schläft auf /die/   Arbeit
         / (6.1) the man   sleeps at /the-FEM-SG-ACC/ work
14   nee nee
         no no

A quick first glance suffices to show that the enhancement of the overall difficulty by the dual task arrangement did not lead to the deployment of telegraphic style. There are a few telegraphic utterances (e.g., "sieben Uhr wecken"/ seven o'clock to-awake, line 2), but the majority of the expressions are finite. The distribution of NF, F, R and the absolute number of utterances in this dual task condition (a5)—summed over the four stories—was: NF = 16%, F = 61%, R = 23%, $n = 57$. The statistical evaluation confirms the first-glance impression. With respect to the distribution of finite and non-finite expressions, there was no significant difference between a5 and a2 ($\chi^2[2] = 7.39$; $p > .005$) or between a5 and a4 ($\chi^2[2] = .95$; $p > .005$). But there were significant differences between a5 and the two interactional conditions (a5 versus a1, $\chi^2[2] = 32.18$; $p < .005$; and a5 vs. a3, $\chi^2[2] = 21.10$; $p < .005$). That means that the enhancement of the task difficulty did not contribute anything with respect to the choice between telegraphic style and a more elaborate way of expressing oneself. The "attenuated-interactional" storytelling with an aphasiologist under dual task conditions showed the same picture as the same condition without dual task constraints, as well as the "attenuated-interactional" storytelling with a confidant instead of an aphasiologist. The logic of a dual task in the cognitive sciences is this: two tasks simultaneously carried out should interfere with each other (that is, the subjects should become worse than in either of the two tasks or in both) if they compete for common processing resources. If there is no interference effect, then the two tasks do not compete with each other or the dual task is not difficult enough. In any case, it is hard to make anything out of a null effect, as in our case. However, storytelling and the choice reaction time task *did* interfere with each other: patient W's speech became markedly worse in a5 as compared with a2. One fairly direct way of assessing this deterioration is the scoring of incorrect grammatical elements. In a2 patient W produced only 3 incorrect elements out of 48 (6%) and in a5 20 elements out of 66 (30%). The difference is significant ($\chi^2[1] = 9.96$; $p < .01$). Thus, the interfering choice reaction time task did have an effect on W's speech; but it did not make her switch over to telegraphic style—*quod erat demonstrandum*.

In summarizing, it might be useful to combine all results in one table (table 10.2), thereby grouping the experimental conditions according to a higher or lower percentage of telegraphic utterances. For transparency's sake, the results are also simplified and only the percentages of NF ("telegrams") are presented.

The two conditions with some sort of ordinary interaction (a1 and a3) go together and the three conditions where the interaction between patient and tester is minimized (a2, a4, and a5) go together. It does not appear to matter

TABLE 10.2 Percentages of Telegraphic Utterances (NF) of Patient W in 5 Conditions

a1 = Informal conversation with aphasiologist	a3 = Interactional storytelling with confidant	a2 = Storytelling under formal test conditions with aphasiologst	a4 = Storytelling under formal test conditions with confidant	a5 = Storytelling under formal test conditions with aphasiologist, dual task
73	52	24	10	16

- what the talk-in-interaction is—either free topic or enforced cartoon stories (a1 vs. a3),
- whether the tester is a less or more familiar person (a2 vs. a4), or
- whether the task is comparatively easy or comparatively difficult (a2 vs. a5).

The only relevant factor determining the deployment or non-deployment of telegraphic style appears to be the presence or absence of some form of ordinary interaction. If the use of telegraphic style is due to an adaptive strategy, then this adaptation must be "interactionally motivated" (to translate the question in the title of Heeschen & Kolk, 1994, "Adaptation bei Agrammatikern—interaktional motiviert?").

As straightforward as this result is, the numbers do not tell us anything about what actually is achieved by the adaptation and how it is achieved. To assume that a patient develops adaptive strategies just to converse with a professional aphasiologist (a1), or that he or she does so for the purposes of an enforced—though interactional—construction of some silly cartoon stories, (a3), does not seem reasonable. A detailed look at the practices deployed by patient and co-participant in naturalistic ordinary settings will be useful, because it must be in these day-to-day recurring situations that the patient can plausibly be assumed to develop adaptive strategies. Such a process of exploring and understanding adaptation in the context of mundane interaction can be informed by the corpus of description and analysis of the phenomena of talk and other conduct in interaction among language-unimpaired speakers developed over the last 35 years within the framework of Conversation Analysis.

To this end, we recorded conversations between aphasic patients and an unimpaired familiar co-participant. Patient W was recorded once in conversation with her daughter and once in conversation with her mother. As the experimental investigations reported in the first part of this chapter dealt mainly with a form of storytelling, we decided to find and focus on an episode with story-like characteristics. After having learned (though definitely not understood) what happens with the patient's speech in various conditions of storytelling, and that what happens is obviously due to the global factor "interaction," we now turn to talk-in-interaction in which some telling is done, in which something gets recounted—a little story, perhaps—as it *really* occurred in an unmanipulated situation of talk-in-interaction to explore how telling is managed by an (aphasic) teller and a ("normal") recipient.

If, instead of using actual deployments of talk "as a window into the structure and organization of normal cognitive processes" and language, we wish to use our understanding of language, cognition and other features of the situation of practical action to understand actual conduct in this world, what is it that we have to come to terms with? And how can we use our understanding of the structures of talk and other conduct in interaction in coming to terms with it?

Analytic observations on some excerpts from conversations with patient W

Example 6 comes from a conversation between W and her daughter (D). It took place in the home of W in a working class area of Berlin-West. The daughter had been living there together with her mother and her grandmother since early childhood. She had moved to another place just shortly before the conversation took place. In her early twenties, she is a student of education. She speaks High German with occasional touches of Berlin dialect, as does her mother. The recorded conversation between D and W was not especially arranged for taping. It occurred at a time and at an occasion when D would have visited her mother for a chat anyway.

Example 6

((The just-preceding talk had been about a birthday party in the home of W a few days earlier. W and D exchanged comments on the quality of the salads served at the party, then there is silence for 5 seconds, then:))

1	D:	Wie lange war Karin-	((W unpacking cookies with her
		How long was Karin-	left hand))
		How long did Karin-	
2		õiß doch!	((D moves head toward the
		eat PRT!	cookies, then back to W))
		Go ahead and eat!	
3		wie lange war Karin noch da?	
		how long was Karin still here?	
		how long did Karin stay?	
4	W:	"Zwei" Uhr.	((head forward as
		"Two o'clock"	if confiding))
		Two o'clock.	
5		(0.8)	((W withdraws gaze, then D))
6	W:	"geschlafen"	((W resumes gaze))
		"slept-PP"	
		Sleeping.	
7		(0.5)	((W withdraws gaze))
8	D:	Du bist eingeschlafen, oder was,	((D resumes gaze,
		You have fallen-to-sleep, or what,	then W))
		You fell asleep, or what,	
9		(1.0)	
10	W:	Ja- ä:h, Karin (.) eingeschlafen	
		Ye- ä:h, Karin (.) fallen-to-sleep	
		Ye- uh, Karin (.) fell asleep	
11		(0.7)	
12	D:	>Wo, hier, oder was.<	
		>Where, here, or what,<	
		>Where, here, or what,<	

```
13  W:   õJa:,   lang gelegt              ((W gesturing "lying down"))
         Ye:s, lain-down
         Ye:s, passed out
14          (0.8)
15  D:   hmpfs!

16          (0.2)
17  D:   >Warum< habt ihr      sie nicht aufgeweckt,
         >why<     have you-PL her not   waked-up,
         Why didn't you wake her up,
18          (1.0)
19  W:   !hh ä- ä:hm (1.8) Gernot         ((W gesturing the tickling
         hh ä- ä:hm (1.8) Gernot          motion through line 23.))
         !hh uh- uh:m, (1.8) Gernot
20       {!hhhh/(0.8)} h'm (0.8) Füße gekillert !hh und
         {!hhhh/(0.8)} h'm (0.8) feet tickled-PP !hh and
         {!hhhh/(0.8)} mm (0.8) tickled [her] feet !hh and
21  D:   h_h_
22          (0.5)
23  W:   P:o gekillert
         tushy tickled-PP
         tickled [her] tushy
24          (.)                           ((W doing "negative" head
                                            shakes through line 26))
25  D:   õhihi
26          (0.5)
27  D:   !hhh nich' wachgeworden,
         !hhh not    got-PP-awake,
         !hhh didn't wake up,
28  W:   Nö
```

((Not directly visible in the transcript is W's non-fluency. Her rate of speech is slow, and the speech is halting and full of hesitations. The pauses in W's speech that are marked in the transcript stand out noticeably against this general non-fluency.))

On the face of it, Karin's behavior at the party appears to be "storyable," and, as noted, this was one of the reasons for selecting this episode for this chapter. However, from a conversation analytic point of view, whether something is a story (or narrative) is not a question of fulfilling defining critera for the genre established by analysts beforehand (as in Labov, 1981), but is a matter of the participants themselves, of whether they themselves are oriented to their doings as the construction of a story or a storytelling. Thus, we had better attend to what kind of talk this is and how it is co-constructed to be that.

The talk about salads at the party having been brought to closure and having issued in a silence grown into a lapse, the character of the next spate of talk is indeterminate. There could be more about the party but need not be. D's next turn moves to take up a matter also related to the party and designed for its possible storyability.

1	D:	Wie lange war Karin- *How long was Karin-* How long did Karin-	((W unpacking cookies with her left hand))
2		i_§ doch! *eat PRT!* Go ahead and eat!	((D moves head toward the cookies, then back to W))
3		wie lange war Karin noch da? *how long was Karin still here?* how long did Karin stay?	

The very question "How long did Karin stay?" itself displays an orientation to there possibly being an issue here worth talking/telling about, and very likely one oriented to by both W and D. It does this in part by virtue of turn design. The question format "How long" itself takes duration to be relevant and problematic, as does the durative verb "stay" and its German implementation in the particle "noch" ("stay" serving here as the English rendering of the German "still be there"). In its presupposing Karin's presence at the party in the first place, the question may well invoke an updating of D's previous knowledge about the event (for example, that D was there until quite late and Karin was still there when she left or retired; or that Karin's presence was unexpected, and thus any duration was problematic, etc.). So Karin's question marks this matter as potentially worthy of further talk, of being made something of.[11]

3		wie lange war Karin noch da? *how long was Karin still here?* how long did Karin stay?	
4	W:	"Zwei" Uhr. *"Two o'clock"* Two o'clock.	((head forward as if confiding))
5		(0.8)	((W withdraws gaze, then D))
6	W:	"geschlafen" *"slept-PP"* Sleeping.	((W resumes gaze))
7		(0.5)	((W withdraws gaze))
8	D:	Du bist eingeschlafen, oder was, *You have fallen-to-sleep, or what,* You fell asleep, or what,	((D resumes gaze, then W))
9		(1.0)	

W's response, "two o'clock" (by any measure a late hour), confirms this inexplicitly conveyed problematicity, conveys some measure of its substantial extent, and hints at a sense of the trouble or faux pas involved on Karin's side. Having done so, W looks away, apparently done. But it seems as if she continues resonating what she has done, and knows that it conveys something possibly misleading about what actually happened, because she implies that Karin continuously until two o'clock was sentiently "staying," that is, choosing not to leave or not registering the inappropriateness of not leaving. But that is not what was going on; she passed out, and she only "stayed" in the conscious sense until she passed out. After that, she may still have physically been there, but she was not "staying" in the same sense. So W "returns" to the talk to add "passed out." And that sets the sequel on another course, for dealing with a "passed out" late-staying guest is different from dealing with a conscious late-staying guest—different in its social interpretation, "moral" import, and strategic challenge to the host—and different as an event reported in conversation. With this reply, then, W aligns with the premise of D's question that something is of interest here, something worth talking and telling about. And in case D had not picked that up from the first component of W's response, W has provided the second.

W's answer is somewhat spare. Although a subsentential expression (just the indication of the time) is certainly canonical here, in W's expression at line 4 the preposition "um"/ at or "bis"/ until is lacking ("um 2 Uhr"/ at two o'clock, or "bis 2 Uhr"/ until two o'clock). Although this does not make her utterance ungrammatical, she produces no more than the necessary minimum. On the other hand, the telling of the time is delivered in a special way: W moves her head in the direction of D, thus coming closer to D's ears, and she lowers the volume of her voice, as if she were confiding something particularly delicate, embarrassing, or outrageous. Still, immediately after her turn in line 4 and in the ensuing pause (line 5), she withdraws her gaze from D and looks back to the cookies she is trying to unpack. Thus, a talk-unrelated activity is displayed as the focus of her attention, responded to by D with her own withdrawal of gaze so that a state of mutual disengagement is arrived at (cf. Goodwin, 1986, for the interactional impact of talk-unrelated actions). But then W redirects her gaze to D and adds "geschlafen"/ slept- PP. That the unit "geschlafen" is related to and connected with the preceding utterance is displayed by the fact that it is delivered with the same somewhat lowered voice. As noted, if Karin fell asleep, it is a possible account for the delivery of Karin's late stay at the party as a delicate or otherwise problematic matter. After this, W again looks away to the cookies. But now D's interest is aroused; she redirects gaze to her mother and offers a candidate understanding (line 8) of W's short and spare expression in line 6. Immediately after onset of D's turn, W redirects her gaze from the cookies back to her daughter, and now mutual orientation is re-achieved.

There is nothing deviant from normal, nothing "impaired" in this fugue-like tumble of gaze directions, of engagement and disengagement. Mutual orientation, as well as mutual disengagement, is not automatic but is an achievement that requires coordinated work and negotiations (Goodwin, 1981, 1984). While the character of the sequence is not yet determined, W's special conspiratorial delivery of "Zwei Uhr" and "geschlafen" is not unlike an interest arouser typical of story prefaces (Sacks, 1995, II: 222–228), and in the aftermath of "geschlafen," the two women are sustaining a mutual orientation that prefigures continuation of the talk in progress.

```
8    D:   Du bist eingeschlafen, oder was,      ((D resumes gaze,
           You have fallen-to-sleep, or what,       then W))
           You fell asleep, or what,
9          (1.0)
10   W:    Ja-  :h, Karin (.) eingeschlafen
           Ye-  :h, Karin (.) fallen-to-sleep
           Ye- uh, Karin (.) fell asleep
11         (0.7)
```

In line 8, D probes W's one-word utterance in line 6, specifically by providing a candidate agent of the sleeping, "you." As will be seen in a moment, D is mistaken here; it was Karin. Did D simply misunderstand her mother? Was W's utterance indeed too short—too "agrammatic"? A closer inspection of D's utterance suggests a more differentiated—and possibly barbed—characterization.

First, D gives the word "Du"/ you a mildly contrastive stress; furthermore, the "Du" is delivered with an unusual pronunciation: the vowel "u" is reduced to a schwa. Nevertheless, it is stressed; and a stressed schwa is a fairly recalcitrant occurrence for any phonological theory of German. Thus, the least that can be said is that the offered agent "you" is strongly marked so that it appears to be not only a proposal for the agent but a contrastive one: was it *you* who fell sleep? The deployment of the tag question "oder was"?/ or what? reinforces this putative contrast but marks it as the less likely understanding. What is at issue here may concern what exactly W's conspiratorial manner was alluding to? Whose conduct is it indelicate to refer to? Was it that Karin stayed so late that the mother fell asleep at the party she herself was hosting (an embarrassment, then, for both of them)? Or is it that Karin's sleeping is treated here as hardly believable, as something that needs special reconfirmation. The turn's construction focuses on the first of these (see endnote 18).

D's turn in line 8 contains another element: she replaces "geschlafen"/ *slept- PP* by "bist eingeschlafen"/ have *fallen asleep*. Because the stress on "Du"/*you* marks it as the thrust of D's turn, the introduction of "bist eingeschlafen" comes off as an embedded correction of W's turn (Jefferson, 1987), done en passant while some other action is the prime basis for the turn; and it is accepted in the canonical manner for embedded corrections—it is incorporated en passant in W's next turn at line 10 (a case of the unmarked correction sequence X-Y-Y). But as shown in a moment, there is more to it.

W begins to answer D's question "*you* fell to sleep, or what?" in the affirmative, but cuts off the "ja"/ *yes*, attaches an "editing term," and then intitiates a self-repair to replace her agreement with a correction of D's displayed supposition. W's intial "ja-" reflects an orientation to the normal preference for agreement (Pomerantz, 1984;

Sacks, 1987), one that surfaces in "normal" speakers as well, even when one's knowledge is at variance with it. As is common in such instances, she repairs it and provides a correction in its place—the real agent of the falling asleep, Karin. She incorporates the repaired verb en passant while correcting the person reference (but only the non-finite verb part, the past participle), thereby ratifying the embedded correction of grammar by D.[12]

```
10  W:   Ja- ä:h, Karin (.) eingeschlafen
         Ye- ä:h, Karin (.) fallen-to-sleep
         Ye- uh, Karin (.) fell asleep
11       (0.7)
12  D:   >Wo,     hier, oder was.<
         >Where, here, or   what,<
          >Where, here, or   what,<
13  W:   Ja:,   lang gelegt              ((W gesturing "lying down"))
         Ye:s, lain-down
         Ye:s, passed out
14       (0.8)
15  D:   hmpfs!
```

In line 12, D continues to "unpack" W's one-word utterance in line 6. She asks for the location of Karin's falling-to-sleep ("Wo?") and then adds a candidate ("hier") which, by the tag question "or what," is marked as just one of several alternatives. Given the global context (the birthday party) as well as the specific context (Karin stayed until 2 o'clock and fell asleep), it is plain enough that Karin fell asleep "here" in the sense of "this residence." Unless discriminating between the kitchen in which this conversation is being conducted and elsewhere in the apartment, the question as a locational inquiry is gratuitous. However, D's turn conveys something else. It is delivered in a (slightly) louder voice and with (slight) acceleration. These features together embody ("do") being taken aback—conveying a disapproving stance. The reproach could be directed toward Karin (for her improper behavior) or toward W (for letting Karin behave improperly, for not preventing Karin from falling to sleep here), or to both.

W's response addresses these several possible reproaches. In line 13, W confirms that it was "here" by a "ja" delivered with heightened and louder voice and with an overlong vowel. This "ja" is quite a different object from the one in line 10; it is an almost lexicalized item in German for reconfirming information marked as unusual or unlikely before. It can be glossed as "yes indeed, imagine!" Clearly, W appears not to take D's questions in line 12 as gratuitous but displays understanding for D's taken-aback stance. The second turn component "langgelegt" gives an account of how all this could happen and why she, the host, could not prevent this *malheur*: Karin has "lain down." The German verb "sich langlegen" does not correspond exactly to the English "to lie down" (which would be "sich hinlegen"). It adds a component of urgency, even uncontrollability, for the action of lying down. This, together with W's gesture (moving left hand from left to right at the height of her breast), which is carried out with some verve, suggests that it was not the simple action of just lying down but rather a falling down—in American English (given the party context) "passing out."

Excursus on agrammatism and conversational
practice: argument structure

It might be useful here to stop the turn-by-turn analytic gloss and to take up issues addressed in the first part of this chapter. W clearly produces talk referred to as "telegraphic style" in traditional terminology. All her utterances are subsentential, and not only in response to wh-questions. Indeed, all her utterances are truncated versions of whatever grammatical unit they are designed to instantiate (e.g., lacking the preposition in a prepositional phrase, etc.). D's response to her mother's spare utterances have already been described as "probing" and "unpacking." She formulates and elaborates points that have been "undertold" or compacted by W herself; she talks, so to speak, on behalf of W (although not in the manner described by Sacks [1995] as "collaboratives" and by Lerner [1991, 1996] as "anticipatory completion"). She deploys a practice also found in a conversation between another agrammatic and another healthy co-participant (Heeschen & Schegloff, 1999), and the characterizations in that article are confirmed by the material under examination here, but only at a global level. The particulars and details of these two conversations are quite different. The most conspicuous difference is that W uses *verb forms* as the kernel of her utterances, whereas the patient described in Heeschen and Schegoff (1999) uses *noun phrases*. From an interactional and linguistic point of view, verb forms have two useful properties: (1) associated with a main verb, there is the verb's argument structure so that the participant who undertakes to elaborate the subsentential unit is guided or "navigated" in doing so;[13] (2) in German, non-finite verb forms such as the past participles used by W have to appear at the end of clauses (see appendix 1), thus marking a possible (syntactical) completion—a grammatical property of German that can be a resource for the management of turn taking (Schegloff, Ochs, & Thompson, 1996, p. 29). Let us briefly check whether W and D make these properties relevant in their interaction.

6   W: "geschlafen"   ((W resumes gaze))
          "slept-PP"
          Sleeping.
7   (0.5) ((W withdraws gaze))
8   D: Du bist eingeschlafen,   oder was,   ((D resumes gaze,
          You have fallen-to-sleep, or what,   then W))
          You fell asleep, or what,
9   (1.0)

```
10  W:    Ja-  :h,  Karin (.) eingeschlafen
          Ye-  :h,  Karin (.) fallen-to-sleep
          Ye-  uh,  Karin (.) fell asleep
11        (0.7)
12  D:    >Wo,      hier,  oder was.<
          >Where,  here,  or  what,<
             >Where,                          here, or what,<
13  W:    Ja:,      lang gelegt          ((W gesturing "lying down"))
          Ye:s,  lain-down
          Ye:s,  passed out
```

For the first of these properties, argument structure, D's elaborations of W's utterance "geschlafen" indeed follow, step by step, the frame of the verb's common understood argument structure: who (line 8) and where (line 12). In some psycholinguistic models of sentence production, the verbal lemma (meaning and argument structure) is considered the starting point and cornerstone of the sentence formulation process (Bock & Levelt, 1994), so that W's utterances would reflect an early basic step in the production process, the elaboration of which is then left to the conversational partner. It is tempting—in a virtual reversal of Vygotsky's proposals—to conceive of D's and W's division of labor as an externalization of cognitive processes otherwise located "within" the individual speaker so that we would have here an ideal case of "shared cognition." However, this would fail to account for some of what is going on in W's and D's interaction. D not only achieves the articulation of information not present in the laconic expression of her mother; she simultaneously marks her stances toward the facts she is informed about in co-construction with her mother. And W, in turn, does not only confirm the mere informational components D's elaborations offer her; she also responds to the stances D marked. Thus, the reproach conveyed in D's turn at line 12 is responded to not only by a confirmation but also by a justification (I could not prevent Karin from behaving like this; she simply passed out). And to D's disapproving surprise and disbelief that Karin fell asleep "hier," W responds with a special delivery of "ja," in line 13. Thus, although it is true that D exploits the fact that verbs have an argument structure, she does considerably more at the same time. The need to elaborate and to "unpack" W's key word "geschlafen" becomes an occasion and a resource for other activities on D's part.

Excursus on agrammatism and conversational practice:
Possible turn completion and the treatment of silence

Now we turn to the second of these properties (clause final position of non-finite verb forms). Although grammatical rules—such as the clause-final position of non-finite verbs in German—are not sufficient for the description of units in conversation (Ford & Thompson, 1996), and although conversational units in German can be expanded beyond the non-finite verb, the latter clearly marks a possible (though not necessarily an actual) completion point for a turn. The question then is whether D displays orientation to non-finite verbs in her mother's speech as possibly indicating the turn's end. And this is clearly *not* the case, or at least D does not exploit such positions as places at which to start a next turn of her own. After W's turn in line 10, as well as after her turn in 13 (both ending with a non-finite verb), D begins a next turn only after gaps of silence of considerable length.[14] It seems as if D gives her mother time to add more material, and only if W fails to indicate that she is going to continue does D launch her own utterances. D displays this attitude also in line 05: she withdraws her gaze only after W herself has withdrawn gaze and not directly after the time indication ("Zwei Uhr"), although this is—in this position (an answer to a temporal wh-question)—certainly a potentially complete turn. This "considerateness" of D, this concern about being sure that W has indeed completed what she wants to say, is a common feature of D's conduct in interaction with W, observable in many other episodes and many other occasions not presented here.[15] Although this practice is, in one respect, somewhat problematic as it exposes W as a patient with a dysfluency problem, it can also be characterized as a benign behavior: it at least contributes to avoiding one sort of trouble otherwise endemic to an interactional environment with recurrent inter-turn gaps of silence. This sort of trouble can be seen in an episode of a conversation between W and her own mother (G).

Both mother and daughter of W have been living together with her for many years, since the onset of her aphasia. W's mother is referred to here as "grandmother" (G). G at first declined to participate in the taping, saying that she did not know what to talk about. The first author suggested that W and G could discuss the TV program or whatever they had on their minds, but before finishing this suggestion, G began talking about TV.

Example 7

```
1   G:   Ja, ik wollte sagen,   was  *  guckst'n           ((* G points
         Yes, I would-liketo-say what watch-you-PRT       to TV-room))
         Yes, I wanted to say, what are you gonna watch
2        heute abend        im Fernsehen,  = haste      da
         today in-the-evening on TV,        = have-you there
         tonight on TV,                     = have you
3        schon  was       je- (1.0)* guckt     ((* W withdraws
         already something l-  (1.0)  looked-P          gaze))
         already watched something?
4           (0.5)
5   W:   Ach ja? ä:h,  Grusel (.) [film
         Oh yes? ä:h,  horror- (.)  movie
         Oh yeah? Uh:, a horror    [movie
6   G:                            [ (nein,) Gruselfilm,
                                   (no)   horror-movie,
                                   (no,) a horror movie,
```

```
7         ach [ nein, ich meine jetzt,*          ((* G points to TV-room,
          oh   no,   I   mean now,                W redirects gaze to G))
          oh [ no,   I   mean now,
8         nach dem da
          after this   there
          after what you're watching
9   W:        [""h_h_""
10        (0.8)
11  G:    Ke:vin kennste   ja,    Ke:vin allein zu Hause
          Kevin   you-know PRT, Kevin alone at home
          Kevin  you know,      Kevin Home Alone
12        (0.4)
13  G:    "ham wer auch schon   jesehn."
          have  we also  already seen.
          we've already seen that.
14        (1.0)
15  G:    "(ne) nich  so   doll, wa?"
          (no)  not   that good, what?
          (Not) very good, huh?
16        (1.0)
17  G:    >Dann bringen se<  noch Der Al:te
          then bring      they still  The Old
          >They are still showing<   The Old Man
18        (0.8)
19  W:    >ach nee<                    ((W withdraws gaze))
          oh   no
          >Oh  no <
20  G:    Nee(-) ach nee
          no(-)  oh  no
          No(-)  Oh  no
21  W:    hihhi
22  G:    *Du mit   deinen [Gru:sel-,         ((*W redirects gaze to G))
          You with your      horror-,
          You and  your   [horror-,
22  W:                     [Kevin
23  G:    du  du  m- möcht (est immer) also du willst
          you you m- like      always PRT you want
          You you l-  like    (it all the time) you always
24        lieber     was      zum    Gruseln
          more-gladly something for-the getting-the-creeps
          prefer something that gives you the creeps.
25        haben [ immer
          have    always
26  W:    *[ja   schön hahaha            *((W nodding head
           yes, lovely hahaha             and looking away))
          [Yes, it's lovely hahaha
```

G begins by asking what W is going to watch on TV that evening and whether she has already selected something. W answers G's question with "Gruselfilm"/ *horror movie* (line 5). Immediately before the completion of G's turn, W withdraws her gaze to her lap. It appears that she anticipates (very likely from past history) that her selection will be problematic for G. And her forebodings prove to be justified. Immediately after "Grusel"/ *horror* and overlapping with "film," G launches a strong rejection of W's choice: "No, horror-movie, oh no" (lines 6–7). It is delivered in a somewhat accusatory and angry tone, so that it conveys a component of complaint and reproach beyond the mere rejection of a proposal. W registers it (at line 9) with a bit of laughter overlapping G's second "no," a laugh that may register not only an understanding of G's rejection but also an "admission of guilt" that the proposal was made with an anticipation of its rejection. G now proposes (line 11) an alternative to the horror movie, *Kevin Home Alone*.[16] When there is no uptake of this proposal (at line 12), G speaks again, articulating a possible reason for reservations about this suggestion—that the women have already seen the film (line 13). After this, there is again silence, now for 1.0 sec. As W again fails to provide any response, either to G's suggestion or to the possible grounds for rejecting it, G continues, again with possible grounds for rejecting the proposal, this time a negative assessment of the film (line 15), and this time marking the completion of her turn with an upgraded indication of the relevance of a response by W—the turn-exit device of a tag question ("wa?"/ *what*? in line 15). Again, however, a 1.0-second silence passes (line 16) in which W gives no indication of moving to take next turn. Once again G retakes the floor (line 17), now completing the series of backdowns from her earlier proposal by offering an alternative proposal for the evening's TV watching (*Der Alte*/ the old one—a very innocent, unspectacular, "worthy" detective series.

The silences at lines 12, 14, and 16 deserve an explicit analytic interactional gloss. Preceding line 12, G had offered a proposal for the evening's TV watching, and such an action (a "first pair part" of an adjacency pair) makes relevant next a responsive action (a "second pair part") by its addressee, W. The prime alternative types of response are acceptance and rejection, or, more generally, alignment or disalignment. Instead, G encounters silence. Silence after a first pair part—whatever its particular action—prefigures a non-aligning response, in this case a rejection, a dispreferred option that participants regularly undertake (jointly) to avoid. One way of avoiding it is to anticipate the obstacle and offer it as an account in search of agreement—that is, alignment at least on *that*. Another way to avoid the misalignment is withdrawal of the object of the prospective rejection and its replacement. In the present exchange, then, an account is one type of next move that can be relevant. However, after each increment of silence that follows, it is not W but G who formulates the account or otherwise backs away from the proposal: they already saw the movie, the movie was not so good, here is another proposal instead. G can be taken here as speaking, in a sense, on behalf of W as the party resisting the proposal, showing an alignment of understanding even where there is disagreement on what to do. The silence is taken not as an "aphasiological" silence reflecting some language problem, but as an interactionally meaningful gap of silence, that is, a delay prefiguring a dispreferred action—a common practice in ordinary conversation. And G's recurrent responses to the silences display adjustments and reactions not to language impairment but to misalignment in a project being worked through in interaction. The same effect can also be seen at lines 16–17, where W's non-response in the aftermath of an overt question (the tag-question "wa?" at line 15) prompts the final backdown from the previous proposal and the offering of another. And this time G gets a response, again after a delay (the 0.8 sec at line 1), which here again prefigures rejection. And, in fact, W's response *is* a rejection, indeed is more than a simple rejection; the "ach" marks the rejected proposal as, in effect, having not been apt or appropriate (Heritage, 1998). It is an inapt alternative to a horror movie.[17] In a sense then, the answer "ach nee" is a rejection and at the same time an account of it. G registers the rejection by "nee," but replaces it immediately by what W had actually said, thus displaying an understanding that W did more than just reject the suggestion.

We need not press the analytic gloss of this exchange further. We presented the exchange between W and her mother in juxtaposition with the exchange between W and her daughter to exemplify and discuss two quite different ways in which conversational co-participants can understand the temporal delays that can characterize conversations with Broca's aphasics, can react to them, and thereby incorporate them into quite different interactional trajectories as a result. Although these are just two singular exchanges, we offer them here to instantiate a contrast with potentially much greater provenance. Here is a series of points explicating the juxtaposition:

1. The two episodes are characterized by silences of comparable duration, located in a position conversation analysts call "gaps," that is, after possible completion of a turn constructional unit and, therefore, of a turn.

2. In these exchanges, because of the aphasia of one of the participants, "gap" position may be equivocal by virtue of both grammar (problematic capacity to recognize grammatical possible completion and to mobilize grammatical structure of a next turn) and prosody (often indeterminate contours that do not clearly project or realize possible completion).

3. In the interaction between W and G, many more of these gaps following talk by G are resolved by further talk by G (rather than by W) than in the conversation between W and D, where (following a turn by D) more are resolved by eventual talk by W.

4. In the W/G conversation, the post-gap resumption of talk by G displays treatment of the gap as "disagree-able" rather than dis-fluent by embodying backdown, account, abandonment of position, and so on, that is, responses to perceived misalignment; by contrast, D's post-gap talk does not have this character.

5. So there appear to be two different turn-taking and sequence organizational *gestalten* managing the sequential import of temporal delay at possible turn boundaries:

   a. One is interactional and conventional (in the sense of commonplace), treating gaps as indicative of *interactional* trouble, whether trouble of understanding, alignment, or something else.

   b. The other is medical, custodial, adaptive—treating gaps as the product of *individual* trouble—whether productional or receptive, and specifically *not* to be treated as indicative of interactional trouble. The consequence can be a kind of "kid gloves" display and a continuous orientation to the aphasic interlocutor as "patient," as "troubled," and so on.

6. This contrast is spread over, and manifested in, *stretches of talk*, the joint product of the several parties' participation, and liable to become a diffuse "ethos" (Bateson, 1936) of interaction, a transient or persistent moral climate that can be troubling or comforting, but in any case not specifiable, and hence treatable as unreal, as suspect, as "imagined" by the affected party. And the affected party is vulnerable to facing it, no matter what form it takes: as apparent "testiness" or conflict sensitivity in the conventional interactional stance, or as apparently being "humored" in the other. The alternatives may come to characterize different episodes or phases in a single occasion of interaction, different interactional occasions in a series of occasions, stable characteristics of relationships with different interactional partners, and so forth.

It remains to be seen how robust this contrast turns out to be. But it is one line of consequences whose roots may be traced back to the impact of agrammatism on the organization of turns, thereby on the management of ordinary turn-taking in conversation, and thereby on the interpretation of turn-taking events such as inter-turn silence through the organization of sequences.

Return to the telling

After these comments on W's agrammatism and its possible bearing on ensuing talk, let us resume the explication of example 6.

```
10  W:   Ja- :h,  Karin (.) eingeschlafen
         Ye- :h, Karin (.) fallen-to-sleep
         Ye- uh, Karin (.) fell asleep
11       (0.7)
```

```
12  D:    >Wo,      hier,  oder was.<
          >Where,  here,  or  what,<
          >Where,  here,  or  what,<
13  W:    Ja:, lang gelegt                        ((W gesturing "lying down"))
          Ye:s, lain-down
          Ye:s, passed out
14        (0.8)
15  D:    hmpfs!
16        (0.2)
17  D:    >Warum< habt ihr    sie  nicht aufgeweckt,
          >why< have you-PL her not   waked-up,
          Why didn't you wake her up,
18        (1.0)
19  W:    !hh - ä:hm (1.8) Gernot               ((W gesturing the tickling
          !hh - ä:hm (1.8) Gernot                motion through line 23.))
          !hh uh- uh:m, (1.8) Gernot
20        {!hhhh/(0.8)} h'm (0.8) Füße gekillert !hh und
          {!hhhh/(0.8)} h'm (0.8) feet tickled-PP !hh and
          {!hhhh/(0.8)} mm (0.8) tickled [her] feet !hh and
21  D:    h_h_
```

In line 15, D responds (with a delay of 0.8!) to W's accounts in line 13 with a labial sound (like a puff), which is fairly conventional in German for the expression of disapproval and surprise. With this, D overtly confirms her strongly critical stance toward Karin's improper conduct at the party. But that her critique is not restricted to Karin but extends toward her mother is now shown in the continuation of her turn at line 17. In its formulation of a negative observation (what someone did *not* do; cf. Schegloff, 1988) and in its demand for an account for this "failure," this turn is built as a complaint, addressed *to* her mother, and complaining *about* her mother and other responsible persons at the party ("ihr"/ *you-PL*) and asks why they—once they could not prevent Karin from falling to sleep—did not awake her in order to rescue the situation.[18]

The question/complaint is followed by a pause of 1.0 second in which nothing visible or audible happens except that the two parties remain oriented to each other.[19] The sequence of body-behavioral actions after the silence deserves a more detailed description than could be given in the transcript. W "points" her head to the left, in the direction of a neighboring room, where obviously the whole event took place and where the protagonists were located. There follows a trouble-indicating editing term—a same-turn repair initiation characteristic of a search ("ä- ä:hm"), and then the deployment of a hand gesture expressing a sort of "resignation" (open palm turned upward). Simultaneously with the gesture, W turns her gaze away from D and begins to look downward to her lap. After the gesture, the hand is turned down again and re-positioned to its place on the table near the cookies (its "home position"; Sacks & Schegloff, 1975). These activities occupy the additional gap of 1.8 seconds between question/complaint and its response.

W then delivers a (male) name "Gernot" and, with the onset of this name, she redirects her gaze to D but withdraws it again immediately thereafter—again down to her lap. W's hand is then lifted a bit, moved in the direction of D's visual field, and then launches a pointing gesture down to W's feet. (Both the observer and the co-participant can only guess that the gesture is to the feet because, in carrying out the gesture, W makes her hand and lower arm disappear under table.) With the onset of "Füße gekillert"/*feet tickled-PP* ("killern" is the normal Berlinish verb for High German "kitzeln"), W's hand reappears above the table and again becomes visible. W's fingers are now being rapidly moved in a fashion depicting the activity of tickling and—to anticipate—these tickling movements continue until the end of W's turn in line 23. The interval between uttering "Gernot" (the agent of the tickling) and the onset of "Füße gekillert" (the verb phrase) is two times 0.8 seconds, with a soft "h'm" in between. (Whether the first 0.8 seconds are filled with silence or with breathing activities cannot be determined.)

It appears that W encounters two word-finding problems here—first for the name of the agent and then for the body part (and perhaps also for the activity).[20] W's head nodding/pointing to the place where Gernot apparently acted is certainly insufficient as a clue for D to guess the new referent. But it appears that W did not design the head gesture as an invitation for D to co-participate in the search for the name: after the nod, the head and gaze remain to the right, that is, away from D. This gaze aversion is fairly canonical in the initial phase of a word search (Goodwin & Goodwin, 1986) and seems to display the general preference for self-repair (Schegloff, Jefferson, & Sacks, 1977). And W is indeed able to repair the trouble with the name by herself; she finds and utters it and then reorients herself back to D. But immediately thereafter, W appears to run into a second word-finding problem. What she "has in mind" is indicated by the pointing gesture, but it has already been noted that D cannot see what W is pointing to. It seems, however, that W is carrying out the gesture "for herself," and, as with the search for "Gernot," is not soliciting assistance from her interlocutor in finding the searched-for item.[21] However, this purely cognitive account of what W is doing with the gesture(s) is not fully satisfactory. Although what W's hand does under the table is indeed hidden, the act of deploying the hand to a place where it cannot be seen is itself public and visible. Actually, W makes some effort to make it public; before the hand disappears, it is raised and thus explicitly brought to D's attention. The "hiding act" appears to reinforce what is already displayed by W's gaze aversion, namely, the preference for solving the word-finding problem by herself; it serves to discourage or "disinvite" D from participating in the search.[22] At the same time, it makes manifest that there **is** a problem, and it thereby provides an account for the silence-in-progress—one that may displace alternative possible accounts and interpretations, preeminent among them that the response which is "on the way," but delayed, is a dispreferred or non-aligning one.

After "Füße gekillert," W prepares herself (and displays this preparation) to continue with an inbreath and an "und."

```
19  W:    !hh ä- :hm (1.8) Gernot              ((W gesturing the tickling
          !hh ä- :hm (1.8) Gernot               motion through line 23.))
          !hh uh- uh:m, (1.8) Gernot
20        {!hhhh/(0.8)} h'm (0.8) Füße gekillert !hh und
          {!hhhh/(0.8)} h'm (0.8) feet tickled-PP !hh and
          {!hhhh/(0.8)} mm (0.8) tickled [her] feet !hh and
21  D:    h_h_
22        (0.5)
23  W:    P:o    gekillert
          tushy tickled-PP
          tickled [her] tushy
24        (.)                                  ((W doing "negative" head
                                                 shakes through line 26))
25  D:    hihi
26        (0.5)
27  D:    !hhh nich' wachgeworden,
          !hhh not  got-PP-awake,
          !hhh didn't wake up,
28  W:    Nö
```

The hand—continuing to display the tickling—goes to the neck, a perfectly reasonable body part to tickle in order to awake someone from sleep. At just this point—in midturn—D interpolates laughter into W's talk.[23] What is accomplished through this positioning of the laughter? Its place suggests that it is not reactive to something that has already occurred or been said, but is rather anticipatory laughter, displaying the projection that what will follow in the talk projected to come by W's gesture is a laugh-source.[24] D's anticipatory laughter can be taken as showing W that their minds are together; D can project that W was going to produce a "laughable," and agrees in treating it as something deserving laughter. A display of such convergence might be particularly relevant at this moment, as D's implicit or explicit reproaches in lines 8, 12, and 17 might have created a certain tension. D accepts her mother's justifications that they could not do anything to prevent Karin from falling to sleep ("she sort of fell down," line 13) and that they tried to awake her with tickling, and she shows this acceptance to her mother at a very sensitive point, namely, *before* her mother has actually finished her justification. Almost perfectly simultaneous with D's laughter, W changes the direction of her pointing gesture from the neck to her "tushy" and reinforces the action of bringing this body part into focus by lifting it from her seat. Exposing this delicate body part is certainly an impropriety that can occur only in intimate interaction and serves to confer a sense of intimacy if it were lacking. It is a laughable by which intimacy is offered and confirmed (Jefferson, Sacks, & Schegloff, 1987).

After the interrupting laughter and a short pause (line 22), W brings the unit launched with the "und" before the laughter to completion: "Po gekillert"/ *tushy tickled- PP*. The word "Po" is not an extreme impropriety, but its deployment again marks this as an intimate interaction. Thus, W underlines the amusing and intimate aspect of her showing the tushy by referring to it with a "naughty" word. The utterance of this word comes after the laughter of D and it thus confirms the acceptance of intimacy offered with the laughter. In a sense, not only does D's projection of a laughable comes true, but W makes it come true.

As the starting point of this chapter was agrammatism and telegraphic style, a brief comment on the linguistic form of W's turn in lines 19 through 23 might be apt. The auxiliary for the past participles is lacking, and thus the whole expression technically falls under the rubric "telegram," which is any expression without a finite verb. But, otherwise, W's utterance is quite elaborate compared with her previous ones. In particular, a grammatical subject is present ("Gernot," the agent of the tickling). And the appearance of a subject in an expression in which the finite verb is lacking was already discussed as linguistically somewhat problematic (and rare).[25] How should we understand it at just this juncture of the conversation?

The preceding turn by D to which W is responding is different in various respects from her questions at line 8 and 12. The latter were designed in such a way that a brief answer was, in principle, all that was required. In fact, these questions were formulated as candidate understandings, so that only a "yes" or a "no" (with a correction) would have been sufficient. The question in line 17, however, is not an understanding check or an unpacking of something her mother had alluded to before. As a question, it makes relevant a fuller telling of the events at the birthday party. Furthermore, its formal design does not offer a preformulated format on which W could scaffold her answer. Finally, this is not only a question but also a vehicle for a complaint and a request for accountability—that is, an action requiring not only answering but defense or compliance. All of these features of D's turn constrain W not only to construct her expression by herself. In particular, they make relevant the explication of the agent and the action that constitute the account that responds to the demands of the preceding turn. Thus, the degree of elaborateness of W's expression appears to fit the local interactional contingencies of just this sequential and interactional juncture and is not responsive to, or understandable by reference to, grammatical rules or statistical regularities (for a more general argument along these lines, see Schegloff, 1993).

At the micro-pause in line 24, W begins to produce lateral ("negative") head shakes that persist during D's laughter (line 25) and the pause of 0.5 second at line 26. D's laughter here is an upgrade of her preceding laughter; there is an increase in sonority (the vocalic part of the first laughter resembled a schwa, that of the second one a full vowel), and it is delivered at a higher pitch than the first one, amplifying the display of affiliation with W. In line 27, D responds to W's lateral headshakes and once again anticipates the import conveyed in them: the efforts to wake Karin up were in vain. D's utterance here is striking; it is subsentential and is of the same linguistic format as W's earlier spare and telegraphic utterances. Although this format may well be unmarked in this position and merit no special notice, it may be worth noting its possibly interactionally meaningful import, a sort of linguistic affiliation with W. Although the expression is not delivered with question intonation, it is nonetheless an understanding check of W's account of the outcome of these efforts to "revive" Karin. W reconfirms D's guess with a "nö" delivered with a somewhat amused tone. The special form of the negation—the vowel [ö] instead of the more familiar [e]—again betokens intimacy. Thus, from line 21 through line 28, the interactants do more than just the co-formulation of information concerning the events at the party. Simultaneously, they produce an activity sequence, covering a whole range of stances, from complaint to account to acceptance and alignment.

Summary and discussion

Throughout this example (and, it may be added, throughout the whole conversation) W uses exclusively short subsentential expressions. But this is not because she cannot do otherwise. In the cartoon story tellings, in particular in condition a4, she used grammatically quite elaborate expressions, including a subordinate construction, although the latter cost effort and an enormous amount of time. So what is achieved by the "telegraphic" style in the interaction with her daughter is very active co-construction. W's contributions are generally laconic, abbreviated, undertold, and designedly compact; they prompt in D moves to unpack her mother's spare expressions, including articulating verbally W's non-verbal behavior (e.g., the negative headshakes starting in line 24). This "speaking on behalf of the patient" has also been observed in Heeschen and Schegloff (1999) and, even more dramatically, in Goodwin's (1995, chapter 4 in this volume) various accounts of a more severely affected aphasic. This characterization of the interactional impact of telegraphic style and even more radically reduced linguistic production appears to be corroborated by this case, but only at a very general level. The particulars of the interactions described in Heeschen and Schegloff (1999) and here are quite different. W uses verbs that enable D to reconstruct the missing information by "navigating" along the argument structure associated with the verb. Trajectories composed of verbs followed by reconstruction of the arguments implemented in understanding checks is the most conspicuous linguistic feature of the interaction between W and D and can be observed throughout the whole conversation. But this division of labor in co-formulating information is not the only feature of the verb-argument sequences. D elaborates W's expressions by providing a candidate for a given argument. Her co-formulations become the vehicle for marking her stance toward the co-formulated information.

All this works in a remarkably smooth way due to D's supportive practices, in particular her concern about non-conflictual turn transition. She explicitly marks the completion of her turns wherever possible, and she gives her mother time to initiate or finish her turns. This kind of support is exactly tailored to W's specific language problems, namely, the agrammatics' problems of syntactically parsing the co-participant's turn and of syntactically and prosodically organizing their own turns. In other instances, such as word finding, D appears to respect W's strong preference for self-repair. Although W might not have welcomed her correction in line 8, it was at least designed as an embedded, and thus unobtrusive, correction. Thus, it is not only W who adapts to her language problem (by delivering only very short expressions), but D, too, adapts to her mother's agrammaticism (by elaborating W's expressions, by careful management of turn transition, etc.).

But adaptation seems to be more than just some practices on the part of each of the co-participants. Adaptation is a mutual phenomenon. W adapts by a drastic reduction of the structure of her expressions, but at the same time her short expressions are designed to facilitate D's support (most notably by the use of verbs). We have noted that W's turns are laconic, curt, abbreviated, undertold, designedly compact, and that they prompt moves to unpack them. What forms of compacting are deployed on the one hand to provide the terms for subsequent collaborative unpacking on the other? We can focus on what the aphasic party has left out or on what the aphasic party has put in, and how, and where. The key observation here has concerned the use of verb forms to package the designedly compacted talk, for the resource it provides via argument structure to guide the interlocutor's complementary work of unpacking.

W's frequent use of verbs as the kernel of her subsentential expressions substantially counters one of the most cherished views in aphasiology: Broca's patients have a selective and specific naming problem for activities requiring verbs (see Gainotti, 1998). Is W an exception in her diagnostic group? W participated in a picture-naming test designed by the first author for an entirely different purpose than the one underlying this chapter. In this test, Broca's patients were selectively worse in verb retrieval than in noun retrieval when compared with Wernicke's patients, whose performance for verbs was equally good (or bad) as for nouns: on average, Broca's patients retrieved 82% correct nouns and 37% verbs; Wernicke's averages were 74% and 78%, respectively. W followed fairly exactly the statistical trends of her group: she had 43% correct verbs and 83% correct nouns. On the basis of these results, one would expect anything but the extensive use of verbs for W's linguistic behavior in talk-in-interaction. For the time being, it is hard to see what underlies this divergence between test performance and naturalistic behavior. But W's use of verbs is not an isolated case of such divergence (cf. Schegloff [1999, chapter 2 in this volume] for similar findings regarding pragmatics). In general, it remains an open problem in psycholinguistics (including aphasiology) to what extent experimental results can be attributed to the "natural world, and not to the procedures of inquiry which produced them" (Schegloff et al., 1996, p. 25).[26]

Conclusion

What, then, would we have the reader take away from this chapter?

1. There are now good grounds for systematically entertaining the possibility that results of testing with aphasic and other neurologically affected subjects are at least in part a function of interactional contingencies of the testing situation, and for openness regarding inferences to other, non-specialized "speech exchange systems," including those which massively characterize everyday life. Why this is so is as yet unknown, but it bears on features central to neuro-scientific (including aphasiological) inquiry, diagnosis, and treatment. That testing supplies a window into the brain and ordinary cognitive processes can no longer be taken as given. It should be clear that inquiry into naturally occurring conduct—including (perhaps preeminently) conduct in interaction—is now critical.

2. One strategic site affected by agrammatism is the "transition space"—the boundary area between the possible end of one turn at talk and the possible start of a next. The normal temporal value of the transition space is a beat, but in the conversations examined here and ones like them, this temporality is upset and eventful silences are created by the parties—*all* the parties, for any one of them can end a silence. We have described two different ways in which these temporal variances can be absorbed and woven into the sequential structures of conversation—ways that can have quite different experiential effects on the participants and on the quality of the interaction. These deserve more elaboration than they could be given here, and more grounding in data as well. Indeed, there is reason to believe (if there is any merit to this line of analysis) that these alternative ways of managing temporal "anomalies" in talk-in-interaction are relevant whatever the sources of the anomalies—whether grounded in compromised brain functioning or in compromised mastery of the spoken language. In any case, the anomalies of talk-in-interaction are not to be understood only by their origins; their import is set by what is made of them, and what is made of them can vary systematically.

3. Although one cannot ignore what it is that aphasics can *not* do, it is clear that what they *can* do is important and varies, and that the particulars of telegraphic speech are consequential in shaping its accommodation in conversation. This chapter has barely begun to explore the possibility that reduction to verbal expressions tilts the forms of accomodation toward exploiting argument structure. How do

interlocutors proceed with aphasics whose telegrams take the form of noun phrases? And what other forms remain to be explored?

Wherever these questions, and others we do not yet know enough to ask, may lead, it seems clear that, for a long time into the future, that work will prosper which most incisively explicates what happens when those with compromised neurological functioning encounter the ordinary world of life in its primordial site—talk and other conduct in interaction.

Appendix 1

Remarks on transcription, translation, and German grammar

The transcriptions follow the conventions of Ochs et al. (1996) with four minor modifications:

1. The exclamation mark is used to indicate a specially confirmative delivery of the preceding word. The word is spoken somewhat louder and somewhat shorter than usually, and sometimes either with a particularly high voice or with a particularly low voice. An example can be found in line 35 of example 2a.
2. Words between slashes are incorrectly delivered words referred to as "paraphasias" in aphasiological contexts. The source of the incorrectness can be phonetic, grammatical, or semantic.
3. The distribution of capital letters is determined by the rules of German orthography. They do not indicate enhanced loudness. For the latter, only underlinings are used.
4. Incomprehensible speech is indicated by sequences of x's in round brackets. The number of x's indicates the approximate number of syllables given the rhythm of the speaker.

For the German texts, the conventional rules of German orthography are followed, but without the innovations introduced by the Orthographic Reform from August 1998. Colloquially pronounced words and Berlinisms are also written in normal orthography; that is to say, they are written in such a way that application of the orthographic rules would lead to the actual pronounciation. Punctuation signs do not follow German orthography. They indicate features of intonation as described by Ochs et al. (1996).

Under the German text, an English word-by-word translation is given, written in Italics. If the morphological properties and categories of a word cannot be inferred from the English equivalents, explanatory abbreviations are attached to the English

word (see list of abbreviations). However, in order not to inflate the English translation, this is not always done and not always in an exhaustive way. For example, the
German article is inflected for gender, number, and case. But these categories are
indicated with attachments only in transcriptions in the first part because only in that
part are the grammatical-morphological features of agrammatic speech of particular
interest. But even there, specifications are not always complete. As a general rule, if
nothing is indicated by attached abbreviations, the German word is grammatically
and morphologically correct.

If English requires more than one word for a single German word, these words
are connected with a hyphen. A frequently occurring example is the infinitive. In
German, the infinitive is built by verbal stem plus the suffix -en; thus, in the English
translation, the "to" and the verbal stem are connected. Sometimes a German expression consisting of only one or two words requires an English expression structured
in a totally different way. The words of the English expression are then connected
with hyphens, and the alignment with the German text indicates to which German
word(s) the expressions correspond. An example is "weiterschlafen"/ to-continue-
to-sleep.

On a third line, an idiomatic English translation is given. However, this is not
always done, but only when the word-by-word translation would be very hard to
understand. The reader should not forget that the German original, in particular the
speech of the agrammatic patients, is often also unidiomatic and sometimes hard to
understand. In such a case, no effort was made to make the English idiomatic. This
holds in particular for the experimental storytellings reported in the first part.

Five features of German grammar need special explanations because they might
be fairly puzzling for the English-speaking reader:

1. Spoken German is very rich in particles. Their contribution to meaning is very subtle and cannot be captured by any direct English
   translation. In the word-by-word translation, they are left untranslated
   and indicated by "PRT." Where possible, an effort is made to reflect
   the particles' meaning in the idiomatic translation.
2. In spoken German, the personal pronouns "er, sie, es, sie-PLURAL" /
   he, she, it, they are often replaced by forms of the demonstrative
   pronoun "d-" that, in many contexts, have only a mild demonstrative
   touch. In the English word-by-word translation, they are represented
   by the personal pronoun plus an attached -DEM.
3. The use of the perfect tense in spoken German is quite different from
   that in English. The German perfect tense does not necessarily involve
   aspect and is used in contexts where in English a preterite would be
   used. For example, German "Ich bin vier Wochen in Amerika gewesen"
   has the meaning "I was in America four weeks" and not "I have
   been." In this context also the form of the perfect participle in German

is always distinct from the preterite forms; hence, English forms such as "tickled" have always the attachment "-PP" (for "participle") to avoid misunderstandings.

4. Word order in German is relatively free except for the forms of the verb. In main clauses, finite verb forms have to appear in second position, the non-finite forms (infinitive and participle) in clause-final position. As a consequence, sentences with perfect tense do not only deviate from English with respect to meaning, but also in the word order: "Ich bin vier Wochen in Amerika gewesen" would appear in a word-by-word translation as "I have four weeks in America been."

5. Points 3 and 4 are of particular relevance for understanding agrammatic "telegraphic" speech in German. When a patient tells about an event in the past, he or she would use the past participle without the auxiliary (and mostly without a grammatical subject) and the participle is preceded by its arguments. Thus, in "telegraphese" the elaborate "Ich bin vier Wochen in Amerika gewesen" would correspond to the shorter expression "vier Wochen in Amerika gewesen"/ four weeks in America been. In telling about the present (or the future), the finite forms of the present tense are replaced by an infinitive, which—of course—has to appear at the end of the clause. Thus, the more elaborate "Der Wecker klingelt um sieben Uhr"/ the alarm-clock rings at seven o'clock would correspond in telegraphese to "(der Wecker) um sieben Uhr klingeln"/ (the alarm-clock) at seven o'clock to-ring. Constructions with either an infinitive or a past participle possibly preceded by arguments figure centrally in the speech of the two patients presented in this chapter. The reader would be well advised not to rely only on the idiomatic English translation.

List of Abbreviations

ACC	accusative
DAT	dative
DEM	demonstrative
FEM	feminine
INF	infinitive
MASC	masculine
NOM	nominative
PL	plural
POL	polite address form
PP	participle
PRT	particle
SG	singular

Appendix 2

K describes a cartoon story consisting of four pictures. The first cartoon shows a farmer sowing corn; the second how the corn is growing; the third shows the farmer examining the corn (and he is obviously content); the fourth shows the farmer transporting the corn with a truck. In the corn field, there stands a scarecrow.

01   So, denn, da   /die/   Mais also (1.5) die   der
      So, then, there /the-FEM/ corn PRT (1.5) the-FEM the-MSC
02   der   äh streut   die   Körner (2.5) und der   der
      the-MSC äh scatters the-PL corns   (2.5) and the-MSC the-MSC
03   guckt ach der   (2.0) ((sighs)) der die äh der die die äh
      looks ach the-MSC (2.0) ((sighs)) (series of articles)
04   schreckt Dings also die   äh   die   (xx) /schreck/
      scares   thing PRT the-FEM äh the-FEM (xx) /scare/
05   die   Vögel, /Vöchel/, die   (3.8) die Vögel schrecken
      the-PL birds /Vöchel/, the-PL (3.8) the birds scare
06   /drauf/.   (2.0) die   der   der   guckt (4.8)
      /there-on/ (2.0) the-FEM the-MSC the-MSC looks (4.8)
07   und der   dann weiter
      and the-MSC then further
08   Dann guckt er, dann probiert er, /der/
      Then looks he, then examines he, /the-MSC/
09   probiert er, da   mal dann da   ist   Flaute gewesen
      examines he, there PRT then there has dead-calm been
      (("da ist Flaute gewesen" is idiomatic for *then things were finished*))
10   also fertig,   (2.0) /fertig macht/.
      PRT finished, (2.0)   /finished/.

Notes

1. Compare Schegloff, 1989: 140–144, and in particular:

What occurs in interaction is not merely the serial externalization into some joint arena of batches of talk, hatched in private . . . intentions, and filled out with the docile artifacts of "language." . . . This treats the mind/brain as the scene of all the action, and the space of interaction as a structureless medium, or at least a medium whose structure is beside the point with respect to what is transmitted through it, as the composition of telephone cable is beside the point for the conversations transmitted through it. But interaction is that for which the talk is conceived; its character is shaped by the structure of opportunities to deliver a message in the first place, and so forth." (140)

2. The first section of the chapter reports on collaborative work conducted over a considerable time period by the first author, Max Planck Institute for Psycholinguistics, Nijmegen, and H. Kolk, Catholic University of Nijmegen.

3. In this description and characterization of W's utterance, it is assumed that the preceding expression "der Mann"/ the-MASC-SG-NOM man is self-repaired and substituted by "die Frau"/ the-FEM-SG-NOM woman. Alternatively, one can assume that "der Mann"/ the-MASC-SG-NOM is meant to be the object of "weckt"/ awakes; under this assumption, however, W would produce an incorrect case marking (it should be "den Mann"/ the-MASC-SG-ACC). In addition, the word order in W's utterance would be incorrect (the verb form "weckt" must occur directly after "den Mann"). And as word order errors are very rare in Broca's aphasia, the first description of W's utterance is more plausible. However, all these reconstructions of aphasic utterances and their grammatical scoring are rarely entirely unequivocal. Additional principles must frequently be invoked for deciding between one or the other reconstruction as, for example, the "minimum principle" (Kolk & Heeschen, 1992, pp. 99–100).

4. This sounds as if the tester/experimenter acts in a friendly and considerate way, but one can see it as well as a fairly cruel action from the perspective of ordinary conduct in ordinary conversations: the tester/experimenter systematically lets pass many occasions for possible turn transition and remains systematically silent when the patient has reached a completion point. And as "silence is a terrible thing" (Sacks, 1995/1970, p. 225), the patient frequently finds himself or herself in a situation when he or she must continue to talk, although he or she neither planned nor wanted to do so.

5. It is called "baseline" because in almost all patient files in almost all neurological and neuropsychological institutions with which the first author has had contact at least a bit of speech obtained under this condition is documented.

6. For reasons of comparison, a sample of K's speech obtained under the more formal testing conditions appears in appendix 2.

It is certainly evident—even without further discussion—that K speaks here in a drastically different way than in the conversation with H. His speech in the cartoon story shows all the features described already for W's telling the wake-up story. In particular, K makes not only omissions here but also a lot of errors.

7. Cases like these make quantitative assessments of aphasic speech such as suggested by Saffran, Berndt, and Schwartz (1989) fairly problematic. What, for example, does a score for "sentences" mean if a sentence is defined as any occurrence of a subject and a verb, but if the absence of a subject is sometimes required by the grammatical rules of the language and thus cannot be taken as a sign of the patient's impairment?

8. The first author was asked this question by a friend during a stay in Boston after he had told him that he would leave Boston the next day.

9. The general idea of adaptation is not new in neuropsychology. Jackson's (1884) idea of positive and negative symptoms needs to be mentioned here (for a discussion, see Kolk, 1987), as well as Baillarger's and Jackson's awareness of the influence of the concrete task situation on the speech outcome of aphasics (see Alajouanine, 1960, for a review). Isserlin's (1922) account of telegraphic speech as the result of an economy strategy belongs to this tradition, as does Goldstein's (1948) general neuropsychological approach, according to which symptoms have functions and reflect the organism's efforts to cope with a deficit rather than the deficit itself. But these distinguished authors have never represented the mainstream in aphasiology and neuropsychology. And in more recent times when, for methodological reasons, transparent relations between symptomatic performance and deficit are required (given

a particular goal of impairment studies, see introductory paragraph), the tradition of Jackson, Goldstein, and others has been almost completely forgotten.

10. This choice is not necessarily consciously controlled. Thus, if the adaptivists speak of "choice" or "strategic adaptation" or "adaptive strategy," then it is rather—to use the terms of Heritage, 1990/1991—a strategy$_{cog}$ than a strategy$_{cs}$, although the borderline between them can be a bit blurred.

11. D interrupts her question concerning Karin before it has come to completion and encourages her mother to have one of the cookies from the package W is hesitantly opening, as if she does not dare to help herself to a snack. A somewhat testy stance is conveyed not only by doing this self-interruptively, but also by the virtually untranslatable particle "doch," which here might contribute to having the turn rendered as "Eat it already!" Although not present in the excerpt, it might be useful to know that the problem of overweight and overeating is a recurrent topic in exchanges between W and D. It informs the preceding exchange about the salads at the party. After the inserted injunction, D returns to her original question, repeats it verbatim to show she is saying again what she was in the course of saying before (Schegloff, 1996a), and brings it to completion.

12. Between the agent "Karin" and the verb, there is a noticeable micro-pause for which there are several possible characterizations: First, the aphasiological characterization assumes that the pause is just something that can happen in non-fluent patients. Second, the linguistic characterization notes that if the finite part of the verb is missing, then the grammatical subject as specifier of the verb phrase is not licensed any longer (Cahana-Amitay, 1997; Haverkort, 1999; de Roo; 1999). It is not part of the construction; between subject and non-finite verb there is a break and this is expressed by the pause. Third, one interactional characterization supposes that the hesitant and coda-like delivery of "eingeschlafen" reflects a perturbation in the aftermath of the other-correction in line 8—perhaps prompted by the equivocal need for a repeat of the framing item to complete the correction. Another interactional characterization might be that the separation of the two units in W's turn responds to the fact that two different components or layers in D's preceding turn—the openly asked question for the identity of the agent and the embedded-correction work—are addressed by them, and this interactionally different nature of the two units is reflected by their separated delivery. The aphasiological characterization is certainly the least attractive. Even if, on the basis of quantitative studies, the pause can be associated with a certain probability, this would not explain why it occurred here. The linguistic characterization is not incompatible with the two interaction-oriented ones, which, in turn, are not incompatible with each other. Perhaps, there is something to each of these possibilities.

13. In a forthcoming work, Thompson and Hopper reassess the viability of familiar conceptions of argument structure when juxtaposed with data drawn from ordinary conversation. In its use of the talk of the participants to invoke the relevance of the notion of argument structure in this context, our discussion appears to be compatible with the Thompson/Hopper critique.

14. D's "play it safe" strategy (delay turn transition until she is absolutely sure that W has finished) might be partly due to the fact that W's intonation contours are a bit flat. The risings and fallings are not very sharp, so that they cannot be reliably exploited as cues with respect to turn continuation or turn completion. This "dysprosody" is frequently part of the general non-fluency of Broca patients (Huber, Poeck, & Wenhger, 1989, pp. 111, 113).

15. Note that D's silence after a turn by W is quite different from the "perversely passive" conduct of an aphasiologist described in the first section. First, D does not wait endlessly before taking a next turn, and second, she does not produce continuers after the end of W's turn, providing for W to continue some putative larger discourse unit. That is to say, her conduct is not organized in a manner designed to elicit maximal turns by W; she simply waits a bit to make sure that the minimal turns of W are indeed over.

In D's conduct, there is another indication of her concern to ensure conflict-free and unproblematic turn transition. The two tag questions "oder was?" in lines 8 and 12 were characterized as displaying D's awareness of alternatives; but tag questions are also a common and effective turn-exit device (Sacks et al., 1974), marking very clearly and unambiguously a place relevant for transition and, ordinarily, a selected next speaker. In the whole conversation between W and D, D uses "oder was?" excessively so that one could easily take it to be simply D's stylistic idiosyncrasy. But even if it were, it has interactional impact and is consequential for the organization of the conversation. It spares W a more sophisticated—and in particular a continuing—syntactic analysis of D's turns with respect to completion, or reinforces it.

16. This is the German title (retranslated into English) of the movie *Kevin Home Alone I* (known in the United States simply as *Home Alone*). It was broadcast on German TV some weeks before this conversation took place. The follow-up movie *Kevin Home Alone II* was announced for one of the days following the conversation. From what G is saying, it appears that (she thought) it was to be broadcast the same evening, but she was wrong.

17. Indeed, *Der Alte* is a perfect contrast program to a horror movie, and people with a predilection for the latter can hardly be expected to like *Der Alte*.

18. This complaint against the mother suggests the possibility—not pressed previously—that line 8 ("you fell asleep, or what") was not simply a misunderstanding of the conspiratorial tenor of the mother's previous utterance. It may display a propensity on the daughter's part to level accusations and complaints (of which line 8 is another analyzable instance) against the mother.

19. This is another indicator of D's concern about turn transition. We earlier noted that she marks her own turn completions with tag questions; here we note that she not only gives W time to finish but also to intitiate her turns. This is quite sensitive, given that one of the major problems of Broca's aphasics is the initiation of speech (Goodglass, 1973/1968). It seems the two parties grant each other moments of silence up to 1.0 sec. It is possible that this one second reflects an underlying metric (or metrical adjustment) as described by Jefferson (1989), a conjecture reinforced by noting that, after the 1.0 second of silence, W produces only an aspiration and an "editing term," followed by an additional 1.8 seconds of silence!

20. An alternative line of analysis would focus on the known difficulty previously cited for Broca's aphasics to initiate speech, reinforced here by W's mobilization of an effort to produce a more elaborate expression, an almost full sentence complete with subject noun phrase, and so forth, which may enhance the problems of starting. The line adopted in the text carries its own justification.

21. Such a characterization would square neatly with the theory that gestures serve not (or not only, cf. Kendon, 1994) a communicative function, but the facilitation of word retrieval—in unimpaired speakers (Krauss, Chen, & Chawla, 1996; Krauss, Morrel-Samuels, & Colasante, 1991) as well as in aphasics (Hadar & Yadlin-Gedassy, 1994; Hadar, Burstein,

Krauss, & Soroker, 1998). W could then be understood to be trying to access the word "Füße" by pointing to her feet, whatever else she might also be undertaking to do.

22. The fact that even aphasics are not oriented toward co-participation in the initial phase of a word search has been frequently observed (Klippi, 1996; Laakso & Klippi, 1999).

23. Given what was said about D's careful endeavors to avoid overlap, this is surprising. It would not help to consider the laughter as mere unvoluntary physiological reaction to something funny. Laughter is a socially organized activity, and its form, as well as its positioning, is meaningful in interaction (Jefferson et al., 1987). On the other hand, laughter is not ordinarily treated as interruptive, or as competitive with simultaneously produced talk (Schegloff, 2000).

24. This is reminiscent of a practice described and analyzed by Goodwin and Goodwin (1992): a recipient interrupts an ongoing turn at a point where it is projectable that the speaker is going to produce an assessment, but where it is still unclear what kind of an assessment he or she is going to produce, with an assessment of his or her own. Goodwin and Goodwin characterize this practice as a strong display of agreement or of claimed agreement: the recipient shows his or her confidence that he or she knows in advance what the speaker is going to say and that he or she and the speaker will agree. Similar as well are the anticipatory completions described by Lerner (1991, 1996).

25. Non-finite expressions with a subject do not fit the minimalist linguistic theory of agrammatism (see Cahana-Amitay, 1997; Haverkort, 1999; de Roo, 1999), as the subject belongs—as specifier—to the same phrase as the finiteness features of the verb, which, however, are not present so that the subject is not licensed any longer. As a matter of fact, telegraphic utterances with a subject occur very infrequently in agrammatic as well as in unimpaired speech. According to Hofstede (1992), only 4% of all non-finite expressions have the format "subject + non-finite verb," as compared with 23% for the format without the subject. Thus, statistically, they play a marginal role, and the linguistic theory can be rescued. However, no statistics can help us to understand why such a linguistically recalcitrant utterance appears precisely where it occurs here. To understand this, an inspection of the sequential context of the occurrence is necessary. And, indeed, such an inspection yields immediately an answer, pursued in the text that follows.

26. There is perhaps no more ironic exemplar of this problem than one that returns us to the beginnings of this chapter, and the use of stories and storytelling in testing practices for aphasics. Suppose that we ask whether the talk about Karin's misbehavior at the party should be understood as a story? Surely in the beginning of this episode the two parties do not appear oriented to the construction of a story preface (Sacks, 1974) or other of the described forms for launching a storytelling in conversation. Nor is the further trajectory of the exchange compatible with the proposal that a storytelling is being achieved here. There is, for example, no extended turn of the sort characteristic of stories, with an occasional interpolation of continuers or assessments or news-marks. Although W is the participant who is knowledgeable about the party events, both participants determine the trajectory of the reconstruction of the events, and both contribute, to an equal extent, to the promotion of the telling—D by specific questions and W by the form of her answering. W triggered the whole sequence by "geschlafen"/ *slept* (line 6), but D has thereafter taken the initiative in "steering" the telling itself. Perhaps, this is an interactive format for collaborative storytelling W and D employ. If so, they are not alone, nor are other such collaborators with aphasics alone. Similar or related practices have

been described for storytelling unaffected by brain trauma (cf. Lerner, 1992; Mandelbaum, 1987, 1989, 1993). If this is so, then, retrospectively, the practice of experimentally eliciting whole series of storytellings in the testing practices described in the first part of this chapter becomes even more questionable than previously registered.

References

Alajouanine, T. (1960). Baillarger and Jackson: The Principle of Baillarger-Jackson in aphasia. *Journal of Neurology, Neurosurgery and Psychiatry*, *23*, 191–193.

Bateson, G. (1936). *Naven*. Stanford, CA: Stanford University Press).

Bleser, R. D. (1987). From Agrammatism to Paragrammatism: German Aphasiological Traditions and Grammatical Disturbances. *Cognitive Neurospychology*, *4*, 187–256.

Bock, K., & Levelt, W. (1994). Language Production: Grammatical Encoding. In M. A. Gernsbacher (Ed.), *Handbook of Psycholinguistics* (pp. 945–984). San Diego: Academic Press.

Cahana-Amitay, D. (1997). *Syntactic Aspects of the Production of Verbal Inflection in Aphasia*. Doctoral dissertation, Boston University.

Caplan, D. (1987). *Neurolinguistics and Linguistic Aphasiology*. Cambridge: Cambridge University Press.

Caramazza, A. (1986). On Drawing Inferences About the Structure of Normal Cognitive Systems from the Analysis of Patterns of Impaired Performance: The Case for Single-Patient Studies. *Brain and Cognition*, *5*, 41–66.

Caramazza, A. (1992). Is Cognitive Neuropsychology Possible? *Journal of Cognitive Neuroscience*, *4*(1), 80–95.

Caramazza, A. (1997). Brain and Language. In M. S.Gazzaniga (Ed.), *Conversations in the Cognitive Neurosciences* (pp. 131–151). Cambridge, MA: MIT Press.

Ford, C. E., & Thompson, S. A. (1996). Interactional Units in Conversation: Syntactic, Intonational, and Pragmatic Resources for the Management of Turns. In E. Ochs, E. A. Schegloff, & S. A. Thompson (Eds.), *Interaction and Grammar* (pp. 134–184). Cambridge: Cambridge University Press).

Gainotti, G. (1998). Category-Specific Disorders for Nouns and Verbs: A Very Old and Very New Problem. In B. Stemmer & H. A. Whitaker (Eds.), *Handbook of Neurolinguistics* (pp. 3–11). San Diego: Academic Press.

Goldstein, K. (1948). *Language and Language Disturbances*. New York: Grune and Stratton.

Goodglass, H. (1973[1968]). Studies on the Grammar of Aphasics. In H. Goodglass & S. Blumstein (Eds.), *Psycholinguistics and Aphasia* (pp. 183–215). Baltimore: Johns Hopkins University Press.

Goodglass, H., & Kaplan, E. (1972). *The Assessment of Aphasia and Related Disorders*. Philadelphia: Lea and Febiger.

Goodglass, H., Christiansen, J. A., & Gallagher, R. (1993). Morphology and Ssyntax in Free Narrative and Structured Tests: Fluent vs. Non-fluent Aphasics. *Cortex*, *29*, 377–407.

Goodwin, C. (1981). *Conversational Organization*. New York: Academic Press.

Goodwin, C. (1984). Notes on Story Structure and the Organization of Participation. In J. M. Atkinson & J. Heritage (Eds.), *Structures of Social Action* (pp. 225–246). Cambridge: Cambridge University Press.

Goodwin, C. (1986). Gestures as a Resource for the Organization of Mutual Orientation. *Semiotica*, *62*(1/2), 29–49.

Goodwin, C. (1995). Co-constructing Meaning in Conversations with an Aphasic Man. *Research on Language and Social Interaction, 28*, 233–60.

Goodwin, C. (1996). Introduction to the panel discussion "The Pragmatic Life of Brain Damaged Patients: Situating Language Impairments Within Conversation" at the 5th International Pragmatics Conference, Mexico City, July 4–6.

Goodwin, C., & Goodwin, M. H. (1992). Assessments and the Construction of Context. In A. Duranti & C. Goodwin (Eds.), *Rethinking Context* (pp. 151–189). Cambridge: Cambridge University Press.

Goodwin, M. H., & Goodwin, C. (1986). Gesture and Coparticipation in the Activity of Searching for a Word. *Semiotica, 62*(1/2), 51–75.

Hadar, U., & Yadlin-Gedassy, S. (1994). Conceptual and Lexical Aspects of Gesture: Evidence from Aphasia. *Journal of Neurolinguistics, 8*, 57–65.

Hadar, U., Burstein, A., Krauss, R., & Soroker, N. (1998). Ideational Gestures and Speech in Brain-Damaged Subjects. *Language and Cognitive Processes, 13*(1), 59–76.

Hagiwara, H. (1995). The Breakdown of Functional Categories and the Economy of Derivation. *Brain and Language, 50*, 92–116.

Haverkort, M. (1999). Kenmerk-checking, taalverwerving en afasie. *Nederlandse Taalkunde, 4*(2), 111–124.

Heeschen, C., & Kolk, H. H. J. (1994). Adaptation bei Agrammatikern—Interaktional motiviert? In I. M. Ohlendorf, T. A. Pollow, W. Widdig, & D. B. Linke (Eds.), *Sprache und Gehirn. Grundlagenforschung für die Aphasietherapie* (pp. 125–135). Freiburg: HochschulVerlag.

Heeschen, C., & Schegloff, E. A. (1999). Agrammatism, Adaptation Theory, Conversation Analysis: On the Role of So-Called Telegraphic Style in Talk-in-Interaction. *Aphasiology, 13*(4/5), 365–405.

Heritage, J. (1990/1991). Intention, Meaning and Strategy: Observations on Constraints on Interaction Analysis. *Research on Language and Social Interaction, 24*, 311–332.

Heritage, J. (1998). Oh-Prefaced Responses to Inquiry. *Language in Society, 27*, 291–334.

Heritage, J., & Greatbatch, D. (1991). On the Institutional Character of Institutional Talk: The Case of News Interviews. In D. Boden & D. H. Zimmerman (Eds.), *Talk and Social Structure* (pp. 93–137). Cambridge: Polity Press.

Hofstede, B. T. M. (1992). *Agrammatic Speech in Broca's Aphasia. Strategic Choice for the Elliptic Register*. NICI Technical Report 02-07. Doctoral dissertation, University of Nijmegen, The Netherlands.

Huber, W., Poeck, K., & Weniger, D. (1989). Aphasie. In K. Poeck (Ed.), *Klinische Neuropsychologie* (2nd ed., pp. 89–137). Stuttgart: Georg Thieme Verlag.

Huber, W., Poeck, K., Weniger, D., & Willmes, K. (1983). *Der Aachener Aphasie Test*. Göttingen: Hogrefe.

Huber, W., Poeck, K., & Willmes, K. (1984). The Aachen Aphasia Test. *Advances in Neurology, 42*, 291–303.

Isserlin, M. (1922). Über Agrammatismus. *Zeitschrift für die gesamte Neurologie und Psychiatrie, 75*, 322–410.

Jackson, J. H. (1884). Evolution and Dissolution of the Nervous System (Croonian Lectures). In J. Taylor, G. Holmes, & F. M. R. Walshe (Eds.), *John Hughlings Jackson, Selected Writings, Vol. Two*. (London: Hodder and Stoughton, 1932). Republished by N. J. M. Arts (Ed.). Nijmegen: Arts & Boeve, 1996, 45–75.

Jarema, G. (1998). The Breakdown of Morphology in Aphasia: A Cross-Linguistic Perspective. In B. Stemmer & H. A. Whitaker (Eds.), *Handbook of Neurolinguistics* (pp. 221–234). San Diego: Academic Press.

Jefferson, G. (1984). Notes on a Systematic Deployment of the Acknowledgement Tokens "Yeah" and "Mm hm." *Papers in Linguistics, 17,* 197–206.

Jefferson. G. (1987). On Exposed and Embedded Correction in Conversation. In G. B. Button & J. R. E. Lee (Eds.), *Talk and Social Organization* (pp. 86–100). Clevedon: Multilingual Matters.

Jefferson, G. (1989). Notes on a Possible Metric Which Provides for a "Standard Maximum Silence" of Approximately One Second in Conversation. In D. Roger & P. Bull (Eds.), *Conversation: An Interdisciplinary Perspective* (pp. 166–196). Clevedon: Multilingual Matters.

Jefferson, G., Sacks, H., & Schegloff, E. A. (1987). Notes on Laughter in the Pursuit of Intimacy. In G. B. Button & J. R. E. Lee (Eds.), *Talk and Social Organization* (pp. 152–205). Clevedon: Multilingual Matters.

Kean, M.-L. (1995). The Elusive Character of Agrammatism. *Brain and Language, 50,* 369–384.

Kendon, A. (1994). Do Gestures Communicate?: A Review. *Research on Language and Social Interaction* 27, 275–300.

Klein, W. (1985). Ellipse, Fokusgliederung und thematischer Stand. In R. Meyer-Herman & H. Rieser (Eds.), *Ellipsen und fragmentarische Ausdrücke* (pp. 1–24). Tübingen: Niemeyer.

Kleist, K. (1934). *Gehirnpathologie.* Leipzig: Barth.

Klippi, A. (1996). *Conversation as an Achievement in Aphasics.* Helsinki: Suomalaisen Kirjallisuuden Seura.

Kolk, H. (1987). A Theory of Grammatical Impairment in Aphasia. In G. Kempen (Ed.), *Natural Language Generation* (pp. 377–391). Dordrecht: Martinus Nijhoff.

Kolk, H. H. J. (1995). A Time-Based Approach to Agrammatic Production. *Brain and Language, 50,* 282–303.

Kolk, H. (1998). Disorders of Syntax in Aphasia: Linguistic-Descriptive and Processing Approaches. In B. Stemmer & H. A. Whitaker (Eds.), *Handbook of Neurolinguistics* (pp. 249–260). San Diego: Academic Press.

Kolk, H. H. J., & Heeschen, C. (1992). Agrammatism, Paragrammatism and the Management of Language. *Language and Cognitive Processes, 7,* 89–129.

Krauss, R. M., Chen, Y., & Chawla, P. (1996). Nonverbal Behavior and Nonverbal Communication: What Do Conversational Hand Gestures Tell Us? In M. Zanna (Ed.), *Advances in Experimental Social Psychology, 26* (pp. 389–450). New York: Academic Press.

Krauss, R. M., Morrel-Samuels, P., & Colasante, P. (1991). Do Conversational Hand Gestures Communicate? *Journal of Personality and Social Psychology, 61,* 743–754.

Laakso, M., & Klippi, A. (1999). A Closer Look at the "Hint and Guess" Sequences in Aphasic Conversation. *Aphasiology, 13*(4/5), 345–363.

Labov, W. (1981). Speech Actions and Reactions in Personal Narrative. In D. Tannen (Ed.), *Analyzing Discourse: Text and Talk* (pp. 219–247). Washington, DC: Georgetown University Press.

Lerner, G. H. (1991). On the Syntax of Sentences-in-Progress. *Language in Society, 20,* 441–458.

Lerner, G. (1992). Assisted Storytelling: Deploying Shared Knowledge as a Practical Matter. *Qualitative Sociology*, *15*, 247–271.

Lerner, G. H. (1996). On the "Semi-Permeable" Character of Grammatical Units in Conversation: Conditional Entry into the Turn Space of Another Speaker. In E. Ochs, E. A. Schegloff, & S. A. Thompson (Eds.), *Interaction and Grammar* (pp. 238–276). Cambridge: Cambridge University Press.

Levelt, W. J. M. (1989). *Speaking: From Intention to Articulation*. Cambridge, MA: MIT Press.

Mandelbaum, J. (1987). Couples Sharing Stories. *Communication Quarterly*, *35*, 144–171.

Mandelbaum, J. (1989). Interpersonal Activities in Conversational Storytelling. *Western Journal of Speech Communication*, *53*, 114–126.

Mandelbaum, J. (1993). Assigning Responsibility in Conversational Storytelling: The Interactional Construction of Reality. *Text*, *13*, 247–66.

Menn, L., & Obler, L. K. (1990). *Agrammatic Aphasia: A Cross-Language Narrative Sourcebook*. Amsterdam: John Benjamins.

Ochs, E., Schegloff, E. A., & Thompson, S. (Eds.). (1996). *Interaction and Grammar*. Cambridge: Cambridge University Press.

Pomerantz, A. (1984). Agreeing and Disagreeing with Assessments: Some Features of Preferred/Dispreferred Turn Shapes. In J. M.Atkinson & J. Heritage (Eds.), *Structures of Social Action: Studies in Conversation Analysis* (pp. 57–101). Cambridge: Cambridge University Press.

Roo, E. de (1999). *Agrammatic Grammar: Functional Categories in Agrammatic Speech*. Den Haag: Thesus.

Sacks, H. (1995 [1970]). Stories Take More than One Utterance; Story Prefaces. In Jefferson, G. (Ed.), *Harvey Sacks. Lectures on Conversation* (vol. 2, pp. 222–228). Cambridge, MA: Blackwell.

Sacks, H. (1987 [1973]). On the Preferences for Agreement and Contiguity in Sequences in Conversation. In G. Button & J. R. E. Lee (Eds.), *Talk and Social Organisation* (pp. 54–69). Clevedon, England: Multilingual Matters.

Sacks, H. (1974). An Analysis of the Course of a Joke's Telling in Conversation. In R. Bauman & J. Sherzer (Eds.), *Explorations in the Ethnography of Speaking* (pp. 337–353). Cambridge: Cambridge University Press.

Sacks, H. (1995). *Lectures on Conversation. Volume II*. Ed. by G. Jefferson with Introductions by E. A. Schegloff. Cambridge, MA: Blackwell.

Sacks, H., & Schegloff, E. A. (1975). Home Position. Paper delivered at the Annual Meeting of the American Anthropological Association, San Francisco, CA, November, 1975.

Sacks, H., Schegloff, E. A., & Jefferson, G. (1974). A Simplest Systematics for the Organization of Turn-Taking For Conversation. *Language*, *50*, 696–735.

Saffran, E. M., Berndt, R. S., & Schwartz, M. F. (1989). The Quantitative Analysis of Agrammatic Production: Procedure and Data. *Brain and Language*, *37*, 440–479.

Schegloff, E. A. (1981). Discourse as an Interactional Achievement: Some Uses of "Uh Huh" and Other Things That Come Between Sentences. In D. Tannen (Ed.), *Analyzing Discourse: Text and Talk* (pp. 71–93). Washington, DC: Georgetown University Press.

Schegloff, E. A. (1988). Goffman and the Analysis of Conversation. In P. Drew & A. Wootton (Eds.), *Erving Goffman: Exploring the Interaction Order* (pp. 89–135). Cambridge: Polity Press.

Schegloff, E. A. (1989). Reflections on Language, Development, and the Interactional Character of Talk-in-Interaction. In M. Bornstein & J. S. Bruner (Eds.), *Interaction in Human Development* (pp. 139–153). Hillsdale, NJ: Erlbaum.

Schegloff, E. A. (1993). Reflections on Quantification in the Sstudy of Conversation. *Research on Language and Social Interaction, 26,* 99–128.

Schegloff, E. A. (1996a). Confirming Allusions: Toward an Empirical Account of Action. *American Journal of Sociology, 104,* 161–216.

Schegloff, E. A. (1996b). Turn Organization: One Intersection of Grammar and Interaction. In E. Ochs, E. A. Schegloff, & S. A. Thompson (Eds.), *Interaction and Grammar* (pp. 52–133). Cambridge: Cambridge University Press.

Schegloff, E. A. (1999). Discourse, Pragmatics, Conversation, Analysis. *Discourse Studies, 1,* 405–35.

Schegloff, E. A. (2000). Overlapping Talk and the Organization of Turn-Taking for Conversation. *Language in Society, 29,*1–63.

Schegloff. E. A., Jefferson, G., & Şacks, H. (1977). The Preference for Self-Correction in the Organization of Repair in Conversation. *Language, 53,* 361–382.

Schegloff, E. A., Ochs, E., & Thompson, S. A. (1996). Introduction. In E. Ochs, E. A. Schegloff, & S. A. Thompson (Eds.), *Interaction and Grammar* (pp. 1–51). Cambridge: Cambridge University Press.

Thompson, S. A., & Hopper, P. J. (forthcoming). Transitivity and Clause Structure in Conversation. In J. Bybee & P. J. Hopper (Eds.), *Frequency and the Emergence of Linguistic Structure*. Amsterdam: John Benjamins.

11

GAIL RAMSBERGER
AND LISE MENN

Co-Constructing Lucy

Adding a Social Perspective to the Assessment of Communicative Success in Aphasia

Changing models of disability

Traditional clinical practice in aphasia rehabilitation has been strongly influenced by the medical model. In this approach, rehabilitation emphasis is placed on the person with aphasia, and the desired outcome is a "cure" of the symptoms of aphasia, to the extent possible (Ramsberger, 1994). The medical orientation seems appropriate for people in the acute stages; numerous studies have clearly shown that much recovery of linguistic functioning takes place during the first few weeks or months postonset (Marshall & Phillips, 1983; Pashek & Holland, 1988). However, when significant continued improvement of aphasia symptoms can no longer be demonstrated, the medical perspective loses its relevance for further rehabilitation efforts.

For people with chronic aphasia, another perspective on disability seems more relevant. In recent years, disability activists have argued that disability is best viewed from a social rather than a medical viewpoint (Barton, 1996; Linton, 1998). People may have physical, mental, or emotional differences from some norm, but the degree to which a person is *disabled* by those differences depends on the interaction of that person with the world in which he or she lives. Thus, the disabling nature of aphasia for two people is likely to be different even if their aphasia symptoms are similar in type and severity.

Furthermore, a person with aphasia will experience different disabilities in different aspects or interactions of life. The intervention approach called Supported Conversation for Adults with Aphasia (SCA; Kagan, 1998; Marshall, 1998) is in fact focused on reducing a client's disability by teaching communication techniques to his or her principal conversation partner and to people who deal professionally with aphasic speakers.

Thus, whereas the medical model focuses on the person with aphasia, the focal point in the social perspective is the person and his or her world. No longer is aphasia defined solely in terms of a person's medical etiology, lesion size and location, diagnostic category, and solo linguistic performances. Rather, in a social perspective, aphasia is to be defined also in terms of its impact on communication in real life: "Attention is starting to focus on how the *system* copes, rather than how the aphasic individual adapts in isolation" (Parr & Byng 1998: 848; emphasis original). Such a shift in the way aphasia is viewed requires a corresponding change in assessment and treatment procedures.

Issues in the assessment of communicative ability

Real-life communication takes many forms, has many purposes, takes place in a variety of physical environments, and usually involves at least two individuals. All of these variables—form, purpose, environment, and partner(s)—can be expected to affect communicative success in aphasia. So although traditional clinical practices, such as gathering a connected speech sample while the patient is describing a standardized picture, or asking a series of yes/no questions, may permit easy quantification of performance and be valid observations of certain linguistic processes, performances on these traditional tasks do not reflect the social nature of real-life communication.

Several tests have been developed in an attempt to better capture the nuances of real-world communication (e.g., Communication Abilities in Daily Living [CADL], Holland, 1980; Communicative Effectiveness Index [CETI], Lomas et al., 1989; the American Speech Language Hearing Association Functional Assessment of Communication Skills in Adults [ASHA FACS], Frattali, Thompson, Holland, Wohl & Ferketic, 1995). Functional measures such as these try to gather information about a person's ability to perform specific real-world communicative behaviors (e.g., read the directory of a building, use money, follow directions, and so on). Some (i.e., ASHA FACS and CETI) include assessment of more social dimensions of communication, such as the ability to express agreement or disagreement, to add new information to a conversation, etc. The ASHA FACS includes a rating of "communication sharing" that seeks to quantify the degree of burden carried by communication partners. Generally, however, these functional tests continue to focus only on the person with aphasia and do not consider the contribution of a communicative partner or the dynamics of the interaction between the two. (Despite the name, the ASHA FACS rating of "communication sharing" is defined in essentially the same way as the "severity rating" of the classic Boston Diagnostic Aphasia Examination [Goodglass & Kaplan 1983]). Consequently, functional measures such as these fit best in the medical model rather than the social model of disability.

One-to-one conversation is a communicative context not typically central to functional communication assessment. Yet it is the most important form of communication for all of us. It is through conversation that we most often demonstrate our competence (Kagan, 1995), as well as establish and maintain interpersonal connections. Conversation is the vehicle by which we express what we know and who we are. So it makes sense to begin the development of socially oriented assessment procedures by first looking at conversational interaction.

Researchers have shown a growing interest in the study of conversation in both normal and disordered communication. One line of conversation research, Conversation Analysis (CA), has attempted to understand how meaning is exchanged between conversational partners. This type of analysis has potentially important clinical applications in aphasia (Jordan & Kaiser, 1996). For example, CA of a dialogue between a person with aphasia and his or her spouse might indicate that turn-taking is not equitable, or that the partner is not responding to requests for clarification. The clinician could then initiate therapeutic procedures to facilitate change of these dimensions (see Lyon, 1998, for a description of such a treatment). Presumably, successful modification of qualitative aspects of a conversational interaction would result in improved transaction (i.e., exchange of information) or interaction (i.e., social connection). Kagan (1995) has suggested that the intercourse of "transaction" and "interaction" is the essence of communicative success in conversation. Improving communicative success is the desired functional outcome in a rehabilitation program that seeks to change qualitative dimensions of conversation.

However, there are few tools for evaluating communicative success in conversation. Lyon (1998) describes two nonstandardized scales for quantifying the "interaction" dimension, but we are aware of no procedure that offers a standardized method of gathering reliable data regarding the "transactional (content)" dimension. In this chapter, we will discuss a procedure we have developed that allows us to measure conversational success in terms of the transmission of information to a real conversational partner.

Narratives as conversational interaction

For the purposes of standardization, we needed to create a task that could be duplicated, had results with face validity, and that furthermore had results that could be compared. One of the challenges to developing a standardized objective measure of conversational success is that natural conversation usually does not involve an externally specified goal (Lesser & Milroy, 1993), but judging "success" is hard if there is no goal to measure performance against. Everyday bilateral or multilateral negotiations about plans and responsibilities, such as where to go for dinner or who will host a party, certainly involve definable goals and could potentially be adapted for clinical use. The task that we describe in this chapter, however, was the telling of a story. Within this framework, we were able to use standardized instructions that clearly specified the goal of the conversation to be the transmission of information.

The narratives we are studying are elicited, rather than arising naturally in the course of conversation. Makoto Hayashi (personal communication, November 1998) has drawn our attention to the fact that such narratives may differ in unknown ways from the naturally occurring "story" that M. H. Goodwin defends as an object of study (1990: 229–230):

> For conversation analysts, stories provide crucial data for the study of the interactive organization of multi-unit turns. . . . [S]peakers in everyday life are able to create through the resources of talk a whole theater, animating both characters and the reactions of others to them. . . . [S]tories are in fact extraordinarily complex speech events. . . . [T]hey may contain . . . a range of different kinds of talk and action. Thus, while some of the utterances within a story might report a sequence of events, others will provide the speaker's evaluation of those events. Yet other parts will contain talk that is to be attributed not to the current narrator but rather to the characters being animated within a story.
>
> The diverse voices and events that constitute a story are woven together into a coherent whole through use of syntactic devices of considerable complexity. Such linguistic structure is complemented by an equally vivid use of intonation, gesture, and other paralinguistic phenomena . . . [quoting Voloshinov (1973)]: " . . . [A] speaker never simply reports the talk of another but instead, in the very process of animating that talk, comments on it and shows his or her alignment to it."

Nevertheless, the use of interactive elicited narratives is a major move toward ecological validity in testing. Our task is unlike typical clinical assessment procedures in that specification of the goal and topics of the conversations were the only restrictions we imposed; we did not restrict the non-aphasic partner's responses to back-channel support and neutral "tell-me-more" elicitation. These restrictions are imposed by conventional "medical-model" measures because test designers know, from clinical experience, that the non-aphasic communicative partner contributes some degree of variability to the information transmitted in conversational interactions. In contrast, working from a social model, we wanted to examine the way in which the non-aphasic partner in fact contributes to communicative success. As Goodwin goes on to say (1990: 230), "Finally, stories are told to an *audience*, and although this feature of their organization has frequently been overlooked, . . . both *who* stories are addressed to and *interaction between speakers and recipients during their telling* are quite central to their organization (italics original).

Studying narrative as interaction in the clinic

Therefore, in addition to leaving the non-aphasic communication partner's role unrestricted, we decided to use only pairs of partners who were unfamiliar with each other and to pair each person with aphasia with several communicative partners. We of course wanted the person with aphasia to be the holder of the information to be exchanged, so that she or he would naturally have to play an active role in the conversation. We also needed the information to be standardized so that we could measure how much of it was transmitted. Therefore, we had to present it to the partner with aphasia in a way that had the best chance of being fully understood. For this reason, we decided to use popular television situation comedies; these provide the viewer with both verbal and non-verbal information in a rich supportive context, and, besides that, they are fun.

In selecting the content of the information to be exchanged, we had several criteria also nicely satisfied by the choice of a particular comedy, *I Love Lucy*. First, although we wanted a topic that would provide the opportunity for presentation of new information, we also wanted the non-aphasic communicative partners to enter the conversation with some shared knowledge, as is normal in everyday life; most participants over 35 watched the *Lucy* show in the 1950s or 1960s, and they are now popular with younger participants as reruns. We also wanted a topic that would be highly motivating and reasonably similar to the topics typically discussed in casual conversation between acquaintances or family members, such as at the dinner table. *Lucy* is a family show, centering on personal interactions between two couples in just a few settings, so it is similar to the things that people who know each other talk about. (The ability to conduct casual conversations "about nothing" with total strangers has some value, but it is surely much lower on any scale of personal utility.)

Finally, if successful exchange of information in a conversation was to be measured in terms of the number of correct ideas transmitted to the non-aphasic partner, then we needed to be able to verify the accuracy of these ideas. We did this by asking the non-aphasic partner to retell the story, and we told both conversation partners in advance that this would be required. This is not a typical natural goal for the teller or hearer of a story, but we tried it as a way to provide motivation to both parties.

Talk between two people, even strangers, is embedded in the larger contexts of their lives. Speakers have agendas. In talk-at-work as treated in Drew and Heritage (1992), the exchange is directly part of the work of the institution; but in our *Lucy* stories, we have a conversation embedded in a clinical research setting and, furthermore, a conversation presented to the participants as a prototype of a conversation embedded in a clinical assessment/guidance setting, because they were told that the purpose of the study was to see if this would be a good method for such a use. The narrative task is furthermore "contrived," like all overt assessments and research instruments, in that these people would not normally be talking about this topic, should they, say, have been sitting together in a waiting room with time to kill. We are not yet in a position to know how the agenda of "being a cooperative participant in conversation that one has been asked to hold with a stranger for the sake of someone else's research"—here or in, say, the Switchboard Corpus (Godfrey, Holliman, & McDaniel, 1992)—affects what one says and how one says it. As is usual in the lan-

guage research business, we hope that the observable, controllable, analyzable contrived task is realistic enough so that it affords a valid *index* of the unobservable,
. uncontrollable, unanalyzable behavior that we really want to know about: call it
Conversation Under Glass.

The experimental study

Participants

Five participants with aphasia, three women and two men, were recruited from the
caseload of the University Speech, Language & Hearing Clinic. They ranged in age
from 24 to 69 years (three over 55, two between 20 and 35); three of them were 2 to
3 years postonset of brain injury, and two were 10 years post. They had a variety of
different aphasia types (two with Broca's, one with Wernicke's, and two with global
aphasia). All had moderate-severe to severe aphasias with severity ranging from the
25th to the 50th percentile (for aphasic norms) as measured by the Aphasia Diagnostic Profiles (ADP; Helm-Estabrooks, 1992). Twenty adult student participants were
recruited to serve as communicative partners. They had had no previous experience
in communicating with people who have aphasia, and little to no knowledge about
aphasia (see table 11.1 for descriptive data).

Method

Each of the five participants with aphasia was paired with four different student partners so that there were a total of 20 conversational dyads. Each student participated
in only one conversation, and each conversation between an aphasic participant and
his or her student partners had a different topic. Prior to being introduced to each
communicative partner, the aphasic participant viewed one of four randomly ordered
episodes of the television show *I Love Lucy* ("Lucy is Pregnant," "Bonus Bucks,"
"Pioneer Women," and "Job Switching"). Aphasic participants were told that they
would later be asked to carry on a conversation about the episode. Although they
were encouraged to watch each episode as many times as they needed until they felt
confident they knew the story well enough, no participant asked to watch an episode
more than one time.

Immediately after watching an episode, the participant with aphasia was introduced to an unfamiliar student partner. The students had been informed that the person with whom they would be conversing had aphasia and that they sometimes had
difficulty saying what they wanted to say. Students were also told that their conversational partner had just watched a videotape of an episode of an *I Love Lucy* television show. After the members of the dyad were introduced to each other, they were
told that the objective of their conversation was for the student to learn what hap-

TABLE 11.1. Descriptive Data for Participants with Aphasia

Participant	Sex	Age	Etiology	Months postonset	ADP aphasia severity (%ile)	ADP aphasia type	ADP auditory comprehension (%ile)	ADP lexical retrieval (%ile)	ADP* content units
JC	F	63	Stroke	34	13	Global	25	2	0
JK	M	69	Stroke	120	25	Broca	50	9	0
ET	M	24	TBI	30	27	Global	25	25	7
WK	F	56	Stroke	23	37	Wernicke	25	37	11
KJ	F	33	Stroke	120	50	Broca	50	37	15

*ADP content units = the number of units of correct information spoken while describing a standardized picture.

pened in the particular episode of *I Love Lucy*. They were also told that there were no rules except that they must remain within view of the video camera. They could speak, write, draw, or use whatever means of communicating they chose. They were to signal the camera operator when they believed they had completed the task as best they could. At this point the camera would be focused on the student partner and he or she would be asked to retell the story; the collective success of each interaction would be measured in terms of the number of correct ideas the student included in retelling the story.

These instructions made no mention of the need to avoid including incorrect information. Thus, student partners were free to make any inferences or guesses that they chose.

The conversational interactions and the students" retellings of the stories were video-recorded, and the students' retellings of the stories were orthographically transcribed for later analysis. As mentioned before, communicative success was measured in terms of the number of correct ideas or pieces of information included in the student partners' retellings of the stories. Content units were defined as words that help the listener to create a correct mental picture of the scene being described; they were identified using a procedure we developed in earlier work (Menn, Ramsberger, & Helm-Estabrooks, 1994). This notion of the content unit was, in turn, based upon common psychometric practice (e.g., Wechsler Memory Scale; Wechsler, 1945).

In an effort to gather some idea of the ecological validity of our procedure, family members or friends of the five participants with aphasia were asked to complete a questionnaire adapted from the CETI (Lomas et al., 1989). Questions regarding specific conversational abilities in real life were selected from the original version of the CETI (e.g., getting someone's attention, giving yes and no answers appropriately, having coffee time visits and conversations with friends and neighbors). A 5-point scale was used on which "1" signified that the person was "not at all able" and "5" signified that the person was "as able as before the stroke." Responses to the 10 questions were combined to yield a mean rating for each person.

Results and discussion

The mean number of correct content units produced in each partner's retellings of the *I Love Lucy* episodes (i.e., the indicator of communicative success) varied greatly across subjects (mean = 72.95; range = 15.50–172.75). Success in conversation measured in this way was positively correlated with the mean score from the communication questionnaire completed by friends/family of the participants with aphasia ($r = .90$, $p = .019$). Thus, our procedure for objectively measuring success in conversation appears to have some validity.

Mean scores for conversational success were positively related to aphasia severity as measured by the ADP (Helm-Estabrooks, 1996) ($r = .955$, $p = .011$) (see tables 11.1 and 11.2). However, ADP aphasia severity was not always significantly corre-

TABLE 11.2 Individual Performances on Measure of Communicative Success

Participant	Communicative success: Number of correct content units in partners' retelling of I Love Lucy episode				Number of content units
	"Pioneer Women"	"Job Switching"	"Bonus Bucks"	"Lucy is Pregnant"	
JC	20	3	29	10	15.5
JK	25	25	25	21	24
ET	4	34	39	80	39.25
WK	69	100	43	241	113.25
KJ	200	168	205	118	172.75
Mean number of content units	63.6	66	68.2	94	72.95

lated with communicative success when we looked individually at the four different episodes/interactions that formed the composite score (correlations ranged from $r = .646$, $p = .120$ for "Lucy is Pregnant," to $r = .973$, $p = .003$ for "Job Switching"). This finding reinforces the idea that the disabling nature of aphasia is not solely predicted by the severity of aphasia: other factors must also have played a role. This is consistent with self-reports often provided by people with aphasia: for example, KJ reported that when she goes to the grocery store, she goes at a particular time and day when she knows that a certain clerk will be at the courtesy counter, because she is more successful in communicating with him than with other clerks.

Success in the conversational task also was not significantly predicted by three of the most distinguishing characteristics of aphasia, although lexical retrieval might well prove significant with a larger sample: auditory comprehension ($r = .342$, $p = .573$), lexical retrieval ($r = .870$, $p = .055$), or fluency ($r = .718$, $p = .086$). We did find a significant positive relationship with the number of content units produced when describing the ADP picture ($r = .943$, $p = .016$). Again, however, when we ran separate correlations for the four episodes/interactions that comprised the composite score, this significant positive correlation was evident in only one interaction (correlations ranged from $r = .757$, $p = .069$, to $r = .935$, $p = .010$). Participants JK and JC, who produced *no* content units in the ADP picture description task, were able to successfully convey an average of 24 and 15.50 content units in the conversational task!

With the exception of JK, communicative success in conversation varied greatly across episodes/interactions (by a factor of 20 for ET, 5.6 for WK, 4.7 for JC, and 1.7 for KJ). Three factors may account for this variability: practice effects, differences in the difficulty of the four *I Love Lucy* episodes, or factors associated with the unique combination of a participant with aphasia, a student partner, and the specific story being discussed. However, randomizing the order of presentation of the four episodes controlled for potential practice effects. Although the mean number of content units produced across episodes ranged from 63.6 ("Pioneer Women") to 94.00 ("Lucy is Pregnant"), this difference was not significant ($p = .759$). Thus, the possibility that conversational success varied due to differences in general episode difficulty can also be ruled out. Also, all participants with aphasia were far enough postonset that we would not expect significant changes in their aphasia over the course of collecting data from the four conversational interactions.

The explanations that remain, therefore, are that a given person with aphasia experienced varying success in different conversations because of one or more of the following:

- Varying skill of student partners. As the four conversations of each participant with aphasia were with different conversational partners, the variability observed across conversations for a particular person with aphasia might have been due to differences in the interpersonal or adaptive communicative skills of student partners.
- Difference in the ability of the participant with aphasia to deal with individual episode topics. It is possible that there were individual differences in their ability to come up with ways of encoding the events depicted in the different episodes of *I Love Lucy*. For example, personal relevance and degree of emotional arousal are known to influence performance in people with aphasia. These variables may have differed across episodes on an individual basis.
- Varying skills of communicative partnerships. Performance of both student partners and participants with aphasia may have been influenced by the unique "chemistry" of each partnership. Specific pairings of people may have resulted in unpredicted differences in the strength of interpersonal connections, and this in turn may have shaped the interaction.

Qualitative study: A narrative co-constructed by KJ and an experienced communicator

Quantification of the disabling impact of aphasia on conversation, such as the content unit measure used, offers important information about what is being communicated, but it does not provide the type of information that would help a clinician to know how to lessen the disability for communication with a specific partner, let alone showing what a person with aphasia might need in order to deal with different partners. Therapeutic focus and methods are typically designed on the basis of qualitative information gained from the assessment. If conversation were to be the focus of a rehabilitation program, the clinician would need to know how the conversational exchange succeeded or failed.

In the following section we will discuss two brief examples from a conversation about the episode "Lucy is Pregnant" that KJ had with co-author LM. We include these examples to demonstrate the way in which we would like to expand our current line of research to include procedures to assess how information is exchanged in conversations involving people with aphasia. These are very preliminary (among other things, facial expression and timing are not yet included), and we hope that other members of the growing clinical/CA community will help us to develop this line of research further.

In the process of the interaction between the conversation partners, shared knowledge and possible new information are brought together and integrated. In her narration of the episode "Lucy is Pregnant," the amount of information KJ expresses via words is extremely limited. Yet this small amount of verbal information, together with her resourceful non-verbal expressions, is enough to channel her partner's guessing so that it is rarely far from the mark. KJ's monitoring of her partner's understanding and her partner's direct requests for confirmation of her guesses lead to a relatively efficient reconstruction of the story.

The conversation partner (CP)'s work includes the following:

- using the information in KJ's gestures
- disregarding probable wrong information (which KJ helps with, through supplying gestures to override wrong information)
- disregarding probable irrelevancies, trusting KJ to bring them up again if they were indeed relevant
- distilling likely propositions and testing them, thus depending on the accuracy of KJ's feedback.

The conversation partner's general and particular background knowledge are crucial in making the judgments required to carry out these four steps.

One of the basic tasks of narrative, of course, is establishing reference: who are the characters and what does each one do at each point in the story (Pomerantz, 1987; Schegloff, 1972, 1988). Clark (1992: 132, also pp. 173 ff.) notes that speakers and addressees may do this collaboratively, in several turns, depending on how difficult establishing reference turns out to be. Pomerantz (1984: 156), discussing normal speakers, notes that "poor referencing seems to be a matter that speakers rapidly monitor [themselves] for, easily remedy, and treat as minor." But this "minor" task can be excruciatingly difficult for people with aphasia; at the semantic level, one name will often be substituted for another (like an exaggerated case of the parent who runs through the names of several of his or her children before settling on the appropriate one), and dysarthria or phonemic errors may make names quite unintelligible. In addition, personal pronouns may be difficult to access and may show person/gender

substitutions; finally, dysarthria may nearly obliterate the phonetic distinction between "he" and "she."

KJ has all of these problems—semantic, phonemic, and phonetic—and is quite
aware of them. In spite of this general awareness, however, her ability to monitor
each individual referring expression, and correct it if it is wrong, is poor; she is aware
of that, too. So, rather than insisting on trying to communicate referents verbally,
she uses a particularly effective non-verbal strategy in her "Lucy is Pregnant" narrative: she shows her partner that she is going to refer to each main character in the
story as a dot on a piece of paper and manages to elicit their names—Lucy, Ethel,
Ricky—before she adds the cognitive load of telling the story proper by verbal ap-
proximation, writing a few letters, and miming. Eliciting the names from the non-
aphasic partner, of course, relies on the fact that these names are shared background
knowledge; but, again, real-world conversations have some shared starting points
and in fact rely substantially on mutual knowledge (cf. Clark, 1992, pp. 35 ff.).

To show the qualitative understanding of speaker interaction that is added by
even the most basic CA approach, we present two interactive sequences that communicate key parts of "Lucy is Pregnant." The communication tasks that we have
chosen to discuss here are carried out rather "locally," which makes for easier discussion. Often the sequence of events is spread out over much more of the story,
with many more intervening turns; in those cases, the cognitive load for both partners is probably greater.

In the transcript excerpts, non-speech activities are in square brackets. A bracketed character name such as [Lucy] means that KJ has pointed to that character's
spot on the paper to establish her or him as a referent. This transcript is sketchy by
CA standards, but it shows how much is available from what is little more than a
secretarial rendition of a videotape.

Example 1
1 KJ: OK. Um. Go, um. Woman. I don't know woman. Um Etta? No.
2 CP: Ethel?
3 KJ: Good. Uh, good. Uh. Um. Lucer [Lucy].
4 CP: Lucy.
5 KJ: Talking, talking. Um. Woman tired, um. Um. New food eaten [rubs her stomach].
6 CP: Indigestion?
7 KJ: Yuck. I mean yuck. Um. Woman [sticks out her tongue].
8 CP: [laughs] Did she vomit?
9 KJ: No.
10 CP: Just . . .
11 KJ: I mean happy. I mean yuck.
12 CP: Just . . . just felt . . . felt yucky. OK.
13 KJ: See go doctor.
14 CP: Uh hu.
15 KJ: See go. Um woman. Hummmm. Funny. Sick. Happy. What? Uh oh! New baby. No.

Listening to 1, CP must discount a "new referent" possibility for "woman," as no new referent has been established, and must also take "I don't know woman" to mean "I can't say the woman's name." This could turn out to have been incorrect, but since KJ immediately goes on with "Etta," which might be an attempt to refer to Ethel, CP sets aside the idea of the involvement of a third unnamed woman and guesses "Ethel?" at 2, which KJ confirms.

KJ then establishes reference to Lucy with a [Lucy] point. At 4, CP says "Lucy" to confirm her understanding of KJ's point to the [Lucy] dot. KJ is taken to accept this, for she proceeds in 5 to say: "Talking, talking." CP takes Lucy, rather than Ethel, to be the subject of "talking," because she was mentioned after Ethel. Beause KJ has taken care to establish reference to both of them, however, CP assumes that Lucy is talking to Ethel. Neither CP nor KJ seems to feel any need to verify either of these inferences.

KJ's iteration of "talking" in 5 is taken to indicate that the reported conversation is long; something in KJ's prosody probably cues CP to take the repetition as deliberate and as indicating durative rather than iterated action in the story. This is not made explicit so that it can be checked with KJ, however; presumably CP treats it as too small a piece of information to bother interrupting KJ.

CP takes the referent of "Woman" in 5 "Woman tired" to still be Lucy and assumes that Lucy is also the one with the stomachache; presumably both participants are simply treating Lucy as the established topic. CP's guess "Indigestion?" in 6 has apparently been accepted, because KJ goes on to elaborate it. CP's next guess, based on KJ's miming, is rejected, so the degree of Lucy's intestinal problem has apparently been bracketed by the time we get to 10 "Just." Lines 11 and 12, ending with CP's "OK," are taken as confirming this. CP does not yet make any attempt to deal with KJ's puzzling word "happy" in 11.

CP interprets "see" in 13 "See go doctor" as "she," and both this and "woman" as referring to Lucy, without bothering to check. Lucy's approximate age and marital status, knowledge of signs of pregnancy, and that one may go to a doctor to confirm suspicions of pregnancy are all common knowledge; both KJ and CP rely on the fact that each of them possesses this information. KJ's "No" in 15 will eventually turn out to mean that Lucy is incredulous, as she and Ricky had given up on having children; now "happy" would make sense, although we do not know whether CP remembers that it was part of what KJ had said a few turns earlier.

Example 2
1 KJ: Um. Time. Time. Eight. Um. Rick job. Um. [Lucy]
2 CP: It's eight o'clock.
3 KJ: Eight. Job.
4 CP: OK.
5 KJ: Yeah. Right. Band . . . [Gestures at her body in a sweeping fashion to indicate a dress or skirt.]
6 CP: Yeah. Right. All dressed-up.

7 KJ: Um.
8 CP: Got it.
9 KJ: Li . . . Lisa go. [Lucy] Go. Go, um. Um, job. Um. Um. Um. Job. Um Lu. . . . Me
       job [Lucy.]
10 CP: She goes to where Rick . . .
11 KJ: Ah ha!
12 CP: She goes to where Rick is leading the band.

KJ has undertaken to communicate four pieces of information in 1 ("Time. Time. Eight. Um. Rick job. Um. [Lucy]"): the new time, something about Ricky's job, and the fact that Lucy is involved in this event. CP assumes that the [Lucy] point will turn out to be relevant and deals with the rest of this one step at a time. First, she checks the meaning of "Time. Eight"—not bothering with AM or PM, probably because she assumes that this is all happening in one day. "Job" might, in another setting, have caused CP to assume that "Eight o'clock" was 8:00 AM the next day, but that potential error—to the best of CP's recollection—did not happen here. The shared knowledge that Ricky is a bandleader and works at night could have been involved—it is one use that CP could have made of the word "Job"—but at this point we authors are not certain.

KJ's single word "Time" helps enormously; compare this interaction to the one in Goodwin's chapter 4, where resolving the issue of whether a number refers to time or to numbers of people takes a great deal of interactional work.

KJ apparently confirms CP's "Eight o'clock" by repeating "Eight" in 3 and then reiterates "Job." CP is not yet ready to come up with a guess as to what proposition about the job is being made, so in 4 she just says "OK." KJ begins 5 with "Yeah. Right" and so appears to take CP's "OK" in response to "Job" as a license to proceed, although probably unsure of whether CP has understood anything beyond the literal meaning of "job."

KJ now adds new verbal and gestural information in 5: "Band . . . [Gestures at her body in a sweeping fashion to indicate a dress or skirt]"; CP responds in 6 with a verbalization of the gesture.

The word "Band" serves to remind CP of their mutual knowledge that Rick is a band leader; culturewide common knowledge fills in the facts that band leaders work at night at places where people dance or dine out. This will tie down the 8:00 time as the evening, in case that is still at issue; more important, as there has been a recent [Lucy] point rather than any reference to Ethel, CP takes the gesture indicating being dressed up to be about Lucy.

The information of 1 now might be starting to fall together in a schema, but all CP says in 8 is "Got it." This is meager; KJ has no way to be sure of what CP has really "gotten." C. Goodwin points out to us (personal communication, October 1998) that "in his early lectures Sacks had a lot to say about the difference between claiming understanding and demonstrating it, and this seems in part the issue involved in the elaboration after 'Got it.'"

So KJ takes the responsibility for getting the information articulated. The reason for Lucy's being dressed up, after all, could be that she is going someplace without Rick, or that she is expecting company; "band" has not been woven into any of CP's responses yet. KJ does her best to clarify matters in 9: her two false referring expressions ("Lisa" and "Me") are not a problem, thanks to the use of the [Lucy] points to correct each one. But no new words are available: all she can do is reiterate "Job" and [Lucy], hoping that CP will find an appropriate way to connect the job with Lucy. Fortunately, this works, as we see in 10–12, and CP finally articulates the proposition "She goes to where Rick is leading the band."

Triumph ("Ah ha!") in 12 turns, for the equivalent of "At eight o'clock that night, Lucy goes to where Rick is leading the band."

Potential refinements

In our work so far, we have not measured response latencies, either verbal or non-verbal. Were there pauses, nods, and glances between the words in some of the lines we have treated as single turns? These are probably crucial for the success or failure of communication between some dyads. We base this suggestion on Davidson's (1984: 117) work on silence as a signal of potential rejection of social invitations:

> the [low information] components occurring after a possible completion point may be providing the inviter or offerer with a *monitor space* in which he or she can examine what happens or does not happen there [i.e. the initial stages of the hearer's uptake of what has been said so far] for its acceptance/rejection implicativeness. Given the absence of a response such as acceptance immediately after the possible completion point and in overlap with the tag-positioned components in the monitor space, then an inviter or offerer may take this absence as rejection-implicative, that is, as a display that the recipient is having some trouble or problem with the acceptability of the invitation or offer as it stands so far.

Pomerantz (1984: 156) also discusses silences, in the context of establishing reference:

> If there is some question as to why the recipient has not responded, a speaker may try an easy solution first. He or she may attempt to determine what is wrong by seeing whether the easy solution works. It may not be unlike what mechanics, doctors, and others who routinely diagnose problems do on occasion: try the least costly remedy first.

This idea is likely to be relevant to one of the ways that conversations with aphasic speakers can get off track. We assume that monitoring the addressee for uptake is likely to occur whenever a speaker takes any kind of risk. One kind of risk is in-

curred when the non-aphasic partner offers a guess as to the aphasic person's meaning. If the person with aphasia fails to indicate acceptance of a guess made by the
conversation partner swiftly enough (during the monitor space), the partner may start
to offer alternative interpretations immediately. If the first guess was, in fact, correct, but the partner thinks it was rejected, he or she may go further and further astray.
Fortunately, KJ's comprehension in context and her speed of reaction are very good;
few or no such spirals away from the correct story appear to have occurred in the
interaction we are examining. Other aphasic speakers, however, are not nearly as
effective in steering their partners' guesses.

A similar risk is incurred by the partner with aphasia whenever she attempts to
say something that taxes her communicative ability. If the hearer does not appear to
be comprehending, the aphasic partner may modify what she said immediately, without waiting for explicit feedback, and without actually having monitored what her
output sounded like. Such immediate modification may or may not be helpful, depending on how well the aphasic speaker guesses what has caused the partner's blank
silence.

We believe, then, that a major factor in KJ's success is her ability to check whether
an important point has in fact gotten through to her CP. Furthermore, Heath (1984:247)
notes that "a speaker may elicit a display of recipiency from a coparticipant" and that
"a display of recipiency is itself elicitive." It is possible that one of the ways in which
non-aphasic CPs differ from one another is that some "display recipiency" in ways that
the aphasic speaker can pick up on, whereas other non-aphasic partners fail to do this.
Both partners need to make appropriate judgments as to when to check mutual understanding; as Clark (1992: 174) says, "If the participants stopped to ground every word,
it would take too long to say anything, and yet if they didn't stop often enough, misunderstandings could snowball before they could be repaired." We plan to examine the
videotapes of the 20 interactions described in the first part of this chapter to see if part
of the success of information transfer can be accounted for by how well a given dyad
checks the quality of the information getting across. If this is the case, we will look
further, to see whether the quality of information checking is in turn predicted by such
factors as the production and the uptake of displays of recipiency.

General discussion: Conversation Analysis, diagnosis, and therapy

If the speaker does not explicitly state something, and yet the listener correctly incorporates this information into his or her retelling of the story, then he or she must
have inferred it—that is, he or she made a logical guess based on whatever information was available. The gestures produced by KJ in this sample vary in degree of
transparency, and thus in the degree to which the CP must infer meaning. Pointing to
the blank place on the paper to communicate person required a great deal of infer-

ence the first time it was used, before the beginning of the narrative proper. But once it was clear that this would be the way that KJ would express which person she was speaking about, the demands for inference decreased. KJ used other gestures and produced isolated words, none of which expressed complete ideas. In these cases, the CP had to make some guesses about the missing elements of the utterance. This required the CP to combine the fragments (both verbal and non-verbal) produced by KJ with her own background knowledge and logic.

Two competent non-aphasic people provide fuller information in conversation; much of it may be redundant, given their shared knowledge, but moderate levels of redundancy also reduce the hearer's processing load. (The CA literature [e.g., Atkinson & Heritage, passim] currently refers to a "baseline" [p. 19] or "bedrock" [p. 26] of "ordinary/mundane conversations." We cannot do any better; yet we suspect that this notion, taken seriously, will prove to be as problematic as the notions of "literal meaning" or "grammatical utterance".)

In our narratives, because the information that the narrator can produce is so much less than the audience needs, the hearer's construal—and therefore his or her context—may slew about violently from moment to moment. These violent shifts are reminiscent of the way "context" is redefined for the hearer of some kinds of jokes when the teller reaches the punch line, or for the reader of a detective story as the author's incremental clues are understood. In those cases, hearers know that the narrator is playing a game of withholding information, and they have the choice of being more or less active in trying to guess what twist the story will take, since all will be revealed at the end, and nothing much is at stake. Conversations with language-disordered friends or customers are not games, but the satisfaction people feel at having told and understood a story—just because of the excitement of having overcome obstacles together—is all the more real.

KJ's success in the analyzed conversations shows what a high level of cognitive competence on the part of the aphasic speaker is needed to compensate for the language deficit. KJ is not just listening to what CP has said, but is evaluating every utterance in terms of whether CP has in fact understood and gotten the point that KJ is trying to convey. This requires a continous process of analysis of CP's talk and the active refusal to accept mere claims of understanding (e.g., "OK"); she pushes for demonstrations of knowledge, which can uncover possible misunderstanding. The non-aphasic partner, obviously, also must call on a variety of non-linguistic cognitive resources to make information transfer possible. However, non-linguistic cognitive resources range from nearly intact to severely compromised in people with aphasia: not all of them can match KJ's alert, determined, deliberate, and assertive use of innovative ways to communicate. Finally, normal CPs also vary in their willingness and ability to adapt to the unique demands of communicating with a language-impaired partner.

Clinical assessment focusing on conversational interaction has potentially promising implications for aphasia rehabilitation. Traditional aphasia therapy has been directed at improving the symptoms of aphasia identified through performances on neurolinguistic/neuropsychological tests. Therapy designed on the basis of assessment of conversational interaction may offer a radical change to aphasia rehabilitation that has obvious functional impacts. Combining a measure of communicative success in conversation (such as the one described in the first part of this chapter) with the qualitative information given by a CA account may allow the clinician to determine both the degree of communication breakdown and the reasons why it occurs. Therapy could then focus on improving conversational skills of the individual with aphasia, their communicative partners, or the interaction of the two people.

The participants in our exercises "demonstrably orient" (Heritage & Atkinson, 1984: 20) to the roles of Aphasic and Not Aphasic speaker: Mr. or Ms. "Not" is the one who does the overt guessing. But beyond that obvious fact, what do those roles *entail*? They do not have to be communicative straitjackets, although they often are: Lesser and Milroy (1993) found non-aphasic spouses playing "speech pathologist" instead of helping their aphasic partners to find needed words. Donahue (2000) has found that mainstreamed learning-disabled school children, acting as talkshow "hosts" in an experimental task, were constrained in their interactions with classmate "guests" who were not disabled beyond what their language limitations would warrant; they had learned that, to get along in the classroom, they had to keep to subordinate roles. How serious an issue is this matter of acquired role constraints? So far, we can offer only reflection and speculation, but we think it is worth study, if a method can be found.

Lyon (1998) identified two sources of communication breakdown between a married couple in which the wife had severe global aphasia. First, the husband believed that his wife understood all of what he said; second, the couple did not make good use of the wife's preserved, but presumably alternative, communicative abilities. Lyon, however, designed a therapy that focused on 1) rebuilding the wife's confidence in her ability to communicate, 2) providing both husband and wife with a model of successful communication, and 3) coaching the husband to change his communication style to better facilitate his wife's understanding (e.g., slowing his speech rate, simplifying and reducing the information to be shared, etc.).

A person with aphasia has the right to choose the self-presentation that she or he prefers. The reponsibility of the therapist, then, is to determine the range of the client's possibilities. Self-construal is, after all, constrained by reality—even professional actors fail when cast too far from what their bodies and voices make credible. A person with aphasia may rationally choose a role below what we see as her communicative potential; by choosing silence in some situations, she may even encourage others to see her as able to speak if she should choose to do so.

Conclusion

Communication in conversation involves both "interaction" and "transaction" (Kagan, 1995). The method we have described above offers a means of quantifying "transaction" in a task that can be easily carried out within a therapeutic environment. Our experimental task, with the role of narrator assigned to the aphasic speaker and the audience/re-narrator role assigned to the non-aphasic partner, cuts against the "let me entertain you" or the "I know more than you do" roles that the partner might be likely to assume. The partner with aphasia may have acquired some stake in maintaining a real-life role as The Aphasic, but this interaction with a stranger might be perceived as an occasion for breaking out of that pattern.

Knowing how much information can be exchanged between communication partners when one of them has aphasia is important in assessing the disabling impact of aphasia. Success in our measure rests not just on language but also on the ability to compensate for linguistic limitations by making good use of a wide range of cognitive skills, including monitoring, self-monitoring, inferencing, providing feedback, and recognizing and exploiting non-linguistic opportunities for the expression of ideas.

The information obtained by our measure can be used as an objective, ecologically valid measure of therapeutic outcomes. And because the emphasis of this type of assessment is not linguistic processing (which appears to have a limited time frame in which significant recovery can occur), this method may provide clinicians with a means of documenting progress in people in the chronic stages of their aphasia. These CA techniques should be able to help us get from the quantitative work needed for assessment to the qualitative work needed to design dyadic therapy.

Note

Thanks to the participants in our study, especially KJ, whose extraordinary communicative ability in the face of extremely limited language inspired this line of research. The contributions of Makoto Hayashi were essential. We have incorporated some of Chuck Goodwin's notes verbatim and are very grateful for his editorial feedback, and Bill Bright's as well.

References

Atkinson, J. M., & Heritage, J. (Eds.). (1984). *Structures of Social Action: Studies in Conversation Analysis*. Cambridge: Cambridge University Press.

Barton, L. (1996). *Disability & Society: Emerging Issues and Insights*. New York: Longman Sociology Series.

Clark, H. H. (1992). *Arenas of Language Use*. Chicago: University of Chicago Press.

Davidson, J. (1984). Subsequent Versions of Invitations, Offers, Requests, and Proposals Dealing with Actual or Potential Rejection. In J. M. Atkinson & J. Heritage, (Eds.). *Structures of Social Action: Studies in Conversation Analysis* (pp. 102–128). Cambridge: Cambridge UniversityPress.

Drew, P., & Heritage, J. (1992). Analyzing Talk at Work: An Introduction. In P. Drew & J. Heritage (Eds.), *Talk at Work* (pp. 3–65). Cambridge: Cambridge University Press.

Donahue, M. (2000). Influences of School-Aged Children's Beliefs and Goals on Elicited Pragmatic Performance: Lessons Learned from Kissing the Blarney Stone. In L. Menn & N. Bernstein Ratner, (Eds.). *Methods for Studying Language Production*. Hillsdale, NJ: Erlbaum.

Frattali, C. M., Thompson, C. K., Holland, A. L., Wohl, C. B., & Ferketic, M. M. (1995). *The American Speech-Language-Hearing Association Functional Assessment of Communication Skills for Adults*. Rockville, MD: ASHA Fulfillment Operations.

Godfrey, J., Holliman, E., & McDaniel, J. (1992). SWITCHBOARD: Telephone Speech Corpus for Research and Development. International Conference on Acoustics, Speech and Signal Processing 92, 517–520.

Goodglass, H., & Kaplan, E. (1983). The Assessment of Aphasia and Related Disorders. Philadelphia: Lea & Febiger.

Goodwin, M. H. (1990). *He-Said-She-Said: Talk as Social Organization Among Black Children*. Bloomington: Indiana University Press.

Heath, C. (1984) Talk and Recipiency: Sequential Organization in Speech and Body Movement. In J. M. Atkinson & J. Heritage, (Eds.). *Structures of Social Action: Studies in Conversation Analysis* (pp. 247–265). Cambridge: Cambridge UniversityPress.

Helm-Estabrooks, N. (1992). *Aphasia Diagnostic Profiles*. Chicago: Riverside Publishing Co.

Heritage, J. & Atkinson, J. M. (1984). Introduction. In J. M. Atkinson & J. Heritage (Eds.), *Structures of Social Action: Studies in Conversation Analysis* (pp. 1–16). Cambridge: Cambridge UniversityPress.

Holland, A. L. (1980). *Communicative Abilities in Daily Living*. Baltimore: University Park Press.

Jordan, L., & Kaiser, W. (1996). *Aphasia—A Social Approach*. New York: Chapman & Hall.

Kagan, A. (1995). Revealing the Competence of Aphasic Adults Through Conversation: A Challenge to Health Professionals. *Topics in Stroke Rehabilitation, 2*(1), 15–28.

Kagan, A. (1998). Supported Conversation for Adults with Aphasia: Methods and Resources for Training Conversation Partners. *Aphasiology, 12*(9), 816–830.

Lesser, R., & Milroy, L. (1993). *Linguistics and Aphasia: Psycholinguistic and Pragmatic Aspects of Intervention*. London: Longman.

Linton, S. (1998). *Claiming Disability: Knowledge and Identity*. New York: New York University Press.

Lomas, J., Pickard, L., Bester, S., Elbard, H., Finlayson, A., & Zoghaib, C. (1989). The Communication Effectiveness Index: Development and Psychometric Evaluation of a Functional Communication Measure for Adults. *Journal of Speech and Hearing Disorders, 54*, 113–124.

Lyon, J. (1998). Treating Real-Life Functionality in a Couple Coping with Severe Aphasia. N. In Helm-Estabrooks & A. Holland (Eds.), *Approaches to the Treatment of Aphasia* (pp. 203–239). San Diego: Singular Publishing.

Marshall, R. C., & Phillips, D. S. (1983). Prognosis for Improved Verbal Communication in Aphasic Stroke Patients. *Archives of Physical Medicine and Rehabilitation, 64*, 597–601.

Marshall, R. C. (1998). An Introduction to Supported Conversation for Adults with Aphasia: Perspectives, Problems, and Possibilities. *Aphasiology, 12*(9), 811–816.

Menn, L., Ramsberger, G., & Helm-Estabrooks, N. (1994). A Linguistic Communication Measure for Aphasic Narratives. *Aphasiology, 8*(4), 343–359.

Parr, S., & Byng, S. (1998). Breaking New Ground in Familiar Territory: A Comment on "Supported Conversation for Adults with Aphasia" by Aura Kagan. *Aphasiology, 12*(9), 811–816.

Pashek, G. V., & Holland, A. L. (1988). Evolution of Aphasia in the First Year Post Onset. *Cortex, 24*, 411–423.

Pomerantz, A. (1987). Descriptions in Legal Settings. In G. Button & J. R. E. Lee (Eds.), *Talk and Social Organisation* (pp. 226–243). Clevedon: Multilingual Matters.

Ramsberger, G. (1994). A Functional Perspective for Assessment and Rehabilitation of Persons with Severe Aphasia. *Seminars in Speech and Language, 15*(1), 1–17.

Schegloff, E. (1972). Notes on a Conversational Practice: Formulating Place. In D. Sudnow (Ed.), *Studies in Social Interaction* pp. 16–119. New York: Free Press.

Schegloff, E. (1988). Description in the Social Sciences I: Talk-in-Interaction. *IPrA Papers in Pragmatics 2*, 1–24.

Voloshinov, V. N. (1973 [1929/1930]). *Marxism and the Philosophy of Language*. Trans. L. Matejka & I. R. Titunik. New York: Seminar Press.

Wechsler, D. (1945). A Standardized Memory Scale for Clinical Use. *Journal of Psychology, 19*, 87–95.

INDEX